EUROPE IN TRANSITION: THE NYU EUROPEAN STUDIES SERIES

Lessons from the Economic Crisis in Spain

By

Sebastián Royo

First published in 2013 by
PALGRAVE MACMILLAN®
in the United States—a division of St. Martin's Press LLC,
175 Fifth Avenue, New York, NY 10010.

Where this book is distributed in the UK, Europe and the rest of the world,
this is by Palgrave Macmillan, a division of Macmillan Publishers Limited,
registered in England, company number 785998, of Houndmills,
Basingstoke, Hampshire RG21 6XS.

Palgrave Macmillan is the global academic imprint of the above companies
and has companies and representatives throughout the world.

Palgrave® and Macmillan® are registered trademarks in the United States,
the United Kingdom, Europe and other countries.

ISBN: 978–0–230–11447–0

Permission to quote from the following articles has been granted by
Taylor and Francis:
"After the Fiesta: The Spanish Economy Meets the Global Financial Crisis,"
South European Society & Politics 14, no. 1 (2009).
"Reforms Betrayed? Zapatero and Continuities in Economic Policy,"
South European Society & Politics 14, no. 4 (2009).

Permission to quote from the following article has been granted by
John Wiley and Sons:
"How Did the Spanish Financial System Survive the First Stage of the
Global Crisis?", Governance (November 2012).

Library of Congress Cataloging-in-Publication Data is available from the
Library of Congress.

A catalogue record of the book is available from the British Library.

Design by Newgen Imaging Systems (P) Ltd., Chennai, India.

First edition: April 2013

10 9 8 7 6 5 4 3 2 1

To my twin brother Pepe—I miss you SO much.
You are my inspiration, and your reach has no limits

A man's reach should exceed his grasp, or what is heaven for?
—Robert Browning

Markets can remain irrational longer than you can remain solvent.
—John Maynard Keynes

Contents

Previous Publications

Portugal in the 21st Century: Politics, Society and Economics, 2011.

Varieties of Capitalism in Spain: Remaking the Spanish Economy for the New Century, 2008.

Do Isolamento a Integação, 2004.

Spain and Portugal in the European Union: The First 15 Years, 2003, coedited with Paul C. Manuel.

"A New Century of Corporatism?" Corporatism in Southern Europe: Spain and Portugal in Comparative Perspective, 2002.

From Social Democracy to Neoliberalism: The Consequences of Party Hegemony in Spain 1982–1996, 2000.

Figures and Tables

Figures

Tables

Preface and Acknowledgments

This book has taken me too long to write. I started it two years ago, at a time when the effects of the economic crisis in Spain were not so devastating. Did I know at that time that I was about to embark on a rollercoaster! Writing this book has felt as if I were in the middle of a hurricane, pulled in all directions, sinking from the weight of the storm, and never quite in control. There have been many times when I thought I had completed a chapter, but the fast evolution of events forced me to rewrite it and oftentimes to change my original arguments and conclusions. Even as this book goes to print (September 2012), there are many uncertainties and open questions about what is going to happen in Spain. The conclusions and lessons of this book are, therefore, tentative.

The following pages are the product of these struggles. While it is hard to be positive in the middle of one of Spain's most severe crises in the country's modern history, I am far more optimistic about the prospects for the country than other people are. The crisis has been devastating, yet the solid foundations of the country are still there: the human capital, the most educated generations in Spain's history, the success of Spanish firms and banks abroad, all of which have not been destroyed by the crisis. At the same time, I hope that the crisis will have a cathartic effect that will help the country purge the excesses and mistakes that led it to this situation in the first place. For that to occur, it is essential that we understand what has happened and why, and that we are willing to learn from the mistakes in order to avoid them in the future and move forward. While researching for this book, I have sometimes been surprised by the attempts to blame others (the United States, Germany, Brussels, and even the euro) for the crisis and by the tendency to avoid any self-criticism or assume responsibility for the domestic decisions that contributed to the crisis. If we persist in that pattern, we are bound to repeat the same mistakes. It is my hope that we do not. This book is, I hope, a modest contribution toward that effort.

The economic crisis in Spain has been severely intensified by the global financial crisis that spread throughout the world in 2008 after the collapse of Lehman Brothers. The crisis has also been the by-product of the institutional and political deficiencies of the European Monetary Union project. There is no question about it. Yet, this crisis also has deep domestic roots that can be attributed only to Spain. Much can be written about the global financial crisis, or the Eurozone crisis. That is not the objective of this book. While acknowledging the international dimension and causal components of the crisis, this book is particularly interested in examining the domestic causes and responses to the crisis.

The foundations of this book are rooted in my interest for my country of origin, Spain, and in particular for its political economy. I am fortunate that one of my responsibilities at Suffolk University is to oversee its campus in Madrid. This has allowed me to travel to Spain very regularly and to witness firsthand the effects of the crisis.

Over the years, my thinking about the political economy issues has been influenced by many people. I would like to acknowledge the insight of the following people: Joaquín Almunia, Nancy Bermeo, Katrina Burgess, Cesar Camisón, Michele Chang, William Chislett, Carlos Closa, Xavier Coller, Francisco Conde, Alvaro Cuervo, Omar Encarnación, Enrik Enderlein, Miguel Angel Fernández Ordoñez, Bonnie Field, Mauro Guillén, Peter Hall, Kerstin Hamann, Iain Hardie, Diego Hidalgo, David Howarth, Andrew Martin, Cathy Jo Martin, Felix Martin, Silvia Maxfield, Fernando Moreno, Carlos Mulas, Rafael Myro, Emilio Ontiveros, Andrés Ortega, Sofía Pérez, Charles Powell, Lucia Quaglia, Marino Regini, Joaquín Roy, Vivien Schmidt, Philippe Schmitter, Ben Ross Schneider, Kathleen Thelen, Pablo Toral, Mariano Torcal, José Ignacio Torreblanca, and Amy Verdun.

In particular I want to acknowledge and express my utmost gratitude to Robert Fishman. He has provided feedback on many chapters, which has been instrumental. Robert's seminal work on Spain and Portugal has always been a major source and an inspiration for my research. He has been my intellectual mentor. More importantly, I want to thank him and his wife Julia López for their unwavering support through the years. They have been amazing friends and wonderful colleagues. I am forever indebted to them.

Drafts of chapters of this book have been presented at academic conferences, including meetings of the American Political Science Association, the International Studies Association, the Conference of Europeanists, and the European Union Studies Association. I want to thank all the people who were a part of those panels for their valuable insight and comments. I also want to express my gratitude to David Howarth, Iain Hardie, and Amy Verdun for the workshops that they organized at the University of Edinburgh and the University of Victoria on market-based banking. They were instrumental in my research regarding the impact of the crisis on the Spanish financial sector, and their feedback, and that of all the participants in that project, was invaluable.

Over the years, my research in Spain has been greatly facilitated by the active collaboration of people including former cabinet members, business leaders, entrepreneurs, union leaders, scholars, and national and regional administration officials. They were all extremely generous with their time and interest. I am indebted to them. In particular, I would like to acknowledge the help I received from Emilio Ontiveros, who has been a mentor and an inspiration throughout my academic career. Emily Fritz-Endres has provided editorial and research assistance for the book. She has been simply phenomenal. I would not have been able to finish the book without her help.

This book would not have been possible without the help of and inspiration from a number of people. I owe a great debt of gratitude to the many institutions and people who have supported my research over the years. In particular, I would like to thank my colleagues and students in the Government Department at Suffolk University for providing a cordial and supportive environment, as well as my colleagues and students at the Suffolk University, Madrid campus. Working with them has been an extraordinary experience.

The Minda de Gunzburg Center for European Studies at Harvard University, where I am an affiliate and cochair of the Iberian Studies Group, has also proved to be an exceptionally supportive institution for my research. I want to thank Peter Hall for his constant guidance and inspiration. My greatest academic debt is to him. I also want to thank Patricia Craig, Charles Maier, Grzegorz Ekiert, Elaine Papoulias, and Andrew Martin.

During the past seven years I have had the fortune to work as associate dean of the College of Arts and Sciences at Suffolk University for Dean Kenneth Greenberg. Ken is not only my boss but also an extraordinary person. He has been a mentor and an inspiration, and I have learned a lot from him. Ken has been incredibly supportive throughout my career at Suffolk, and I am forever indebted to him for all the opportunities that he has given me. I feel enormously privileged to work for him and to count him as a dear friend. I would also like to thank President McCarthy. In the few months in which he has been president of Suffolk University, he has brought a new level or energy, commitment, and dynamism to Suffolk that has been simply inspiring. I am very fortunate to work with an amazing group of people at Suffolk University. I publish this book as I start a new adventure at Suffolk University as vice provost for student success.

On a more personal note, I would like to thank all the members of my family. My parents have always been incredibly loving and supportive. They are my role models and the sources of the best in me. My brother Borja has always been a champion of my work. My daughters Abigail, Andrea, and Monica have been a joy and a constant source of happiness. They have taught me the most important lessons of life, and I love them so much. My nieces Zoe and McKenzie have also been a delight, and we always cherish the times that we spend together. Finally, I want to thank my wife Cristina. We have shared 20 extraordinary years. She is an exceptional wife, mother, and professional. Cristina is the best thing that ever happened to me. Nothing that I have achieved, including this book, would have been possible without her love, patience, dedication to the family, incredible hard work, and support.

When I started this book, my twin brother, Pepe, had just passed away after bravely fighting a battle against cancer. He was the smartest, kindest, and the most generous person I have had the privilege to be with, and he was, and still is, the most influential person in my life. I would not be who I am without him, and I would never have accomplished anything without his love, leadership, inspiration, and constant support. I miss him so much, every single day. The pain has not abated. I still feel like I am missing a limb, and I struggle every day to cope with the loss. There is not a single day that I do not think of him, and that he is not with me. He is part of my life, of my memories, and of who I am. Poet Pablo Neruda once said: "To feel the love of people whom we love is a fire that feeds our life." I have been inspired by my brother, and I feel I should carry on those things that were so important to him. I try every day. I dedicate this book to him.

SEBASTIÁN ROYO
Boston, Massachusetts
September 2012

Abbreviations

ABS	Asset-Based Securities
AMCE	Acuerdo Para la Mejora del Crecimiento y del Empleo (Agreement for Improvement in the Quality and Growth of Employment)
ANC	Interconfederal Agreement on Collective Bargaining
BBK	Bilbao Bizkaia Kutxa
BBVA	Banco Bilbao Vizcaya Argentaria
BFA	Bankia-Banco Financiero y de Ahorros
BNG	Bloque Nacionalista Gallego (Galician Nationalist Bloc)
CAM	Caja del Mediterráneo
CC	Coalición Canaria
CCOO	Comisiones Obreras
CC-PNC	Coalición Canaria-Nueva Canarias (Canarian Coalition-Canarian Nationalist Party)
CEOE	Confederación Española de Organizaciones Empresariales
CEPYME	Confederación Esapañola de la Pequeña y Mediana Empresa
CGPJ	General Council of the Judiciary
CIS	Centro de Investigaciones Sociológicas (Center for Sociological Research)
CiU	Catalan Convergencia i Union (Convergence and Union)
CME	Coordinated Market Economy
CNMV	Comisión Nacional del Mercado de Valores (National Stock Market Commission)
COMPROMÍS-Q	Coalició Compromís
CPI	Consumer Price Index
ECB	European Central Bank
EFSF	European Financial Stability Facility
EMU	European Monetary Union
ERC	Republican Left of Catalonia
ERE	Expedientes de Regulación de Empleo
ERM	European Rate Mechanism
ETA	Basque Euskadi Ta Askatasuna

EU	European Union
FDI	Foreign Direct Investment
FGD	Fondo de Garantia de Depósitos
FLA	Fondo de Liquidez Autonómico
FRB	Federal Reserve Board
FROB	Fund for Orderly Bank Restructuring
FTSE	Financial Times and Stock Exchange.
GBAI	Geroa Bai
GCI	Global Competitiveness Index
GDP	Gross Domestic Product
ICO	Instituto de Crédito Oficial
INE	Instituto Nacional de Estadística (National Institute of Statistics)
IPO	Initial Public Offering
IU	Izquierda Unida
LME	Liberal Market Economy
LORCA	Ley de Órganos Rectores de Cajas de Ahorros (Law of the Governing Organs of Saving Banks)
MAFO	Miguel Angel Fernández Ordoñez
MEDE	European Stability Mechanism
NA-BAI	Nafarroa Bai
OECD	Organisation for Economic Co-operation and Development
OMT	Outright Monetary Transactions
PM	Prime Minister
PNV	Basque Nationalist Party
PP	Popular Party
PPP	Purchasing Power Parity
PSOE	Partido Socialista Obrero Español (Spanish Socialist Workers' Party)
R-D-I	Research-Development-Innovation
SGP	Stability and Growth Pact
SIP	Sistema Institucional de Protección (Institutional Protection System)
SIVs	Structured Investment Vehicles
SMEs	Small and Medium Enterprises
UGT	Unión General de Trabajadores
UN	United Nations
UNCTAD	United Nations Conference on Trade and Development
UPyD	Unión Progreso y Democracia (Union Progress and Democracy)
VAT	Value Added Tax
VoC	Varieties of Capitalism
VP	Vice President
WI	Wage Increase
WTO	World Trade Organization
YPF	Yacimientos Petrolíferos Fiscales

Introduction: Spain at a Crossroads

Between 1996 and 2007, the Spanish economy was one of the fastest growing and the most successful economies in Europe. High levels of immigration, low interest rates, and the liberalization and modernization of the Spanish economy all contributed to this spectacular performance. This success, however, came to a halt in 2008, and in 2012, Spain is still suffering a very painful economic recession. While the global economic crisis has been a significant contributing factor in this downturn, this book shows that domestic imbalances largely help account for the current economic problems. In the context of Spain's membership in the EU and the EMU, the book examines the reasons for the crisis, analyzes the government's responses, and draws some lessons from the Spanish experience.

The crisis has had an earth-shattering effect in Spain at all levels: economic, political, institutional, and social. Yet, there are different interpretations about the causes and culprits for the crisis. According to one narrative, countries with a historic inability to manage their public finances (e.g., Spain, Portugal, Greece, and Italy) were unwisely allowed into a monetary union anchored by Germany, which has a history of fiscal and monetary probity. These countries took advantage of record low interest rates that led to bubbles. But they failed to address competitive challenges and neglected the structural reforms required for EMU membership. When reality struck them, they tried to undo the effects of decades of fiscal mismanagement by taking advantage of low interest loans from stronger countries. In response to the crisis, they insisted on developing a fiscal union and reforming the EMU institutional framework. From this perspective, these countries want more money from the rich nations to maintain their "unjustified" standards of living and to work less but retire earlier. The supporters of this view consider the crisis a "morality play, a tale of countries that lived high and now face the inevitable reckoning...sin and its consequences is their story, and they are sticking to it."[1]

However, another possible interpretation is that nations in the periphery (Spain, Portugal, Italy, Greece) were encouraged to join a poorly designed EMU by the rich countries, which designed and dominated it. The rich countries (Germany, France) came up with the fiscal rules, but they were the first to break them and get away with it. In the years prior to the crisis, they encouraged their banks, which lacked good profitable opportunities within their stagnant domestic markets, to lend recklessly to the countries in the periphery. When these investments failed, their governments bailed out the banks by lending funds to the debtor countries in order to pay back the banks. They imposed draconian conditions on the debtor countries with unprecedented losses of sovereignty. Each narrative has elements of truth, and depending on which one anyone supports leads to different conclusions about responsibility and appropriate responses to the crisis. This book seeks to shed light on this debate.

In 2012, Spain became the fourth country in the Eurozone to seek an international bailout. Despite the Spanish government's attempt to portray as a victory the decision to seek up to €100 billion in EU rescue funds for domestic banks in difficulties, the reality was more complex. While the agreed-upon EU loans are different from other EU rescue plans because they would be used to only recapitalize banks, the government had resisted any EU assistance since it was voted into office only the previous December. Yet, the rapidly deteriorating conditions of several Spanish financial institutions, notably Bankia, concerns over developments in Greece and market pressures accelerated this outcome. It remains to be seen whether this bailout will be enough. Initial signals from the markets were mixed, and the country's borrowing costs reached record unsustainable levels in the summer of 2012.

Market instability in the Eurozone and the unsustainable borrowing costs for countries such as Spain led to ECB's decision, announced on September 6, 2012, to purchase Eurozone countries' short-term bonds in the secondary markets, as part of the new program dubbed OMT, requiring governments applying for aid from the Eurozone rescue funds to comply with conditions in exchange for the support. In September 2012, merely two months after asking for assistance for its banks, Spain was still considering whether to apply for this aid.

As this book goes to print, Spain is "dancing" toward a rescue. The Spanish government seemed to be taking steps to request this assistance, and reports suggested that the ECB and the European Commission were working with the Spanish government on a reform package. PM Rajoy acknowledged in an interview with the *Wall Street Journal* on September 26, 2012, that he was ready to request a bailout as long as the conditions were reasonable and the yields remained very high for a significant period of time, thus hurling the Spanish economy. He admitted that in such a case "he could give 100% assurances that I would request it."[2]

The Spanish government, facing regional elections in the Basque Country, Galicia, and Catalonia, was keen to avoid the humiliation of requesting another bailout and having European authorities dictate the conditions of a rescue. In anticipation, and in order to maintain an appearance of sovereignty, the government unveiled at the end of September 2012 new reforms to restrict programs allowing people to take early retirement as part of the government's efforts to rein in the country's debt and shore up its shrinking economy, as well as to create an independent agency to monitor compliance with budget targets, new job-training programs, and a legislation to sweep away many onerous governmental regulations. As part of these negotiations with the EU, the government was also trying to avoid at all costs the imposition of any additional austerity measures, rightly focusing on initiatives to spur growth. The challenge for both the Spanish government and the European authorities was to craft an agreement that would help the country regain its competitiveness while laying the foundations for sustainable growth.[3] By January 2013, the Spanish government had not yet decided whether to apply for this aid.

As of October 1, 2012, the crisis seemed far from over; therefore, it was premature and speculative to anticipate what may happen in the near future. However, some things seemed to be clear by then.

First, Spain's situation did not mirror that of Greece, Portugal, or Ireland. There has been a tendency to lump these countries together and to view the crisis as caused by fiscally irresponsible governments. The reality, however, is that Spain's public finances were in robust shape prior to the European sovereign debt crisis: public debt was only 36.3 percent of GDP, and the country had budget surpluses from 2003 through 2007. The deficits were the consequence of the crisis, in response to which the previous government implemented an €8 billion public-works stimulus. This, combined with the fall in revenues, blew an enormous hole in the public accounts.

The key problem for Spain was the private sector debt, driven by record low interest rates after the country joined EMU and fueled by reckless banks' investments and loans, which are now bringing them to their knees. Indeed, the debt of the private sector (households and nonfinancial corporations) was 227.3 percent of GDP at the end of 2010. This situation was aggravated by lack of competitiveness and current account imbalances. In the end, high external indebtedness, the fragility of the financial sector, and further declines in asset prices led to the summer 2012 EU financial rescue.

Second, austerity is not enough. The Eurozone experiment designed to show that a procyclical increase in fiscal austerity in a deep recession can lead to growth and debt sustainability is failing.[4] The Spanish economy is shrinking at a faster rate than forecast for reasons outside the country's control: public debt increased from 36 percent before the crisis to an expected 84 percent by 2013, and total debt increased from 337 percent of GDP in 2008 to 363 percent in mid-2011. In this context, further adjustment of the deficit will exacerbate market tensions. The search for so-called credibility cannot obscure the reality that the current course of action is just not credible, as it yields a result opposite to its intension. It is not only clear now that countries cannot spend what they do not have, but it should also be evident that there will be no solution to the crisis without growth. Unfortunately, the current Eurozone policies of fiscal retrenchment miss the vital point that markets are acting rationally when they bet against countries with low growth and uncompetitive economies. Lamentably, there is no growth strategy in the near horizon.

In this regard, the main problems for Spain are: the feeble outlook for growth (the Spanish economy is expected to contract by 1.8 percent in 2012), high external indebtedness, and private sector debt. The country's sovereign debt was downgraded repeatedly, and unemployment is reaching record levels at over 25 percent (above 50 percent among young people). Structural weaknesses—overregulated product and labor markets, poor productivity, and low educational attainments—continue to inhibit growth and weigh on market assessment.

Since PP's government came to power at the end of 2011, it has been fighting a battle with the markets to convince them of their commitment to austerity and structural reforms but, so far, with little positive results. Since then, all indicators deteriorated pretty much: the yields reached record levels (7.75 percent), as have insurance prices to cover the possible default on Spanish Treasury bonds; the stock markets recorded one of the worst performances in years (compared to other EU countries); and capital flight reached new heights.

Spain found itself at the heart of a Eurozone experiment designed to demonstrate that a procyclical increase in fiscal austerity in a deep recession can lead to growth and debt sustainability. The markets, however, did not seem to believe that such a combination is feasible. What Spain faces is a problem of solvency, not of liquidity, even when it does what the markets expect. IMF's managing director, Christine Lagarde, is on record stating that "when we look at what Spain has already done and is committing to do, there is not much more that we would be asking from Spain if it was with a program with the IMF"; she defined the PP government policies as "very, very brave" and the right ones to make "the Spanish economy more agile, flexible and capable of restoring growth, to help people create new jobs."[5] Yet being a model student is not paying off for the country. The government has both financial and credibility deficits and found itself playing catch-up with the markets to no avail.[6]

Third, Spain needs to put its house in order. As late as 2012, the tendency to believe in an entrenched Anglo-Saxon (or sometimes German) conspiracy to undermine the country persisted. Indeed, there is a feeling among Spaniards that the country and its banks are being unfairly picked on by the markets and the EU. This is a very convenient excuse, especially given that analysts, who for years have been stressing the weaknesses of the Spanish economy and the banking system, as well as its dependence on the construction sector, have largely been proven right.

The reality is, however, that since the crisis started, Spanish governments systematically underestimated the country's property crash, the effects of increasing unemployment, the rising debt-to-GDP ratio, and the impact that these problems would have on the banking sector. The Socialists overestimated the capitalization of Spanish companies, the resilience of the

Spanish financial system, the strength of the countercyclical dynamic provision system, and the openness and competitiveness of the Spanish economy. Pedro Solbes, the VP and finance minister, wrote in September 2008: "Fortunately, we have room for maneuver and will help offset the social costs of the downturn while maintaining the investment in infrastructure and education needed to enhance future productivity. We are convinced that in 2010 our economy will enter a new period of sustainable strong growth benefitting from our structural transformation."[7] Time would prove him wrong.

Unfortunately, the Conservative government's responses have not fared much better. Upon taking power, it believed that it could replicate the success of the Aznar administration that was able to fulfill the Maastricht criteria allowing Spain to become a founding member of the EMU. According to José Ignacio Torreblanca, they tried to execute a "hail Mary" in the form of deep cuts and structural reforms to try to convince the Germans that Spain could be trusted and that the country could avoid financial calamity. Unfortunately, that "shock and awe" strategy has not worked. The domestic and international contexts were dramatically different. This time around, the crisis in Spain cannot be understood outside of the Eurozone crisis. Back in the 1990s, Europe was growing, and Spain was able to benefit from its exports (which is not the case during this crisis) and confidence has been sorely lacking.[8] If anything, the PP government policies were also mired in parochialism, often showing more concern about political interests than doing the right thing.

There is growing consensus that Europe needs a "German Marshall Plan" modeled on the vision that America implemented in Europe after World War II. However, the political will is lacking, and Spain is still waiting. Europe informed many of Spain's decisions at the end of the dictatorship, and Spanish citizens still look to Europe with admiration and gratitude hoping that the solution to the country's current problems will come from across its borders. Nowadays, the perception abroad is that Spain has lived beyond its means. The country needs to put its own house in order, recognize the mistakes that have led it to this state, and make the necessary reforms to ensure that these errors are addressed.

Anatomy of the Crisis: The Pain in S-pain

The economic impact of the crisis has been devastating for the country (see table I.1). Spain went again into recession during the fourth quarter of 2011, and its economy contracted 0.4 percent in the second quarter of 2012. Unfortunately, the crisis is far from over. According to the IMF, the economy will contract again in 2013 by 0.6 percent, the largest contraction among the EU's largest economies (only Italy is expected to contract but by far less: 0.3 percent). The deficit is expected to reach 5.9 percent of GDP and the public debt 96.5 percent.[9]

Table I.1 Main Economic Indicators, Spain (2007–2013)

	Units (%)	2007	2008	2009	2010	2011	2012	2013
GDP, constant prices	Change	3.479	0.888	−3.74	−0.07	0.71	−1.826	0.125
Gross national savings	Of GDP	20.999	19.512	19.201	18.698	18.35	18.526	18.538
Inflation, average consumer prices	Change	2.844	4.13	−0.238	2.043	3.053	1.893	1.561
Unemployment rate	Of total labor force	8.263	11.327	18.01	20.065	21.638	24.2	23.9
General government structural balance	Of potential GDP	−1.131	−5.056	−9.06	−7.331	−6.5	−3.402	−3.136
General government net debt	Of GDP	26.7	30.802	42.501	49.689	56.948	67.021	71.777
Current account balance	Of GDP	−9.995	−9.623	−5.2	−4.604	−3.706	−2.143	−1.721

Source: IMF, World Economic Outlook Database, April 2012.

By September 2012, unemployment reached 25.2 percent (or 5.8 million unemployed), and over 50 percent among young people. This extraordinarily high rate of youth unemployment is threatening the self-esteem and potential of young people and social cohesion. Furthermore, public debt was also reaching new records and was still growing, from the original estimate at the beginning of 2012 of 79.8 percent for the year to a revised 85.3 percent of GDP, largely as a result of the banking bailouts. The EU Commission expects that it will surpass the 100 percent of GDP threshold in 2020. The deficit was expected to reach 7.4 percent by the end of 2012, 1 point higher than the projections.[10] And the projections for 2013 were still brutal. While the government expects the economy to contract by 0.5 percent, the employers' association, CEOE, estimated that it will shrink by 1.6 percent. According to the government projections, unemployment will reach 24.3 percent, but the CEOE projects an increase to 26.5 percent.[11]

High unemployment and lower wages caused by the economic crisis pushed many mortgage holders to the brink. According to the Bank of International Settlements, real house prices in Spain rose by 106 percent from the beginning of EMU to the peak in June 2007. Between then and April 2011, they fell by 18 percent. In the first quarter of 2012, they fell 13 percent, the worst decline to date. Expectations, however, are that the entire original house price increases may be reversed, so prices would have to fall 40 percent from that level.[12] The number of vacant properties reached over 1 million units, and the market is oversupplied, which will continue driving down prices. Property prices are also plummeting, which means that hundreds of thousands of borrowers are in negative equity and cannot easily sell to escape debt. And the commercial property market has all but collapsed with the number of transactions falling by more than 80 percent in the three months before July 2012. Only three property transactions were registered in Spain during the second quarter of 2012 (€67 million) down from 58 million in the previous quarter (€260 million).[13]

The labor market situation also continued to deteriorate rapidly, and the new labor reform approved in 2012 was unable to stem the bleeding. In the six months since approval, contracts fell 4.4 percent compared with the first six months of 2011, with decreases in all types of contracts. The ratio of indefinite contracts over the total reached a new minimum in August 2012 (6 percent), touching the levels of 1994, and the number of temporary contracts also decreased by 4.6 percent. The new entrepreneurship contracts represented only 0.7 percent of all the contracts signed during that period. After four months during which unemployment seemed to decrease a bit, it grew again in August 2012 by 17.8 percent, and the number of workers affected by collective dismissals increased by 45.5 percent between March and June 2012.[14]

The country's difficulties were also manifested by its struggle in raising cash at reasonable costs to fund its debt; the yield for ten-year government bonds reached a record high of 7.75 percent on July 25, 2012, a level widely considered unsustainable and which led other countries (such as Portugal and Ireland) to request a bailout. The country's external debt (the result of the record-level current account deficits in the first decade of the euro) reached 92 percent of GDP in 2011, one of the highest in the euro area; Spain will need to borrow €385 billion until the end of 2014 to cover its budget deficit and other needs.[15]

Another example of the disastrous consequences of the crisis is that 20 percent of the companies closed since the beginning of the crisis in 2008 (24 percent of the small ones closed in 2011). Of course, the reality is far more complex and not everything is so negative, as there are still companies that are navigating the crisis successfully, both domestically and internationally, and there are sectors of the economy (such as the tourist sector) that are still performing well.[16]

The social costs of the crisis have also been enormous. Economists estimate that as many as 1.7 million of Spain's 16 million households have no salary earners. Consequently Spaniards are increasingly resorting to survival tactics, like sorting through trash. With unemployment reaching record levels, as well as more and more households with unemployed adults, the scavenging problem has become so pervasive that some supermarkets have resorted to installing locks in their trash bins as a public health precaution. According to a Caritas report, a Catholic charity, it had fed nearly one million hungry Spaniards in 2010, more than twice as many as in 2007. This figure increased by 65,000 in 2011. And 22 percent of Spanish households were living in poverty, and 600,000 had no income whatsoever. Income inequality and poverty are also increasing. In 2011, inequality reached its highest level since 1995. In

2009, only three countries (Latvia, Lithuania, and Romania) had the worst record for income inequality.[17] Per capita income fell again in 2010 as a result of the economic crisis: it decreased from 103 percent of the EU average to 100 percent in 2010 (at the beginning of the crisis it stood at 105 percent). In 2010, it was eight points below the Eurozone average and was ahead of only smaller countries such as Greece, Portugal, Slovenia, and Latvia. The crisis reversed the process of convergence, and per capita income stood in 2010 at the same level as in 2002, eight years earlier. The main reason for this development has been the dramatic surge in unemployment.[18]

Hunger fueled more and more protests and prompted initiatives like Robin Hood raids on supermarkets organized by a group of mayors and agricultural unions in Southern Spain. Indeed, the economic crisis also reignited old social conflicts over the land. Jobless farmworkers, led by union leaders, such as the mayor of Marinaleda, José Manuel Sánchez Gordillo, started occupying uncultivated land properties in Andalusia, adding a new volatile dimension to the crisis. The confrontation over land ownership was one of the factors leading to the Spanish Civil War in the 1930s, when the elite resisted land reform. Agrarian reform (or the lack thereof) was one of the missing elements in the country's transition to democracy.[19] These problems are expected to get worse in the coming months as the economy continues to deteriorate further.[20]

Another consequence of the crisis has been the increasing migration, reversing the phenomena that took place in the decades that followed the country's accession to the EU. According to the government statistics agency INE, since 2009, when the crisis intensified, the number of Spaniards in their late teens, twenties, and early thirties leaving the country increased by 52 percent, from about 12,000 to nearly 20,000. Even more disturbing is the fact that the flight is starting to include members of the country's educated and entrepreneurial elite. For instance, according to official statistics, 30,000 Spaniards registered to work in Britain in 2011, a 25 percent increase from a year earlier.[21]

The financial crisis continues unabated, and the uncertainty over the real situation of the Spanish banks has not diminished, as shown by the increase in capital flight: between July 2011 and July 2012, Spaniards and Spanish companies reduced their deposit in Spanish banks by €85 billion (of that, 55 billion was a net withdrawal and 15 billion were moved outside of Spain); in July 2012, Spaniards withdrew a record €75 billion from their banks (a net capital outflow of €56.5 billion, up by 40 percent from May). The capital outflow in the first half of 2012 reached €220 billion, the equivalent of about a fifth of the country's GDP.[22] And Spanish banks lost a record 10.5 billion in the first half of 2012, largely as a result of the regulators' request for higher provisions.[23] The liquidity issues of Spanish banks' problems are reflected in their dependence on the ECB; in May 2012, they borrowed a new high of €324.6 billion.

In addition, the problems of the financial sector also have a serious impact on credit, which has been drying up even further, despite the fact that the banks still have a healthy €2.3 trillion in overall deposits, according to data from Morgan Stanley. The 5.2 percent (or €1.648 billion) interannual fall in credit between September 2011 and 2012 was the highest since the Bank of Spain started collecting these statistics in 1962, a half-century ago. Most of these credit cuts are directed to companies and families, while credit to the public administration has reached new records.[24] The economy will hardly get out of the recession until credit flows again, but banks are naturally concerned about the increase in nonperforming loans (in July 2012, the rate of questionable loans reached 9.86 percent, €169.3 billion, a new record), as well as the growing demands for higher capital requirements from the regulators.[25]

And the premium risk is choking the SMEs; according to the ECB data, the cost of loans of up to €1 million with duration between one and five years (the typical one for SMEs) reached 6.5 percent in Spain in July of 2012. The same loan in Germany would cost 4.04 percent and in France, 4.14 percent. This further hinders the competitiveness of Spanish companies.[26]

Moreover, according to the stress tests of the country's 14 largest lenders published on September 28, 2012, conducted by the consultancy Oliver Wyman and aided by the Big Four auditors under the supervision of the ECB and the IMF, Spanish banks will need €59.3 billion in new capital. Seven of the fourteen lenders were deemed to fail in stress scenarios. These were largely the banks that were nationalized or took state aid, such as Bankia, the country's fourth largest lender, which will need to take 24.7 billion in capital. But Banco Popular, Spain's sixth biggest bank by assets, in an adverse scenario would need to raise €3.2 billion. While there was hope that the publication of these results on September 28, 2012, would restore confidence among investors in Spanish banks, there was still widespread skepticism about the validity of the exercise, with many observers fearing that the stress scenarios were weak.[27] On the positive side, the three largest banks (Santander with €25.2 billion, BBVA with 11.1 billion, and Caixabank with 5.7 billion) passed the stress test and need no additional capital.[28] Santander was able to raise $4 billion in its Mexico unit, IPO, in September 2012.

The country still has a long way to go to address the loss of competitiveness suffered during the boom years. Between the introduction of the euro and 2008, unit labor costs in the manufacturing sector, the strongest indicator of the economy's competitiveness, increased in Spain 12 percent more than the Eurozone's, and 24 percent more than Germany's (see figure I.1). According to some estimates, this suggests a 15 percent overvaluation.[29] During that period, the country's productivity decreased by 7 percent compared to the Eurozone's, and 22 percent to Germany's. The collective bargaining system largely focused on maintaining the purchasing capacity of salaries, instead of targeting productivity.[30]

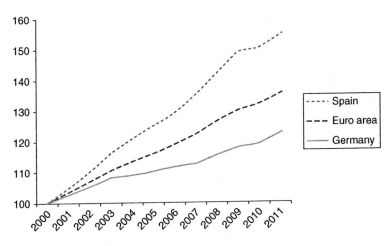

Figure I.1   Labor Costs (2000–2011)
Source: IMF, World Economic Outlook Database, October 2012.

According to the *World Economic Forum*'s annual 2012 competitiveness ranking of 144 countries, Spain was still placed thirty-sixth. The report highlights the vast differences between the best and worst performing nations in the Eurozone, stressing that the process of convergence among Eurozone economies has reversed and is one of the causes of the current difficulties of the Eurozone. According to the report, "one of the shared features of the current situation in all these [Southern European] economies is their persistent lack of competitiveness and their fore their inability to maintain high levels of prosperity…Over all, low levels of productivity and competitiveness do not warrant the salaries that workers in Southern Europe enjoy and have led to unsustainable imbalances, follow by high and rising unemployment."[31]

The performance of the education sector has also left much to be desired: almost one in every three people between the ages 18 and 24 are early school dropouts (this represents double the EU average), and according to OECD, results of Pisa's test in reading, math, and scientific knowledge are poor; there is no university in the top 150 in the main rankings; up to 35 percent of university students drop out before graduation and only a third complete on time.[32] In 2012, 47 percent of Spaniards had only completed primary education (24 percent in the EU and 26 percent in the OECD): 22 percent high school (48 percent in the EU and 44 percent in the OECD) and 31 percent university degrees (28 percent in the EU and 30 percent in the OECD); the graduation rate in high school was 48 percent and in professional training, 28 percent; and 26.5 percent of youths between 18 and 24 years old did not study beyond mandatory education. The problem is not just insufficient resources: average annual public spending per student in public education in Spain is comparatively higher—$10,094 in Spain, $8,307 in the EU, and

$8,329 in the OECD.[33] Research, development, and innovation spending, at 1.38 percent, is significantly lower than the EU average.

The crisis also exposed the financial incontinence of the regional governments and municipalities, which are also in serious dire straits. The regional governments' combined debts is €140 billion, of which €35 billion matured in 2012. Catalonia is the highest indebted one with a debt of €43.9 billion (or 22 percent of its GDP), followed by Valencia (€21.3 billion or 20.8 percent of its GDP) and Castilla-La Mancha (18 percent of its GDP). Madrid has the lowest debt (17.1 billion or 9.1 percent).[34]

As a result of the crisis, the central government has set new limits for each of the 17 regions where 2012 debt must not exceed 15.1 percent of their local GDP.[35] They have been ordered by the central to cut their own budget by 1.5 percent of GDP in 2011 and by 0.7 percent in 2013. Yet, most expect them to miss these targets and project a combined deficit of 2.2 percent of GDP. The regions are struggling to cut their budget deficits, have been shut out of the credit markets, and are crippled by mountains of debt accumulated during the boom years. On Tuesday, August 28, Spain's most economically important region, Catalonia, asked the national government for more than €5 billion in emergency financing, underscoring these struggles, tapping into the €18 billion fund set up by the central government to help regional governments meet their debt repayment obligations.[36] Valencia and Murcia quickly followed and requested aid from Spain's central government. On Tuesday, September 25, 2012, Andalusia, Spain's most populous region, also requested a 4.9 billion rescue; on Thursday, September 27, Castilla-La Mancha requested another €845 million becoming the fifth region to announce that it would tap into the emergency fund. Of the €18 billion emergency fund, these five regions have already requested 16 billion by September 2012.

The economic crisis has also evolved into a constitutional crisis. In September 2012, the Catalonian government announced a snap election in November, and the Catalonian parliament voted in favor of a referendum on independence, which may open the way to Catalan secession. The country, trapped in the worst economic recession since the 1970s, is now contemplating the potential dismantling of the plurinational state established during the transition to democracy to replace the centralized and repressive structure of the Franco years. So far the crisis brought down governments throughout Europe (including in Spain); it now poses, in the case of Spain, a threat to the survival of a nation-state. The success of the Spanish football national team (la Roja, or the red), which won an unprecedented two successive European championships and a world cup during an eight-year span, was celebrated widely throughout the country. At some point, it seemed like it could have served as a metaphor to show that Spaniards were able to overcome difficulties and achieve new heights when they worked together. Unfortunately, it was merely an ephemeral phenomenon that brought Spaniards from all regions together. National identity issues and historical resentments still run deep.

Catalonia, with its 7.5 million inhabitants (16 percent of the Spanish population), amounts to one-fifth of the country's economic output (with a $260 billion economy, it is roughly the size of Portugal), but it is heavily indebted (by far Spain's most indebted region, with $4 billion of the $181 billion debt owed by the 17 regional governments), and Catalans feel that the main reason for their trouble is that the central government takes too much of the region's income to redistribute it to other poorer regions. This conveniently ignores the region's recent struggles: its per capita disposable income and labor productivity grew more slowly than the Spanish average.[37] As noted before, in August 2012, it was forced to request €5 billion in emergency aid from Madrid to meet its refinancing obligations. The 2010 decision by the Constitutional Court to strike down enhancements to Catalan home rule approved by the Catalan parliament in 2006 as part of a reform of the region's statute intensified the clamor for independence.[38] The economic crisis has further fueled resentment toward the central government.

On September 11, 2012, to celebrate the *Diada*—the anniversary of a Catalan defeat at the hands of Spanish troops in 1714—hundreds of thousands of Catalans gathered for a proindependence rally in Barcelona. The PP government, which holds the purse (e.g., with the exception of the Basque Country, financing of regional governments is ultimately at the discretion of the central government), has been accused of trying to use the crisis to push for recentralization, and it has threatened to intervene in the regions and take over their governments unless they adhere to the tight budget targets and reject the Catalan government's demands for an agreement on a new tax revenue redistribution plan (Catalonia currently hands over to Madrid €18 billion a year, which is 9 percent of the economic output, and the Catalonian government sought a similar agreement with the Basque's government, which transfers up to 10 times less per capita to the central government than Catalonia). A poll conducted for the regional government in June 2012 found 51 percent of respondents now wanted independence.[39]

Bad news continued piling up. *What brought the country to this situation?*

Understanding the Crisis: "It's the Politics, Stupid"

Who is to blame? Fingers can point in all directions, but it is a collective failure. The country squandered the privileges of EMU membership, and a lot of the resentment from its European neighbors comes from that. But it is not just the Spaniards' fault. While it is true that a series of Spanish governments bears a large part of the responsibility for mismanaging the economy and finances of the country (particularly at the local and regional levels), there are also other culprits. European banks, for instance, also fueled the real estate bubble because they continued to lend money to Spaniards; and the subprime crisis in the United States ignited an unprecedented global financial crisis with severe effects on the European and Spanish economies.

In addition, the fundamental institutional design problems of the EMU, which did not include a fiscal union, a European joint bank regulator, or a system to deal with financial institutions in stress, also go a long way in explaining the crisis of the Eurozone. Spain, like Ireland, is suffering the consequences of these deficiencies; the country's financial crisis has precipitated a national debt crisis because it cannot afford to bailout its own financial institutions. The EMU also lacked effective mechanisms to control the member states' finances and to penalize those who violated the budget rules. And this did not start with the current crisis; when the euro was first introduced, the Germans and the French were the first ones to argue vehemently for the rules to be watered down to avoid spending cuts. Eurozone countries minimized these risks and are now dealing with the consequences of their hubris, while they are trying to make the institutional changes (a fiscal union and a European-level bank regulator), but in a much more difficult political and economic environment.[40]

Furthermore, investors also share some of the blame; they underpriced the risk of Spanish debt before the crisis, but now they overreact to even minor events causing havoc with the borrowing costs of the country and thus on its economy. European governments, including the German and French, also lent money to Spain so it could be used to buy German exports. The financial regulators also overlooked the problems of the banks and cajas, and failed to act decisively to address them. The national governments in Spain did little to address the bubble and to shift the existing economic growth model. What we are witnessing today at the national and European levels is a blame game that underscored the erosion of the principles of cooperation and solidarity that have underpinned the process of European integration.

As much as there has been a fixation with the economy, with economic policies and with the economic responses to the crisis, it is impossible to understand what has happened without focusing on the politics. In the case of Spain (and the Eurozone as well), it is only appropriate to update the famous campaign slogan, "it's the economy, stupid," that James Carville coined during the first Clinton presidential campaign with a new version, "it's the politics, stupid." The politics of the crisis, both at the domestic and European levels, have been simply abysmal. Indeed, four years into the crisis, it is still perplexing that the political leaders of the country do not have a clear and coherent diagnosis of the crisis, that they keep blaming others for what is happening to the country and fail to assume any responsibilities (after almost eight years in power, Soraya Rodriguez, the Socialist speaker, in a response to the question "many say that the PSOE demonstrates against [the PP] measures to confront a situation that has been in fact created by the PSOE government," answered that "when there was a Socialist government the clear economic difficulties that we confronted were the consequence of a global crisis, not of poor management," and added later in the interview "surely we could have done things better, we do not say that we were perfect,")[41] that they do not yet have a credible long-term plan on how to get the country out of the crisis, and that they insist on austerity and undermine the decisions (such as investment on R-D-I and education) that would set the path for a sustainable future growth. In this regard, the crisis exposed the deficiencies of a political class, supported by its political parties, which developed its own particular set of interests and instruments to sustain it through a system of rent-seeking based on crony capitalism.

Politicians in Spain have been blamed for the real estate, infrastructure, and the renewable energy bubbles, and for the collapse of the cajas, which ultimately led to the EU bailout.[42] According to an influential article titled "Theory of Spain's political class," published by Cesar Molinas in the Spanish daily El País, the roots of the current problems originate in the transition to democracy when politicians adopted a proportional representation voting system with closed, blocked lists that sought to consolidate the party system by strengthening the internal power of the party leaders and adopted the decentralization of the Spanish state. The consequences of these decisions have been enduring. The choice of voting system and blocked lists resulted in a professional political class owing its allegiance to the leaders of the party (which are the ones that place them in the voting lists and/or give them public jobs for the compliance and submission). This has led to a structure in which there is very little contestation within parties and in which loyalty, rather than merit or competence, rules. At the same time, the decentralization process—originally designed as a top-down process, became a bottom-up one led by local and regional elites—has led to the creation of 17 regional governments, as well as thousands of public agencies and companies that became instruments of political patronage. The subsequent decentralization of political parties that followed the political one led to the emergence of regional, local elites that took over the local and regional institutions, including the cajas, whose boards were quickly filled with political appointees who used their position for their own personal gain and/or as a clientelist instrument to finance their projects.

According to Molinas, these developments help account for three of the main bubbles leading to the current crisis: real estate, renewable energy, and infrastructure. The better known bubble is the real estate one: Spain, as we will discuss throughout the book, experienced one of the largest real estate bubbles (and larger than the ones in Ireland and the United States). Between 1997 and 2007, the construction sector grew at an annual rate of 5 percent. During that decade the housing stock increased by 5.7 million new houses, the equivalent of almost 30 percent of the existing stock, and prices increased by 191 percent. In 1998, the construction sector represented 14 percent of total employment in Spain, twice as much as Germany, and five points higher than the UK. This bubble was largely a consequence of the record low interest rates that followed the country's accession to the EMU, as well as other global economic imbalances. However, politicians also played a crucial role; they not only decided where new buildings could be built but also, through the cajas, which they now controlled, provided the funding.

In 1998, the Aznar government approved a new law regulating the land that multiplied the "irrational exuberance" of the construction sector, because it declared that all land could potentially be used for construction unless it was expressly prohibited. This law favored an extraordinary boom in the sector, but contrary to the government's expectations, according to which increasing the stock of houses would reduce prices, it led to a speculative bubble during which people bought houses not because of their low prices but because of the expectation of ever-growing prices and hefty profits (particularly in the context of record low interest rates that facilitated credit and made other investment less attractive).[43] This law led to the continued reclassification of land by the municipalities, which were largely dependent on construction to generate revenue and gave more and more permits to build. This system created a perverse outcome that led not only to the construction bubble but also to the widespread corruption to fund political parties and personal fortunes. In addition, Spain's burgeoning debt problem has its roots in the construction sector boom. The ballooning tax revenues from the building bonanza encouraged municipalities and regional governments to go on a spending spree not only of infrastructure projects including hospitals and schools but also of unnecessary ones like unused swimming pools or airports (see below for specific examples).[44]

Similarly, Spain also experienced a bubble in the renewable energy sector. The energy sector in Spain is a minefield; it has an accumulated deficit of €24 billion as a result of the difference between the costs assumed by the electricity companies to produce electricity and the tariffs paid by most consumers. Politicians, viewing the push toward renewable energy as an opportunity to place Spain at the forefront of these technologies and the fight against climate change, made a big push for subsidies to promote this sector. As a result of these efforts, Spain became the world's third biggest producer of wind power, after the United States and Germany, with an installed capacity of 20,661 megawatts in April 2011. In fact, more than 11 percent of Spain's electricity came from wind power in 2008. Moreover, in 2005, Spain became the first country in Europe to require the installation of photovoltaic electricity generation in new buildings and the second in the world to require the installation of solar hot water systems. The costs, however, have been enormous: the country represents 2 percent of the world GDP, but pays 15 percent of the world's renewable energy subsidies; in order to pay for these subsidies, Spaniards pay the highest electricity rates in Europe (between 2006 and 2011, electricity prices for domestic consumers, according to Eurostat, excluding taxes, increased 69.9 percent, where in the EU they grew only 19.9 percent and in the Eurozone, 13.1 percent; despite this dramatic increase, the deficit between costs and tariffs has increased), which in turn hinders the competitiveness of Spanish companies. This bubble can be explained, again, by the collusion between politicians and businesses to extract resources from consumers and taxpayers, also leading to widespread fraud and corruption.[45] The government announced in September 2012 a new law proposal to reform the energy sector that seeks to collect an additional €3 billion in new taxes to close the deficit. The problem with this solution, of course, is that it will increase prices (the companies will pass along the increased costs to industrial consumers) and thus hinder competitiveness.[46]

The infrastructure bubble, according to Molinas, can also be attributed to the political class. It was caused by billions of euros spent in infrastructure projects that in many cases were unjustified and benefitted only the construction companies and the intermediaries involved in the projects. They were also approved by the local and regional governments (in many instances they granted the construction and the concession to the same companies that presented themselves as license holders, but held little capital) and often funded, yet again, by the cajas. There are now more than €3 billion in debt, most of which would have to come from the taxpayers.

Many refer to these years as the "prodigal years." The crisis exposed the astonishing degree of superfluous (and sometimes irresponsible) spending during that time. Examples abound. In Castellón, they built a new but empty (never had a single arrival or departure) €150 million airport, around a theme park (Mundo Ilusión) and housing estates to support it that was not built.[47] In Alicante, they planned a City of Light, a mega-movie studio, and spent €325 million (largely financed by the regional caja, CAM, which collapsed in 2011) of taxpayers' money in a project that is now defunct: its water canyons are dried, and the studio's 54 acres of plots are almost deserted. In Valencia, according to the left-wing Esquerra Unida party, Mr. Calatrava's designs were selected without competition while his commission grew to 12 percent ($115 million in fees) of the construction cost from the initial 3 percent without public notice (now the region has a 27.3 percent unemployment).[48] In Lanzarote, they opened a 385-room, luxurious, all-inclusive resort partly financed by EU development funds, and local courts declared it an illegal structure. Twenty-two hotels had their initial building licenses retroactively annulled by the Canary Islands High Court (the European Anti-Fraud Office opened an investigation).[49] In Ciudad Real, the Ciudad Real Central, one of the country's most modern and largest international airports that cost €450 million (€1 billion when publicly funded infrastructure and running costs are included), is known as the "silent airport" because only one airline runs two flights a week to Paris and four to Barcelona with help from the regional government subsidies (it has been in bankruptcy proceedings since 2010), and among Caixa Galicia's investments was a yacht crew at the disposal of its chairman. These are all symbols of the wasteful spending that has sunk Spain deep into a recession and a financial crisis. They are monuments to the financial folly that emerged from the property boom and were exacerbated by bad regional and local politics.

The importance of and the damage caused by the political control over the cajas cannot be overstressed. In a country in which the finance sector has been criticized as oligopolistic and unresponsive to the needs of the rest of the economy (Pérez 1997) and in which small companies and entrepreneurs largely depend on financing from banks and cajas, access to funds is crucial, and it often led to what has been described as "incestuous relationships." Restrictive lending to SMEs was precisely one of the reasons that accounts for the poor labor market performance of the country because it undercut these firms' efforts to create jobs and innovate (Fishman 2010, 293–299). The decision by the cajas to channel funding disproportionally to the construction sector (both to construction companies and real estate developers) and toward private mortgages (their reticence to lend to SMEs outside of the construction and real estate sectors) was critical to fuel the bubble in that sector (see Serra Ramoneda 2011).

The collapse of the cajas affected thousands of small savers throughout the country who had invested their life savings in toxic products sold by the cajas (i.e., the so-called *preferentes* or preference shares: a convertible debt instrument that plunged in value and has led to many protests and lawsuits, and despite the fact that they were very complex instruments, too risky to be marketed to consumers, some cajas even sold them to illiterate clients). Their fate accelerated the collapse in trust for institutions that prior to the crisis were at the heart of communities across the country. These were institutions modeled on foundations that collected savings in their areas, lent the money to local businesses and homebuyers, and used part of the profits to invest in charitable work. Their purpose was not to generate profits for shareholders but to redistribute surplus income through social work. Unfortunately, in many cases they fell in the hands of local and regional politicians eager to use them to finance their own projects.[50] Now that they have been largely swept away in nationalizations and mergers over the past three years, there are no other institutions that can play such a crucial social and cultural role in these communities. Unfortunately, as discussed in great detail in chapter 6, many of their managers have been implicated in large payoffs and other scandals.

These developments, according to Molinas, can be largely attributed to the collusion between the political and economic elites who developed a system to "extract" resources from taxpayers for their own benefit. They developed the rent-seeking mechanisms that have allowed them to extract these resources, and they have colonized the institutions that make these decisions, as well as the ones (i.e., the cajas) that provide the funding to implement them. Their selfish interests took prevalence over the general ones. This explains why they failed to articulate a clear diagnosis of the crisis (except blame each other and/or other external forces—the global crisis, such as the EU, Brussels, and Germany), why they failed to assume any responsibility for the crisis, not even an apology, and why they have failed to develop a clear strategy to overcome the crisis beyond waiting for others (the EU/ECB) to come up with solutions and/or wait until it is over. This collusion also explains the resistance from the political and economic elite to reforms because they would jeopardize the existence of the extractive rent-seeking mechanisms that became the main source of rent for most of them. As a result, reforms were often equated during the crisis with fiscal consolidation (budget cuts and tax increases) and masked decisions (like the cuts in education, research, development, and innovation) that will be detrimental to the future competitiveness of the country.[51] The growing capital flight also symbolized the selfishness of the country's elites: in one month (July 2012), they withdrew €74.2 billion from Spanish financial institutions, the largest amount since 1997, and between July 2011 and 2012, the net fall in deposits reached 55 billion.[52] If the elites do not trust the future of the country and pull out their capital, can the regular citizens believe in its future?

But the problem, as convenient as this "theory of Spain's political class," is not only with the political class and the extractive political and economic elites but also with a civil society that tolerated such abuses and repeatedly voted for politicians accused of corruption. As widespread as it became across the country to blame politicians (who became favorite scapegoats for everything that is wrong with the country), this fixation also offered a convenient excuse to overlook Spanish citizens' collective responsibility of the crisis. In many ways, it would be far easier if political parties and the political class could be blamed for everything. However, this explanation fails to account for citizen and voter behavior. Were these parties and these politicians imposed? Who voted for them? Who failed to hold them accountable? Who ignored the rampant corruption and continuing scandals? Who questioned their decisions? Who wondered where the funds for those scandalous projects came from? These are all important questions that also need to be answered. The crisis exposed a passive society that failed to hold its political class accountable, that was not vigilant, and that was more interested in perpetuating and living the "fiesta" than in asking the tough questions challenging the status quo. As long as the society benefitted (and who did not benefit during the bubble years?), it did not question the situation.

With this behavior, many see one of the enduring legacies of Francoism. Political participation and political dissatisfaction in Spain has been a subject of extensive research (Pérez Díaz 1993; Torcal 2002; McDonough, Barnes, and López Pina 1998; Maravall 1997; Morlino and Montero 1995). These studies emphasize the exceptionally low rates of civic engagement and political participation in Spain, the very low understanding of important political issues among Spanish citizens, and the systematic distortion of the public sphere. Fishman (2004) brilliantly explored the paradox of a country in which collective protests end up "disengaging" rather than "engaging" and in which the public sphere often elicits disappointment, despite the high number of expressed grievances.

The crisis, if anything, proved the conclusion that Spain has a largely apolitical society: the "emperor has no clothes." Indeed, a recent European poll shows that Spain is, together with Portugal, the European country in which there is the least interest in politics: only about 30 percent of the population shows some interest in politics; in studies about political commitment, Spain scores high only in the "demonstrations" variable. In other words, Spanish citizens are "reactive"; they mobilize ad hoc demonstrations when specific interest that affects them are touched but later disconnect very rapidly at the same speed with which they were compelled to exhibit on the streets.[53] The expectations raised by the May 15 movement (in many ways similar to the "Occupy Wall-Street" and "We are the 99" movements in the United States, see chapter 5), with its indictment of the political class, did not prove lasting. Voters continued voting for the traditional parties, and the percentage of absenteeism or null votes increased very marginally in successive elections. This lack of citizens' responsibility, not just the politicians', also needs to be accounted for. If there is an important lesson from the crisis, it is that citizens need to assume their responsibilities. It is time for Spanish citizens to stop merely protesting and to start engaging, to channel the high level of popular energy toward becoming real citizens who hold their governments and politicians accountable for their acts and decisions. Only time will show whether the crisis has any such effect.

Spanish society is now confronting one of its worst crises in its recent history, yet it does so from a position of pessimism. Polls show that the crisis led to a profound sense of demoralization and a crisis of self-esteem, with Spaniards being increasingly pessimistic about their future. According to polls from CIS, the assessment of the future evolution of economic conditions has deteriorated markedly in less than one year: 32.8 percent of the respondents felt that it would worsen by November 2011 and 40.5 percent, by July 2012, and 48.6 percent felt in July of 2012 that their personal economic situation was worse than before.[54] In some ways, the crisis has led observers to look at what happened in 1898, when Spain lost its last colonies (Cuba and the Philippines) in the war against the United States.[55] This "disaster" was the spark of a profound reflection about the country's political structures, and it ignited a debate about the need to reform them to allow Spanish people to fulfill their political aspirations. It would take almost a century of political turmoil, and a bloody civil war, to fulfill that goal. With the transition to democracy in the 1970s, it seems that the country had finally found the political system that would allow it to move forward and complete the processes of democratization and modernization, while resolving some of the country's historical challenges (such as dealing with the aspirations of its three historical regions: the Basque Country, Galicia, and Catalonia). The crisis has placed this achievement into question. The enormous progress of the past three decades stalled and is now being questioned. The crisis is viewed as a deep humiliation by the Spanish people and has a profound demoralizing and debilitating effect, both at the individual and collective levels. One of the manifestations of this phenomenon is the generalized resignation and sense of apathy against the crisis. Another is the yearning for the past, particularly for the transition years in which politicians were willing to work together and overcome their differences in pursuit of the common good, something lacking during the current crisis.

The sense of vulnerability is acute and the perception among Spaniards that they no longer control their destiny is widespread and entrenched (a recent poll indicated that 72 percent think that economic decisions are made in Brussels).[56] Even the governments (both the Socialist and the Conservative) seem resigned to the notion that they lost all their autonomy to design and execute the politics to respond to the crisis. This strategy has been disastrous; it may have helped in trying to save their own legitimacy, but it has been at the expense of the legitimacy of the measures they adopted. At the same time, it reinforces the pervasive sense of a government losing control, and it is hard to avoid the feeling that even the government does not believe in those policies (and even seem to accept beforehand that they will not work), yet it accepts them because there is no alternative in order to avoid the country's collapse.[57] The sense of impotence is so acute that a government that has been in power for less than a year feels like one approaching the end of its term. When one walks the streets of Madrid it is hard to escape the conversations about the *prima de riesgo* (the bond spread and yields), and people seem fixated with the possibility of a bailout.

In this regard, the repeated complaints about unfair treatment by markets is a self-defeating strategy. As it has been repeatedly stated, political leadership is about how well you play the hand that you have been dealt with. Both the Socialist and the Conservative governments faced a dire economic situation, but in some ways, they were in a stronger position than that of some other European countries (like Greece). Unfortunately, they have fumbled their aces and have followed and committed unforced error after another: they failed to address the problems on time, they did not do enough to clean the financial sector, and they may have tried to cut too much too fast, thus further depressing the demand. The main problem, however, has not been the economic decisions but the political ones. The repetition of cacophonous, and sometimes even contradictory, messages have not only alienated Spanish voters but also scared investors to end European governments. Both the Socialist and the Conservative governments failed to recognize that markets and investors were listening to what they were saying and observing what they were doing. Oftentimes it seemed like they were addressing their own core supporters without fully understanding that their words would be spread worldwide and would further undermine the confidence of investors in the country (an example described in chapter 2 is when Budget Minister Montoro stated in parliament that the government may not have funds to pay for the public sector wages, or when Foreign Minister García Margallo declared the ECB "a clandestine bank," or when he likened the Eurozone to the Titanic and implicitly warned the wealthy Germans that "if the Titanic sinks, it takes the passengers with it, including those in first class").[58] The lack of common purpose in the country is palpable. Panic is in the air, and the best reassurance is a greater sense of decisiveness and competence.[59] Unfortunately, they have been largely missing throughout the crisis.

The loss of international prestige, and not only in the EU where Spain is now associated with the peripheral "failure" countries but also in Latin America, which for decades was perceived as a model and is now often ridiculed and abused (the nationalization of YPF), an Argentinian energy company, is an extreme example of this), has also contributed to this sense of pessimism.[60]

Moreover, failure of the governments to fulfill their electoral programs and commitments (in fact, the feeling is that they lied to the voters and hid their true intentions), combined with increasing inequalities and uneven distribution of the pain caused by the crisis, and the failure of the economic policies applied so far have only intensified these feelings of pessimism, hostility, and disappointment.[61]

Furthermore, Spanish society confronts the crisis from a position of extreme weakness, depending on the decisions from other countries (and international institutions, such as the ECB), fragmented (one of the consequences of the crisis, as noted in the introduction, has been the intensification of regional tensions), and largely alienated against the country's political class. The historic lack of cohesion of the country has resurfaced again and has further hindered any attempt to develop a national-level collective solution to the crisis. In addition, the crisis is not just a political crisis but a "crisis of politics"; in the absence of decisive leadership from the Left and the Right, politicians (and political parties) are not only perceived as incapable of solving the country's problems, but they are also considered part of the problem, with the fear that this feeling may become entrenched and may contribute to delegitimize the democratic process and/or derive into more radicalized and populist discourses.[62] The emergence of the May 15 movement, discussed in chapter 5, is just another example of this dissatisfaction with the political class.

Throughout 2012 there have been increasing mobilizations all over the country protesting the government economic policies. Their organizers are not just the trade unions but new groups that are using social media to organize demonstrations, and they have been quite successful in bringing hundreds of thousands out on to Spanish streets. However, it is still early to know whether this remobilization of Spanish society, which had been lulled into complacency during the boom years, will be a sustainable phenomenon. In many ways, it resembles the activism of the transition years in the second half of the 1970s when people actively mobilized in support of democratization and political rights, but it is also very different, far less structured, experimental and amorphous, and also is largely bypassing politics (led by groups such as Coordinadora #25S, Economists Against the Crisis, Single Mothers, Judges for Democracy, International Solidarity, and the 15-M Indignants movement) and the traditional institutions that have been tarnished by the crisis.[63] They organized social summits to design the strategy to mobilize citizens in response to the crisis. The common element that brought them all together was the dismantling of the welfare state and the retreat on social rights, which affects them all. While these demonstrations were overwhelmingly nonviolent, in the fall of 2012, there were a few instances of violence as a new movement, "Occupy Congress," organized by Indignants, mobilized to protest against the "kidnapping of democracy." On September 25, 2012, 20 people were arrested and more than a dozen injured in one of these demonstrations, which continued without incident throughout the rest of the week. The social conflict was expected to intensify throughout the fall and winter of 2012.[64]

Also, Spain is facing not only a political and economic crisis but also an institutional one. Indeed, a salient feature of the crisis is the extent to which the country's institutions, established during the democratic transition of the 1970s, have been battered. One of the worst consequences of the crisis, beyond the dramatic social and economic costs, has been the delegitimization of institutions at all levels. The discredit of institutions is running wide and deep, partly as discussed above, not only because they have been colonized by the political elites regardless of qualifications but also because Spanish citizens have tolerated it: they have been willing to live with dysfunctional institutions as long as they benefited from them, rather than risking institutional changes that could work against them.[65]

In this regard, Spain seems to have fallen into the category of countries in which institutions have become extractive and concentrate power and authority in the hands of a few. In a recent seminal work, Acimoglu and Robinson (2012) showed that nations thrive when they develop "inclusive" political economic institutions and fail when they have extractive ones that concentrate power and opportunity in the hands of the elites (73–79). They show that inclusive economic institutions

> that enforce property rights, create a level playing field, and encourage investments in new technologies and skills are more conductive to economic growth than extractive economic institutions that are structured to extract resources from the many by the few... [inclusive ones] are in turn supported by, and support, inclusive political institutions, [which] distribute political power widely in a pluralistic manner and are able to achieve some amount of political centralization.

They conclude that "it is politics and political institutions that determine what economic institutions a country has" (43). According to their view, the role of inclusive political institutions is to promote sustainable economic growth, which requires innovation. Therefore, they need to protect and empower citizens to innovate and invest and need to foster Schumpeter's process of "creative destruction," which is conducive to innovation.

Unfortunately, the crisis in Spain exposed an institutional model that in many cases unleashed an extractive model of crony capitalism. A central problem, as noted by Molinas, was the colonization by the new political elites that emerged since the transition of critical institutions, such as the

Constitutional Court, the Bank of Spain, the CGPJ, or the CNMV. These institutions became politicized and largely lost legitimacy. As a result, institutions that should have played a central role holding politicians accountable largely failed to fulfill that responsibility and instead have become transmission belts of the politicians (and worse, in many cases part of a patronage system), validating their (often questionable) decisions and giving them a free pass.

The problem extended to political institutions such as the Spanish Congress, which failed to fulfill its accountability role. The Senate is predominantly considered useless (despite the fact that it is considered the regional chamber, in the previous legislature it did not introduce a single amendment to the half dozen regional statutes that were approved by the Congress); and Congress (the lower chamber) is dominated and instrumentalized by the party that holds a majority. They largely appear as spectators of the crisis, since both the Socialist and the Conservative governments often resorted to decrees for most of their measures, and the PM rarely spoke (particularly Rajoy) in parliament. Parliamentary rules allow the government with an absolute majority to avoid debates or even full disclosure, and they can veto calls from the minority parties requesting the presence of cabinet ministers for questioning. During its first eight months in power, the PP has submitted to Congress 27 royal decrees that only require the validation of Congress without any opportunity for amendments. The PP government allowed only eight of them to be processed as law proposals. Since 1978, there has never a year in which a government approved as many decrees as this year (2012). During that period, PM Rajoy went to Congress only when obligated (i.e., during the control sessions and after the two European summits). All the other parliamentary requests to question him have been rejected. When the €65 billion austerity package was rammed through Congress in July 2012, he was absent from parliament (and during the debate, one of the PP deputies caused a political storm when she greeted the cuts for unemployed by saying *que se jodan*—let them screw themselves).[66] And in 2012, there was not a State-of-the-Nation debate. In one hour, it approved 10 billion worth cuts in health and education. That summer, while the German Bundestag was debating the conditions for the financial rescue to Spain, the Spanish Congress was on recess, and it had not voted even on that memorandum (the only way it was vetted was in a commission attended by Minister Guindos, but without a vote). The Spanish daily, *El País,* submitted a request for information on official trips from members of Congress; initially it received a positive response, but three months later, it was informed that the secretary general had decided that such information could not be released, and that it would have to wait for the implementation of the new Law of Transparency. And there are no firm plans to change any of this: the Socialists have, now that they are out of power, presented some proposals to change the electoral law and the internal functioning of Congress, but the PP is not making it a priority to address them. Five legislatures ago a group finished a proposal with the support from all parties to reform the bylaws, but the initiative was stopped by the PSOE and the PP, and it has not been reopened. In sum, the walls that currently surround the Spanish Congress are the metaphors of separation between the legislative powers and the citizens.[67]

And the problem is compounded by the fact that PM Rajoy speaks rarely, not just in parliament, but in public or to the press. This vacuum, and the absence of a single voice on economic matters (with the two economic ministers Montoro and Guindos often expressing contradictory messages), intensifies the lack of leadership. The government has also been criticized for its meddling in the main state broadcaster after several journalists considered critical to the PP departed on acrimonious terms.[68] No one questions the government's legitimacy, but its democratic sensibility is lacking.

The lack of transparency (or truth) is simply staggering. For instance, when the government announced another austerity package in July 2012, details emerged in English in the Treasury's web site, aimed at investors, rather than in parliament. The Spanish version that emerged later contained a 10 billion discrepancy over expected revenue increase.[69] The credibility of the government has also been seriously eroded throughout the crisis. The deficit figures are a good example: the Socialist government announced before it left power in November 2011 that the deficit was 6 percent; shortly after coming to power, the PP government claimed that it was false and that it would be close to 8 percent; in March 2012, it announced that it was 8.5 percent; two weeks later, the Madrid municipality and its regional government announced a mistake on its figures and the deficit was revised to 8.7 percent; in September 2012, the INE announced that the figure was understated and that the correct one was 9.1 percent; two days later, the government of the Valencia region announced that its deficit was 3 billion higher, increasing the country's total to 9.4 percent; and we are still waiting for the final data from the other regional governments, which may push up the deficit to 11 percent.[70]

The PP promised not to increase taxes, but they did it within a few weeks after winning the election; it was not going to lower dismissal costs, but it approved a labor reform that lowered the cost of justified dismissals to 20 days per year worked with a maximum of 12 months; it promised that it would not lower public servants' salaries, but it approved an increase in their working hours that was the equivalent of 6 percent per hour worked and later approved the elimination of the Christmas bonus pay (the equivalent of 7 percent of the salary); it was not going to increase the VAT, but it has applied the largest increase (three points to the general one to 21 percent and two points to the reduced one to 10 percent) since that tax was introduced; it was not going to reduce unemployment benefits, but it has; and it was not going to make cuts in health and education, but it has approved the largest cuts in decades. And the government keeps blaming the inheritance it received from the Socialists. After 10 months in power, that excuse no longer seems credible. It either lied about its real plans or did not know, but either option seems unacceptable.[71] How can we expect any confidence from investors and markets?

In addition, time after time investigative commissions have worked as forums to express grievances, but rarely as places in which people have been held accountable, or that had led to any significant political and/or criminal responsibilities. The recent commission that looked at the collapse of Bankia is just an example of this diluted (if not nearly useless) role: former leaders of the bank, former political leaders (including the former minister of finance Salgado), and the former governor of the Bank of Spain were all questioned about the disaster. They all gave their own reasons, largely blaming others for the outcome, yet nothing substantive came out of the process (which is still under judicial review). For instance, Bankia's former chairman, Rodrigo Rato, questioned by the parliamentary panel, underlined the extent to which his decisions were regularly approved by auditors, financial consultants, regulators, and the Bank of Spain's inspectors, and directly contradicted the testimony of Miguel Ángel Fernández Ordoñez, the Socialist-appointed Bank of Spain governor, who had stepped down a few weeks earlier, and who had claimed during his testimony that he had not pressed Mr. Rato to merge Caja Madrid with the Valencian Bancaja to form Bankia. Mr. Rato declared that in June 2010 he was called to the Bank of Spain and in effect was forced to negotiate with Bancaja.[72] Recent reports show that Caja Madrid gave loans to customers who lacked the resources to pay back.[73] The fourth largest financial institution collapses and is no one responsible?[74] How can we be surprised that a government that seems incapable of engaging its own citizens, or institutions such as the Congress, can inspire any confidence on markets and investors? That sums it all.

This colonization extended to public companies and agencies, including the cajas, which were staffed (and led) by acolytes of the politicians with no educational background or professional experience in the field, who were appointed for their loyalty and allegiance to their political patrons. Under their leadership, they became piggy banks and instruments for regional and local leaders of all parties to distribute patronage. It should not be surprising, therefore, that many of their decisions led to the current disaster.[75] As discussed in greater detail in chapter 6, the real estate boom at the heart of the crisis was fueled by the cajas, and the property burst blew holes in their balance sheets that are the heart of the current financial crisis. The government's response to the crisis of the cajas also leaves many questions unanswered: Why did it give 16 billion to CAM or 23 billion to Bankia instead of letting them fail? Why did it recently give 5 billion to Bankia instead of waiting for the EU funds?

Other institutions that should have played a vital role to build up confidence, both domestically and internationally, such as the Bank of Spain (which initially was widely praised, as discussed in chapter 6), have been dragged to the mud of partisan warfare throughout the crisis, and its governor Miguel Angel Fernández Ordoñez was compelled to resign before his term expired amidst the controversy of Bankia's collapse and his failures in managing the financial crisis. This was another instance of damaging politization of the institutions and dereliction of responsibility from the two leading parties: by appointing as governor someone who did not have the appropriate background but was politically closely linked to the Socialist government that appointed him (he had long been associated with the Socialist Party and had served in several government positions throughout his career) and also by failing to provide the necessary regulatory oversight over the institution.

The battering has previously reached untouchable institutions like the monarchy, which no longer seems like the unifying force that it was in the past. King Juan Carlos was revered for his role in bringing democracy to the country. Now, however, Spaniards are questioning their king and scrutinizing his lifestyle and the lack of transparency. The controversy over the king's elephant-hunting trip to Botswana in the spring of 2012, in which he broke his hip, generated a public outcry because it exposed a murky world of business contacts and details about the king's lifestyle (including speculation about his relationship with a German princess who accompanied him in the trip) at a time of national crisis. It led to an unprecedented public apology, but the damage was already done. The royal family's estimated fortune at up to €1.79 billion had been the subject of growing scrutiny. The safari was organized by a Syrian magnate who had worked together with the king on a 9.9 billion bullet train contract that the king had helped broker in 2011 for a Spanish consortium in Saudi Arabia. This controversy has been compounded by an influence-peddling case aimed at the king's son-in-law, Iñaki Urdangarín, who stands accused of using a nonprofit foundation to embezzle public money for sporting events and to use his position to bypass standard bidding procedures. A growing number of Spaniards, including some smaller parties, are using the crisis as a further reason to challenge the monarchy. According to polls, most Spaniards, however, still support him and value his role as a representative of the country and an unifying force, yet they yearn for more transparency.[76]

Another crucial institution, the family, which has been a stabilizing force and which has played a crucial role in the provision of welfare, also seems to be fraying as unemployment increases and the entire members of the family lack any source of income. More and more families are leaning on their elderly relatives (pensions are among the very few benefits that has not been slashed). The situation is so dire that many families are removing their relatives from nursing homes, so they can collect their pensions. A survey from *Simple Lógica* found a sharp increase in the number of older people supporting family members: in February 2010, 15 percent of adults, 65 years or older, said they supported at least one relative, and in the survey conducted two years later, the number had increased to 40 percent; the association of private nursing homes has reported that 76 percent of its members had vacancies in 2009, while that number had increased to 98 percent in 2011. There is more and more evidence that retired people willing to share their pensions to support their families have been the silent heroes of this economic crisis. This may be one of the reasons why conflict in the streets has not been even more intense.[77]

Unfinished Business

As we have seen, Spain is confronting many crises. A crisis that started as an economic storm has evolved into a full-scale political and institutional crisis, and it is now the only country in the world that is contending simultaneously with an economic, financial, sovereign debt and a political, institutional, and constitutional crisis.

Indeed, old wounds are reopening and new sources of political tensions are emerging. While the country's more visible challenges are economic (the growing public debt, the steep deficit, the negative growth, the increasing poverty and inequality, the high and unsustainable borrowing costs, the record unemployment, and the lack of competitiveness) and financial (Spanish banks will need almost €60 billion in capital, according to the latest stress tests of the country's largest 14 institutions), the economic crisis has also unmasked a deeper crisis of the state that has exposed its political, institutional, and regional structures. It has brought to the fore the weaknesses of a political and economic system that has been taken over by a political oligarchy that has allied with the economic and financial ones, with insufficient controls from a passive civil society. The country needs a review of the structures established during the transition to democracy and a profound overhaul of its economic and political system.

Indeed, Spain needs to reform its inefficient local and regional administrations, many of which are already bankrupt, that have brought the country to its knees. They were responsible in 2011 for two-thirds of public expenditures: €234 billion versus 118 billion from the central government, excluding the 23 billion from Social Security. The misuse of these funds has been one of the central reasons for the crisis. Despite the misguided impression to the contrary, high salaries or pensions are not the main problem—60 percent of employees earn less than €1,000 a month, the so-called *mileuristas,* and the average pension is only €785, 63 percent of the EU average—nor are the working hours.

One of the main problems has been the unsustainable state model, which has been appropriated by the political and economic elites, and has been the source of a patronage system that has led to endemic corruption and nepotism (and to the growth of the informal economy, which is estimated at close to 20 percent of GDP).[78] In this regard, the expansion of self-government that followed the democratic transition of the 1970s led to duplications and inefficiencies. Can the country afford 17 ombudsmen, 200 embassies, 50 public TVs with 10,000 employees (most of them with substantial losses),[79] 30,000 public official cars, 4,000 public companies that employ 520,000 people, often created with little fiscalization as instruments of clientelism?

All of that represents around €120 billion, or 11.4 percent of GDP.[80] The regions accounted in the first quarter of 2012 form almost 19 percent of the country's general deficit. These reforms are unavoidable because there is no longer money for all that.

It is not possible to understand what brought the country to its current predicament without blaming the lack of strong and independent institutions, the absence of separation of powers, the feeble and often politicized judiciary, the weak parliament, the electoral system that benefits some political parties at the expense of others, or the closed-list model that allows parties to exercise strict control over the electoral lists (thus premium loyalty over accountability) at the expense of the citizens. They have all been revealed inadequate and have been battered by the crisis.

At the political level, the growing gulf between citizens and parties need to be addressed. Politicians can no longer be deaf and blind to the country's general interests. They need to be less self-serving and more accountable. This will require a reform of the electoral law and the revision of the closed-list system that gives so much power to party's apparatus at the expense of accountability. Decentralization fostered the development of a clientelistic system around the politicians who have evolved into a bigger leech on the public purse. Local and regional governments have spawned homegrown parties, companies, administrations, and interest groups that live off public money. This system has created so many interests that it has become one of the main obstacles to change. The raison d'etre of many of these groups is merely the extraction of public funds, for which they are not accountable. Changes to this system would thus endanger their self-perpetuation. More fiscal self-discipline is necessary (the constitutional amendment passed in 2011 requiring the regions to observe tight deficit and debt limits, and local governments to submit balanced budget, as well as the creation of a supervisory agency to help ensure budgetary compliance by public administrations and the drive to streamline regional and local bodies in order to avoid expensive duplications announced by the government on September 27, 2012, will contribute to this goal). The country needs to settle the regional question. The balance of power between the central government and the regions has been in an almost constant state of renegotiation since the constitutional settlement of 1978. The stability that characterizes other federal systems has been largely absent in Spain, and one of the main consequences of austerity has been that national unity (and social cohesion) is crumbling.[81] The country needs to reform its constitution to settle it once and for all. Renewed calls for the establishment of an asymmetrical federal system need to be considered. The recent demands for independence from Catalonia make the problem only even more urgent.

At the institutional level, reform also needs to become a priority. The judicial system, which has also been penetrated by political interests and which is plagued by inefficiencies and slow-moving courts, needs to be strengthened. And the educational system, which has resulted in comparatively low performance records despite comparatively higher funding, needs to be over-hauled to prepare students for the demands of the twenty-first century.

From an economic standpoint, despite ever-growing evidence that it is not working and it is making the crisis worse, the Spanish government is still persisting with the excessive austerity favored in the Eurozone. It is worth emphasizing, yet again, that Spain had a budget surplus and low debt before the crisis. Deficits emerged after the economy tanked and revenues decreased. Even the IMF has recognized that spending cuts in severely depressed econo-mies may reduce confidence in investments because they may accelerate the pace of economic decline.[82]

Nevertheless, the government announced the 2013 budget at the end of September 2012, which will take nearly €40 billion out of the economy to reduce the public deficit and meet the EU-imposed target of 4.5 percent of GDP for that year (down from 6.3 percent in 2011). And all this, despite increasing difficulties in meeting the deficit targets and obscenely high unemployment levels. The projected increase in social spending caused by the recession is almost entirely offset by the 9.7 billion increase in interest spend-ing due to the higher borrowing costs to finance the growing debt. Social conflict is intensifying as a result of the austerity. Spain still needs to regain competitiveness, a painful process that will take years (although unit labor costs have already come down 4.4 percent since the beginning of the crisis, and the country is beginning to see cost effectiveness that provides hope for further improvements).[83] The crisis will end when the country's living stan-dards are aligned with its productivity. In this regard, structural reforms are as important as the tax increases and spending cuts, including the pending energy liberalization and educational reform. But this pain is being greatly magnified by the harsh spending cuts. What the Spanish economy needs is a looser policy that would let the country's economy breathe while it adjusts to structural reform. It needs support from the EU and the ECB to reduce its borrowing yields and to focus more on growth. Unfortunately, this seems unlikely as Spain (and the other periphery countries in crisis) confronts the EMU political imperatives (i.e., the opposition of countries such as Germany), with the political pressures coming to a head within the country.[84]

The future of Spain is vital to the future of the EU, and the country has become a proxy for the survival of the Eurozone. Paradoxically, while the Spanish government is giving the markets most of what they demand, there are still lingering questions about the Spanish economy and its capacity to regain its competitiveness to grow. This explains the rollercoaster moves in the Spanish ten-year yield, which moved up above 6 percent again at the end of September 2012.[85]

As indicated in the preface, this book goes to press with this lingering question: whether the government would ask for European aid for the state, not just for Spain's banks. Olli Rehn, the EU commissioner for monetary affairs, declared during a visit to Madrid on October 1, 2012, that Europe stood "ready and willing" to act in response to a possible bailout. However, before the end of September, PM Rajoy had taken full advantage of the drop in interest rates that followed the ECB's announcement to resist pressures to request the EU aid. Yet, the markets' patience seemed to be running out, and by the end of September 2012, investors were intensifying, again, the financial pressures on the Rajoy government: the country's Ibex's share index, which had rallied over the summer, ended down 3.9 percent and the FTSE Eurofirst 300 index dropped 1.7 percent; the interest rates on Spain's ten-year bonds approached 6 percent for the first time in months. With €20 billion in Spanish bonds due in October 2012, many observers predicted that the Spanish government would request assistance to help cover about half of the €180 billion that the government need over the following year.[86]

The 2013 government budget, one of the most draconian in the country's history, seemed to bring PM Rajoy's government closer to asking for this aid.[87] On September 27, 2012, the government announced its fifth round of budget cuts and tax increases in nine months. The government still claimed that it did not know what conditions the EU might impose in return for a bailout, but this reform package was widely considered as the instrument that would pave the way for a new EU bailout and Spanish sovereign debt purchases by the ECB as part of its proposed OMT program. Under the 2013 budget plan, government spending would be slashed by 8.9 percent, and tax receipts would increase from €170 billion to €175 billion; government spending would fall about €40 billion, or 0.8 percent of GDP.[88] The objective was to bring down the deficit from 8.5 percent of GDP in 2011 to 4.5 percent in 2013. The day after, Oliver Wyman presented the results of the banking stress tests summarized earlier: 7 of the 14 banks audited will need close to 60 billion of additional capital.

Once again, the reaction from the markets was mixed amidst concerns that taking out some €40 billion in the middle of a deepening recession would further slow down the growth (the government expects that Spain's economy will contract 1.5 percent in 2011 and 0.5 percent in 2013, a forecast that many observers consider too optimistic) and increase the chances that the country would find itself in a debt spiral. Unless a clear growth strategy emerges (both within Spain and the Eurozone), the rest is largely rhetoric.

Moreover, Spain faces debt refinancing needs of €38.6 billion in 2013, 10 billion more than what was budgeted for 2012, underscoring the country's difficulties containing its borrowing costs.[89] The fact that Spain has not yet received any of the funding promised for its banks and that Germany and other northern European countries seemed to be backtracking on the decision adopted at the June 29 Eurozone leaders' summit, in which they agreed "to break the vicious circle between banks and sovereigns," added to the uncertainty. Germany now claimed that the banking union should not deal with any legacy risk but only with problems that arise in the future. If this is confirmed it would add billions of euros to the Spanish debt. This is yet another instance of Eurozone leaders muddling through.[90] It is time to accept that the markets do not seem to be questioning only the reforms or the will of the Rajoy government but also the will of the German one.

In addition, there are lingering concerns about the continuing slide of the real estate sector, which may not have reached bottom, and its impact on the banks' accounts. There was also skepticism about the conservative assumptions used by Oliver Wyman in the latest round of stress tests. Moody's estimated that those banks would need between €75 billion and €105 billion. The final test of investors' confidence will be the ability of the Spanish government to attract private investors to the newly created "bad bank" that will absorb the toxic real estate assets of Spanish banks.[91] The price at which those assets are transferred to the bad bank will be very important to reassure investors that there is a floor for the price of those assets.[92] The government's decision not to cut or even freeze pensions (in fact it plans to increase payouts by 1 percent) was also perplexing: pension expenditures represent the single biggest line item in the Spanish government budget at 40 percent of public spending and 9 percent of GDP. Once again, from the markets' perspective, it seemed that political considerations (there are 10 million pensioners who can vote) trumped the government commitment to austerity.

Nevertheless, imposed austerity on the Spanish government was not working. Yet, as late as October 2012, there was still little recognition, in Madrid, Berlin, or Brussels, that returning Spain to solvency would require new policies to encourage economic growth through less rigid fiscal targets. Spain cannot grow until it is competitive; however, it cannot grow while engaging in austerity. The challenge is how to square that circle.

The solution to the country's problems demands recognition that this has been a collective failure, which requires a constructive collective response.[93] The crisis has not been solely caused by external factors, nor has it been the result of a "series of unfortunate events" or accidents. It has been the consequence of specific actions (and inactions) from individuals and institutions, and as such they could have been avoided. More importantly, it has also been the result of an entrenched culture (*la cultura del pelotazo*) that has allowed these things to happen and that has failed to hold political and economic leaders accountable. The crisis should lead Spaniards to review and redesign the institutional practices and cultural elements that have brought the country into such disrepair. Who audits the auditor? Who holds the political and economic elites accountable? The country needs to strengthen the institutional mechanisms that will control the politicians and regulators. Institutions such as the Constitutional Court, the General Counsel of the Judiciary, the Bank of Spain, the CNMV, and the Energy Commission need to be depoliticized and given the resources to hold politicians and regulators accountable.

Spain needs fundamental changes that require an ample majority to carry through the political, fiscal, and economic changes in ways by which they are accepted by the majority that they are just and fair. For instance, if structural reforms are necessary to address the country's competitiveness problems, the government could consider fiscal policies as an instrument to address the most negative consequences of those reforms and to compensate those groups that may have been negatively affected by them. Only this way it may be able to gain the necessary social support.[94] Unfortunately, so far, both the Socialist Party and the PP have played a partisan game rather than building consensus. The PP government needs to forge a national consensus urgently and take advantage of the growing calls for a national pact (even Rajoy had called for a "common effort" during the electoral campaign), akin to the Moncloa Pacts of 1977 that underpinned the transition to democracy, that include the nationalist parties. Such a pact would not be a sign of weakness, but rather a vital instrument to steer the country out of the recession. Indeed, in order to recover trust and credibility, Spaniards first need to agree among themselves, and what Spain needs today is sensible compromises aimed at resolving the pressing disagreements of the moment.[95] Unless they stop pointing fingers and blaming each other (as well as others outside of Spain), and accept that they need to share the cost of any solution, the crisis will not end (or it is bound to repeat itself). This is the time for POLITICS in capital letters. Time is running out.

Objectives of the Book

This book seeks to address a series of interrelated issues. First, it describes the performance of the Spanish economy during the past decade (2002–2012). Second, it analyzes the basis of the success during the 1997–2007 period. Third, it examines the imbalances that made that success unsustainable, as well as the factors that hindered the implementation of the necessary economic reforms to transform the existing economic growth model. Fourth, it studies the economic and political consequences of the crisis, as well as the performance of the Spanish financial sector during the crisis. Finally, based on the analysis of the Spanish experience, it draws some lessons that would be of interest for other countries from a normative standpoint.

From a domestic standpoint, this book challenges the interpretation according to which the responses of European countries to the pressures associated with globalization and the process of European integration are uniform. Contrary to this prediction, this book shows that Spain globalization and European integration have promoted rather than undermine alternative domestic responses. While technological changes, capital market integration, and postindustrialization have affected the balance of power between governments and private actors and have triggered new political realignments, they have also influenced the interests and strategies of the actors and have led to new strategies and patterns of change. These developments have not only led to particular economic policies and preferences, but they have also precluded the implementation of alternative policy options and have often hindered the necessary reforms.

Furthermore, the book also addresses the impact of European integration on Southern European/peripheral economy. The recent performance of the country shows that EU and EMU membership have not led to the implementation of the structural reforms necessary to address the country's economic weaknesses (i.e., dependency on the constructions sector and erosion in competitiveness). On the contrary, the book will make the case that EMU contributed to the economic boom, which was fueled by consumption and record low interest rates, thus facilitating the postponement of necessary economic reforms. Indeed, the Spanish experience shows that the process of economic reforms has to be a domestic one led by domestic actors willing to carry them out.

The book explores one of the core questions facing the new Europe, namely the sustainability of the EMU in the context of sharp differences in economic performance and levels of competitiveness. Spain shows the pitfalls of monetary integration of less competitive economies, used previously to high inflation and high interest rates. These countries are likely to experience an explosion in consumer spending and borrowing, because lower interest rates and the loosening of credit will likely lead to a credit boom. This development resulted in further losses in external competitiveness, together with a shift from the tradable to the nontradable sector of the economy, which had a negative impact on productivity. How can these issues be addressed to make EMU sustainable?

What Is Unique about This Book?

The focus of the book is, first, Spain. There are very few books published in English that examine the Spanish economic transformation over the past two decades and the challenges that the country faces in the new millennium. Moreover, the book incorporates the Spanish European integration experience, which to date has been studied largely from the standpoint of literature on political transitions to democracy, into the literature on European political economy. The Spanish experience within the EU and the EMU offers one of the few instances in which the integration that took place in an economic, political, and institutional context was markedly different from that of the other European states.

At the same time, the book evaluates the impact of EU/EMU accession on the Spanish economy. EU membership initially brought its own problems to the Spanish economy. While the difficulties of the 1980s and early 1990s were successfully overcome, fresh challenges have emerged in the new millennium. Entry to the EU has so far brought many advantages to the country. Spain has benefited extensively from the EU's cohesion policies, which have contributed to improve the physical infrastructure and capital stock of the country. At the same time, Spain's trade with the EU has expanded dramatically over the past 25 years, and foreign investment has flooded in.

One of the main consequences of these developments has been a reduction in the economic differentials that separated the country from the European average. Yet, its EMU membership, as noted above, has presented significant challenges that remain to be addressed.

The Spanish experience with EU/EMU integration also illustrates the economic, social, institutional, and cultural challenges of this undertaking and will provide useful lessons for other countries. While integration has had very positive effects, the process of integration has also brought significant costs in terms of economic adjustment, loss of sovereignty, and cultural homogenization. Furthermore, EU integration does not guarantee success. Indeed, Spain has suffered an intense economic downturn since 2008 and is experiencing serious budgetary and fiscal problems that are hampering its economic growth and are likely to do so for the foreseeable future.

The book also examines the performance of Spain's financial sector during the crisis. Indeed, initially one of the few positive surprises of the global financial crisis in Spain was the performance of its financial sector. Spanish banks, contrary to its counterparts all over the world, appeared to have escaped the direct effects of the global financial crisis during the first stage of the crisis. It is important to understand why. There is consensus that the stern regulations of the Bank of Spain played a key role in this outcome. The regulations made it so expensive for financial institutions to establish off–balance sheet vehicles, which have sunk banks elsewhere, that Spanish banks stayed away from such toxic assets. However, the depth of the crisis and the collapse of the real estate sector eventually caused a massive crisis in the financial sector that led to the nationalization of several institutions and a EU financial bailout. This dramatic turn of events also needs to be explained.

At a time when there are increasing doubts about the future of EMU, this book sheds light on the impact of monetary integration on a "peripheral" economy. It will show that in the case of Spain, EMU membership has contributed to prevent capital flight and has helped to avoid a repetition of the attacks on the peseta. Without the euro, the huge trade deficit would have already led to capital flight, devaluation of the peseta, inflationary spiral, increases in interest rates and risk premium (with the associated impact on the cost of the debt), and implementation of more restrictive monetary and fiscal policies. However, the Spanish experience also shows the pitfalls of monetary integration of less competitive economies with an inflationary history. These countries are likely to experience a credit boom, driven by potentially overoptimistic expectations of future permanent income, which in turn may increase housing demand and household indebtedness, and lead to overestimations of potential output and to expansionary fiscal policies. The boom also led to higher wage increases that were caused by the tightening of the labor market, higher inflation and losses in external competitiveness, together with a shift from the tradable to the nontradable sector of the economy, which had a negative impact on productivity.

The book also addresses the challenges of EMU membership based on the Spanish experience. In the case of Spain, the insufficient responsiveness of prices and wages, which have not adjusted smoothly across sectors, has led to accumulated competitiveness loses and large external imbalances. The book will stress the need to implement supply-side reforms in order to make the country's economy more competitive.

Theoretical Framework

This book is positioned within the VoC debate about LMEs and CME (Hall and Soskice 2001). According to the VoC literature, Spain is characterized by strong strategic coordination in financial markets but not so in the field of labor relations (Royo 2008). In this regard, some have claimed that Spain is moving toward the Anglo-Saxon model because the lack of articulation of its institutional ideal precludes the evolution toward a CME (see Molina and Rhodes 2007). Contrary to this prediction, this book shows that, at least in some instances, in Spain the global financial crisis has promoted rather than undermined coordination among economic actors.

At the same time, the book considers the Spanish experience during the crisis within the framework of the VoC literature. While some countries have converged toward deregulation as a result of the combined processes of globalization and European integration, this book shows that differences persist. Indeed, in the case of Spain, the crisis has led to extensive regulatory intervention that has served to reinforce the preexisting model. The analysis of the Spanish experience during the crisis confirms the thesis that coordination is a political process. It shows that institutional change is a political matter and that successful coordination depends not only on the organization of the social actors but also on their interests and strategies. Indeed, in a context of structural changes, we have to examine the political settlements that motivate the economic actors, and we need to look at the evolving interests of capital and the structural and political constraints within which economic actors define and defend their interests (Royo 2000; 2008). Finally, this book develops further the VoC literature, by highlighting the role of micro and macro domestic political economy institutions in laying the foundations of the crisis and its subsequent development, as well as the responses to the crisis.

Moreover, the book is situated within the broader, comparative political economy literature (see Royo 2013a). Some scholars have sought to place the politics of financial reform in Spain in a historical context. Sofía Pérez (1997) and Arvid Lukauskas (1997) have already challenged the widespread assumption that international market forces alone explain domestic financial reforms in Spain. Both claim that in Spain domestic politics played an even larger role than international pressures. Pérez contends that domestic elites, particularly a group of reformers within the central bank, seized on liberal economic arguments and developed new patterns of accommodation with private bankers to promote reforms. She emphasizes the oligopolistic nature of the sector, arguing that this system generated significant costs for Spanish firms outside the finance sector.

Lukauskas also examines the role of public officials in the evolution of financial regulation in Spain, but he is more favorable to its political class. He claims that they undertook financial liberalization, despite opposition from powerful groups, to achieve political goals; democratization gave them a strong incentive to improve economic performance through financial reform in order to compete for votes. He attributes their banking policies to an electorally based desire to secure economic outcomes, such as growth, by pleasing the median voter.

More recently, in another seminal piece, Robert Fishman (2010) has analyzed the economic consequences of Spain's banking system and has shown how the country's poor employment performance has also been rooted in its financial system. Fishman argues that the Spanish policymakers' approach was molded by its path to democracy, which shaped the political handling of banking and of financing for SMEs.

In addition, according to the standard typology of the varieties of financial capitalism, national financial systems can be divided into "bank based" and "market based" depending on the dominant sources of LME finance (Zysman 1983). This literature focuses on national systems as governments and/or LMEs as agents of change. Indeed, the transformation of national financial systems is largely seen in terms of the rise of shareholding capitalism and as a move away from bank-financed capitalism—an analysis that points to the implications of the end of "patient capital" for other elements of the national variety of capitalism. According to this view, banks are static, so any changes in their activities, and the implications of those changes, are largely neglected. In other words, it tends to overlook the important role of banking and banks, and their contribution to change (Hardie and Howarth 2011). This book seeks to address this shortcoming by focusing on agency (the operation of Spanish banks) in order to explain changes in national financial (and specifically banking) systems during the first phase of the global financial crisis. Yet, while the focus is upon the activities of banks, it is also necessary to understand the institutional framework that has shaped banking activities in Spain.

This book builds on these contributions and stresses the agency of domestic actors in shaping national financial system change. It uses a comparative, historical analysis approach to explain the response of the financial sector to the first phase of the global financial crisis. This holistic analysis will contribute to a more complete understanding of the national varieties of capitalism.

To do so, it puts the Spanish financial institutions in context, while following a comparative, historical analysis that looks beyond the typical VoC approach to include a wider range of considerations, including historical learning processes, strategic decisions, and cultural arguments. It addresses four of the alleged weaknesses of the VoC approach, namely, neglect of the state, disregard for dynamics of change, divorce of the (financial) firm from national contexts, and incapacity for dealing with countries that do not fit easily into CMEs and LMEs. This analysis offers a compelling alternative to state- and market-driven conceptions of financial regulations and reform.

Finally, the book is also rooted in the political economy literature on institutions, ideas, and interests. These are categories typically used by comparative political economists to define a policy constellation. Each one of them has been the focus in three major approaches in the comparative political economy literature. However, in this book, they are not treated as separate variables but as "social representations" (Jenson and Merand 2010). This is so because of the "codependent" connection among the three variables, as they are intertwined and need each other (Jenson 2010, 8; Heclo 1993). Indeed, instead of looking at the relative weight of ideas, interests, and institutions separately, they will be considered "synthetically and sequentially" (Blyth 2002, 170), as each one of them is constitutive of the others. This book will claim that these variables help account for the economic difficulties that Spain has experienced.[96]

Organization of the Book

Chapter 1 examines the performance of the Spanish economy in the years that preceded the global financial crisis and analyzes the weaknesses of the Spanish economic model, and the domestic imbalances that precipitated the crisis, once the Spanish economy was hit by the global crisis. Chapter 2 looks at the responses of the Socialists and Conservative governments to the crisis. It describes the major initiatives that both governments undertook to address the crisis and analyzes the result of these initiatives. It shows a pattern of tardiness and shortsightedness on the part of both governments, which often reacted too late to the crisis and with insufficient actions. It describes their responses as largely a reactive approach driven by pressure from the markets and the country's neighbors.

Chapter 3 analyzes the stickiness in economic policymaking. The unsustainability of an economic growth model largely driven by construction and consumption had been often stressed in the years prior to the crisis, including by leaders of the Socialist opposition party before they won the 2004 election. Yet, when the Socialist won the elections they did little to change the existing economic model. This chapter explains this paradox. Chapter 4 examines the country's fiscal policies in the years prior to the global financial crisis, from 2000 to 2008, focusing on three main variables to account for its fiscal policies and fiscal performance: institutions, ideas, and interests. Contrary to the widespread assumption that the crisis in Spain is a crisis of irresponsible public spending, this chapter shows that was not in fact the case. However, fiscal prudence was short-lived. Indeed, when the global crisis hit the country the deficit and debt started spiraling out of control. The chapter examines the reasons behind this performance shift, and it looks at the alternatives that the government could have pursued.

Chapter 5 considers the political and electoral impact of the crisis, and its effects on the social concertation process and the labor reform process. Chapter 6 analyzes the impact of the global crisis on the Spanish financial system between 2008 and 2012. As noted earlier, the Spanish financial system experienced a notable positive performance during the first stage of the crisis. In the past year, however, this changed and it is now suffering one of the worst financial crisis in the country's modern history, which led to the EU financial bailout. Yet the chapter shows that, the crisis is largely concentrated in a particular set of institutions, the *cajas de ahorro*. Overall, the performance of the largest Spanish financial institutions has been positive throughout the crisis. The chapter examines why and contends that this response was largely driven by institutional, political, and cultural factors. The book closes with some lessons from the Spanish experience during the crisis.

CHAPTER 1

From Boom to Bust: A Miraculous Decade (1997–2007)?

Introduction

In 2011, Spain commemorated 25 years of EU membership. For Spain, the EU symbolized modernization and democracy. The European integration process has facilitated the reincorporation of the country into the international arena; contributed to the legitimacy of the new democratic regimes; acted as a buffer in controversial issues (such as decentralization and the implementation of economic reforms); and facilitated and accelerated the process of convergence and modernization of financial, commercial, and manufacturing structures. The concept of Europe became a driving force that moved reforms forward, and it was a fundamental factor for bringing together political stabilization, economic recovery, and democratic consolidation.

EU integration was the catalyst for the final conversion of the Spanish economy into a modern, Western-type economy. The economic liberalization, trade integration, and modernization of the Spanish economy started in the 1950s and 1960s with the implementation of the stabilization plan in 1959 (Estefanía 2007, 53–116), and Spain became increasingly prosperous over the two decades prior to EU accession. Yet, one of the key consequences of Spain's entry into Europe has been that its membership has facilitated the modernization of its economy (Royo 2008; Tovias 2002). The actual accession of Spain after 1986 compelled the country to adopt economic policies and business strategies consistent with membership and the *acquis communautaire*. At the same time, EU membership facilitated the microeconomic and macroeconomic reforms that successive Spanish governments undertook throughout the 1980s and 1990s.

The overall economic results have been very beneficial. Since 1986, Spain has closed the wealth gap with the richest European countries. In the first 20 years of its EU membership, per capita income grew 20 points, 1 point per

Table 1.1 Compliance of the EMU Convergence Criteria (1996–2006)

		Spain	
%		1996	2006
Inflation	change	3.6	3.5
General government deficit	GDP	4.6	-1.8
General government gross debt	GDP	70.1	39.8
Long-term interest rates	change	8.7	3.82

Source: Commission and EMU Reports, ECB.

Table 1.2 Divergence of GDP Per Capita (1980–2006)

	1980	1985	1990	2000	2006
EU totals (%)	100.0	100.0	100.0	100.0	100.0
Spain	74.2	72.5	77.8	81.0	97.2

Source: EU.

year, to reach close to 90 percent of the EU15 average. By 2007, Spain had already reached the EU25 average, a process that was accelerated by the fact that the country has grown on an average 1.4 percentage points more than the EU between 1996 and 2007 (see table 1.1). At the same time, the integration with Europe also deepened; by 2007, 90 percent of the FDI, 87 percent of the tourists, 74 percent of the exports, and 66 percent of the imports came from the EU.

Yet, the process of nominal convergence has advanced at a faster pace than real convergence. The country's income levels remain behind the EU average (see table 1.2).

Moreover, Spain became one of the founding members of the EMU, and its impact has also been positive for the country; it contributed to macroeconomic stability, imposed fiscal discipline and central bank independence, and lowered the cost of capital dramatically.

Spain in the 1990s and 2000s: The Miraculous Decade

Before the global crisis that hit Spain in the spring of 2008, the country had become one of Europe's most successful economies (Royo 2008, 8–12). While the performance of other European countries was slow or stagnant, Spain performed much better at reforming its welfare systems and labor markets, as well as at improving labor market flexibility and lowering unemployment. Indeed, over the decade and a half prior to 2008, the Spanish economy was able to break out of the historical pattern of boom and bust, and the country's economic performance was nothing short of remarkable. Propped by low interest rates and immigration, in 2008, Spain was in its fourteenth year of uninterrupted growth, and it was benefiting from the longest cycle of continuous expansion of its economy in modern history (only Ireland in the Eurozone has a better record), which contributed to the narrowing of per capita GDP with the EU.[1]

Unemployment fell from 20 percent in the mid-1990s to 7.95 percent in the first half of 2007 (the lowest level since 1978), as Spain became the second country in the EU (after Germany, which has a much larger economy) to create the most jobs (an average of 600,000 per year during that decade).[2] The Spanish economy grew a spectacular 3.9 percent in 2006 and 3.8 percent in 2007. As we have seen, economic growth contributed to per capita income growth and employment. Indeed, the performance of the labor market was remarkable; between 1997 and 2007, 33 percent of total employment created in the EU15 came from Spain. In 2006, the active population increased by 3.5 percent, the highest in the EU (led by new immigrants and the incorporation of women in the labor market, which increased from 59 percent in 1995 to 72 percent in 2006), and 772,000 new jobs were created. The public deficit was also eliminated (the country had a *superavit* between 2005 and 2006, which reached 1.8 percent of GDP, or €18 billion, in 2006), and the public debt was reduced to 39.8 percent of GDP, the lowest in the past two decades.[3] The construction boom was also remarkable; more than 400,000 new homes were built in and around Madrid between 2002 and 2007.

The overall effects of EMU integration were also very positive for the country. One of the key benefits was the dramatic reduction in short-term and long-term nominal interest rates: from 13.3 percent and 11.7 percent in 1992 to 3.0 percent and 4.7 percent in 1999, and to 2.2 percent and 3.4 percent in 2005.[4] The lower costs of capital led to an important surge in investment by families (in housing and consumer goods) and businesses (in employment and capital goods). Without the euro, the huge trade deficit that exploded in the second half of the 2000s would have forced a devaluation of the peseta and the implementation of more restrictive fiscal policies.

The economic success extended to Spanish companies, which now expanded beyond their traditional frontiers (Guillén 2005). In 2006, they spent a total of €140 billion ($184 billion) on domestic and overseas acquisitions, coming in third behind the UK and France.[5] Of this, €80 billion were spent to buy companies abroad (compared with the €65 billion spent by German companies).[6] In 2006, Spanish FDI abroad increased 113 percent, reaching €71,487 billion (or the equivalent of 7.3 percent of GDP, compared with 3.7 percent in 2005).[7] In 2006, Iberdrola, an electricity supplier, purchased Scottish Power for $22.5 billion to create Europe's third largest utility; Banco Santander, Spain's largest bank, purchased Britain's Abbey National Bank for $24 billion; Ferrovial, a family construction group, concluded a takeover of the British BAA (which operates the three main airports of the UK) for 10 billion pounds; and Telefónica bought O2, the UK mobile phone company.[8] Indeed, 2006 was a banner year for Spanish firms; 72 percent of firms increased their production and 75.1 percent their profits, while 55.4 percent hired new employees and 77.6 percent increased their investments.[9]

The country's transformation was not only economic but also social. The Spanish became more optimistic and self-confident (a Harris poll showed that they were more confident of their economic future than their European and American counterparts, and a poll by the Center for Sociological Analysis showed that 80 percent were satisfied or very satisfied with their economic situation).[10] Paraphrasing a famous campaign to promote the country, Spain was "different" again and, according to a poll, for Europeans it had become the most popular country to work in.[11] Between 2000 and 2007, some 5 million immigrants (645,000 in 2004 and 500,000 in 2006) settled in Spain (8.7 percent of the population compared with 3.7 percent in the EU15), making the country the biggest recipient of immigrants in the EU (they represent 10 percent of the contributors to the Social Security system). This is a radical departure for a country that used to be a net exporter of people, and more so because it has been able to absorb these immigrants without falling prey (at least so far) to the social tensions that have plagued other European countries (although there have been isolated incidents of racial violence) (Calavita 2005).[12] Several factors have contributed to this development.[13] First, economic growth, with its accompanying job creation, provided employment for the newcomers while pushing down the overall unemployment. Second, cultural: about one-third of the immigrants came from Latin America and they shared the same language as well as part of the culture, which facilitated their integration. Third, demographic: an ageing population and low birthrates. Finally, the national temperament, characterized by a generally tolerant attitude, marked by the memory of a history of emigration, which made the Spanish more sympathetic to immigrants (according to a recent poll, no fewer than 42 percent state that migration had a positive effect on the economy). The percentage of children from mixed marriages increased from 1.8 in 1995 to 11.5 in 2005.[14]

These immigrants contributed significantly to the economic success of the country in that decade because they boosted the aggregate performance of the economy: they raised the supply of labor, increased demand as they spent money, moderated wages, put downward pressure on inflation, boosted output, helped the labor market to avoid shortages, contributed to consumption, and increased flexibility in the economy with their mobility and willingness to take on low-paid jobs in sectors such as construction and agriculture in which the Spanish were no longer interested.[15]

Indeed, an important factor in the per capita convergence surge after 2000 was the substantive revision of the Spanish GDP data as a result of changes in the National Accounts from 1995 to 2000. These changes represented an increase in GDP per capita of 4 percent in real terms (the equivalent of Slovakia's GDP). This dramatic change was the result of the significant growth of the Spanish population since 1998 owing to the surge

Table 1.3 Economic Summary, Spain (2000–2008)

	Units	Scale	2000	2001	2002	2003	2004	2005	2006	2007	2008
GDP, constant prices	National currency	Billions	546.886	566.82	582.146	600.179	619.784	642.192	667.991	691.807	697.727
GDP, constant prices	Annual % change		5.053	3.645	2.704	3.098	3.267	3.615	4.017	3.565	0.856
GDP per capita, constant prices	National currency	Units	13,582	13,919	14,090	14,288	14,517	14,797	15,149	15,415	15,294
Output gap in % of potential GDP	% of potential GDP		1.898	1.474	0.293	0.132	0.501	1.403	2.876	3.937	3.106
GDP based on PPP share of world total	%		2.146	2.178	2.177	2.168	2.128	2.109	2.087	2.062	2.017
Inflation, average consumer prices	Annual % change		3.484	2.827	3.589	3.102	3.053	3.382	3.562	2.844	4.13
Unemployment rate	% of total labor force		13.873	10.553	11.475	11.48	10.97	9.16	8.513	8.263	11.327
Employment	Persons	Millions	16.412	16.931	17.338	17.878	18.51	19.267	20.024	20.626	20.532
General government balance	National currency	Billions	−6.161	−4.361	−3.312	−1.622	−2.862	8.759	19.847	23.259	−41.874
General government balance	% of GDP		−0.978	−0.641	−0.454	−0.207	−0.34	0.964	2.016	2.209	−3.847
Current account balance	% of GDP		−3.959	−3.941	−3.259	−3.509	−5.251	−7.357	−8.972	−10.01	−9.592

Source: IMF, World Economic Outlook Database, October 2009.

in immigration (for instance, population grew by 2.1 percent in 2003). The key factor in this acceleration of convergence, given the negative behavior of productivity (if productivity had grown at the EU average, Spain would have surpassed the EU per capita average by 3 points in 2007), was the important increase in the participation rate, which was the result of the reduction in unemployment, and the increase in the activity rate (proportion of people of working age who have a job or are actively seeking one) that followed immigration growth and the incorporation of female workers into the labor market. Indeed, between 2000 and 2004, the immigration population multiplied threefold.

As a matter of fact, most of the 772,000 new jobs (about 60 percent) created in Spain in 2006 went to immigrants.[16] The immigrants' motivation to work hard also opened the way for productivity improvements (in 2006, Spain experienced the largest increase since 1997, with a 0.8 percent hike). It is estimated that in the four years prior to the crisis, the immigrants contributed 0.8 percentage points to the GDP.[17] Immigration represented more than 50 percent of employment growth and 78.6 percent of the demographic growth (as a result, Spain led the demographic growth of the European countries between 1995 and 2005 with a demographic advance of 10.7 percent compared to the EU15 average of 4.8 percent).[18] They also contributed to the huge increase in employment, one of the key reasons for the impressive economic expansion. Indeed, between 1988 and 2006, employment contributed 3 percentage points to the 3.5 percent annual increase in Spain's potential GDP (see table 1.3).[19]

The Basis for Success

EU/EMU Membership

What made this transformation possible? The modernization of the Spanish economy in the two and a half decades prior to the global financial crisis has been intimately connected to the country's integration in the EU (Royo 2008, 35–58). Indeed, European integration was a catalyst for the final conversion of the Spanish economy into a modern, Western-type economy. Yet, membership was not the only reason for this development. The economic liberalization, trade integration, and modernization of the Spanish economy started in the 1950s and 1960s, and Spain became increasingly prosperous over the two decades prior to EU accession. However, one of the key consequences of its entry into Europe was that it accelerated the modernization of the country's economy. Spain also benefited extensively from European funds: approximately €150,000 million from agricultural, regional development, training, and cohesion programs.

Indeed, since its accession in 1986, the Spanish economy has experienced profound economic changes. Among other factors, EU membership has led to policy and institutional reforms at the macro and micro levels that have led to macroeconomic stability and the strengthening of competitiveness of the productive sector. These reforms led to the liberalization (of a number of goods and services markets, as well as the labor market), privatization, and the adaptation of competition policy to EU regulations, all aiming at rolling back the presence of the government in the economy and at increasing the overall efficiency of the system.

The combined impetuses for lowering trade barriers, the introduction of VAT, the suppression of import tariffs, the adoption of economic policy rules (such as quality standards or the harmonization of indirect taxes), and the increasing mobility of goods and factors of production that comes with greater economic integration boosted trade and enhanced the openness of the Spanish economy. After 1999, this development was fostered by the lower cost of transactions and greater exchange rate stability associated with the single currency.

Indeed, EMU membership has also been very positive for the country; it contributed to macroeconomic stability. Overall, EMU membership (and the Stability Pact) provided the country with unprecedented stability because it forced successive governments to consolidate responsible economic policies, leading to greater credibility and improved ratings of Spain's pubic debt (and consequently to lower financing costs).

The EU contributed significantly to this development. During 1994–1999, EU aid accounted for 1.5 percent of GDP in Spain. The percentage of public investment financed by EU funds has been rising since 1985 reaching average values of 15 percent for Spain EU funding, allowing rates of public investment to remain relatively stable since the mid-1980s. The European Commission estimated that the impact of EU structural funds on GDP growth and employment was significant: overall, these funds, given their impact on the demand side (i.e., public works) and on the supply side (they increased the productive capacity of the Spanish economy), contributed to economic growth. It is estimated that, on an average, these funds have added 0.4 percentage points to yearly economic growth during 1989–2006, or the equivalent of €600 per habitant per year.[20] These funds contributed significantly to reduce regional disparities and foster convergence within the EU. As a result, major infrastructure shortcomings were addressed; road and telecommunications networks improved dramatically both in quantity and quality. In addition, increased spending on education and training contributed to upgrade the labor force. In sum, these funds played a prominent role in developing the factors to improve competitiveness and to determine the potential growth of the least-developed regions (Sebastián 2001).[21]

Policy Stability

Another important factor to account for the country's economic success was the remarkable economic policy stability following the economic crisis of 1992–1993. Indeed, there were few economic policy shifts throughout the

1990s and early 2000s despite changes in government. Between 1993 and 2008, there were only two ministers of finance, Pedro Solbes (1993–1996 and 2004–2009) and Rodrigo Rato (1996–2004); the country had only three PMs (Felipe González: 1982–1996, José María Aznar: 1996–2004, and José Luís Rodríguez Zapatero: 2004–2011). This pattern was further reinforced by the ideological cohesiveness of the political parties in the government and the strong control that party leaders exercised over the members of the cabinet and parliament deputies.

In addition, this stability was reinforced by consensus between the Conservative and the Socialist leaders regarding fiscal consolidation, as well as the need to hold firm in the application of restrictive fiscal policies and the achievement of budgetary fiscal surpluses. As a result, a 7 percent budget deficit in 1993 became a 2.2 percent surplus in 2007, and public debt decreased from 68 percent of GDP in 1998 to 36.2 percent in 2007.

Other factors that contributed to this success include limited corruption and fairly clean politics,[22] a relatively open and flexible economy, and the success of Spanish multinational corporations: the *Financial Times'* list of the world's largest multinationals included 8 firms in 2000 and 14 firms in 2008. They all contributed to the success of the Spanish economy.

The Domestic Imbalances

The economic success was marred by some glaring deficiencies that came to the fore in 2008 when the global financial crisis hit the country, because it was largely a "miracle" based on brick and mortar (Martinez-Mongay and Maza Lasierra 2009).[23] The foundations of economic growth were fragile because the country had low productivity growth (productivity contributed only 0.5 percentage points to potential GDP between 1998 and 2006) and deteriorating external competitiveness.[24]

Moreover, growth was largely based on low-intensity economic sectors, such as services and construction, which are not exposed to international competition. In 2006, most of the new jobs were created in low-productivity sectors such as construction (33 percent), services associated with housing such as sales and rentals (15 percent), and tourism and domestic service (30 percent). These sectors represented 75 percent of all the new jobs created in Spain in 2006 (new manufacturing jobs, in contrast, represented only 5 percent). The temporary labor rate reached 33.3 percent in 2007, and inflation remained a recurrent problem (it closed with a 2.7 percent increase in 2006, but the average for that year was 3.6 percent); thus the inflation differential with the EU (almost 1 point) had not decreased, reducing the competitiveness of Spanish products abroad (and consequently Spanish companies lost market shares abroad).[25]

In addition, family indebtedness reached a record 115 percent of disposable income in 2006, and the construction and housing sectors accounted for 18.5 percent of GDP (twice the Eurozone average). House prices rose by 150 percent since 1998, and the average price of a square meter of residential property went up from €700 in 1997 to €2,000 at the end of 2006, even though the housing stock had doubled. Many wondered whether this bubble was sustainable.[26] The crisis that started in 2008 confirmed the worst fears.

Between 40 and 60 percent of the benefits of the largest Spanish companies came from abroad. Yet, in the past few years, this figure decreased by approximately 10 percentage points, and there was a decline in FDI of all types in the country, falling from a peak of €38.3 billion in 2000 to €16.6 billion in 2005.[27] The current account deficit reached 8.9 percent of GDP in 2006 and was over 10 percent in 2007 making Spain the country with the largest deficit in absolute terms (€86,026 million) behind only the United States; imports were 25 percent higher than exports, and Spanish companies lost market shares over the same period. The prospects were not very bright as the trade deficit reached 9.5 percent in 2008.[28]

In a list of 44 indicators (including economic performance, reform, employment, and research), Spain (together with Portugal and Greece) was among the worst-performing countries in the EMU in a majority of those areas.[29]

One of the consequences of EMU membership for Spain was the convergence of interest rates, which declined by more than 12 percentage points since 1996. This led to record low interest rates (negative in real terms) and an explosion of credit and mortgages in the country. Over the past decade and a half, financial deregulation, rising incomes (linked to the lower unemployment rates), growing immigration, and strong demand from foreigners (it increased sixfold compared to the first half of the 1990s) who purchased real estate in Spain, all led to an upsurge in real estate demand. Consequently, real estate prices increased by 130 percent between 1997 and 2007, and the ratio of average house prices to average incomes were comparatively much higher than in other countries. According to some estimates, prior to the 2008 crisis, construction made up almost 17 percent of GDP and residential construction represented an average of 13.5 percent between 1985 and 1995.[30] The bubble in the housing market was estimated at 30 percent, and it led to another bubble in the construction sector, generating 20 percent of all the employment created in Spain in the decade prior to the 2008 crisis. The US market grew moderately in comparison. This situation led some observers to talk about a "real estate bubble." While the empirical evidence was inconclusive, there was no question that this situation was risky. Since most mortgages had variable rates, the savings rate was very low, and the rate of indebtedness of Spanish families increased (before 1990 it represented 60 percent of disposable income, and since then, it has grown to 110 percent); mortgage holders were quite vulnerable to interest rate increases from the ECB.

Furthermore, the real estate boom overshadowed the lack of competitiveness of the Spanish economy. According to the GCI, 2007, Spain was placed twenty-ninth in the world, and in some of the categories computed in the ranking (e.g., the quality of public institutions), its performance was poorer than in previous years (it was ranked twenty-third in 2005 and twenty-fifth in 2007). But, the degree of competitiveness is a critical variable to establish the potential for growth and development of economies in the short- and medium-term because it helps determine the share of domestic demand that is satisfied with products from abroad and the share of external demand that is satisfied with internal production. In this regard, the loss of competitiveness of the Spanish economy was a very worrisome development. The current account deficit was a key symptom of Spain's loss of competitiveness. The current account deficit reached 8.3 percent in 2006 and 9.1 percent in 2007. To place these figures in perspective, the deficit at that time in the United States was 5.8 percent.

Several reasons explain the evolution of the trade deficit before the 2008 crisis.[31] Increasing internal demand led to a growth in imports, while exports were hindered by the appreciation of the euro, the crisis in the larger European economies, and the growing competition from other countries. Furthermore, the current account deficit showed the disequilibria between savings and private investment. While the public sector was no longer in deficit, the private sector showed a large deficit (particularly the one from nonfinancial societies).

In addition, Spanish exports were concentrated in a few markets. Seventy percent of Spanish exports go to the EU15. Yet, the average growth of Spanish markets in the five years prior to the crisis was 4.5 percent, while global markets grew by 7 percent. The slow growth of European economies during those years had a deleterious effect on Spanish exports. Another problem was the limited degree of technological sophistication of Spanish products; most Spanish exports were labor intensive making them vulnerable to cost-based competition. Indeed, high-technology exports represented only 8 percent of the total (less than half of the EU15 average).

Inflation was also a contributing structural problem that aggravated the loss of competitiveness because it undercut the ability of Spanish exporters to compete with other European countries. In the decade prior to the crisis, the inflation rate exceeded that of the Eurozone by an average of more than 1 percentage point each year. This inflation differential is largely attributed to the barriers to service sector entry, particularly in the gas and electricity sectors, as well as collusive practices, commercial restrictions, and inefficient productive and commercial structures.[32]

The lack of competitiveness was compounded by the fact that Spain entered the euro at an undervalued exchange rate and subsequently lost against the Eurozone because of above-average wage increases and inflation. Unit labor costs continued to rise, not so much because of higher nominal wages (which grew moderately) but because of a fall in productivity.[33]

Productivity in Spain grew only an average of 0.3 percent between 1997 and 2007, one whole point below the EU average, placing Spain at the bottom of the EU, ahead only of Italy and Greece. The most productive activities (energy, industry, and financial services) contributed only 11 percent of GDP growth.[34] Yet, over the past decade Spain did not address its fundamental challenge: declining productivity. As a matter of fact, real wages decreased in Spain two years in a row between 2004 and 2006 and according to the November 2007 IESE-Adecco ILCA report, between 1997 and 2007, Spanish salaries increased only 1.4 percent due to poor productivity growth.[35]

Low productivity was a significant endemic problem. While we know little about what determines productivity growth in advanced economies, some of the reasons for the lackluster productivity performance of the Spanish economy include (Royo 2008, 72–73) heavy regulation, public spending (i.e., public sector productivity shows a decline), low rate of investment, low skill levels in human capital, poor infrastructure (e.g., congestion in roads or problems in retail and wholesale distribution), mediocre performance in innovation and expenditure on R&D, poor intellectual property protection, poor science base (e.g., reduced number of scientific publications), and weak presence in high-technology industries. This drop can also be explained by a massive wave of immigration that had lower levels of education and increased the total working population (thus reducing average workers' contribution to GDP).

Another weakness was in the labor market. While unemployment fell and Spain became the second country after Germany in the EU to create the most jobs in the decade preceding the crisis, the participation rate, which was 5 percentage points lower than EU's in 1997 (62.4 percent versus 67.7 percent, respectively) had, by 2007, increased to 70 percent—the EU average. Yet, these impressive results could not mask the underlying weaknesses: the temporary rate grew from 30.8 percent in 2004 to 33.6 percent in 2006, the highest by far in Europe; there were wide disparities in the quality of work between men and women; and the industrial relations framework did not provide firms with the necessary flexibility (either internal or external) to deploy and organize their labor force.[36]

The extremely high temporary rate was the mechanism for employers to avoid high dismissal costs. However, there were profound consequences: it discouraged employers from investing in their workers; it limited the commitment of employees toward their firms; it hindered the development and implementation of training programs, with negative consequences on productivity; and it stifled innovation and worker mobility. Job insecurity also led to a lack of enterprise among young people with university degrees.

In addition, according to several reports, Spain remained among the least flexible economies. The *Euroíndice Laboral*, published by the IESE for Adecco, looked at three variables (contracts, working time, and dismissal restrictions) to identify Spain as the country in the EU with most labor rigidities and one of those with the highest dismissal costs, ahead only of Greece.[37]

Spain also lagged well behind in other critical areas (Royo 2008, 78): since most employment is in sectors based on intensive- and low-qualified labor, only 36 percent of Spanish employees work with new technologies; the percentage of the population that participates in professional training programs is merely 5.8, well below the EU average of 9 percent. Spain is listed twentieth in the GCI in the area of innovation capacity and technological development of firms; and while investment in R&D increased over 1998–2003 by an average of 7.6 percent, the percentage of investment in R&D (at 1.1 percent of the GDP) is still less than the EU average of 1.93 percent. This is reflected in the number of patents published. The largest percentage of all patents published in Spain, by sector, is in chemicals, materials, and instrumentation (43 percent), followed by telecom and electronics (16 percent), food and agriculture (12 percent), automotive and transport (11 percent), pharmaceutical and medical (10 percent), and energy and power (4 percent). Moreover, the country's poor record in innovation is deteriorating further. Although Spanish scientists account for 4 percent of the world's published research, the country lags behind other European countries in innovation league tables based on patent filing.[38]

Education also was a glaring weakness. Spanish students are below OECD averages in reading and comprehension, math, and sciences. Half of the Spaniards do not complete secondary education, and 28 percent of the students have repeated a grade at least once (the OECD average is 13 percent).[39] Furthermore, no Spanish university is ranked in the top 200 in the Shanghai Jiang Tong University Ranking of World Universities (2006); Spain spends only 1.3 percent of its GDP (or €1,700 per student) in higher education; it has one of the most dense student populations in universities (44,800 students on an average); and R&D in and connection of the education sector with the market are insufficient.[40]

While there is overall consensus that the country needs to improve its education system, invest in R&D to increase productivity, as well as modernize the public sector, and make the labor market more stable (i.e., reduce the temporary rate) and flexible, the government did not take the necessary actions to address these problems. Spain spent only half of what the OECD spends on an average on education; it lagged behind most European countries in investment in R&D; and it is ranked twenty-ninth by the UNCTAD as an attractive location for R&D. Other observers note that Spain is failing to do more to integrate its immigrant population; social divisions are beginning to emerge (see Calavita 2005).[41]

By the summer of 2008, the effects of the crisis were evident; since then, the country has suffered one of the worst recessions in history (Royo 2009b).

The Unfolding of the Economic Crisis

These imbalances rushed to the fore in 2007–2008 when the real estate market bubble burst and the international financial crisis hit Spain. In just a few months, the "debt-fired dream of endless consumption" turned into a nightmare. By summer 2010, Spain was facing the worst economic recession in half a century. According to government data, 2009 was the worst year in recent economic history: GDP fell 1.6 percent and unemployment figures crossed 4 million. Consumer confidence was shattered, the implosion of the housing sector reached historic proportions and threatened to extend for several years, and the manufacturing sector continues to suffer.

Initially, the government was reluctant to recognize the crisis, which was becoming increasingly evident as early as the summer of 2007, because of electoral considerations: the country had general elections in March 2008. And after the election, it was afraid to admit that it had not been entirely truthful during the campaign. While this pattern has been quite common in other European countries, in Spain, the increasing evidence that the model based on construction was already showing symptoms of exhaustion in 2007 compounded this mistake. Yet, the Spanish government refused to recognize not only that the international crisis was affecting the country but also that the crises in the country would be aggravated by the high levels of private indebtedness. As late as August 17, 2007, Finance Minister Solbes predicted that "the crisis would have a relative small effect" on the Spanish economy.

When it became impossible to deny what was evident, the government's initial reluctance to recognize and address the crisis was rapidly replaced by frenetic activism and the introduction of a succession of plans and measures to confront it, and deal with the unprecedented dramatic surge of unemployment (Royo 2009b).

There is general consensus that the Spanish government was slow to recognize and react to the crisis. As a result, a few precious months were lost, and the government prepared budgets for 2008 and 2009 that were utterly unrealistic. As a matter of fact, as late as 2010, the situation continued to worsen. The most significant decline was in consumer confidence, hammered as it was by financial convulsions, increase in unemployment, and scarcity of credit. As a result, household consumption, representing 56 percent of GDP, fell 1 percent in the last quarter for the first time in the past 15 years, contributing sharply to the deterioration of economic conditions. According to the Bank of Spain, this decline in household consumption was even more important during the recession than the deceleration of residential investment, which also fell by 20 percent, driven down by worsening financial conditions, uncertainties, and drop in residential prices. So far, the government actions have had limited effect in stemming this hemorrhage (see table 1.4 for the impact of the crisis).

Table 1.4 The Impact of the Crisis (2007–2013)

	2007	2008	2009	2010	2011	2012*	2013*
GDP, constant prices	3.479	0.888	−3.74	−0.07	0.71	−1.826	0.125
Output gap in percentage GDP	3.843	2.387	−2.693	−3.319	−3.069	−4.457	−4.338
Gross national savings	20.999	19.512	19.201	18.698	18.35	18.526	18.538
Inflation, average	2.844	4.13	−0.238	2.043	3.053	1.893	1.561
Unemployment rate	8.263	11.327	18.01	20.065	21.638	24.2	23.9
Government structural balance	−1.131	−5.056	−9.06	−7.331	−6.5	−3.402	−3.136
General government gross debt	36.301	40.173	53.929	61.173	68.471	79.041	84.027
Current account balance	−9.995	−9.623	−5.2	−4.604	−3.706	−2.143	−1.721

*Estimates
Source: IMF, World Economic Outlook Database, April 2012.

Conclusion

The European integration process facilitated and accelerated the process of convergence and modernization of financial, commercial, and manufacturing structures in Spain. Overall, the impact of membership has been very beneficial. European integration accelerated the reforms, but at the same time, it allowed for an orderly implementation that benefited from the experiences and support of other European countries, as well as from their financial support. The impressive rates of economic growth experienced by Spain during the past 20 years were closely connected with EU membership. The sharp decline in interest rates that resulted from EMU integration, the transfer of European funds to Spain, the implementation of more orthodox fiscal policies, and the opening of the Spanish economy are all examples of outcomes associated with European membership. Without the euro, the exorbitant trade deficit would have forced devaluation, as well as the implementation of more restrictive fiscal policies.

Yet, the Spanish experience shows that EU membership is no substitute for the domestic implementation of reforms, which should proceed further in areas such as labor, product, and capital markets. Successful convergence and increasing competitiveness hinge to a considerable degree on the ability and willingness of Spanish leaders to implement reforms in the face of domestic resistance. Lack of political willingness to reform coupled with sluggish growth hindered the convergence process. Those who thought that EU/EMU membership would cure all ills of the Spanish economy learned that the EU has limited direct power to enforce outcomes.

Indeed, the experience of Spain in the EU shows that the indirect influence of EU recommendations on policy and demonstration effects has been greater than direct action. Hence, it is not surprising that European states, and particularly Spain, are failing to live up to the ambitious targets established at the European Council of Lisbon in March 2000, which aimed at making the EU more competitive. While EU membership will facilitate (and in many cases ameliorate) adjustment costs and will provide impetus for reforms, the experience of Spain shows that this is no substitute for the implementation of domestic reforms. In Spain, insufficient progress brought economic stagnation.

By the summer of 2008, the effects of the crisis were evident, and since then, the country has suffered one of the worst recessions in history, with unemployment reaching over 24 percent at the end of 2011 and more than 5.2 million people unemployed. This collapse was not fully unexpected. The global liquidity crisis caused by the subprime, and the surge in commodities, food, and energy prices, brought to the fore the imbalances in the Spanish economy: the record current account deficit, persisting inflation, low-productivity growth, dwindling competitiveness, increasing unitary labor costs, excess consumption, and low savings. These realities all set the ground for the current devastating economic crisis (see Royo 2009b). We turn next to the government's response to the crisis.

CHAPTER 2

Responding to the Crisis:
A Chronicle of a Foretold Failure

Responses to the First Stage of the Crisis (2007–2009)

The economic imbalances of the country roared to the fore in 2007–2008 when the real estate market bubble burst and the international financial crisis hit Spain. Since then, Spain has been facing the worst economic recession in half a century. Year 2009 was the worst in recent economic history: GDP fell 1.6 percent (three points less than the previous year); unemployment reached almost 4 million people (15.9 percent of the active population); and the public deficit increased over six percent (from 3.4 percent in 2008). Originally, the crisis was expected to last "only" until 2011, destroying on an average 600,000 jobs annually and increasing the unemployment rate to over 16 percent. The reality was far worse; unemployment reached over 24 percent in 2012, and the economy slipped back to recession in 2011, 2012, and is expected to be the only Eurozone country to be in recession in 2013. Consumer confidence has been shattered, the implosion of the housing sector has reached historic proportions, and the manufacturing sector has also been suffering.

As noted in chapter 1, despite the fact that the economic crisis was becoming increasingly evident as early as summer 2007, the government was initially remiss in recognizing the crisis because it was facing general elections in March 2008, which it expected to win, and it did not want to hurt its electoral prospects with negative news regarding the economy. Yet, even after the election, it was reluctant to admit that there was a crisis, due to concern that it could be accused of not having been entirely truthful during the campaign. At the same time, it overlooked the fact that there was increasing evidence that the economic growth model, largely based on the construction and real estate sectors, was already showing symptoms of exhaustion. And to compound the problem, the government (starting with the finance minister) continued minimizing the potential domestic impact of the international financial crisis on the Spanish economy.

However, the sudden collapse of the construction sector precipitated the crisis: between the summer of 2007 and April of 2008, building permits were down 40 percent, cement consumption was down by more than 10 percent, the number of property transactions had fallen by 15 percent, and the construction sector had eliminated 100,000 jobs.

Shortly after being reelected in March 2008, PM Zapatero outlined to parliament his government's priorities for the next four years, promising emergency measures to reactivate the Spanish economy. Among his proposals, he included speeding up the completion of government infrastructure projects, such as high speed trains; promoting more state-subsidized housing; extending government guarantees to some mortgage securitizations; developing a state rental agency to help developers sell their empty homes; retraining programs for construction workers; reducing at least 30 percent in red tape; and rebating €400 for all contributors that year (2008) to "help families and boost the economy." At that time, the government started to acknowledge that the global financial crisis was affecting Spain: "we have to face with realism a period of economic slowdown."[1]

When it became impossible to deny their apathy, the government's initial reluctance to recognize and address the crisis was rapidly replaced by frenetic activism. They implemented a succession of plans and measures to try to confront and address the unprecedented dramatic surge of unemployment. Table 2.1 summarizes the main actions taken by the Zapatero government in 2007 and 2008.

In the initial stages of the global financial crisis, the Spanish economy was in better shape than that of many other countries. As we will see in chapter 6, its financial sector was not as contaminated by the subprime crisis, and the fiscal conservatism of the preceding decade, which had been translated into budget surpluses and relatively low debt (37 percent of GDP), provided an initial fiscal cushion against the mounting crisis. However, when the financial crisis intensified and the credit markets dried up, Spain became one of the countries severely affected by the crisis, with the implosion of the construction sector and the sharp decline in consumption. The severity of the crisis was highlighted by the dramatic surge in unemployment, which increased 36 percent in just one year (from 8.3 percent to 11.3 percent, or almost 1.3 million jobs), and is expected to increase to 18 percent by 2010. According to the government's forecasts, the situation was only expected to get worse (see table 2.2 for the government's forecast).

As we outlined in the previous chapter, the sharp deterioration of the labor market was particularly striking. It was largely caused by the economic crisis and the collapse of the real estate sector, and aggravated by a demographic growth pattern based on significant migratory flows; in 2007, 3.128 million immigrants lived in the country, of which 2.745 million were employed and 374,000 unemployed. In 2008, the number of immigrants

Table 2.1   The Response of the Zapatero Government to the Crisis (2007–2008)

Chronology of the Crisis	Responses from the PSOE Government
August 9–11, 2007: Stock market crash caused by the subprime	July 13, 2007: Cabinet approves of the €2,500 baby-check.
September 18, 2007: First reduction of interest rates by the Fed	August 17, 2007: Solbes announces that the crisis will have a "relative small effect" in the Spanish economy.
December 19, 2007: The ECB inserts 350 billion in the financial system	August 14, 2007: Zapatero asks the banks to continue providing credit to real estate companies.
January 21, 2008: Worldwide stock market panic. The Ibex falls 7.54%	October 19, 2007: Reform of the professional training system.
March 9, 2008: General election in Spain	December 4, 2007: Zapatero announces the elimination of capital gain taxes.
March 16, 2008: The Fed approves the purchase of Bern Stearns by JPMorgan	January 9, 2008: In the middle of the electoral campaign Zapatero promises full employment. Caldera announces a new program to hire and train unemployed workers from the construction sector.
June 1–7, 2008: Spanish truck drivers go on strike against increasing oil prices	January 27, 2008: Zapatero proposes a €400 reduction in the income tax.
June 30, 2008: First public deficit, after three years of surplus.	February 25, 2008: Solbes promises the elimination of the cost to extend mortgages.
July 11, 2008: The oil barrel price breaks a new record: $147.8 per barrel	April 18, 2008: Cabinet approves the "Extraordinary Plan for Orientation, Professional Training and Work Insertion," which focuses on the rehiring of unemployed workers. It includes a €201 million plan to rehire unemployed workers; the hiring of 1,500 "employment orientation leaders," assistance for unemployed with low income; subventions for geographical mobility; and €350 during three months for the unemployed with "special difficulties."
July 14, 2008: The real estate company Martisa declares bankruptcy	April 19, 2008: Package of anticrisis measures: Increase of guarantees from the ICO and the treasury to fund SMEs and protected housing.
July 30, 2008: Inflation reaches 5.3%, the highest level in 16 years	June 23, 2008: Zapatero announces new measures like the freezing of compensation for high administrative officials, a new model for the AENA, and soft credits to replace vehicles 15 years old and older.
September 15, 2008: Lehman declares bankruptcy	July 7, 2008: Sebastián announces the "Plan VIVE," which includes €1.2 billion until 2010 to renovate the automobile park. It provides help to those who want to buy a new car, and saves interest payments of up to €1,040 per car.

continued

Table 2.1 Continued

Chronology of the Crisis	Responses from the PSOE Government
October 2, 2008: The United States approves the first financial rescue package	**July 29, 2008**: Sebastián presents the Energy Saving Plan to reduce oil dependency and energy consumption. It includes 31 energy saving initiatives to promote energy savings and sustain industrial activity, including a plan to distribute 49 million low-electrical consumption bulbs among Spanish households; a 20% reduction of speed limits in road access to cities; the extension of subway service hours; incentives to the production of electrical cars, with the aim of reaching 1 million units by 2011; and plans to improve the acclimatization of public spaces.
October 8, 2008: World central banks cut interest rates in a coordinated way	**August 4, 2008**: Extraordinary meeting of the Council of Ministers. New impulse to the law to increase competition in the service sector; reduction of the timeframe that companies have to declare the environmental impact of their operations; elimination of 81 bureaucratic steps to open new companies with the goal to reduce the average timeframe from 25 to 14 months.
October 10, 2008: Worldwide stock markets suffer one of the worst weeks of their history	**October 7 and 13, 2008**: Presentation of the Spanish rescue plan: creation of a €50 billion fund to purchase assets from financial institutions, increase of guarantees to banking deposits to €100,000, new €100 billion guarantees to emit new debt.
October 12, 2008: European countries announce multimillion rescue packages	**November 8, 2008**: Plan to allow unemployed workers with family responsibilities to delay during two years the payment of half of their monthly mortgage installments; the government will advance the money to the banks. New €1,500 bonus plan to support the hiring of unemployed workers; further capitalization of the unemployment subsidy system to allow for the initiation of entrepreneurship activities. Extension to six years of the period in which investors can invest their savings in housing accounts (until 2010).
October 31, 2008: The Bank of Spain announces that the Spanish economy suffered negative growth in the third semester	**November 14, 2008**: The cabinet approves a revised Plan VIVE that increases to €30,000 the funding limits to purchase a vehicle and extends it to other beneficiaries, and applies it to used vehicles.
November 4, 2008: Worst unemployment month in history	**November 27, 2008**: Zapatero announces new measures against the crisis including an extraordinary investment plan of €11 billion (or 1.2% of GDP), with €8 billion assigned to subsidize public works by the municipalities.

Table 2.1 Continued

Chronology of the Crisis	Responses from the PSOE Government
December 10, 2008: The Bush administration declares that it would step in to prevent the "precipitous collapse" of the US auto industry; Ready to use $700 billion fund to help ailing industry	**January 16, 2009**: Spanish government announces the economic projections for 2009. Worst recession in five decades.
January 20, 2009: President Obama's inauguration. Negotiations on new stimulus package	**January 18, 2009**: Solbes declares that "we have used the entire margin that we had against the crisis."
February 10, 2009: Secretary Geithner presents new US financial rescue plan	**February 13, 2009**: Government approves an emergency €1.5 billion budget cut, spread across most ministries, to help fund the rising cost of unemployment. The Ministry of Development is the one affected the most with €300 million in cuts.
February 13, 2009: Stimulus Bill approved in the United States	**February 13, 2009**: Government approves new €4 billion assistance plan for the motor industry. State aid will be denied to companies that cut their workforce without union agreement.

Source: Author and *El País*, November 9, 2008: 26.

Table 2.2 Government Economic Forecast (Variation in Percentage)

	2008	2009*	2010*	2011*
GDP real	1.2	−1.6	1.2	2.6
GDP nominal	4.7	0.0	3.3	5.0
Private consumption	0.5	−1.5	0.7	1.3
Public administration consumption	5.1	2.1	1.5	1.7
Gross capital formation	−1.8	−9.3	−1.2	4.4
Domestic demand	0.7	−3.2	0.4	2.2
Exports	2.9	0.3	3.6	4.6
Imports	0.6	−4.6	0.4	3.0
Contribution of external sector to growth	0.6	1.6	0.9	0.4
Employment	−0.4	−3.6	0.2	1.4
Unemployment rate (% of active population)	11.1	15.9	15.7	14.9
Productivity	1.6	2.0	1.1	1.1
Public deficit	−3.4	−5.8	−4.8	−3.9

*Forecast

Source: Ministry of Economy and Finance.

increased by almost 400,000 to 3.523 million (representing 55 percent of the active population growth), but 580,000 were unemployed, an increase of 200,000. To place these figures in perspective, in October 2008, the number of unemployed native-Spaniards increased by 400,000 while the number employed, contrary to what happened with the immigrants, decreased by 130,000. Only in the construction sector did unemployment increase (170 percent between the summer of 2007 and 2008) and the manufacturing and service sectors (which was also battered by the global crisis, lower consumption, and lack of international competitiveness) were unable to incorporate these workers.[2]

Because the Spanish government was slow to recognize and react to the crisis, a few precious months were lost causing the government to prepare an unrealistic budget for 2008 (and 2009) without responding to the rapidly deteriorating circumstances. In an effort to compensate for the initial lack of action, the Zapatero government moved fast in 2008 and presented five major plans to address the effects of the crisis in a document entitled "Spanish Plan for the Stimulus of the Economy and Employment" (see table 2.3).

These initiatives, however, did not pay off and the crisis continued accelerating faster than its remedies. As a matter of fact, at the beginning of 2009, things only got worse. While the Spanish economy grew by 1.2 percent in 2008, economic conditions deteriorated sharply in the last quarter due to the intensification of the global financial crisis. During that last quarter, economic growth decreased 0.8 percent driven by the sharp drop of domestic demand (2.4 percent) and employment (3 percent). This data confirms that the Spanish economy was officially in recession after two consecutive quarters with negative economic growth. The most significant declines were in consumers' confidence, shattered by the financial convulsions, the increase in unemployment, and the scarcity of credit. As a result, household consumption, representing 56 percent of GDP at that time, fell 1 percent in the last quarter of 2008 for the first time in the previous 15 years, contributing sharply to the deterioration of economic conditions. According to the Bank of Spain, this decline in household consumption was a more important factor during the recession than the deceleration of residential investment, which also fell 20 percent, driven down by worsening financial conditions, uncertainties, and the drop in residential prices.

Nevertheless, the government actions had limited effect stemming this haemorrhage.[3] Many of the approved measures took too long to be implemented and some were not directly related to the crisis. Furthermore, in some cases, the implementation of these initiatives was hampered by the insufficient collaboration from the regional governments that held legal implementation responsibilities in many economic areas. For instance, the €201 million plan to rehire workers from the construction sector, hire 1,500 employment orientation leaders, and support unemployed with particular incomes was under the purview of the regional governments, but it was unclear until months later whether the initiatives delivered; similarly, the

Table 2.3 The Spanish Plan for the Stimulus of the Economy and Employment

Support to Families	*Promotion of Employment*
€400 deduction in individual income tax (€11.4 billion in two years)	Public investment plan to create 300,000 jobs (€11 billion)
Elimination of the estate tax (€1.8 billion)	Hiring of 1,500 orientation leaders to help unemployed find jobs
Delay in the payment of mortgages for unemployed	€350 subsidy to unemployed without access to unemployment benefits for three months
Extension of the limit of two years to purchase a house for subscribers of housing saving accounts	€1,500 bonus for the hiring of unemployed with family responsibilities
Advance in the personal income deductions for families with low incomes	Increase to 60% of the amount from the unemployment benefits that can be used to become an autonomous worker
Two-year extension of the time limit to sell a house and take advantage of fiscal benefits	
Support to Companies	*Support to Banks*
Reduction of corporate taxes from 32.5% to 30% (€5.3 billion)	Fund to purchase assets (€50 billion)
Development of ESystem to accelerate the devolution of the VAT tax.	Guarantees for the emission of debt (€200 billion in two years)
Increase to €10.9 billion of the ICO funding to support business plans	Increase of deposit guarantees to €100,000
One-year delay in the devolution of the principal from ICO loans	*Structural Reforms*
Increase to €5 billion of the ICO budget line to fund Official Protected Housing, and opening of a new €3 billion line to promote the housing rental market.	Opening of a new negotiation round with political groups to reform service, telecommunication, energy, and transportation sectors
New €10 billion fund to fund companies with liquidity problems	Opening of the process to revise the Pacto de Toledo about the pension system

Source: "Una transfusión de 80,000 millones frente a la recesión," *El País*, November 30, 2008, N7.

implementation of the professional training system reform started in October 2008, but took months to come into practice.

In other cases, the actual effects of the measures were more limited than anticipated. For instance, the €400 income tax rebate or the €2,500 baby-check did not have the expected expansive effect because people were reluctant to spend. Other initiatives, such as the flexible application of corporate taxes to avoid hurting companies during the implementation of the new Accounting Plan, or the new option to receive the VAT rebate each month, provided only temporary relief; others, like the 2007 reform of the corporate and income tax systems, provided individuals and companies with additional resources (€7.3 billion), but were drowned by the magnitude of the crisis.

The package of measures to support the financial sector, which provided €100 billion in guarantees and €50 billion for the acquisition of toxic assets, also had very limited impact. The initiatives to provide liquidity to citizens and real estate companies to ameliorate the crisis in that sector were deemed insufficient; in other cases (like the housing plan), they were hampered by the scarcity of credit. The "Plan VIVE," established to fund the purchase of new vehicles, had to be redesigned after 100 days because it failed, and finally began to show limited results at the end of 2008. The government also fulfilled its commitment to increase investment in infrastructure, yet the legal bidding processes to initiate these infrastructure projects moved far slower than required and the number of these projects fell by 17 percent compared with the previous year. Finally, the government took actions to alleviate the liquidity problems of SMEs, like the expansion of ICO's, preferential credit lines from €11 to €600 million, or the increase of Treasury guarantees from €1 billion to €3 billion for these companies. Yet the scarcity of credit still hurt them. And the range of potential assistance continued narrowing due to lack of funds. Even Finance Minister Pedro Solbes acknowledged that Spain has "used all the leeway that we had in public spending." It was not a positive picture overall.

Notably, as we will see in chapter 6, one of the few positive developments was the initial performance of the Spanish financial sector during the crisis. During that period, contrary to their counterparts all over the world, Spanish banks appeared to have escaped the direct effects of the global financial crisis. Their consensus was that stern regulations of the Bank of Spain played a key role in this outcome. It made it so expensive for financial institutions to establish off–balance sheet vehicles, and forced banks to set aside "generic" bank provisions during the good years, which provided Spanish banks with a countercyclical mechanism that was essential to overcome the first stage of the current crisis. Banco Santander, for instance, built more than €6 billion of generic loan loss provisions. This strategy was praised globally since the crisis started and sheltered Spanish banks from the initial worst effects of the crisis.[4] Unfortunately, as we discuss in chapter 6, it proved short-lived and the country would need a financial bailout.

The crisis continued unabated through 2009 and political difficulties intensified for the Zapatero government. On March 1, his Socialist Party obtained a historical triumph in the Basque Country's elections. Paradoxically, this was counterproductive at the national level; Basque nationalists lost power for the first time in 29 years and, as a result, the six national deputies of the PNV decided that they would no longer support the Zapatero government. Consequently the Socialist Party lost control of the national parliament and the ability to pass the laws it wanted, thus complicating the legislative agenda.

While waiting to see the impact of the December stimulus package, at the end of March, PM Zapatero announced his intention to launch a fresh round of public spending if it was needed to pull the Spanish economy out of the recession. He still insisted that Spain had fiscal room for manoeuvre ("we have an ample margin with our debt") because its government debt was still only 38–39 percent of GDP, well below the EU average (notwithstanding the fact that the country's deficit was expected to reach 7 percent of GDP in 2009). PM Zapatero stated that his intention to launch a "coordinated and selected effort" concentrated on energy saving and renewable energy, biotechnology, and life sciences. While it was not clear how such initiatives would help bring down unemployment (which was already at 14 percent), he claimed that energy saving was a "major structural reform" that would create jobs, reduce Spain's oil-dependence, and reduce external deficit.[5] All this when the government had already spent €8 billion on emergency job creation programs between 2008 and 2009.

PM Zapatero's optimism, however, was quashed immediately by his own finance minister Pedro Solbes, who claimed just a day later that there was no room for fiscal stimulus plans in Spain. He expected the deficit to be well above the 3 percent EU limit, and hence stated that "in these conditions, I and the rest of my colleagues from the Eurozone believe that there is no room for further stimulus plans." This public disagreement fueled rampant speculation that PM Zapatero was preparing to sacrifice Solbes (who had been brought in for his credibility as an orthodox safe pair of hands to manage the Spanish economy after the Socialists' surprising victory in 2004) in a cabinet reshuffle. In the midst of this dispute, the government approved on March 27 draft legislation to adopt the EU's services directive, which involved modifying 47 separate laws and eliminating various regulations in an effort to make Spain's economy more flexible and competitive, but less bureaucratic.[6]

The rumors were confirmed shortly afterward. PM Zapatero replaced his finance minister on April 7 and made five other cabinet changes in a "new push" to cope with the economic crisis. The finance portfolio was handed to Elena Salgado, who was at the time minister of public administration. In the end, Solbes' decision to question the wisdom of Spain's costly fiscal stimulus plans led to his dismissal.

Meanwhile, negative news continued piling up. According to the April 2009 labor survey, unemployment jumped by more than 800,000 in the quarter to rise above 4 million for the first time. The jobless rate of 17.4 percent was double the EU average and already half the EU jobs lost during the crisis were in Spain. This confirmed again the structural nature of Spanish unemployment; during the previous 30 years, the rate dipped only once below 8 percent and exceeded 20 percent in the mid-1980s and mid-1990s. Most economists continued blaming the high level of protection enjoyed by permanent employees and the structure of the wage bargaining system (largely based on sectoral and regional negotiations), inherited from the Franco regime. Since companies could not adjust wages, they resorted to temporary contracts (unsurprisingly, Spain has the highest rate of temporary work in the OECD, about one-third of the workforce) and when demand decreased they adjusted the number of employees. This system also had a pernicious effect because employers had little incentive to train workers, with consequent impact on their productivity, innovation, and loyalty to company.[7] The crisis was also affecting the tourism industry, one of the centerpieces of the Spanish economy, as cash-strapped tourists avoided Spain. Companies in the sector (including Iberia, the air carriers) saw their profits halved and suffered some of the worst fallouts in decades.

The opposing PP took advantage of the situation and continued criticizing the administration severely. Until 2009 it was not able to capitalize on the crisis and was marred by local and regional scandals. The party's leader Mariano Rajoy was particularly critical of the "untenable rise in Spain's indebtedness" and pushed for more austerity. However, starting that spring, the PP started gaining ground on the Socialists, confirmed by their victory on the June 7 European election, in which they won with a victory margin of nearly 4 percentage points over the Socialists. The government, still somehow in denial, continue pitching "green shots" and trusted that the year's fiscal stimulus measures (equivalent to more than 2 percent of GDP) would somehow pay off. Minister Salgado started to admit their inability to continue running budget deficits indefinitely: "we are going to retire this fiscal stimulus as soon as our growth is at normal figures...perhaps 1.5 or 2 percent...of course we are very much committed to austerity and to the sustainability of our finances." Even the Bank of Spain, in the words of its director-general José Luís Malo de Molina, continued claiming that "the level of debt is still very comfortable," but admitted that "what is worrying is the speed of the deterioration...the worsening of finances could lead to a situation in which it may be necessary to raise taxes or cut costs when the economy has not recovered from recession."[8] On June 12, the government increased fuel and tobacco duties worth €2.3 billion and decided to buy almost exclusively the Spanish government's debt with the €58 billion surplus of its Social Security system.

In the midst of intensifying pressures to restrain the growing deficit, which was expected to reach 10 percent of GDP in 2009, the EU Commission gave Spain further breathing room and extended the country's timeframe to meet the 3 percent deficit limit by one year, that is, till 2013. Meanwhile, the government started to consider ways to close the widening fiscal gap and discussed an increase in capital gains tax, while claiming that they were "not contemplating raising income tax rates" and that they intended "to preserve income from work." Supporting this tax increase, PM Zapatero added that "if a crisis comes, you then have to develop your social policies, it seems reasonable that an important part of society should make a small effort to help those in difficulties," while insisting that the government would restore budgetary stability and "fulfil the stability pact."[9]

The decision to raise taxes was confirmed on September 27, when the government approved an austerity budget for 2010 and unveiled tax increases designed to raise an extra €11 billion per year to cut the deficit. The budget outlined spending cuts, increases in income and capital gain taxes, and increased interest income. It abolished the €400 annual tax rebate granted just two years earlier, increased the main VAT rate by 2 percentage points to 18 percent (keeping the rate for basic foods unchanged at 4 percent), and raised tax rates on unearned income by 1 percent to 19 percent, as well as increasing taxes by three points to 21 percent for annual earnings above €6,000, signaling that they were targeting the rich and not the middle classes (in Minister Salgado's words, "those with the most should make the biggest contribution").[10] This happened at a time when the EU Commission demanded a tax break that fueled a spate of Spanish international mergers, and acquisitions in Spain would be abolished. The PP lambasted these decisions claiming that they were a recipe for more unemployment, more deficits, and more taxes. They ended up doing the same after winning the election.

The response from the markets was also scathing. Standard & Poor, which had already stripped Spain of its triple-A sovereign credit rating in January of that year (they stood at AA+ for long-term and A-1 for short-term debt), affirming the rating in October but revising the outlook from "stable" to "negative" because of the likelihood of more prolonged economic weakness and further deterioration of public finances than previously anticipated (the deficit was expected to reach 10 percent that year and the debt to increase to 67 percent of GDP). This was widely interpreted as a strong criticism of the government's inability to curb its deficit: "reducing Spain's fiscal and economic imbalances require strong policy actions, which have not yet materialized." S&P expected that Spain "would experience a more pronounced and persistent deterioration in its public finances and a more prolonged period of economic weakness versus its peers...with trend GDP growth below 1 percent annually."[11]

The government reacted, again, stating its confidence in meeting the EU targets. PM Zapatero, in his legendary characteristically optimist vein, sought to reassure nervous investors by predicting that the country's return to growth was imminent and promised a dose of austerity to reduce the deficit. He claimed that the stimulus packages helped stave off economic recession by saving thousands of jobs and emphasized that Spain's public debt would still be nearly 20 percentage points below the EU average. However, he admitted the importance of meeting the EU deficit targets: "we are very aware that this effort by the state is of a temporary nature and must not endanger fiscal sustainability in the medium term...the return to growth and the expected fiscal consolidation will allow us to fulfil the objectives of the [EU] stability pact in 2013."[12] Time would prove him wrong; while the government insisted that the crisis was over, data indicated that it was just warming up. Indeed, things were about to get much worse come the new year.

The government started the new year (2010) with fresh austerity measures, unveiling a radical plan to narrow its budget deficit by a total of €50 billion over four years. Half of that amount would come from spending cuts including a near-freeze on hiring for the civil service in 2010. It also announced an increase of the retirement age from 65 to 67 to be introduced gradually starting in 2013. The government, however, still ruled out cuts in Social Security payments, education spending, research and development, or foreign aid.[13]

Meanwhile, unemployment continued soaring: in December 2009 the number of unemployed increased by nearly 55,000 to reach nearly 4 million, thus making 2009 the year with the highest unemployment level since 1997, and the highest among large Eurozone economies (the EU average was 9.8 percent). The problem was particularly acute among young people: unemployment level jumped from 17.5 percent in 2006 to 42.9 percent by the end of 2009. Young Spaniards suffered disproportionally the brunt of the recession because most of them worked under temporary contracts. Unsurprisingly, the government's popularity continued eroding as a result of this barrage of negative impacts. New polls showed that support for the PP was at 43.6 percent, more than 5 percentage points ahead of the Socialists with 38.5 percent.

Despite the dismal prospects (the IMF predicted that Spain would be the only big developed economy not to grow in 2010), the government continued with its optimistic outlook. At the World Economic Forum in Davos, PM Zapatero described it as "shocking" that Spain was being criticized by the likes of the United States, the UK, or Germany when it had avoided spending any funds on bank recues; in Washington, DC, he added that "Spain has a strong and solid financial system." Meanwhile his deputy María Teresa de la Vega still claimed that "we have control of the ship, we have a plan."[14] They still refused to address the markets' concern: how could the country reign on its deficit while regaining its competitiveness and growth? So far, markets remained unimpressed amid doubts that the government had either the will or the power to push through the necessary fiscal reforms to cut the deficit and improve competitiveness.[15]

A Policy Reversal: 2010–2011

The crisis continued unabated and in January 2010, Spain's unemployment rate topped 4 million for the first time since the current recording system started in 1996. Almost 125,000 people registered as unemployed in January 2010, pushing the total to about 4.05 million. Most of the lost jobs (82 percent) were from the service sector. The government's proposed austerity was expected to make matters worse in the short term. Support for the government continued crumbling in the face of this crisis and there was a growing loss of confidence abroad in Zapatero's fiscal policies. New polls indicated that voters rated Rajoy for the first time more highly than PM Zapatero and 43.4 percent of voters supported the PP compared with only 37.5 percent for the PSOE, and the gap started widening rapidly. The government found itself trapped in a catch-22: the more the PM adopted measures to placate international investors, the higher the discontent among Spaniards who vigorously opposed the austerity measures (this opposition was particularly strong among leftist voters and trade unions). In response, the government tried to regain the initiative and find some support. In early February, the government hosted a meeting with employers and trade unions to begin negotiations about the labor market with the aim to create more jobs. Yet, speculation of an early election was rampant at the time.

In the midst of increasing pressure from its European partners and the markets, the government continued pushing forward and shifted tactics to focus largely on austerity. PM Zapatero now claimed that his government would implement its austerity plan to cut the deficit "whatever the cost," and expressed his willingness to introduce harsher measures if necessary. Evidence to the contrary notwithstanding, he still claimed that his government had a "plan—a credible quantifiable plan—which we have already begun to implement.... Let's wait and see how we end 2010 and where we are on the budget and whether we are meeting our targets and, of course, if we have to make more cuts or demand more austerity then we will do so." This represented a clear policy reversal of the government, but by now he was willing to say anything to placate the markets. He admitted as much: "we have had to make a huge effort in public expenditures to provide social protection to our unemployed citizens and to bolster production and activity as far as we were able. But now that the deficit has got to a point that is unsustainable, we are equally determined and we do have a three year plan to bring it down." He finally, but reluctantly, admitted to mistakes: "we were not right in our forecast but neither was anyone—though that isn't something that helps." He confessed that "from here to the elections [in 2012] our policy is going to have to be one of austerity and cost cutting... there is no other way. And, to date, our commitments to reduce the deficit in the year 2010 are being complied with impeccably." He finally admitted the need to reform the labor market, but still wanted to find a way to reach consensus favoring a negotiated agreement with the unions and employers "that includes more flexibility while preserving the rights and guarantees of employees." Yet, he still refused to give up his optimism: Spain would "not fall back into the second division of nations.... Now we are going through a difficult time, but we are going to get out of this. We'll leave it behind and if we do things well we'll be the stronger for it."[16]

Good intentions aside, Spain was also being affected by the crisis in Greece. Fears about contagion intensified in the spring, and were compounded by yet another downgrade from S&P on April 28, 2010, by one notch from AA+ to AA, thus dealing a blow to the country's frantic efforts to separate itself from the crisis in Greece. As a result, the stock market continued falling. All this led to renewed rumors of an ongoing negotiation for an IMF rescue package of €280 billion, forcing PM Zapatero to dismiss them categorically as "complete insanity," while declaring these rumors as "simply intolerable" because of the damage that they had on Spain's interests, adding that "we can't spend all day paying attention to speculation." However, the government's insistence that it did not have a public debt problem (public debt at 55 percent was still about 20 percentage points below the EU average), while ignoring the private debt, only intensified concerns about the private debt (total gross external debt stood at 170 percent of GDP and the net figure, 90 percent), which further eroded confidence.[17] Moreover, markets also viewed Spain as moving too slowly on crucial reforms, and the government had shown little inclination to force change on the population (for instance, the government's proposal to push up the retirement age to 67 from 65 to help cope with the costs of rapidly aging population was put on an backburner after a series of protests).[18]

Following a week "from hell" in which the country suffered constant attacks from the markets, and saw interest rates increase and the stock markets fall by 14 percent, the worst performance in its history, the government was finally forced to take radical steps. On May 12, 2010, PM Zapatero announced in Congress a brutal austerity package. It included, among other measures,[19]

- **Public sector:** Reduction by an average of 5 percent of civil servants' salary in 2010 and freezes for 2011. This reduction would be proportional to the salary, thus having a greater effect on those with higher salaries. Cabinet members' salaries were reduced by 15 percent. It was estimated that this reduction would save €2.4 billion in 2010 and could reach 3 billion if other public institutions (Congress and the 17 regional parliaments followed through with a similar reduction).
- **Pensions:** Pension increases were suspended for 2011 (with the exception of the noncontributing and the people who received the minimum pension—30 percent of pensioners receive the minimum pension).
- **Retirement:** The transition regime from Law 40/2007 that allowed for early retirement was abolished.
- **Baby-check:** The €2,500 benefit per baby being born was eliminated.
- **Medical drugs:** Drug packages would be adjusted to include only the prescribed doses.
- **Dependency:** The retroactivity policy to receive benefits included in the Law of Dependency was eliminated, but the government announced its commitment to ensure all requests would be decided within six months to minimize the negative impact.
- **Official foreign development aid:** Reduction of €600 million between 2010 and 2011 (this figure had already been reduced by 1 percent in 2009).

- **Public Investment:** Reduction by €6.05 billion in national public investment for the next two years (in addition to the 5 billion for 2010 already included in the Austerity Plan). This decision would cause a delay in the completion of public works, expected to last between six months and one year.
- **Regional governments and municipalities:** Budget reduction of €1.2 billion (in addition to the 1 billion already cut the previous January).

These measures were approved by the Council of Ministers the following Friday and were implemented immediately. The objective was to save €15 billion in one and a half years.

These decisions, defined by PM Zapatero as "indispensable and equitative," caused a political cataclysm. The president who had sworn he would not touch social benefits in the middle of the crisis and who had held onto social peace as a lifejacket to survive the recession was forced to do a complete turnaround due to pressure from the markets, as well as its European and US allies (even President Obama put pressure). Initially the government had planned to do the adjustment in 2011 and announce it in June as part of the 2011 budget discussion. However, events during the week of May 3–9, beyond the government's control, forced this action; the escalating premium, the sharp decline in the stock market, and the decision by the ECB (its president, Jean-Claude Trichet, spoke against the possibility that the ECB would purchase sovereign debt) precipitated the situation.

The spring 2010 Eurogroup meeting of heads of government focused largely on Greece, but Spain's problems were on everyone's mind and PM Zapatero reached out to other Eurozone leaders pushing for a European mechanism that would protect countries from speculative attacks by the markets. The plan was finally approved at the following Ecofin meeting, but during the subsequent press conference PM Zapatero did not give any hint of what was about to happen in Spain. His focus was still on the need for growth and all indications seemed to point toward sticking with the austerity plan approved the previous January: "our deficit reduction process, necessary and unavoidable, must be supported by economic growth. In order to reduce the deficit faster, which to a large extend affects public investments, we cannot put in jeopardy our economic recovery. And less so now that we have had positive growth in the first quarter and we have finally come out of the recession." To judge from his press conference, it seemed like PM Zapatero was resisting any additional cuts. Regardless, it all became moot when Finance Minister Salgado attended the Ecofin meeting on Sunday and its European counterparts, including the German one, demanded further cuts. According to some sources, they demanded cuts equivalent to €30 billion between 2010 and 2011, and Salgado was able to bring it down to 15 billion (5 billion in 2010 and 10 billion in 2011). The Spanish government worked around the clock during the days prior to PM Zapatero's announcement to decide how to achieve that target. That Tuesday, he even received a call from president

Obama expressing his concerns for Spanish problems and requested additional sacrifices. Before he made it public in Congress, he communicated the plan to the unions, who expressed their complete opposition.[20] The package was approved by one vote in parliament. Economists reacted skeptically to the plan because it relied heavily, yet again, on economic growth forecasts that were seen as overly optimistic.

Mobilizations against the plan started almost immediately, as then thousands of civil servants joined protests across Spain against the public sector pay cuts and to call on the government to rescind the legislation covering public sector salary cuts.

A few days later (on June 23), in a report about the Spanish economy, the IMF warned the government of the weak and fragile status of the economy, and called on Spain to implement urgent and far-reaching reforms in the labor market as well as for the financial system to support the ambitious program of fiscal consolidation approved by the government. The IMF was also very critical of the collective bargaining system, tied to the inflation rate, which limited the internal flexibility of enterprises. It stressed the need to address the dysfunctional labor market, the deflating property bubble, the large fiscal deficit, as well as the high degree of indebtedness of the private sector, the external indebtedness, the weak competitiveness, and low productivity growth.

The government followed through on these demands and on June 16, in preparation for a EU summit and the visit from the IMF chief, Strauss-Kahn, PM Zapatero's government announced long-awaited changes to the country's rigid labor laws to address the 20 percent unemployment rate, which continued repressing consumer demand and draining public resources. It approved a decree to reform the labor market by giving employers more control over how to deploy workers and make it a little cheaper to dismiss permanent employees (and hopefully easier to rehire). At the same time, it strengthened the rules allowing for excessive use of temporary workers (see chapter 5). The government, unable to reach an agreement with unions and employers, was forced to impose the decisions unilaterally. The reform, however, ended up not satisfying anyone. Employers declared it an insufficient "mini-reform" while unions protested vehemently and announced mobilizations. They called for a general strike on July 29.

In addition, the Bank of Spain continued pushing to accelerate the pace of financial sector consolidation. It set a June 15 deadline for applications from the cajas to receive capital from the fund established the previous year to encourage mergers in the overcrowded sector (the so-called FROB). This allowed it to determine how much money is needed to disburse from the FROB and also stepped in to rescue two lenders—Caja Castilla-La Mancha and Cajasur (see chapters 6). Government officials also pushed for the publication of the results of stress tests on banks in Europe to defend Spain's solvency and fend off persisting speculation regarding a possible €250 billion sovereign bailout package.

Markets seemed to respond positively to all these actions, and Spain was able, again, to raise money at reasonable margin (i.e., on June 15, it sold €5 billion worth of 12-month and 18-month Treasury bonds at average yields of 2.3 percent and 2.8 percent respectively). Yet, access to capital was still closed for many Spanish companies. Francisco Gónzalez, BBVA's chairman, admitted as much; small or weak financial institutions found themselves frozen out of bond markets and denied the short-term funding that they so desperately needed for the operations.[21]

The annual state of the union's address in Congress showed the increasing isolation of the government. During his speech, PM Zapatero called on Spaniards to endure the austerity imposed by his government and embrace economic reforms for the sake of Spain's future: "I want to tell you that this is a transcendental moment for Spain, a crucial moment for its immediate future and for the coming decades.... We need to adopt measures to reduce the impact on our economy of the worst crisis that we have known, and at the same time we need to drive forward the most intense economic transformation of our country in recent times." He announced that the economy had grown during the second quarter of 2010 and reaffirmed the official prediction of a slight annual contraction of 0.3 percent for the year (other observers raised it to 0.8 percent). The perception was that international financial markets and Spain's EU partners, who had been irate at his government's refusal to accept the severity of the crisis, had largely imposed his policy U-turn. Opposition parties were virtually unanimous in heaping scorn on the government, with the opposition leader, Mariano Rajoy, leading the charge: "you are not fit to govern.... The best service that you can therefore do for your country to cut short this ordeal is to dissolve parliament and call a general election."[22]

After a relatively calm summer in which the government seemed to be rewarded by the markets for its commitment to meet the deficit targets with lower borrowing costs, Minister Salgado unveiled in September what she defined as "the most austere budget of recent years" for 2011, confirming the government's determination to stick to its deficit reduction plans. She announced an increase in income tax for the rich (the top marginal rate would rise 1 percentage point—from 43 percent to 44 percent—for incomes over €120,000 and two points—from 43 percent to 45 percent—for incomes above €170,000), the abolition of a special capital gains tax exemption for the investment funds used by wealthy Spanish families to manage their assets (the so-called *Sicavs*), and cuts in ministerial expenditure by an "extraordinarily large" 16 percent. The revenue expected from these measures was limited (the income tax increase was expected to generate between 170 million and €200 million), but it sent a strong signal to the Socialists voters that the government felt their pain (the general strike called by the unions was scheduled for the following week). Minister Salgado also announced a small downward revision of the 2009 budget deficit (putting it at 11.1 percent, instead of 11.2 percent of GDP) and reiterated her commitment to reduce the deficit to 9.3 percent in 2010 and 6 percent in 2011.[23]

The general strike of September 29 (the first since 2002) was less successful than feared. It had become a "necessary ritual" for the unions, who feared that their support among workers would further erode (they claimed to have 1.2 million members and to represent 80 percent of the workers) if they did not challenge the government's austerity. Yet, while they claimed victory, they could not point out the specific concessions they expected to extract from the government.[24]

Embattled PM Zapatero responded to his growing isolation and sinking popularity with another government reshuffle. New polls showed the Socialists with about 29 percent support and the PP with 43 percent. In an attempt to defuse popular discontent over his policies and allow his government to survive until the next scheduled general election in March 2010 he decided to slim the cabinet, eliminating the ministries of housing and of equality (who had been persistently attacked by the PP) and reducing the number of cabinet posts by five, as well as promoting loyal Socialists. Alfredo Pérez Rubalcaba, the interior minister who eventually would replace PM Zapatero as candidate in the general election, was promoted to deputy PM. In his by then legendary optimistic vein, he stated that he wanted to "strengthen the government's political discourse" and claimed that "this would be the government of reform, of the definite recovery of the economy and of employment." Observers, however, were skeptical of the reformist claim and suspected the government was turning Left, abandoning its reformist impulse; the new minister of labor, Valeriano Gómez, was close to the trade unions and had participated in the general strike against the government's labor reform while the new environment minister, Rosa Aguilar, had been a member of the Communist Party and the leftist IU for decades.[25]

Despite all this, the battle within the government intensified throughout the late fall and early winter of 2010, and market turbulences continued amidst fears of a possible Irish bailout (Ireland was struggling with the implosion of its real estate sector and its banks were collapsing in turn) and concerns regarding the Spanish economy's ability to grow and reduce its deficit. The Spanish government continued stating categorically that the country was not in a position to be rescued and PM Zapatero stated: "I should warn those investors who are short selling Spain that they going to be wrong and will go against their interests."[26] Meanwhile, an electoral campaign was taking place in Catalonia to elect the regional government and parliament. This was yet another election lost by the Socialists reinstating the Conservative nationalists of CiU (Convergencia i Unio) to power (see chapter 5).

As the end of 2010 neared, the Spanish government diligently tried to disassociate the country from Ireland's debt crisis defending that its problems could be resolved without resorting to the rescue package approved for Ireland. It restated its pledge to cutting the budget deficit and to reforming the country's pension system. PM Zapatero stated that "the commitment to cut the deficit is one which must be fulfilled exactly as promised, because on it depended the confidence on our economy that will pave the way for economic recovery and the growth of employment."[27] To calm investors, the government unveiled an "action plan" for the following 15 months, approved by the cabinet in late November. Nevertheless, contagion fears persisted as the government tried to fight a battle to convince investors that there was no further need for a bailout after the €80 billion rescue agreed for Ireland on November 20–21. Minister Salgado continued insisting that the country was "doing everything it had promised to do with tangible results." The EU Commission also defended Spain and argued that speculation against the country was unjustified. Yet, markets remained unconvinced; it was no longer only about austerity, but also about growth, and many wondered how the Spanish economy would grow with more austerity. It was a vicious circle hard to break away from.

In yet another attempt to try to regain the initiative, PM Zapatero hosted 37 business leaders on November 27 in order to promote confidence in the Spanish economy and dispel any notion that the country would need a bailout, as well as demonstrate a joint commitment to fiscal discipline and economic reform. The summit brought together senior ministers and the leaders of companies employing 1 million people with turnover equivalent to 40 percent of Spain's economic output. Many of these leaders had been critical of PM Zapatero's management of the economy since the start of the crisis, but most seemed convinced that if the austerity plan was implemented properly, it would be sufficient to restore confidence in the country's public finances. The gathering was an opportunity for the government to present a unified front and to reemphasize the three pillars of the government's crisis strategy: austerity and the reduction of the budget deficit; reform of the banking system through mergers among the cajas—due to be completed by December 24; and structural reforms. PM Zapatero declared it a success: "this is a day that has strengthened confidence.... We have reinforced our commitment to the economic stability of Spain and to recovery." The government restated its commitment to reform the pension system, extending the retirement age from 65 to 67 early in 2011, announced a plan to launch a National Competitiveness Commission, and committed to more transparency to placate the increasingly frenzied international debt markets (according to a new plan, the Finance Ministry would report monthly on Spain's public debt and the regional governments would have to give budget updates quarterly).[28]

As the year came to an end, confidence remained elusive. Consumer surveys anticipated that overall spending during the forthcoming holiday season would be reduced for the third consecutive year; it fell sharply from €951 per household in 2007 to an average 655 in 2010 with expenditure on meals at less than half the level of 2007. Clearly the 4 million unemployed were dragging down consumption. Aggravating the sense of doom, a building worker, who lost his job and ran out of money, shot four people in Olot.

Even municipalities, in an attempt to meet deficit targets, were forced to spend less on Christmas lights.[29]

The OECD also told Spain to reform the country's inadequate market competition and dysfunctional labor market. In a downbeat survey published on December 20, uncompetitive product markets and scarce waters were added to the list of issues that should be addressed by the Spanish government. While crediting Spain for making moves in the right direction (i.e., removing of a national requirement for a license to open a shop, or the decision to grant independence to telecom, energy, and postal services regulators), the OECD stated again that Spain should reform its labor market, continue cutting its budget deficit, and also liberalize product markets to foster competitiveness. It claimed that lack of competitiveness was a main reason ("unsustainable domestic demand boom driven by residential and business investment resulting in rising private debt" was another) for the country's escalating record of unemployment. According to the OECD, "progress in product market regulation can improve competitiveness both by strengthening productivity and lowering prices. This could allow a faster reallocation of resources to the most efficient and fast-growing sectors" (2010, 14).

The year ended on a somewhat more positive note when the administration announced that the government and the autonomous regions were on track to meet the official budget deficit target of 9.3 percent of GDP in spite of elections in 13 of the 17 regions that year. The final deficit was expected to be "somewhat better" than the target and unemployment fell by 0.25 percent from November (which was still at 20.7 percent). Ideally, this news would provide some relief for the embattled Spanish economy.

However, 2011 started with renewed concerns about the country's ability to reduce its deficit, leading PM Zapatero to issue a stern warning to the country's autonomous regions, demanding that they curb public spending and debt creation (they count for half of public spending, mainly on health and education, with the central government disbursing about a third and Social Security the rest). He reiterated that the central government would strictly enforce deficit targets and act against any region that would deviate: "at the end of the day, who is accountable? It is the central government, isn't it? And we have to spearhead, lead the way forward with the control of public spending for the autonomous regions. And they have to deliver. They have to fulfil those obligations, because if they do not, the government will act." Concerns about the regional governments' ability to control their debt were justified; according to the Bank of Spain, their debt had doubled to €115 billion since 2008, 15 percent of the total (the central government's debt was at 541 billion). For instance, Catalonia, one of the richest regions, needed to raise €10–11 billion in 2011 to cover deficits and repay earlier loans (it had accumulated an estimated €3 billion in arrears). In 2010, the deficit reached 3.6 percent of regional output, 50 percent above the central government's limit for the autonomous regions that year, and was expected that the projected Catalan deficit for 2011 would require a further €2.6 billion bailout (the Catalan government argued that it was "structurally underfunded and demanded a revision of the revenue compact").[30] This forced the Ministry of Finance to impose new transparency rules and new ceilings. PM Zapatero stressed that the government held the tools to control such profligacy: "we have powerful instruments. No autonomous regional government could actually issue debt without the backing, without the authority of the central government. So we have the key." He also called for the harmonization of business laws and the reduction of the administrative burden on businesses across Spain, in order to alleviate the problems caused by different sets of regulations, too much red tape, and difficulties getting licenses.[31] The month of January ended on a positive note when the government and the unions agreed on a pension reform that would raise the retirement age from 65 to 67.

At the same time, while the government continued pushing for a restructuring of the unlisted cajas (see chapter 6) and the rapid recapitalization of the financial sector, investors remained concerned about the weakness of many of the cajas and worried that they could sink the Spanish economy. In response to this concern, the government pushed for mergers (see chapters 6). As a result, the number of cajas was cut from 45 to 17.[32] These mergers also sought to rationalize their operations and reduce costs. Moreover, in order to increase transparency and avoid doubts over the sovereign creditworthiness of the system, the government also demanded that they publish their real estate exposure by the end of January 2011. Their recapitalization was effected largely from money from FROB, an state guaranteed entity with the ability to rise up to €99 billion. PM Zapatero still insisted that the need for public capital would be "very limited," thus it could be done with private capital.[33]

Meanwhile, the government continued to turn every stone to reduce expenses. At the end of February, it announced a plan to cut the motorway speed limit starting on March 7 to 110km per hour from 120 km per hour to save petrol following the upheaval in northern Africa and the increase in oil prices. It stressed that this cut was temporary and linked the decision to the emergency situation in the region. It was estimated that this change would cut oil consumption by about 15 percent and diesel by 11 percent (Spain is almost completely dependent on imported fuel, and every $10 rise in oil prices costs an extra €6 billion). To further reduce oil consumption, the government also announced plans to cut the price of commuter and short-distance rail tickets by 5 percent and increase the proportion of biodiesel used in diesel oil from 5.8 percent to 7 percent.[34]

Despite this frantic agenda, negative news continued piling up. Moody's downgraded Spain's sovereign credit rating in March by one notch to Aa2 (two notches below the top level and the same as that from S&P), thus reviving investors' fears. Consequently, the euro tumbled and Spanish government bond prices fell, while the yield on its ten-year debt rose to 5.55 percent, the highest since January.[35]

On April 3, 2011, PM Zapatero, in power since 2004, announced he would not be the Socialist Party's candidate for the general election that was due in March 2012. By then, he had lost support from a large part of his voters (the PSOE was facing a double-digit deficit in opinion polls behind the PP), as well as the one from the trade unions. His personal popularity rates had plummeted to historic lows for a Spanish head of government as people blamed him for mismanagement of the crisis, as well as for his unjustified overoptimism and unrealism about the country's economic prospects. He was gambling that his decision to drop out would bolster his party's chances to stay in power (and to limit the damage on the May 22 regional and municipal elections). In his message announcing the decision, he stated that "we are already in positive growth, we have stabilized the debt market risks, we are out of danger and we are close to the final issue, which is to create jobs. We are close, very close." He added that the prospect of Spain suffering a similar sovereign debt crisis to that of Greece or Ireland was now "99.9 to 100 percent ruled out."[36] Time would prove that his optimism was, yet again, deeply misguided and unjustified. The country was not out of the woods.

The intensification of the crisis throughout the early spring now spread to Portugal and forced it to request a bailout. However, surprisingly, this new bailout did not lead to increases on the yield on Spanish debt (as had happened when Ireland requested the bailout). On the contrary, the spread between German and Spanish bonds surprisingly narrowed to about 175 billion on Monday, April 11. This seemed to show that Spain was finally decoupling from the other peripheral economies, and seemed to confirm the steady restoration of the country's reputation among investors. The government's success reducing the deficit from 11.1 percent of GDP to 9.2 percent in 2010 (Portugal had failed to achieve this), as well as the perception that the country's financial woes and the cost of recapitalizing the cajas would be manageable (Moody's estimated that it would cost €120 billion in its worst case scenario, which would represent only a quarter of the Irish costs, and the Bank of Spain's estimates were eight time lower), contributed to this renewed confidence in the Spanish economy.[37]

Even the IMF maintained that Spain was a "completely different" case from the rest of the troubled Eurozone periphery. The IMF global financial stability report alerted Spanish households, still laden with debt caused by the burst of the real estate market, of challenges and yet it praised the government for its pension and labor market reforms, as well as for the financial restructuring and recapitalization plans put in place to address the weaknesses of the country's financial system. The IMF claimed that Spain's fiscal and financial reforms distinguished the country from the other peripheral economies.[38] Unfortunately, all this proved to be a temporary development.

Despite the positive news, the government was still somehow determined to continue putting its foot in its mouth. Following reports that China Investment Corporation, a sovereign wealth fund, was considering a €9 billion investment in the country's troubled cajas, after PM Zapatero met

Chinese leaders in April, the government was forced to make an embarrassing clarification denying the reports and confirming that it was too early to name "specific amounts of investment."[39]

The unemployment situation continued deteriorating throughout the spring. It increased by 214,000 in the first quarter of 2011, as the proportion of adults unemployed rose to 21.3 percent, up from 20.3 percent in the previous quarter, and reaching 4,910,200 at the end of March, hitting the highest level in 14 years. The level of youth employment (those under the age of 25) climbed to almost 40 percent. The government responded with a plan to offer incentives to companies to declare their unregistered workers as part of an initiative to increase tax receipts and clamp down on the informal economy (it is typical for unemployed people to claim unemployment benefits while receiving cash for informal work). Unsurprisingly, retail sales were also down 8.6 percent.

One of the important manifestations, given the depth of the crisis and the impact of unemployment, was the new surge of emigrants leaving Spain in search of job opportunities elsewhere (reversing the pattern of migration of the previous decade). According to official data, 118,000 people left the country in the two years before April 2010, pushed out by unemployment. However, some of these people left not because of unemployment but seeking high pay and in search of good living conditions. This exodus was different from the one in the 1950s and 1960s, when thousands of largely unskilled Spaniards moved to northern Europe to escape the country's misery. These were largely educated and skilled Spaniards, which raised concern of a "brain drain."[40]

The dire situation, particularly for young people, led to an unexpected wave of protests, coordinated virtually via Twitter and Facebook, which led to the emergence of the so-called May 15 movement of indignados (indignated). It was started on May 15 by a loose group of dissatisfied young Spaniards calling themselves "Real Democracy now," and was inspired by uprisings in the Middle East. They organized demonstrations that rapidly spread across the country. The movement swelled into an amorphous prochange uprising that condemned the domination of the political system by the two leading political parties, called for electoral reforms, and protested against the government's response to the crisis.[41] One of the main causes for indignation was precisely the record level of youth unemployment, but many participants espoused other causes: feminism; anarchism; the capitalist system; judiciary; political corruption; electoral system; nationalization of the banks; and support for additional subsidies for the arts. Hundreds gathered in Puerta del Sol, the heart of Madrid (the protest fever spread to many other cities as well), to demonstrate against the two main parties; many decided to continue the protests indefinitely and stayed there for weeks setting up temporary camps until they were forcefully expelled by the police. While there were questions about the fledging popular movement's significant impact at the polls (the demonstrations took place at the same time as the regional and municipal elections in the country), the overwhelming victory of the PP seemed to confirm that their impact had been limited and that most of the protesters had not voted.[42]

The electoral results were a resounding defeat for the governing party (see chapter 5). From Barcelona, through Castilla-La Mancha, to Seville, the Socialists lost a slew of regional polls and experienced its worst electoral performance since the establishment of democracy. The Socialists earned just 27.8 percent of the vote and trailed the PP by 10 points. The results added political volatility to an already uncertain situation, as the PP demanded the resignation of PM Zapatero and called for an early general election (which he refused); they intensified concerns about the government's commitment to austerity under a new political climate and its ability to control regional government spending, particularly now with most of them under the opposition.

Market nerves about Greece and about the Spanish government's commitment to rigorous deficit reductions pushed up the yields again in late May, killing any notion that Spain had finally decoupled from the other bailed-out countries. The Bank of Spain governor alerted the government that the country needed to continue cutting its budget deficit and implement economic reforms. The heavy electoral defeat of the Socialist Party in the regional elections only added to markets' jitters. In a typical fashion for incoming administrations, the victors decried the mismanagement of their predecessors and declared the inherited finances of their regions a complete mess. In Castilla-La Mancha, one of the 17 autonomous regions, the secretary general of the PP declared the region "totally bankrupt," and another PP leader classified it as "the Greece of Spanish regions."[43] Although the region represented only 3 percent of Spain's GDP, these comments reverberated across Spain's frontiers.

More and more reports were surfacing about corruption and money misspent during the boom years (for instance, in Castilla-La Mancha there were claims regarding a new airport that cost €1 billion, but virtually had no flights). Many started to demand a revision of the decentralized system established during the democratic transition, and argued that it was expensive, bureaucratic, and led to inefficient and costly duplications (a new report from Funcas showed that the number of public employees had increased from between 400,000 and 700,000 to as many as 3.2 million in the decade prior to 2010). Many of the regions were expected to overshoot the official deficit targets for the year (Catalonia's, as we have seen, was expected to reach twice the official target despite drastic cuts) and, in addition to that debt, there were questions about the debt of public sector companies and the total amount of unpaid bills.[44] No wonder credit rating agencies and international investors were nervous.

The stride of negative news for the government and the country continued into the summer, when EU officials indicated in a report, published on June 7 as part of the 27 country-specific evaluations of EU government budget and reform programs established as an element of the EU's revamped efforts to avoid future crisis, that Spain had adopted overly optimistic economic growth assumptions in its budget plans and ran the risk of its public pension system destabilizing government finances. While praising the government's efforts to rein in spending and fix the cajas, the report made it clear that these efforts were insufficient and that the government had to go even further. It also gave warning about the future of many cajas, questioned the effectiveness of the government's merging and reorganization plan, and alerted of the need for discipline among the regions' governments. It called for a reduction of Social Security contributions to reduce labor costs and an increase of VAT or energy to compensate. The government immediately rejected these suggestions (Minister Salgado indicated that they were "not going to follow that recommendation in the short term"), and claimed that the EU supported the government's strategy.[45] This report was closely monitored by the markets and added to an already cloudy scenario for the country.

As part of a new drive to reassure financial markets that Spain could decouple from the troubles of the other periphery countries, the government approved a new round of budget cuts to public spending on July 24, 2011, and, since oil prices had decreased, it lifted the temporary highway speed limits originally imposed to save energy and money. As part of this austerity package, the government imposed a 3.8 percent cut in the state budget for 2012 and set a spending limit of €117.4 billion (still less severe than the 7.9 percent cut of 2011). It estimated that the economy would grow by 2.3 percent in 2012 (a figure widely considered as too optimistic, which reinforced the well-established pattern to build the budget on unrealistically positive assumptions), and unemployment was expected to fall from 21 percent to 18.5 percent.[46]

However, the IMF piled up the negative news when it claimed in another report that the repair of the Spanish economy was still incomplete and alerted of the "considerable" risk of further setbacks. Following a pattern that by then had become quite common, the IMF praised the government for its austerity efforts and reforms, yet continued calling for further reforms: "Unwinding imbalances accumulated during the long boom and reallocating resources across sectors will take years and many policy choices. And some of the underlying problems of the Spanish economy, especially weak productivity growth and the dysfunctional labor market, remain to be fully addressed" (IMF, July 2011, 2). While it anticipated modest export-led growth, it pointed to sizeable risks: "On the downside, the key medium term risk is an intensification of domestic headwinds, and in the near term, rising concerns about sovereign risks in the euro area" (IMF, July 2011, 30). According to the IMF, Spain was not still "out of the danger zone." On the contrary, "the outlook is difficult and risks elevated," as "many of the imbalances and structural weaknesses accumulated during the boom remain to be fully addressed" (IMF, July 2011, 5). The IMF also alerted that fiscal consolidation was "based on optimistic macroeconomic projections and there is a risk of some regional governments missing their targets," and called for "additional action"; it stressed the need to complete the financial sector reform, as well as "a bold strengthening of labor market reforms to substantially reduce unemployment, and following through on the structural reform agenda to spur productivity and employment." Finally, it emphasized the need for consensus, something that has been largely missing throughout the crisis: "Such a comprehensive strategy would be helped by broad political and social support" (IMF, July 2011, 2, 30–31).[47] The government, in the voice of Minister Salgado, in its positive interpretation of the report, expressed its satisfaction: "the IMF signals risks, but it gives a very positive assessment."[48]

In the end, the government's attempts to reassure international bond investors with a combination of austerity and reforms were repeatedly dwarfed by the larger context (concerns about a possible debt default by Greece intensified that summer), and by these reports, which insisted on the need to accelerate the reforms and consolidate the austerity efforts. Increasing social unrest only deepened these concerns. The young demonstrators who launched the May 15 movement continued camping out by the thousands in Spain's major city squares for most of May and June, protesting the economic crisis, unemployment, and political corruption. The movement generated an army of volunteers, very active and visible in trying to prevent foreclosures and blocking evictions. On June 20, thousands of Spaniards marched in Madrid, Barcelona, and other cities to protest against austerity measures, in addition to attacking Brussels and the "pact for the euro" agreed on in March to strengthen economic coordination in the Eurozone. There were also a few isolated violent incidents that were captured by the international media, alarming observers further.[49]

Bond yields continued rising throughout the summer keeping Spain in the line of fire. The yield on ten-year bonds rose to 6.3 percent in mid-July, a record since the launch of the euro. Yet, the government still claimed that things were under control, and PM Zapatero insisted that there were no need for worries over the country's finances: "from the point of view of financing the treasury, the state, there is absolute tranquility," while calling for a "firm, coordinated, clear and rapid European response."[50]

The European stress tests to banks run by the European Banking Authority, published in mid-July, seemed to provide a much needed oxygen tank for Spain. They showed that Spain's leading banks were the strongest performers in the stress tests, which was expected to relive the pressure on the country. BBVA topped the stress tests with a core tier one capital ratio of 9.2 percent, even after modeling for a potential range of economic problems (see chapter 6).

However, the huge gross external debt burden (€1,744 billion) and the dependence on foreign financing still placed Spain in a vulnerable position, and the pressure continued on the country's sovereign debt. At the same time, the Bank of Spain reported that the economy grew by 0.2 percent in the second quarter of 2011, a year-on-year growth rate of 0.7 percent, quashing any expectation that the government's forecast of 1.3 percent growth for the year could be achieved. Thus, the government's ability to deliver its budget deficit reduction targets without further austerity measures was hampered.

After months of resistance, the ECB finally decided to act directly that summer in the sovereign crisis, and Spain benefitted from the ECB's emergency purchases of Spanish sovereign bonds. However, despite months of calling for ECB's intervention, the government claimed, in the words of Minister Salgado, "we don't need them to come and help us. We must earn ourselves a position of leadership in the European Union by implementing the right policies." And it responded, yet again, with new budget measures worth €5 billion to ensure it would meet 2011's deficit reduction targets of 9.2 percent. It changed the scheduling of advance corporation tax payments by large companies to try to collect an additional €2.5 billion in 2011 and reduced spending on pharmaceuticals by the health system to save another €2.5 billion. The PP responded accusing the government of "playing tricks" with the budget numbers.[51]

Spain found itself in an undesired and untenable position trying to impose sufficient austerity measures to soothe fears of default among international bond investors, while simultaneously avoiding spending cuts to the extent that it could hinder growth. The rising yield rates confirmed these concerns and led to a new threat by Moody's at the end of July to further downgrade.

In an attempt to rescue his party's grim chances at the polls and to force through economic reforms, PM Zapatero decided to call an early general election, on November 30, 2011 (deliberately, the anniversary of Franco's death, in a twisted attempt to remind voters of the dangers of the Right), four months ahead of schedule, announcing it on July 29. Polls seemed to suggest that the Socialists would suffer a sweeping defeat. No matter how it was presented, the early call was an admission of defeat. His government's credibility was in tatters after three years of gruesome crisis, and all attempts to reassure international bond investors were gaining little traction, as Spain battled worse conditions in the international bond markets. Furthermore, the Socialists did not have an absolute majority in Congress, and increasing opposition to the government policies was making it unlikely that it would have the necessary votes to pass essential budget legislation in Congress. When PM Zapatero made the announcements, he stated: "Certainty is stability," and claimed "on January 1, the new government must work on economic recovery and on reducing the deficit."[52] The Socialists had chosen an old pair of hands, Alfredo Pérez Rubalcaba, a former deputy and interior minister who had also served under PM González, as the PM candidate for the election.

The reaction from the markets was mixed. On the one hand, an early election could paralyze the government, which would stay on in a care-taking capacity for another three months, thus increasing political risk and potentially hindering the ongoing fiscal consolidation and reform efforts. On the other hand, if the PP gained an absolute majority, as all polls seemed to predict (it was ahead by 14 percentage points), the new government would have the votes to march through any reform and/or austerity measure through Congress, plus it could count on the support of business leaders. The immediate response resulted in even more turbulence in the bond markets caused by yet another big selloff of Spanish debt that pushed yields of benchmark ten-year Spanish bonds that peaked at 6.45 percent and the premiums reaching euro-era records of 404 basis points. While the government dismissed the tensions as "transitory" or "speculative," PM Zapatero decided to delay a planned summer holiday amid fears (though denied categorically by the government) that the country would require a bailout.

The months prior to the general election were marked by persistent tensions in the markets. At the end of August, and in response to market pressures and EU demands (which were expressed and agreed in a EU summit the previous July 21), the government introduced a constitutional amendment to limit the public deficit and push for a balanced budget that would force public administrations to abide by a maximum deficit. In order to allow for a certain flexibility, the final deficit figure, however, was not enshrined in the constitution. The parties agreed that it would have to be approved by a new organic law (the PP passed this law the following April). With this constitutional amendment, Spain followed Germany, which included it in its Basic Law in 2009 (article 109), and had already capped its deficit in its constitution. The EU intent was to have all 17 Eurozone members adopt similar constitutional principles. It was negotiated between the PP and the PSOE at the end of August, and approved by the Spanish parliament on September 2 in a record time, so it could be completed before parliament was dissolved on September 27. Only the PP and the PSOE voted in its favor; on the day of the vote, four of the smallest parties abandoned their parliamentary seats as a sign of protest against the way in which the reform had been negotiated and adopted. It was yet another indication of the erosion of institutions, one of the collateral effects of this crisis, and a fitting end to that legislature session.

The PP leaders could not hide their impatience to take over the running of the country and took every opportunity to lambast the outgoing administration for its disastrous management of the economy. Yet, it was clear that the margin of manoeuvre would be limited and that the new government would have to implement and enforce the same unpopular policies as those implemented by the Socialists. The PP candidate and party leader, Mariano Rajoy, insisted he would tell the truth to Spaniards during the electoral campaign: "we are in a very difficult situation, that tough times are coming, and that we are all going to have to tighten our belts." And, he claimed that they would run the economy with far more competence and rigor than the Socialists.

The Responses from the PP Conservative Government (December 2011–August 2012)

As described in more detail later in the book (see chapter 5), the Conservative PP came to power in December 2011, and its leader Mariano Rajoy became the sixth PM of Spain post-Franco democracy. In this election, Spanish voters chastised severely the previous Socialist administration under PM Rodriguez Zapatero for its economic mismanagement. The PP won an absolute majority and, armed with this majority (which Zapatero did not have), they sought to implement a process of reforms to overhaul the Spanish economy, starting with the labor market.

PM Rajoy unveiled his government program during his inauguration debate in Congress on December 19, 2012 (see table 2.4).[53] It was based on fiscal austerity and rapid reforms aimed to extract the Spanish economy from its financial and economic crisis. During his speech, he outlined plans to cut the deficit, create jobs, clean up the banking system, eliminate bureaucracy, and restore Spain's reputation abroad. He admitted that the outlook could "not be more sombre," and described three main goals: budgetary stability, cleaning up of the financial sector, and structural reform with particular focus on the labor market. His ultimate goal was to make the Spanish economy "more flexible and competitive."

He announced a government decree for December 30 that would enact urgent fiscal measures, including a provisional 2012 budget that would be followed by a budget stability law in January, and a full 2012 budget by March. At the time, it was estimated that the country would need to cut €16.5 billion more from the budget to meet the approved budget deficit of 4.4 percent of GDP. Rajoy stated that spending would be cut in all areas except pensions, which, in accordance with his electoral program, would increase at the same level as inflation; most hiring in the public sector would be frozen, and public enterprises would be restructured and/or closed. He announced that he had "no intention to raise taxes," something that he would later fail to do.

As indicated above, the PP had already agreed with the Socialist government to change the constitution to entrench long-term budgetary prudence in line with EU demands; Rajoy announced a new stability law to implement by 2020 the commitment to reduce the country's debt progressively to 60 percent of GDP (it stood at 67 percent in 2011), while limiting structural deficits to 0.4 percent of GDP.

In addition, Rajoy described his government plans to clean up bank's balance sheets and force them to disclose latent or hidden losses on their books caused by the collapse of the real estate market. He also mentioned that this would involve a push for mergers and consolidation, as well as regulatory and supervisory changes to the Bank of Spain's powers, within the first six months of the government's tenure.

He announced his aim to introduce a law to reform the labor market in the first quarter of 2012 thereby improving the collective bargaining system

Table 2.4 Summary of PP Government Commitments Announced during the Inauguration Debate (December 19, 2012)

Policy Area	Proposal
Pensions	Increase pensions in January 2012 to meet inflation levels
Early retirement	Bring closer the real average retirement age (63.5 years) to the legal one (67 years); allow retired people to receive a partial pension while working part-time
Holidays	Eliminate the so-called bridges and move mid-week holidays to Mondays
Social Security	One year of free Social Security for those who employ firsttime workers younger than 30 years old
Employment in public sector	Zero level of replacement with the exception of policy and military forces, as well as basic public services
Public administration	Austerity: deficit capped at 0.4% of GDP after 2020 for all administrations and sanctions for noncompliance
Public administration debts	Establishment of a new procedure to compensate the public administration debts with companies and autonomous workers
Banks' real estate holdings	Banks should sell the real estate holdings to clean up their accounts and update the value of these assets
Banks' mergers	Promote a second round of consolidation and mergers in the sector
Regulators	Reduce the number of regulators, restructurings of their competences, and a new system to name regulators with further intervention from parliament; changes to the supervisory role of the Bank of Spain.
Employment	Fiscal reduction of €3,000 per contract
Housing	Reestablishment of housing income tax deductions
Corporate taxes	Companies with up to €12 million in business will be allowed to use the special regime with a rate of 20%. Increase to €500,000 to apply the reduced rate of 25%
Education	Three years of high school, promotion of bilingual education (and trilingual education in the historic autonomous regions)
Teaching	Changes in the system to access teaching to promote merit
VAT	Autonomous workers and small enterprises will not pay VAT until the bill has been fully paid
Transparency	Approval of a Transparency law within the next six months
Television	Revision of the public TV model to allow new management models
Institutions	Renewal of the members of the Constitutional Court, Accounts Court, the Ombudsman, and public TV counselors
Other	New law of mediation and arbitrage, reestablishment of the Ministry of Agriculture

Source: "Rajoy anuncia un plan urgente y amplio de reformas sin concretar," *El País*, December 20, 2012.

by decentralizing it and giving more power to individual employers while simultaneously promoting flexibility and competitiveness; taking initiatives to promote entrepreneurship, including tax benefits for small companies; implementing plans to reform education, energy policy, and justice; and reducing the number of regulatory bodies for strategic sectors of the economy. At the same time he attacked some entrenched Spanish habits, like the costly tradition of creating long weekends around holidays (the so-called *puentes* or "bridges"), and stated that the government planned to move mid-week holidays to the nearest Monday.

The response from the markets was quite positive: in a bill auction on Tuesday, December 20, 2012, the interest cost of six-month bonds more than halved to 2.4 percent from 5.2 percent the previous month; the three-month yield fell even further, from 5.1 percent to 1.7 percent. The following weeks and months became a race against time to implement all these plans. To do so, he chose a former manager of Lehman Brothers and deputy finance minister under the Aznar administration, Luís de Guindos, as minister of finance and competitiveness, and Cristobal Montoro, a former budget minister under Aznar, as the minister responsible for the budget and public administration.

On December 30, the government announced immediate cuts of €8.9 billion in annual public spending, in addition to tax raises worth €6 billion.[54] The cuts came from departmental spending in addition to subsidies to political parties and trade unions among other items. The government also announced that pensions would increase by 1 percent in 2012 in accordance with expected inflation, and that civil wages would be frozen. In addition, it imposed "temporary tax increases," including income and property taxes, to raise an extra €6 billion per year, with wealthy property owners paying the most. At the same time, it warned of a major deficit overshot; the 2011 budget deficit was expected to reach 8 percent of GDP, much higher than expected, and a full 2 percentage points (or €20 billion) above the target agreed with the EU, which was far worse than even the most pessimistic observers had estimated, effectively making it much harder for Spain to meet its 4.4 percent deficit target. Minister Montoro announced that the final figure would be unknown until February and blamed the 17 autonomous regions for the overshot. This somewhat perplexing announcement (why announce a deficit figure when they were not sure of the final data?), and the decision to increase taxes (in contradiction with the party's electoral promise) set an ominous tone.

One of the major initial decisions taken by the PP government was the approval of a new labor reform. On February 10, the government announced an "extremely aggressive" labor reform as defined by Minister Guindos (see chapter 5 for additional details on this reform). Contrary to PM Rajoy's commitment ("the PP does not intend to make dismissals cheaper"), the new law made dismissals cheaper and created new labor contracts while eliminating, changing the structure of collective bargaining.

Subsequently, the government also announced and approved a new financial reform, the third in three years since the crisis started. It required additional provisions from banks of €50 billion to clean up their toxic assets (the Bank of Spain estimated at the end of 2011 that they held 184 billion in toxic assets). The additional provisions were calculated from increasing to 80 percent the percentage of land covered in the case of nonpayment (and 65 percent for unfinished houses, and 35 percent for finished ones). Banks would have until the end of 2012 to comply. The government also strengthened the FROB, and limited to €600,000 the salary of bank and cajas managers, but to €300,000 to groups controlled by the FROB. Spanish parliament approved the reform on February 16 with support from the PSOE, PNV, CiU, and abstention of the PNV, a rare occasion in which there was significant consensus on reform.

By the end of February, the deterioration of the fiscal situation became evident. On February 27, the government announced that the public deficit had reached 8.51 percent of GDP in 2011, well beyond the 6 percent agreed with the EU, and higher than the estimate made by the government after it took power in December. And this happened in spite of the series of supposedly harsh austerity measures (including tax rates and a 5 percent cut in civil service pay [see above]) that had been introduced by the Zapatero administration in May 2010. Eurostat validated the 8.5 percent deficit on April 23: only Ireland (13.1 percent) and Greece (9.1 percent) had a larger deficit within the Eurozone. Most of the overshot (1.64 percentage points of the 2.51 total) came from the autonomous regional governments, which failed to achieve their official targets. The worst was Castilla-La Mancha, whose regional deficit reached 7.3 percent of GDP. Finally, the real estate market continued in free fall in the fourth quarter of 2011 and home prices sank by 11.2 percent from a year earlier.[55]

With the economy projected to shrink 1 percent according to the EU (1.5 percent according to the Bank of Spain), the government started pressing the European Commission to ease the country's strict budget target for 2012 (4.4 percent of GDP), arguing about the risks of too much austerity. The government was concerned that too much austerity would further hinder growth, and also that it may imperil its program of longer-term reforms. The Commission argued, however, that Spain had to complete its 2012 budget first, which was expected to be released at the end of March. It also viewed with consternation the increasing politization of what was considered a technical issue (the EU had recently approved new fiscal rules to contain the debt crisis), with many policymakers sensitive over what had happened in 2003, when the Eurozone decided to water down its fiscal rules at the behest of the French and German governments, which is viewed as one of the reasons for the bloc's current woes.

Social unrest intensified as well, putting further pressure on the government. A demonstration held in Valencia by students and parents against education cuts was quelled by police using force, triggering days of protests across the city, branding the schools as symbols of the pitfalls of austerity. In previous crises, social strains had been mitigated by the cash generated in the underground economy and the cushion of support provided by extended families. However, the severity of this crisis made these mechanisms insufficient; for 1.6 million households, year 2011 ended without a single member holding an official job.

In a surprising unilateral move, which proved to be a tactical and strategic mistake, PM Rajoy announced on March 2 that Spain intended to breach its budget target for this year, delivering the news hours after joining fellow EU leaders to sign a new fiscal contract intended to ensure Eurozone member states' commitment to disciplined finances and prevent the debt problems that had led to the crisis. He claimed that the 4.4 percent deficit target was no longer realistic given the country's gloomy economic outlook, and stated that he had not informed the EU Commission of his plans because "this was a sovereign decision that Spain has taken." The new target was set at 5.8 percent of GDP, down from the 8.5 percent from 2011, but well above the 4.4 percent target set by the EU. He still confirmed the government's commitment to achieve the 3 percent target set for 2013 and to bring the country back to compliance with the EU deficit rules.[56] The EU Commission eventually corrected Rajoy and established a target deficit of 5.3 percent of GDP for 2012.

This decision took place amidst growing concerns about the country's rising public debt. While still manageable at 67 percent of GDP, it was growing quickly with each annual deficit, and could grow even faster by contingent liabilities from bank bailouts, the unpaid bills from the regional and municipal governments, or the debts from public enterprises. The government had already agreed to pay €35 billion in overdue bills owed to suppliers by municipalities and regional governments. Credit was still lacking; loans to Spanish business and individuals shrank by 4 percent in January. This was the sharpest monthly fall in more than two years despite the fact that banks were awash in cash because of the ECB's generous loans programs. Since the ECB began cutting rates of three-year loans to troubled European banks in December 2011, Spanish financial institutions were among the most enthusiastic recipients; between December 2011 and the end of March 2012, they borrowed about €200 billion at 1 percent interest.

The combination of escalating fiscal austerity to deal with the debt problem, a worsening real estate burst, and the recession were already threatening to set off a vicious economic circle in Spain akin to the one that brought the other rescued countries to their knees. The market started to feel that way; the country's ten-year bond yield, the best real time gauge of how private investors view the country's prospects, jumped to 5.4 percent by late March, from 4.9 percent at the end of February. And much worse was to come.

The government tried to mitigate the foreclosure problems and announced on March 9 a new code of good practices to help those that could not pay their mortgages. The final objective of this initiative was to allow mortgage holders who fulfilled the requirements to return their houses and complete the payment on the credit.[57] This was a significant change; in Spain, when mortgage debtors cannot make their payments, which was more recurrent given the escalating unemployment, the law denies them two recourses available in other countries such as the United States: they cannot hand in the keys to the bank and walk away; and they cannot discharge their debt in bankruptcy. On the contrary, they remain personally liable for the full amount of the loan after foreclosure; especially when penalty and court fees are added, they can easily find themselves on the street with thousands of euros in debt.[58] The government wanted to pressure financial institutions to sign the new code, and hoped it would be applied retroactively. At that time, there were 300,000 judicial foreclosure processes open (an additional 150,000 had already been executed). Banks and financial institutions reacted negatively, as they felt pressured to sign the code, despite its voluntary nature.

The end of March brought further negatives for the Rajoy government. On Sunday, March 25, 2012, Andalusia, one of Spain's largest regions, went in for regional elections. Despite opinion polls predicting the PP victory, the party failed to win an absolute majority that would have allowed it to wrest control of the region from the Socialist, which had run the region since the post-Franco restoration of democracy. The government had intentionally decided to postpone the 2012 budget until after the Andalusian elections, for fear that too much austerity would dent the PP's popularity and prevent the party from scoring an absolute majority. This politically motivated decision was widely criticized within and outside of Spain. With 50 seats, the PP won more votes than the Socialists for the first time in over three decades, but the combination of seats from the Socialists (47) and the leftist IU (12; double its representation from four years ago), allowed the Left to form a coalition government and stay in power. This failure was a significant setback for the PP government. Andalusia's deficit was more than double the official target in 2011 (unemployment was 31 percent), and the government would now face further difficulties controlling the regional budget and reaching consensus in order to reform regional and state governments.

The week closed with a general strike on March 29 called by the trade unions to protest against the labor reforms implemented by the Rajoy government. Thousands of workers abandoned big industrial companies and stalled air and rail transportation across the country. While the unions declared the strike a success and claimed that it was bigger than the previous national stoppage in September 2010 (though employers and the government challenged the unions' figures), the government reaffirmed its commitment to staying the course, because in Rajoy's own words, "it was obliged to make reforms to modernize the country."[59]

The government confirmed its determination by presenting the day after the general strike what Minister Montoro termed "the most austere budget" since the restoration of democracy. The new budget established tax rises for companies and individuals (in contradiction with the PP electoral's commitment) and drastic reductions in government spending, with the aim of bringing Spain's public finances under control, as well as averting a bailout by the EU and the IMF. Austerity measures for 2012 amounted to €27 billion. About 15 billion of the deficit reduction is yet to come in spending cuts with 12 billion from revenue-raising measures. The government expected to raise €12.3 billion in new taxes (5.3 billion from corporate taxes and 2.5 billion from a controversial temporary amnesty on tax evasion, which was appealed by the Socialists to the Constitutional Court[60]), while cutting ministry budgets by 17 percent to €65.8 billion in 2012. These measures would allow the government to reduce the public sector deficit from 8.5 percent to 5.3 percent of GDP in accordance with EU demands. Yet, there were concerns about the ability of the central government to force the 17 autonomous regions to meet their deficit targets as well, and about how realistic the projections and budget assumptions were given the perverse effects that tax increases could have in a shrinking economy.[61] Observers criticized the composition of the cuts and the reliance on a one-off tax amnesty to raise €2.5 billion.

Pressure on Spain intensified throughout the spring despite the insistence by the government and EU officials that Spain's banks would not need an injection from the Eurozone's rescue fund. As part of the financial reform approved in February, the government gave banks until March 31 to present recapitalization plans to insulate them from further market shocks. While most observers still believed at the time that additional provisioning and capital requirements would be largely met through private sector solutions, there was still rampant speculation that many banks would require a deep write down of questionable housing loans followed by an infusion of capital from the Eurozone rescue fund. EU Commissioner Oli Reihn denied this possibility and confirmed that there was no pressure on Spain to accept aid.[62] Time would prove otherwise.

While sovereign bond prices continued spiralling out of control (the yield on the ten-year benchmark reached 5.8 percent in early April and the risk premium over German bonds increased by more than 4 percentage points or 400 points); the stock market prolonged its free fall, while the government tried to soothe the markets, announcing on April 9 reforms of the health and education systems, to rationalize spending in the autonomous regions. The goal was to save at least 10 billion of public spending by rationalizing health and education through the elimination of overlaps and the improvement of efficiency in public services. The government also announced later an initiative to ban business transactions in cash involving more than €2,500, as part of a broader campaign against tax evasion that was expected to raise more than 8 billion in 2012 (the so-called informal economy was estimated to be worth almost a fifth of GDP). Furthermore, as part of the plan to reorganize the provision of health services and reduces costs, the government also announced in mid-April a plan to require patients to pay more for their prescriptions.

The pressure from the markets, however, was still unrelenting. A few days later, Spain's borrowing costs rose to levels not seen since the previous January (the ten-year bonds traded to yield above 6 percent for the first time since the ECB began flooding the region's banks with €1 billion in cheap credit in December 2011), and the stock market fell by 3 percent, raising further concerns that Spain would require a bailout. Markets were increasingly concerned about the negative impact of austerity on growth and the perverse loop in which the country found itself: the more austerity the deeper the recession. The country found itself at the heart of a Eurozone experiment designed to demonstrate that procyclical increase in fiscal austerity in a deep recession can lead on to growth and debt sustainability. The markets, however, did not seem to believe that such a combination was feasible. It was a problem of solvency, not of liquidity.

Still, the government insisted that it would not be distracted by short-term market fluctuations and would stick to the austerity program needed to put Spain back on track to meet the EU deficit target. Guindos reiterated that Spain "does not need a rescue at this time," and the Commission insisted that there had been no discussions on assisting Madrid with aid from the €500 billion recue fund.[63] Meanwhile, PM Rajoy continued urging his European counterparts to stop pointing the finger at Spain (the Italian PM Monti blamed Spain for the latest falls in Italian sovereign bond prices; French president Sarkozy used Spain as an example of left-wing mismanagement—the Spanish Socialists had run the country for the previous four years—in his presidential reelection campaign against his Socialist rival, Hollande), and to work together to strengthen the Eurozone: "We all got problems. We in Spain are working to solve ours and help the Eurozone, and we expect others to do the same and be cautious in what they say. We all have a great responsibility. We want a strong Europe and a strong Euro." He insisted that Spain did not need help to finance itself: "That is not the case for Spain, nor will it be the case for Spain in the future, I want to make it clear. . . . For this I request the greatest possible prudence and sense of responsibility. . . . What is good for Spain is good for the Eurozone."[64] The government had both a financial deficit and a deficit of credibility, and it found itself playing catch-up with the markets to no avail.[65]

On April 12, the government pushed through parliament a "budgetary stability law" obliging Spain to cut its annual budget deficit to zero by 2020, from €90 billion or 8.5 percent of GDP in 2011, and to limit total public debt to 60 percent of GDP at the end of 2012. The PSOE voted against it, claiming it went beyond the constitutional amendment that both parties agreed upon the previous September (see above). This law will allow the central government to intervene in errant regions to ensure compliance, and it was a response to markets' and EU concerns that the central government could not reign on its "out of control" regions. The crisis generated a new debate about the outcomes of the decentralization process initiated during the democratic transition of the 1970s; hardliners were using it as an opportunity to criticize the autonomous regions system, perceived as having generated inefficiencies and duplication of public services, as well as multiplicity of regional regulations.[66]

Nevertheless, despite all the frantic action, the crisis continued intensifying throughout the spring and the government was forced to admit that the country was "undergoing a crisis of enormous proportions." In mid-April, it was announced that Spain had lost €32 billion on foreign investment in public debt in one year (from 54.8 percent in 2010 to 50.4 percent in 2011), and that development was accelerating; the relative weight of international capital in the country's treasury bond market declined from 50.48 percent in December 2011 to 37.54 percent in April of 2012 (13 percentage points), and 61 billion in the first three months of the year. Bond yields were still stuck at 10 percent. This was a clear signal of lack of confidence on the Spanish economy on the part of foreign investors. By April, the number of new mortgages reached the lowest levels since the crisis started; it decreased 45.7 percent vis-à-vis the previous year. Unemployment continued its unstoppable race, reaching 5.63 million people (or 24.4 percent) that month, close to the 1994 record (the number of unemployed increased by 729,000 in one year, as the jobless rate neared one in four). Real estate prices were down by 25 percent, about 300,000 properties had been repossessed since the crisis started in 2007, and there were 1.9 million units on sale and 3.9 that could go on the market in the coming years), with estimates that the glut would cause home prices eventually to fall by up to 60 percent.[67]

The credit rating agencies continued punishing the country, exhibited by Standard & Poor (S&P) who delivered yet another blow to Spanish confidence by cutting the country's sovereign credit rating by two notches, anticipating that the ongoing recession would extend to 2013. S&P specifically mentioned the need to provide extra financial support for weaker banks, a problem already highlighted the same week by the IMF.

The government continued pounding on its European allies for assistance, rarely with subtlety. Foreign Minister Margallo, one of the most outspoken members of the government, stated on Spanish radio that "this is like the Titanic. If there is a sinking here, even the first class passengers drown." From the government perspective it was doing everything that could be done by applying a brutal cure to the economy with policies that have a negative impact in the short term, yet its European partners were not doing much to help the country. On April 23, it became official, according to the Bank of Spain, that the country had lurched into recession for the second time since 2009, with GDP falling by 0.4 percent in the first three months of 2012, adding a 0.3 percent to the previous quarter. The prediction for the year is that the economy will shrink by 1.7 percent. At the same time, Eurostat confirmed Spain's budget deficit of 8.5 percent for 2011, proving the reliability of Spanish statistics (there was speculation that the data was adapted).[68]

Nevertheless, the government still insisted on its commitment to cut the deficit in line with EU targets, claiming that the labor reform would eventually help create jobs, and that the financial reforms, with higher capital requirements and bad loan provisions, would be enough to avert the need for a EU-financed rescue of the financial sector. Many investors and observers, however, remained skeptical, and on April 16, Spain crossed the first red line when the yield on the country's ten-year bonds increased to 6.07 percent, and the risk premium reached 435 points. The IMF seemed to confirm these doubts when it stated on April 25 that "to preserve financial stability, it is critical that these banks, specially the largest one [in reference to Bankia], take swift and decisive measures to strengthen their balance sheets and improve management and governance practices." This statement renewed predictions that the government would be forced to intervene with Bankia and other lenders (see chapter 6). All this took place in the face of increasing social unrest, as thousands of Spaniards took to the streets across the country to protest austerity and commemorate the anniversary of the May 15 Movement, with about 70,000 indignados taking the central squares of Madrid, Barcelona, and other cities.

Yet, the government continued its efforts to reign over the country's public finances and was able to extract adjustment from the regional governments of €18.34 billion (most of it, €13.071 billion, in budget cuts) during a tense Political Counsel that took place on May 16 during which the government approved the adjustment plans of the autonomous regions in a highly fought and celebrated pact. With the government under pressure from its European partners, it went as far as to threaten to seize control of some of the regions' budgets (among the most troubled: Asturias, Valencia, and Andalusia). The autonomous regions, hard-pressed for liquidity, requested the creation of hispabonds, a joint emission of debt from the autonomous regions with the collateral of the Treasury. The government, however, refused to commit and postponed the decision to the following summer (eventually deciding to create a liquidity instrument to help the regions).

Meanwhile, the financial crisis intensified in Spain with the collapse of Bankia (see chapter 6), and Minister Guindos announced the drafting of two independent advisers to examine the books of all Spanish banks. The goal was to restore international confidence in the country's lenders. Moreover, the government continued with its reformist agenda. On May 25, the government announced a new law to liberalize the opening of retail stories, a highly regulated sector up to this time. Later, it approved measures to give retail stores the flexibility to schedule their own business hours in certain cities (something that was highly regulated up to that point).

By the late spring/early summer, deteriorating economic conditions and the intensification of the banking crisis that led to the country's financial bailout (see chapter 6) combined to derail the government's reform agenda that was placed on the backburner. The government now focused on a new brutal austerity package.

July 2012

On Wednesday, July 11, 2012, the Spanish government unveiled its fourth set of austerity measures in its seven months in power, which was described as the hardest adjustment of the democratic period. They were designed to achieve Spain's deficit targets convened with the European Commission's within the framework of the Excessive Deficit Procedure. These measures included, among others,[69]

- A significant increase in tax revenues, including VAT, corporate income tax, personal income tax, and excise duties;
- A substantial review of the unemployment benefit regime and of Social Security contributions;
- Measures to increase the efficiency of the public sector and to reduce the public sector wage bill; and
- A frontloading of the sustainability factors in the pension system.

Specific highlights of this package included €65 billion worth of tax increases and public spending cuts (the equivalent of 6.5 percent of GDP), in order to secure European aid to support the Spanish banking system. The goal of the package was to reduce Spain's budget deficit by €80 billion over the next two and a half years, building on previous cuts: Zapatero's government imposed €15 billion in two years; Rajoy already adopted €27 billion in cuts in December 2011. This new adjustment package included a rollback of unemployment benefits; an increase in VAT from 18 to 21 percent; cuts in state funding to unions by 20 percent; scrapped property tax breaks; caps and cuts in salaries and bonuses for some public sector workers; the sale of state-owned airport and railway assets; and cuts to local governments. During the speech in Congress during which he announced the largest adjustment package since the transition to democracy, PM Mariano Rajoy issued stark warnings about the risk to Spain's future (see table 2.5).

According to the government the estimated impact of these measures would be approximately €13.5 billion in the remainder of 2012, €22.9 billion in 2013, and €20 billion in 2014. This calculation excludes the valuation of the impact of further measures, including Energy and Environmental taxation, which the government was planning to announce at a later date. These measures were in addition to those already announced in the 2012 Central Government Budget in April 2012, and to the economic and financial plans presented by the autonomous regional governments in May 2012. This package was approved by the central government and would enter full force immediately, with the exception of the VAT tax increase, which would be implemented starting that September (2012).

This new austerity package rendered obsolete the country's budget for 2012, just two weeks after it had been formally approved, showing, yet again,

Table 2.5 New Austerity Measures (July 10, 2012)

Policy Area	Description
VAT	The regular type increases from 18 to 21%; the reduced one from 8 to 10%; and the super-reduced that taxes essential goods (like bread or vegetables) stays at 4%. As a result of this increase, the government expects to collect €22.1 billion. Taxes to tobacco and the environment will also increase.
Other taxes	Changes to the staged payment system of the Corporate Tax system. Social contributions will go down 1 percentage point in 2013, and another one in 2014. Taxes on employment will also be reduced.
Unemployment benefits	The regulatory base used to calculate the unemployment benefit is reduced from 60% to 50%. As a result, the amount will be reduced after the sixth moth for new beneficiaries. The amount is calculated based on the contribution during past 180 days of employment. Once unemployed the person receives 70% of that amount, and after six months, 60%. From now on, the unemployed would receive only 50% after the sixth month. The goal is to promote active search for employment. The measure will reduce the average unemployment benefit (which stood at €813.9) currently received by 1.349 million unemployed. The goal is to reduce the cost for the central government's budget, one of the fastest growing ones during the crisis. There is also a plan to reduce bonuses to hiring.
Pensions	The government plans to bring to the Toledo Pact a new law proposal to reform the pension system and accelerate the sustainability factor and address anticipated retirements.
Civil servant salaries	Elimination of the bonus Christmas pay in 2012, 2013, and 2014, with an estimated saving of €4 billion. This would represent a reduction of 7% in their gross annual salary, and a saving of 4 billion for the government. The workers may recuperate the savings after 2014 through a pension fund. The government announced later that this elimination would not apply to civil servants who earn less than 1.5 of the minimum wage, or €962.

Work days	Reduction of the number of days of free disposition (the so-called *moscosos*), and the number of union representatives liberated will be based on whatever is established by law.
City hall representatives	Reduction of 30% in the number of city hall representatives. Mayor and councilors will have to publish their salaries, and their retributions will be homogenized. The annual budget law will establish parameters based on the characteristics of the municipality. The role of provincial deputies (*diputaciones provinciales*) will be strengthened to guarantee the provisions of public services. The expected savings would reach €3.5 billion. The role of the municipal comptroller will also be strengthened to improve the control over local budgets.
Taxes on energy	Taxes on energy will be changed to reduce the deficit caused by the current tariff system (the difference between the production costs and what users pay, which currently stands at 24 billion)
Housing subsidies	Tax incentives on the purchase of housing will be phased out during 2013. The government had reestablished retroactively this incentive in December 2012 shortly after coming to power (it had been eliminated by the Zapatero government in 2011 for those who earned more than €24,000). It represented €2.5 billion.
Expense from ministries	The government approved a new adjustment in ministries budgets of €600 million.
Political parties	20% cuts in the subventions received by political parties, unions, and business organizations in the 2013 budget (added to the 20% cut already approved for 2012)
Public companies	The government announced a new reduction and the elimination of local public companies, to avoid duplication of services. It will take place in the context of a second phase of the Restructuring Plan for the Public Business Sector and Foundations.

Source: El País, July 11, 2012.

the rapidly shifting circumstances and the constant need to adopt new measures in the context of a rapidly deteriorating situation. The government, once again, was a few steps behind: in four months, the central government budget's deficit reached 3.41 percent, practically the amount forecasted for the entire year.

The July 11 announcement followed an EU agreement finalized earlier that week allowing Spain an extra year to meet its deficit reduction targets and to iron out the conditions to disburse the €100 billion in aid to the ailing banking sector. The EU action was prompted by the difficulties that Spain was encountering in funding its sovereign debt, with international investors pushing the country's borrowing costs to euro-era highs. The markets initially had a positive reaction and Spanish government bonds fell by 14 basis points at 6.70 percent, having been above 7 percent earlier in the week.

This latest austerity package was a complete turnaround on the government promises. PM Rajoy admitted: "I said that would reduce taxes and I am increasing them... the circumstances have changed and I have to adapt myself to them." His government repeatedly pledged he would not waver on his commitment to reduce the deficit to 5.3 percent of economic output for 2012, yet the EU allowed Spain to reduce the target to 6.3 percent and was given an extra year to come within the 3 percent agreed limit. The list of contradictions is already legend (see table 2.6).

The risk, yet again, was that an additional round of austerity would strangle an economy, forecasted to shrink by 1.7 percent in 2012, which was already suffering the highest rate of unemployment in the Eurozone. While there was consensus that too little fiscal consolidation could roil the markets, there was increasing awareness that too much austerity also would undermine the country's recovery and further erode markets' confidence. The main concern centered on the potential impact of these measures on consumer spending (VAT collections were already down by 10 percent this year). Spain needed both austerity and growth, a difficult circle to square.

Furthermore, the combination of private sector deleveraging and austerity risked exacerbating capital flight at a time when Spain needed capital to increase credit and investment. Unfortunately, as shown in chapter 6, Spain faced a particularly unholy combination of challenges because of the size of its banking sector relative to the economy and the depth of the banking losses.

The social impact of additional austerity was also an important concern. This latest package was announced as thousands of miners, most of whom had spent weeks marching nearly 300 miles from the Asturias region, marched in Madrid center to protest against austerity measures including cuts to coal subsidies that threatened the survival of their mines. Protests intensified in the days following the approval of the package, with civil servants taking to the streets to protest the cuts, sparkling small skirmishes in confrontations with the police.

A crucial challenge for the Rajoy government was to convince Spaniards that, however much these measures may contradict his electoral promises

Table 2.6 The PP "Policy Shifts"

Policy Area	Commitment from PM Rajoy/PP	Action
VAT increase	" I am not like you...You increased the VAT to people and did not have it in your program...If I do not have it in my program I will not do it" (Electoral debate, November 2011)	VAT increased in July 2012
Civil servants' salaries	"I will freeze civil servants' salaries instead of lowering them because Spain needs consumption and investment" (March 2012)	Christmas bonus eliminated and working hours increased
Unemployment benefits	"I will not modify the unemployment insurance" (November 2011)	Cuts in unemployment benefits in July 2102
Income tax and housing deductions	"I will leave it very clear so none is mistaken. We will oppose any tax increases. Increasing taxes today mean more unemployment and more recession, and an additional screw to the already damaged economy of families and companies" (September 2011)	Direct taxes increased in December 2011: between 0.7% and 7% based on the rate. In 2012 and 2013 this affects 17 million taxpayers and represents a €300 increase for an average salary. Retentions to savings also increased between two and six points, with a new cap of 27%. The IBI increases between 4% and 10% for 25 million of real estate assets. Finally, tax subsidies for housing eliminated in July 2012.
Labor reform	"The PP does not intend to reduce dismissal costs, but instead to promote that indefinite contracts become the general rule" (September 2011)	Labor reform in February 2011 establishes a dismissal with 20 days of compensation per year worked with a maximum of 12 months while increasing the accepted causes for dismissals to include poor financial results like a drop in sales. Companies can also change unilaterally salary and working conditions.
Fiscal amnesty	"Nonpresentable, antisocial and unfair...We tell citizens who pay that we are going to increase their taxes, and to those who commit fraud that they will be forgiven" (June 2010)	Amnesty fiscal: those who committed fraud can now launder their money paying only 10% in taxes. Interests and fees are commuted.

continued

Table 2.6 Continued

Policy Area	Commitment from PM Rajoy/PP	Action
Health copayment	"I will use the scissors everywhere except in public pensions, health and education" (November 2011)	Copayment of medical drugs approved on April 20 based on income, including for pensioners. With general character they will pay 10% of the price of the medications with a cap of between 8 and €18. Health services are limited for illegal immigrants.
University fees	" I will use the scissors everywhere except in public pensions, health and education" (November 2011)	University fees increased: students have to pay between 15% and 25% of the real cost of the degree (before they paid 15% on average), and the number of working hours for professors is also increased, as well as the number of students in classrooms.
Fulfillment of deficit objectives	"Our objective is to move forward with the fiscal consolidation and fulfill impeccably our budget deficit objectives" (December 2011)	The EU requested a 4.4% deficit for 2013; Rajoy announced unilaterally (and without approval from the EU) that the objective for the year would be 5.8%; the EU rejected it and approved a 5.3% one.
Euphemisms	"To say always the truth, even when it hurts, without any embellishments and excuses: to call bread, bread, and wine, wine" (Inauguration speech December 2011)	Amnesty fiscal = "a regularization law"; Labor reforms = "introducing flexibility to the conditions to avoid dismissals" Health cuts = "progressive copayment of drugs"; VAT tax increase = "increase of indirect taxes in hacienda terms."

Source: "Rajoy no mintió, son las circunstancias," *El País*, July 11, 2012.

and public statements, they were unavoidable and would ultimately have positive consequences by positioning the country on a new path of growth. His trump card throughout the crisis was fear of the potential consequences of a full-scale bailout. During the speech announcing these measures, he adopted Churchill's tone ("I have nothing to offer but blood, sweat and tears"), insisting, yet again, on blaming the previous government and his political inheritance ("the excesses from the past have to be paid in the present"), presenting these measures as unavoidable ("there is no alternative") because the country "needs to borrow money" and is trapped "in a vicious circle that it needs to break." He described the current times as "crucial" for Spain, a period "that will determine the future of the country," and expressed his confidence that these sacrifices would pay off giving a "reward" down the line. The president asked Spaniards to trust him, a hard task, given the damage to his credibility only 6 months after coming to power, because he was doing the exact opposite of his promises.

The initial reaction from the markets to the austerity package seemed positive; in the first bond auction after the package approval (on Tuesday, July 17, 2012), Spain paid significantly lower interest rates to raise short-term money (Spanish Treasury sold €2.6 billion, in 12-month bills at an average interest rate of 3.9 percent, down from 5.07 percent in the previous auction on June 19. Spain also sold €961 million in 18-month bills at a rate of 4.24 percent, down from 5.10 percent), which seemed to suggest that the austerity package offered some reassurance to nervous financial markets. The borrowing costs, however, were still high amidst concerns regarding the details of the rescue for Spain's banks, which were yet to be determined, and persisting fears that the banking bailout was a prelude to a rescue of the sovereign. Even Minister Guindos acknowledged as much when he emphasized that Spain was still under attack in the bond markets, recognizing that foreign investors were increasingly avoiding bond auctions, leaving only domestic buyers to buy Spanish debt.[70]

And the volatility intensified, fueled by continuing uncertainty regarding Spain's public finances, and disconcerting statements from members of the government. For example, Minister Montoro stated during a parliamentary debate that "there is no more money in the public coffers to pay for public services.... If we do not increase tax revenues we are jeopardizing the payroll for civil servants, which is what is happening at the autonomous regions and the municipalities.... Civil servants know it and they are willing to sacrifice to push Spain forward." The response from the markets was immediate: the risk premium vis-à-vis Germany increased that day from 559 (bp) basic points to 576, close to the 586 record of the euro era, established on June 18, 2012.[71]

And things only got worse in the following weeks, exhibiting further concern that more austerity would only hinder growth. Even as Eurozone finance ministers approved a loan package of up to €100 billion for Spain to repair its banks, the country's bond yield continued rising, reaching new records. To make matters worse, the government reviewed its forecast and announced that it expected the economy to contract 0.5 percent in 2013 (instead of growing 0.2), with unemployment remaining around 24 percent. Furthermore, the decision by some of the autonomous regions (notably Valencia, Catalonia, and Murcia), which had found themselves closed out from the capital markets, to seek support from an €18 billion emergency fund created by the central government in July to help the regions (the so-called FLA),[72] only intensified fears regarding the state of the country's public finances.

These fears were not wholly unjustified: Valencia had a debt stock of €20.7 billion and had to refinance 8.1 billion in 2012 (2.9 billion in the second half of the year); Andalusia had debts of 14.3 billion and has to find 2.4 billion in the second half of 2012; and Catalonia, with an economy equivalent in size to

Portugal, had a total debt of 41.8 billion, with 13.5 billion maturing in 2012, and 3.7 billion in the second half. And this liquidity problem turned into a political "duel" between the central government and the regions (the government decided to reserve the additional room granted by the EU Commission regarding the deficit target entirely for the central government, thus putting even more pressure on the regional governments for cuts; plus it threatened to take over running those autonomous governments that would not fulfill the targets). All this threatened to break the longstanding (but unstable) balance between the central government and the regions, with many in the regions claiming that the PP had an agenda to recentralize and wanted to use the crisis to roll back the democratic transition devolution settlement.[73] As an overall result, Spain's borrowing costs soared above 7.5 percent (on July 23, Spain's interest rate on ten-year government debt spiked to 7.51 percent, its highest level since the single currency was introduced in 1999, a level that many observers feel could eventually shut Spain out of public markets and force it to seek a bailout); and the stock market suffered some of its worst days in years (stocks hit new lows for the year, down by about 30 percent, with banks and conglomerates leading the way).[74]

Meanwhile, in Madrid the government faced an onslaught from the previous governor of the Bank of Spain (Miguel Angel Fernández Ordoñez), and the former minister of finance (Elena Salgado) in the Spanish parliament. Called to declare the collapse of Bankia, they used the opportunity to criticize the government policies, with Mr. Ordoñez claiming that "in the first half of the year we have witnessed a collapse of confidence in Spain. Now we are not only worse than Italy, but worse than Ireland, a country that has been rescued." Yet Minister Guindos, who traveled to Germany and France to hold discussion with his counterparts on July 24 and 25, still insisted that his nation would not seek a government rescue.[75]

The ECB and the European leaders reacted calmly to the new storm. Before acting, they wanted to see the effect of the implementation of the banking bailout (full implementation of which was expected to be completed by September), plus there were no more available funds (the new EU €500 billion rescue had yet to be formally adopted and implemented because the German Constitutional Court was not expected to decide on it until September). And the ECB was resisting pressures to resume the large-scale buying up of government bonds on secondary markets that it began in 2010 (it already spent €210 billion without arresting the crisis, and the program was frozen since the beginning of 2012). ECB leaders argued that any bond buying should be done by the bailout funds that had been developed by the Eurozone leaders to support countries in difficulties.[76]

However, at the end of July, during the peak of the storm, the ECB was finally heard. Following days of intense market turmoil and concern that Spain's borrowing costs had reached unsustainable levels and may force the country to request a sovereign bailout, Mario Draghi, the ECB president, told a conference that it was "ready to do whatever it takes" to preserve the single currency, and challenged the markets: "believe me, it will be enough." His comments triggered a rally and the yields on Spanish bonds dropped 45 bp to 6.93 percent.[77] Unfortunately, it proved to be short-lived, as he did not indicate what actions the ECB may take. Wolfgang Schäuble, German finance minister, continued challenging widespread speculation about any Spanish request for support, while ruling out the purchase of sovereign bonds. He rejected the notion that Spain was "desperate" because of the increasing borrowing costs and instead praised Spain for making "all the necessary decisions," including increasing VAT and cutting civil service pensions"; "the financial markets are not acknowledging these reforms yet, but that will come." On July 30, he met with US Treasury Secretary, Timothy Geithner, and they discussed the "considerable efforts" being made by Italy and Spain "to pursue far-reaching fiscal and structural reforms"; Italian PM Monti continued praising the Spanish government actions, claiming that Italy and Spain were "starting to see the light at the end of the tunnel."[78]

The news were still grim, however. At the end of July, Spain published the national employment statistics, which showed that 5.69 million people ended the second quarter of 2011 jobless, raising the unemployment rate to a record 24.6 percent (compared to 24.4 percent in the first quarter). Youth unemployment rose to 53 percent that quarter, up 1.3 percent from the previous quarter, and a whopping 7 percentage points from the previous year. This increase in unemployment underscored the challenge facing the Rajoy government; it had to clean up public finances to reassure investors, at the same time as turning around an economy sinking deeper into recession. It was trying to square the circle, and its decisions were not making it any easier on those suffering the brunt of the crisis: in the previous three months, the public sector eliminated 63,000 jobs; and as part of the €65 billion austerity package, the government had lowered unemployment benefits. In July, there were 1.7 million households without jobs. The IMF, in a new report, continued praising the government, but warned that the deficit reduction "would have a significant impact on growth, especially in 2013," and anticipated that GDP would contract by 1.2 percent, double its previous forecast of 0.5 percent. The lack of confidence in the Spanish economy was also illustrated by the massive amount of capital flight. In May 2012, the month in which Bankia imploded, €41.2 billion left Spain. In the previous 11 months, €259 billion had left the country.

In March, the government announced a law project for transparency and good governance to maintain an image of control of public accounts (both regional and municipal ones), and on July 27, the cabinet approved a Transparency Law project that included criminal sanctions (including jail time) of between one and four years for those who falsify public accounts (including any other document or information that includes economic data), or for anyone who divulges false information through any media.[79]

The severity of the crisis and the unpopularity of the government measures also had an impact on the government support. A poll published by *El País* on July 28 showed that support for the PP declined from 46.4 percent to 30.0 percent. They lost 14.6 point in only eight months, an unprecedented record in Spain according to all polling agencies, and just in July, support dropped 7 points. The poll also showed that support for the PSOE only increased by 1.6 points, confirming the continuing dissatisfaction of voters with the Socialists.[80] Another poll from the CIS confirmed the decline; the PP lost 8 percentage points between November 2011 election and August 2012 (36.6 percent versus 44.6 percent), and this poll was conducted before the latest cuts. The PSOE increased its support only by 1.2 percent.[81]

To make matters worse, some of Spain's leading banks, in an attempt to set aside more money to cover loans that could potentially default, reported significantly lower earnings that same month: Caixabank's profit fell by 80 percent as it set aside $4.45 billion against problem real estate loans; Banco Popular reported a 42 percent decline after reserving €4.1 billion; and Banco Santander reported a sharp drop of 51 percent in profits, as well, after reserving €2.78 billion, and announced cuts in their top managers' salaries.[82]

In the end, nothing seemed to work. The sharpening contraction in Spain in 2012 showed that the austerity, which both PM Zapatero and PM Rajoy claimed was needed to win the confidence of the EU and the international bond markets, was not working. Both governments tried to do virtually everything demanded of them, including one of the most ambitious labor reforms seen in Europe since World War II, with the expectations that both the EU/ECB and international bond markets would reward them with lower financing costs, but it did not happen. Painful reforms and fiscal austerity would work only if Europe's sovereign debt crisis could be calmed. The IMF recognized as much: "the success of this strategy in restoring confidence, jobs, and growth depend critically on progress at the European level in strengthening the currency union" (IMF, July 27, 2012).[83]

Conclusion

As shown throughout the chapter, the story of the Spanish governments' response to the crisis is a story characterized by denial, procrastination, fragmented and insufficient responses, euphemisms (if not outright lies), contradictions, lack of coordination with European partners and institutions, absence of minimal consensus among the leading political parties, and unfulfilled promises and commitments. And the list goes on and on. Since the crisis started, both the Socialists and the PP governments had a deficit of credibility, and found themselves playing catch-up with the markets. History will judge them harshly.

The Socialists first denied the crisis claiming it would not affect Spain, then minimized it arguing that the impact would be minimal. PM Zapatero and his cabinet refused to say the word "crisis" in spite of strong evidence of the housing market collapse, deepening recession, and the global financial crisis. It was only in 2010 that he finally admitted that the crisis was the "deepest and most serious since the 1930s."[84] Furthermore, from the start of the crisis until 2010, PM Zapatero and his government not only spent freely on emergency job creation plans, but were also persistently too optimistic regarding Spain's economic prospects, making the government's responsibility of persuading Spaniards of the need for austerity far more difficult. Their forecasts were typically overoptimistic and often simply wrong; the 2009 budget deficit figure of 11.4 percent, for instance, was almost 2 percentage points higher than the official estimate of just two weeks earlier, and growth estimates (on which more of their forecast depended) were typically unrealistic (i.e., the economy was expected to grow by 3 percent in 2012).

As a result, they reacted too late, and by the time they did, they did not do nearly enough to address what the crisis demanded. When they realized it, it was way too late, and they could only play catch-up. Eventually, the circumstances overwhelmed the government, and hence it was compelled in May 2010 to make a dramatic policy turnaround that destroyed its credibility and led to its historical electoral defeat the following year. The Socialists left power under a terrible cloud of mismanagement and incompetence, which would drag the country down for years to come, leaving an unprecedented dreadful legacy to the new government.

Unfortunately, the Conservatives have not fared much better, at least so far (summer 2012). Somehow, they came to believe that the problem was the Socialists themselves: their incompetence and their lack of credibility. Once they were gone from power, the markets would welcome the new government's reformist agenda, and its efforts would be rewarded with access to capital in addition to lower interest rates to finance the country's funding needs. Unfortunately, things were not so simple. Market's skepticism was (and is) well entrenched and rooted in the lack of confidence that Spain can get away from the vicious loop in which it finds itself: can a procyclical increase in fiscal austerity in a deep recession lead to growth and debt sustainability? So far, the response from the markets has been a resolute "no."

The range of mistakes in just six months in power is simply astonishing, starting with the clumsy handling of the 2012 budget, delayed until after local elections in Andalusia in March, and following with the unilateral announcement that its deficit would be 5.8 percent of GDP, not the 4.4 percent agreed upon with the EU. These are just two examples that led to the erosion of their international standing and credibility. The apparent lack of coordination between ministers Guindos and Montoro (the perception is that they constantly contradict each other), and the lack of leadership from PM Rajoy, only intensifies the problem. There is always a learning curve for any new government. The problem for Spain is that the country was already very hard-pressed for time and does not have the leeway for the amateurish mistakes made so far by the Rajoy government. Every mistake, contradiction, improvised statement, or out of place political declaration has led to new poundings from the markets in the form of higher yields.

Furthermore, the repeated pattern to blame the Socialists for the legacy that they left behind (as disastrous and indefensible as it was), as well as the well-established approach to accuse the markets for not rewarding the country as it deserves, or to blame its EU partners for not doing the right thing, only increases skepticism, generates further uncertainty, and erodes the standing and credibility of the government both within and outside Spanish borders.

The government demonstrated its lack of clear principles (see table 2.6 on "Policy Shifts"), constantly manifesting its impotence, as well as its disgust with the measures that it is "forced" to implement. Furthermore, it tends to ask for acts of faith from Spanish citizens, markets, and European partners alike: "you all have to trust that what we are doing (even though we do not like it, and there is no choice) will work, and will help push the country out of the recession." Can one be surprised that the markets respond the way that they do? Spain needed better action.

Finally, the crisis led to constant and mutual recriminations between the two leading parties, trying to blame each other and decrying the mismanagement of whomever was in power at the national or regional level. Trying to score points at their opponents' expense became a typical pattern, regardless of the negative impact that many of the vindictive and vicious back and forth accusations had on their credibility, and even more importantly, on the perceptions of credit rating agencies and international bond market investors. If anything, the crisis demonstrated that there is a dual culpability, as both parties shared responsibility over the management of the regions and the central government in the years preceding and during the crisis. Both often governed with genuine incompetence, particularly at the regional and local level. The unwillingness to find common ground through the crisis (the most notable exceptions being the constitutional reform of September 2011; Rajoy's support for Zapatero's financial reforms and banking aid, with the exception of his last one, in which he abstained; and Rubalcaba's support to the PP's first financial reform) also were laid down at their feet. It shows that they placed their political interest over the country's. Both suffered as a result.

In the end, neither the Socialist nor the PP proved to have much influence (or success) over the constituency that mattered most during the global financial crisis: international sovereign bond market investors. As much as they tried to provide reassurance with austerity and reforms, so far they have largely failed. Good intentions are not a good substitute for adequate and timely decisions, competence, transparency, strong coordination, and good communication.

CHAPTER 3

The Challenges of Economic Reforms: Zapatero and Continuities in Economic Policymaking

Introduction

This book claims that a central explanation for the crisis was based on the successive policies of the government and their failure to change an unsustainable growth model based on consumption and construction, as well as their neglect in addressing the shortcomings of the Spanish economy described in chapter 1. *Why did the Zapatero governments fail to do so? Why did they largely continue the economic policies of the Conservative government?*

PSOE's victory in the March 2004 general election brought a new generation of Socialist leaders to power, led by PM José Luís Rodríguez Zapatero. Before the electoral campaign, he asked a group of leading economists, coordinated by Miguel Sebastián, to develop the economic program for the electoral campaign. This program advocated for a policy shift of moving the country away from a growth model largely based on consumption and construction into one based on value added and productivity.

When Zapatero became the PM, he decided to name Pedro Solbes, who served in the same capacity in the previous Socialist administration in the early 1990s, as his VP and minister of economics and finance. Solbes came to power with a strong reputation as a fiscal conservative and his macroeconomic policies proved consistent. In fact, as we will examine in this contribution, his economic policies did not diverge significantly from the policies that the Conservative government had implemented in the previous eight years (which, in turn, were a continuation of Solbes' policies of the early 1990s). Indeed, this chapter argues that macroeconomic policy is one of the few policy areas that seemed largely above partisan politics, with little dissension between the two leading political parties. They had largely accepted this economic model for over two decades.

What factors explain this degree of continuity? While in other policy areas the Socialists' policies depart from previous administrations, this chapter shows that in the economic policy realm during the years prior to the 2009 crisis, there was remarkable continuity, not just between the PP and the PSOE administrations, but also with the policies of previous administrations dating back to the transition to democracy. This continuity in economic policymaking was a departure from other policy areas in which the new Socialist government implemented radically ambitious policies, leading to what other scholars have referred to as a "second transition" (Field 2011). Indeed, it is hard to talk about a "second transition" in the economic policy realm.

This chapter is grounded in the literature on political economy of policy reform (Williamson 1994; Maravall 1997). Continuity in economic policy serves as the dependent variable and with particular focus on fiscal, labor, and social policies (since Spain is a member of the EMU, its monetary policies are no longer in the hands of the national government). I seek to highlight continuities in the economic arena, challenging the notion of a second transition, and I attempt to explain these long-term continuities (since the transition to democracy) as well as the short-term ones (between Zapatero and the previous Conservative administration).

The continuity in economic policies between the first Zapatero administration and the previous Conservative government (a period running from 1996 through March 2008) was based on two main factors: first, inertia driven by economic success: When the Socialists won the election in 2004 the Spanish economy was in the midst of one of the most successful economic periods of its modern history, highlighted by the country's largely unexpected accession to the EMU as a founding member. Therefore, despite the electoral promise to move away from a model based on consumption and construction, the Socialist government largely stuck to the formula "if it is not broken, do not fix it."

Second, this continuity was also rooted in policy stability based on ideological/programmatic consensus (fiscal consolidation was adopted as a mantra by both leading political parties), as well as personnel continuities and stability at the top skeleton of economic policymaking, both within the Ministry of Economics and the Bank of Spain.

While these two variables help explain the continuities between the Aznar and Zapatero administrations in economic policies, it is important to note that this degree of continuity has not been a new phenomenon. On the contrary, there has been a high degree of continuity and consensus in this area since the democratic transition, in particular since the Socialist Party's victory in 1982. This chapter also examines the longer-term historical reasons behind these continuities. First, Europe and the process of European integration have played a central role in Spanish policymaking since the transition to democracy and have conditioned significantly the economic policies and decisions of successive governments since the late 1970s.

Social bargaining in economic policymaking since the democratic transition has also contributed toward this continuity. Indeed, there has been a pattern of cooperation in economic and social policymaking among the social actors (government, trade unions, and employers' association) that led to the institutionalization of social bargaining. Though there were breakdowns in this process, the overall institutionalization has contributed to a higher degree of consensus in the social and economic policymaking realms, which, in turn, resulted in greater continuity and stability in economic policies across administrations (see chapter 5).

The chapter is divided into three parts. First, it outlines the main aspects of Zapatero's economic policies, focusing largely on macroeconomic policies. The second section examines each of the factors that helps explain patterns of continuity in economic policymaking. The last section closes with some remarks about the current economic crisis.

The Economic Policies of the First Zapatero Government

When the Socialists came to power in 2004, they found an economy that was growing very rapidly. Indeed, as discussed in chapter 1, between 1996 and 2008, the Spanish economy experienced high rates of economic growth, averaging close to 3 percent annually (see table 3.1). This growth was based on

Table 3.1 Economic Summary, Spain (2004–2008)

	Units	2004	2005	2006	2007	2008
GDP, constant prices	Annual % change	3,267	3,615	3,887	3,662	1,158
GDP, current prices	National currency	19,700,354	20,940,793	22,278,313	23,410,932	24,007,025
Output gap, % of potential GDP	% of potential GDP	1,898	2,614	3,734	4,268	2,740
Inflation, average consumer prices	Annual % change	3,053	3,382	3,563	2,844	4,130
Unemployment rate	% of total labor force	10,970	9,160	8,513	8,263	11,325
Employment	Persons (millions)	18,510	19,267	20,024	20,626	20,469
General government balance	% of GDP	−0,340	0,964	2,020	2,214	−3,824
Current account balance	% of GDP	−5,251	−7,357	−8,930	−10,079	−9,557

Source: IMF, World Economic Outlook Database, April 2009.

the following foundations: high levels of consumption, which grew 3 percent on an average during 1998–2008 driven by low interest rates, lower levels of debt, a reduction in unemployment, and high population growth pushed by immigration. An additional factor was the increasing investments in housing, which grew over 4 percent and in capital resources, 2 percent. This level of growth, however, was possible only because of the increase in the level of family debt; as Spaniards took advantage of real interest rates that were close to zero, as well as the willingness of banks and financial institutions to finance mortgages in the absence of more profitable opportunities (and the guarantee of the increasing expected value of properties) (Royo 2009b).

By the end of its second term, the Aznar administration was credited with Spain's successful integration into the EMU, macroeconomic discipline, and a long period of economic expansion that has contributed to close the gap with the country's European richer neighbors. However, these accomplishments glossed over the imbalances and fragility of the growth model based on private consumption, with high levels of debt and little investment in production.

During the Aznar years, the Socialists stressed that the model of economic growth was based on unsustainable imbalances rooted in the persistent inflation caused by excessive demand and unresponsive supply, which benefits from the lack of competition in most Spanish goods and services markets, as well as the loss of competitiveness highlighted by a rapidly growing current account deficit caused among other factors by the strong euro, the absence of endogenous technology, high consumption of energy and raw materials, and low productivity.

The concern about the fragility of this model was reflected in the PSOE's electoral program, which had been developed by a "think tank" that included, among others, a group of leading economists such as Pedro Solbes, Miguel Sebastián, David Vergara, David Tagua, and Rafael Domenech. The electoral program emphasized these problems and proposed measures to rectify them in order to place the economy on a new path toward a more sustainable growth model. However, when they won the election and came to power, this emphasis was sidelined. The appointment of Pedro Solbes as VP and minister of economics and finance set the pattern because, not only did he have the support of the old-guard of the PSOE who had served under González, which gave him significant political clout despite the fact that he was an independent, but also because of the long-established tradition since the early 1980s that any economic policy had to go through the Ministry of Economics and Finance.

The macroeconomic guidelines adopted by the new government turned out to be similar to those of the Aznar/Rato-Aznar's minister of economics and finance. Originally, these guidelines were developed with the objective to allow Spain to join the EMU as a founding member, and were formalized in the Stability Program the Aznar government presented in December 1998. These were annually reviewed. These guidelines reflected the macroeconomic orthodoxy of the late 1980s and were based on three key elements (Editorial Board 2007):

1. The applicability of the open economy (or Mundell-Fleming) model, according to which monetary policy is ineffective to control cycles in the context of fixed exchange rates (like the Spanish one, which is part of the Eurozone; 70 percent of its economy is dependent on Eurozone countries) and fiscal policies are efficient only in the long term.
2. The validity of the rational expectation (or Lucas) models, according to which economic policies have to be predictable and subject to rules in order to avoid distortions. Therefore, in the case of Spain, which is part of the EMU, macroeconomic policy should pursue budgetary discipline, and, if possible, this should be guaranteed by law. This principle led to the approval of the Budgetary Stability Act, passed in 2001, but subsequently modified to add flexibility.
3. The belief that large public deficits crowd out investment from the private sector and make it more difficult and expensive to access capital.
4. The firm belief, rooted in neoclassical theories, that intervention in markets creates only distortions and inefficiencies.

Consequently, economic policies in Spain, starting with the last González administration of the early 1990s, were based on these orthodox principles paving way for exhaustive fiscal discipline, some relaxation in labor and goods market regulations, and acceleration of the opening of the economy.

When Solbes returned to power in 2004, he stuck with these principles. Therefore, the budgetary process was largely based on one goal: achieving a surplus. This was perceived as an adequate approach for an economy driven by high demand and consumption that faced structural inflationary pressures and a significant deficit in the balance of payments. Public spending increased in all areas (supported by growing revenues generated from the fast growth of economy). Yet this increase was limited and most of it has been by the autonomous regions, which manage almost 30 percent of total public spending.

When considered on the basis of the guidelines mentioned above, it is not surprising that the macroeconomic policies followed by Zapatero/Solbes have provided a strong continuity with the previous administration. It was only in the last two years of its first term in office that the Socialist administration focused more on supply-oriented measures to impact the growth model and tried to develop a more modern system to allocate resources and promote overall productivity, rather than following the traditional approach of promoting only specific activities. Therefore, the last two budgets of the first term increased spending in areas such as education, research and development, and infrastructure. This policy shift was driven by the approval of a *National Reform Plan* that sought to address the Lisbon Strategy for EU growth. The Plan, subtitled "Convergence and Employment," had two main goals: to achieve a similar employment rate and income per capita convergence to that of the EU average by 2010.

Furthermore, the orthodox nature of Zapatero government's approach to economic policy was also reflected in its taxation policies (Editorial Board 2007). It followed the PP, which made tax reform and the lowering of taxes a highlight of its economic accomplishments. Even before he was elected, Zapatero famously stated that "lowering taxes is also leftist." The Socialist administration approved two reforms: the first in 2006 reduced the income brackets from five down to four and the marginal rate by 2 percentage points; and it established a new 18 percent fixed rate for all capital gains. The second reform of 2008 was smaller and had more of an electoral focus. In four years, the government reduced income and corporate taxes, eliminated the capital gain tax, and approved measures like the controversial baby-check that gave €400 to families for every baby born. The overall effect of these reforms, however, was to further erode the progressiveness of the taxation system.

In sum, there is consensus that the economic policies implemented by the Zapatero government during his first term remained in the framework of neoliberal orthodoxy and that they achieved limited reforms. The rest of the chapter will examine in greater detail the reasons for the continuity with the policies of the Aznar era. The first part focuses on the short-term reasons (economic success and leadership continuities) and the second on long-term reasons (EU integration and social bargaining).

Explaining Patterns of Continuity in Economic Policies

Short-Term Reasons
The economic "miracle." As outlined in chapter 1, between 1995 and 2007, Spain became one of Europe's hitherto most successful economies (Royo 2009b). While other European countries were stuck in the mud, Spain performed much better at reforming its welfare systems and labor markets, as well as at improving flexibility and reducing unemployment. It seemed for a time that during this decade, the Spanish economy was finally able to break with the historical pattern of boom and bust, and the country's economic performance was nothing but short of remarkable. As late as 2007, the Spanish economy still grew a spectacular 3.9 percent. Propped by low interest rates and immigration, Spain was (in 2008) in its fifteenth year of uninterrupted growth and was benefiting from the longest cycle of continuing expansion of the economy in modern history (only Ireland in the Eurozone had a better record).

Economic growth contributed to per capita income growth, which almost reached the EU25 average (97.7 percent) in 2007. At the same time, the performance of the labor market was also spectacular: between 1998 and 2008, 33 percent of all the total employment created in the EU15 was created in

Spain and unemployment fell from 20 percent in the mid-1990s to 7.9 percent in the first half of 2007 (the lowest level since 1978).

The public deficit was also eliminated (the country had a *surplus* between 2005 and 2007) and the public debt was reduced to 39.8 percent of GDP in 2007, the lowest in the past two decades. The construction boom was also remarkable; more than 400,000 new homes were built in and around Madrid between 2003 and 2008. This economic success extended to Spanish companies, which expanded beyond their traditional frontiers. In 2006, they spent a total of €140 billion on domestic and overseas acquisitions, putting the country third behind the United Kingdom and France (Royo 2009b, 20–21).

Spain's transformation was not only economic but also social. Since 2000, some 5 million immigrants settled in Spain (8.7 percent of the population compared with 3.7 percent in the EU15), making the country the biggest recipient of immigrants in the EU. These immigrants contributed significantly to the economic success of the country because they boosted the aggregate performance of the economy; they raised the supply of labor, increased demand as they spent money, moderated wages, and put downward pressure on inflation, boosted output, allowed the labor market to avoid labor shortages, contributed to consumption, and increased more flexibility in the economy with their mobility and willingness to take on low-paid jobs in sectors such as construction and agriculture, in which Spaniards are no longer interested.[1] The performance of the Spanish economy during the first Zapatero administration is outlined in table 3.1.

As indicated throughout the book, this economic growth, which started in the second half of the 1990s, was boosted by the considerable fall in interest rates when nominal short-term interest rates converged to those set by the ECB. They fell more rapidly than inflation and their impact was further boosted by the simultaneous processes of financial liberalization and increasing competition that took place at the same time, contributing to the increase in domestic demand and, in particular, housing demand. The expansion these years was largely driven by the internal demand. This boom coincided with a period of international expansion.[2]

Observing the performance and success of this proven model, the Zapatero administration was reluctant to diverge from the policies of the previous Conservative government and stuck to the formula, abandoning its electoral pledges.

Policy stability. Another crucial factor that accounts for patterns of continuity is the remarkable level of economic policy stability in the country, particularly after the crisis of 1992–1993. Indeed, there have been few significant economic policy shifts throughout the 1990s and the 2000s, despite changes in government. Policy stability, in turn, was the result of two main factors: leadership continuities and policy consensus between the two leading political parties.

Indeed, as we saw in chapter 1, one of the main explanations for this degree of policy stability was the fact that between 1993 and April 2009, there were only two ministers of economics and finance: Pedro Solbes (1993–1996 and 2004–April 2009) and Rodrigo Rato (1996–2004) and three PMs (Felipe González, José María Aznar, and José Luís Rodríguez Zapatero). Furthermore, this continuity was also supported by the tradition to leave economic policies in the hands of the minister of economics, which, in turn, led to a more technocratic approach.

In addition, as a rare occurrence, Pedro Solbes, minister of finance under a Socialist government in the early 1990s when the process of fiscal consolidation started, became minister of finance again in 2004 after the Socialist Party won the general election; he remained in the position until April 2009 when he stepped down following differences with Zapatero over the course of policies in addressing the dramatic economic crisis. He was replaced by Elena Salgado as VP and minister of economics and finance.[3]

Both Solbes and Rato are technocrats, pragmatists, and lack strong ideological attachments. Firm believers of European integration, they understood the importance of applying economic policies consistent with Spain's European goals (i.e., EMU membership and the fulfillment of the SGP). For Rato, EMU membership became his paramount goal and allowed him to build the consensus needed to implement the (painful) necessary measures to fulfil the Maastricht criteria. This process had already started under the previous Socialist government with Solbes in the economic helm, and even Rato recognized in private that he had largely followed the policies Solbes initiated.

Solbes was not even affiliated with the Socialist Party and had served for a long time in Brussels working for the EU in different capacities. When Zapatero was elected, his choice was Solbes. At that time, Solbes was serving as the EU Commissioner for Economic and Monetary Affairs, a position in which he had served practically from the time he left his position as minister of finance in the previous Socialist administration in 1996.

As a fiscal hawk, a reputation he developed during his first tenure as VP under PM González and holding position in the EU as defender and enforcer of the SGP, he had the credentials and the credibility to reassure those who may have been concerned with the economic direction of the new Socialist government. He was a safe pair of hands that could guard against the most progressive elements of the party and the government. His power as VP was reinforced by the fact that Zapatero recognized his own lack of interest and expertise on economic matters. It is, therefore, not surprising that there was a high degree of continuity between both administrations in economic policy.

More importantly, policy stability was reinforced by the fact that each of the previous three governments had completed its mandate and there had been no early elections. Moreover, the power of the minister of economics and finance was also reinforced vis-à-vis other cabinet members because both of them also served as deputies of the PM under the Conservative and Socialist administrations. This pattern was further strengthened by the ideological cohesiveness of these parties and the strong control that party leaders exercised over all the members of the cabinet and parliament deputies.[4]

In addition, as indicated in chapter 1, this stability was reinforced by the shared (rare) agreement among the Conservative and Socialist leaders regarding fiscal consolidation (the balance budget objective was established by the PP in November 2002 through the Budget Stability Law), as well as the need to hold firm in the application of conservative fiscal policies and the achievement of budgetary fiscal surpluses.[5] It was accepted that increases in government consumption adversely affect long-term growth and that, while fiscal consolidation may have short-term costs with regard to activity, they can be minimized if consolidation is credible by implementing consistent decisions that deliver solid results. As a result of this approach, as shown in table 3.2 and discussed in greater detail in chapter 4, Spain was transformed from being a country with a somewhat lax reputation in terms of fiscal discipline to a paradigmatic model of a country applying the budget surplus policy mantra, which led to three consecutive budget surpluses years (2005–2007) and the reduction of the general government debt from 63.9 percent in 1995 to 36.2 percent in 2007.

Long-Term Reasons
Social bargaining. An important factor that helps account for continuity in economic policy since the democratic transition has been the process of social bargaining, which played a crucial role in maintaining macroeconomic stability (see chapter 5). This section aligns with the dominant views about concertation and social pacts in the 1990s and 2000s. Indeed, there is an extensive literature that has highlighted functional explanations for the return to social pacts and their contribution to macroeconomic stability (see Pérez and Pochet 1999; Hancké 2002; González and Gutiérrez 2002; Rhodes 1998: Traxler 1997; Hassel and Ebbinghaus 2000; Molina and Rhodes 2007; Royo 2000). In the view of these scholars, the cooperation of employers and unions is essential for the pursuit of active social policy and in order to avoid inflationary wage-price spirals. At the same time, effective concertation contributes to reduction of uncertainty, fosters acceptance of reforms and restructuring, and allows for greater efficiency in the implementation of economic reforms (De la Dehesa 1994, 135–136).

Table 3.2 Fiscal Position, Spain (1995–2008)

	1995	2001	2002	2003	2004	2005	2006	2007	2008
General government balance	−6.3	−0.5	−0.5	−0.2	−0.3	1.0	2.0	2.2	−3.1
General government debt	63.9	61.6	52.5	48.7	46.2	43.0	39.6	36.2	38.6

Source: IMF, World Economic Outlook Database, various years.

Since 1994, these agreements have become instruments through which the social actors have tried to resolve collective action problems through social concertation. In this regard, the return to concertation has to be explained in terms of functional domestic responses to the macroeconomic challenges posed by European integration and more specifically EMU (see Royo 2008, 101–143). Indeed, attempts at reform have largely been a top-down political exchange process in which the social actors resorted to social bargaining as an instrument to address conflicts and increase the governability of the system (Molina and Rhodes 2007, 231).

Unions supported them as a defensive strategy to retake the initiative, affirm their role as political actors, and influence policy outcomes. Employers, for their part, finally realized that their long-term success hinged on the ability of the national system in which they operate to provide the collective goods they need to compete effectively—such as professional training or wage coordination and wage moderation. Finally, the Aznar and Zapatero governments, recognizing that social bargaining fosters acceptance of reforms and restructuring and facilitates their implementation, supported this process to achieve social peace and wage moderation. Despite breakdowns, the institutionalization of this gradualist approach contributed to policy continuities across administrations since the transition because it advocated negotiations and political socialization, as well as the search of consensus among the economic actors (Royo 2002, 203–208).

The overall impact of these agreements has been positive. Indeed social bargaining, through its contributions to social peace (the number of strikes between 2002 and 2008 oscillated between 669 and 810 per year) and wage moderation (see table 3.3) played a part in the fulfillment of the convergence process laid down in the Maastricht Treaty. This generated a new virtuous circle characterized by sustained rapid growth, improving fiscal position, lower unemployment, and higher investment and productivity, which, in turn, promoted rapid growth.

Therefore, it is not surprising that the Zapatero government, which learned from the experiences of the González administration in the late 1980s and early 1990s the perils of challenging the unions, feverishly pursued social bargaining with the social actors; this, in turn, led to a higher

Table 3.3 Seven Years of Collective Bargaining: Salary Increases and CPI (2002–2008)

	2002	2003	2004	2005	2006	2007	2008
CPI	4.0	2.6	3.2	3.7	2.7	4.2	1.4
WI	3.9	3.7	3.6	4.0	3.6	4.2	3.6

Note: CPI: From December to December; WI: Negotiated in collective agreements.
Source: INE.

degree of consensus and continuity with the economic and social policies of previous governments.

Consensus over European integration. European integration has been another key factor to explain continuities in Spanish economic policy for over two decades. Indeed, European integration has been considered by many scholars an important external source for domestic policymaking, particularly in Southern European countries (Marks 1997; Harrison and Corkill 2004; Almarcha 1993; Closa and Heywood 2004; Royo and Manuel 2005).

In the particular case of Spain, the processes of democratization, Europeanization, and economic modernization are deeply intertwined. After decades of relative isolation under an authoritarian regime, the success of the democratic transition paved the way for full membership in the European Community in 1986. The European Community epitomized, in the eyes of Spanish citizens, the values of liberty, democracy, and progress absent in Spain for decades. Europe was a unifying element and integration was supported by all the leading political parties. This initial consensus has remained largely consistent since then. Polls consistently show that Spaniards are among the most enthusiastic supporters of the EU.

The decision to be a member of the EU, however, has had significant policy implications. Indeed, the transfer of sovereignty entailed by EU and EMU membership limits significantly the range of economic policies that can be implemented at the national level: they affect taxation policies (for instance, countries cannot exceed the deficit and debt levels specified by the SGP); the regulation of markets such as the labor market and financial markets; completion of regulations in goods and services; and supply policies. These constraints are further reinforced by the fact that the Spanish economy is an open economy, and, therefore, subject to restrictions imposed by international markets, as well as by the fact that many powers were transferred to the autonomous regions, which currently control around of 30 percent of public spending (Editorial Board 2007).

In Spain, the expectation of European integration influenced to a large extent the decision to continue liberalizing and reforming (De la Dehesa 1994, 137). In addition, from an economic standpoint, EC/EU accession brought significant changes (Royo 2007, 35–58). Under the terms of the accession agreement signed in 1985, Spain had to undertake significant steps to align their legislation on industrial, agriculture, economic, and financial polices to that of the European Community. This meant that Spain had to phase in tariffs and prices, and approve tax changes (including the establishment of a VAT that the rest of the Community already put in place. This process also involved, in a second phase, the removal of technical barriers to trade. Hence, the accession of Spain to the European Community in 1986 forced the political and economic actors to adopt economic policies and business strategies consistent with membership and the acquis communautaire (including the custom union, the VAT, the Common Agriculture and Fisheries Polices, the external trade agreements; and later the Single Market, the ERM, and EMU).

However, EU membership also facilitated the micro and macroeconomic reforms that successive Spanish governments undertook throughout the 1980s and 1990s. In a context of strong support among Spanish citizens for integration, membership became a facilitating mechanism that allowed the government to prioritize economic growth rather than social modernization and hence, to pursue difficult economic and social policies (i.e., to reform their labor and financial markets) with short-term painful effects. Moreover, the decision to comply with the EMU Maastricht Treaty criteria led to the implementation of macro and microeconomic policies resulting in fiscal consolidation, central bank independence, and wage moderation.

Indeed, as outlined in chapter 1, since 1986, the Spanish economy underwent profound economic changes following European integration. EU membership led to policy and institutional reforms in the these economic areas: monetary and exchange rate policies (first independent monetary coordination, followed by accession to the ERM, and finally EMU membership); reform of the tax system (i.e., the introduction of the VAT and reduction of import duties); and a fiscal consolidation process. These changes led to structural reforms processes aimed at macroeconomic stability and strengthening of competitiveness of the productive sector. On the supply side, these reforms sought the development of well-functioning capital markets, the promotion of efficiency in public services, and the enhancement of flexibility in the labor market. As a result, markets and prices for a number of goods and services were deregulated and liberalized; the labor market was the subject of limited deregulatory reforms; a privatization program was started in the early 1980s to roll back the presence of the government in the economy and to increase the overall efficiency of the system; and a competition policy was adapted to EU regulations.

In the past decade and a half, the country's accession to the EMU also played a critical role in the economic policies of successive governments. For instance, during the first half of the 1990s, the conditions established by the Maastricht Treaty imposed significant budgetary restraints on Spain's fiscal policies, and the leading political parties ferociously pursued fiscal consolidation under the growing consensus that lax monetary policies had played a significant role in the slowdown of the convergence process prior to EC accession. Once Spain became a founding member of EMU, although monetary policies were no longer in the hands of its national governments, both under the PP and PSOE administrations, fiscal consolidation was the mantra (until the implosion of the economy in the fall of 2008), well beyond the constraints imposed by the SGP. This has also been an important factor in explaining continuities in economic policies.

Conclusions

This chapter highlighted continuities in the economic arena, which challenged the notion of a "second transition" in the economic policy realm, and attempted to explain these continuities. While social bargaining contributed to create a favorable domestic environment for reforms, European integration provided the external anchor and justification for the implementation of fiscal discipline. At the same time, economic success and consensus among key economic policymakers and social actors across administrations and party lines led to policy continuities though making reforms more difficult. Indeed, in spite of the large number of structural reforms and a sustained period of economic growth, the Spanish economy has not deviated significantly from a low-skill, low-cost production system.

Consensus (and sometimes dogmatism) worked well in the short term contributing to the credibility of the government policies in the medium- and long-term. However, there are disputes over whether a more accommodating policy would have been positive to upgrade the productive base of the country with investments in necessary infrastructure and human capital. The maintenance of the balanced deficit paradigm as a goal on its own may have blinded the PP and PSOE governments of the benefits of investing in new technology areas in which Spain still lags behind. While the Zapatero administration tried to do this in the last two years of its first term, this effort has been clearly insufficient.

If Aznar was criticized for his government's obsession with the zero deficit and the insufficient reforms to address the imbalances of the growth model, the same could be said about Zapatero's first term. Indeed, Zapatero's policies largely failed to address the core problems of the Spanish economy: the inflation differential, the loss of competitiveness, and the low productivity of labor. Therefore, from an economic standpoint, referring to this first term as a period of "continuity" seems justified. Hence, his critics accused him of failing to correct significantly Spain's "social underdevelopment."[6]

In the end, the degree of continuity in economic policies of the past decade may have been detrimental given its failure to address the fundamental imbalances of the Spanish economy. As seen in chapter 1, success was marred by some glaring deficiencies, because it was largely a "miracle" based on bricks and mortar (Royo 2009b). The foundations of economic growth were fragile because the country had low productivity growth (productivity contributed only 0.5 percentage of points to potential GDP between 1998 and 2006) and deteriorating external competitiveness. These imbalances were unsustainable and led to the implosion of the economy propelled by the global financial crisis that started in 2007 (*Economist* 2008).

It was in the context of this devastating economic crisis that the second Zapatero administration tried to revert to the original goal to change the economic model. Toward this the government worked on two fronts. On one hand, it negotiated a social pact with unions and employers to adopt measures to confront the crisis. The process, however, broke down during the summer of 2009 when the CEOE demanded inclusion in the negotiations of a labor reform to reduce dismissal costs (see chapter 5). Legislatively, the government drafted a new law for a sustainable economy that focused on three axes: economic, social, and environmental sustainability. These reforms, however would be hampered by the lack of funds (the country's deficit was expected to exceed 10 percent of GDP in 2009), which forced the government to unveil tax increases designed to raise an extra €11 billion per year.

The goal was to increase productivity by increasing the capital intensity of production. The government understood that in order to be innovative and, in turn, achieve higher productivity four main conditions need to be met: first, investment in capital technology (i.e., information systems and telecommunications); second, a new culture of entrepreneurship, innovation, and risk-taking; third, human capital with strong skills and flexibility to adapt to new technologies and processes based on a model of continuous training; and, finally, a flexible and adaptable industrial relations framework.

The scope of these reforms reflects the daunting challenge still facing Spanish governments. However, the lack of political willingness to implement these reforms prior to the 2008 crisis hindered the convergence process with Europe and further eroded the competitiveness of the Spanish economy. History shows that successful reforms must fulfill several requirements (De la Dehesa 2009): first, they should originate from the government, who should lead the process; second, the ruling and opposition parties should share a vision of the future allowing them to reach consensus on reforms; and, finally, civil society and the social actors should support the reforms. Successful convergence with Europe and increasing competitiveness hinged to a considerable degree on the ability of Spanish leaders to implement reforms in the face of domestic resistance. Unfortunately, as the current crisis so eloquently exposes, lack of progress in implementing these reforms brought economic stagnation and a worse scenario.

CHAPTER 4

The Limits of Fiscal Convergence

Introduction

One of the most generalized misinterpretations regarding the crisis in Southern Europe is attributing it to wildly mismanaged finances. Many policymakers across Europe still insist that the crisis was caused by irresponsible public borrowing, and this, in turn, led to misguided solutions. In fact, with very few exceptions, notably Greece, that interpretation is incorrect. As a matter of fact, in Spain the current crisis did not originate with wildly mismanaged finances. On the contrary, as late as 2011, Spain's debt ratio was still well below the EMU average: while Spain stood at less than 60 percent of GDP, Greece stood at 160.8 percent, Italy at 120 percent, Portugal at 106.8 percent, Ireland at 105 percent, Belgium at 98.5 percent, and France at 86 percent.

Indeed, the fiscal position of Spain prior to the crisis was reasonably robust, as it run a budget surplus in 2005, 2006, and 2007. It was only when the crisis hit the country and the real estate market collapsed that the fiscal position deteriorated markedly and the country experienced huge deficits. But prior to 2007, Spain seemed to be in an enviable fiscal position, even when compared with Germany (see figure 4.1).[1]

The problem in Spain was the giant inflow of capital from the rest of Europe; the consequence was rapid growth and significant inflation. In fact, the deficit was a result, not a cause, of Spain's problems: when the global financial crisis hit Spain and the real estate bubble burst, unemployment soared, and the budget went into deep deficit, caused partly by depressed revenues and partly by emergency spending to limit human costs. As described in chapter 2, the government responded to the crisis with a massive €8 billion public works stimulus. This decision, combined with a dramatic fall in revenue, blew an enormous hole in the public accounts resulting in a large deficit. In addition, the bursting of the real estate bubble led to large falls in output as well as in tax revenues.

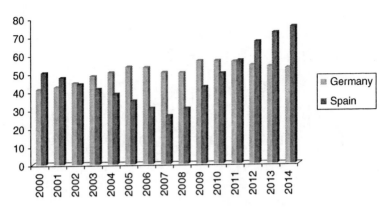

Figure 4.1 Net Public Debt: Germany and Spain (2000–2014)
Source: IMF, *World Economic Outlook*

Also, the conditions for the crisis in Spain were created by excessive lending and borrowing of the private sector. Yes, the problem was not public debt, but the private one. Indeed, Spain experienced a problem of ever-growing private sector debt, which was compounded by the reckless investments and loans of banks (including the overleveraged ones), and aggravated by competitiveness and current account imbalances. In Spain, the debt of private sector (households and nonfinancial corporations in particular) was 227.3 percent of GDP at the end of 2010; total debt increased from 337 percent of GDP in 2008 to 363 percent in mid-2011. One of the main difficulties for many countries during the global financial crisis was that private debt had been piled on deficits of governments, turning a financial crisis into one of sovereign debt. Ireland served as a prime example when it was forced to nationalize its banks, and Spain, as will be shown in chapter 6, faces similar challenges.

This chapter seeks to challenge the misconceptions regarding Spain's fiscal performance and looks at the factors that help better understand what made it possible for the country to outperform countries with a longer history of fiscal probity in the years prior to the crisis. Three issues stand out: first, prior to the crisis, Spain was a model of fiscal probity, and PM Aznar went as far as to lecture other European countries (including Germany, which at the time was in violation of the SGP) in the late 1990s, about their fiscal performance. *How was Spain able to do so well?* Second, the stellar performance in the years prior to the global financial crisis did not prevent the country from experiencing very serious difficulties after 2008. *What should have Spain done to prevent this?* Finally, if irresponsible public borrowing was not the main cause of the crisis, *what was it?* This chapter will show that below the public debt and financial crisis there was a balance of payment crisis caused by the misalignment of internal real exchange rates.

This chapter analyzes Spain's fiscal performance during the years prior to the crisis. This performance is explained based on three main variables: institutions, ideas, and interests. These are categories typically used by comparative political economists to define a policy constellation. Each one of them has been treated as three major approaches/focuses in the comparative political economy literature. However, in this chapter they are not treated as separate variables but as "social representations" (Jenson and Mérand 2010). This is because of the "codependent" connection among the three variables, as they are intertwined (Jenson 2010, 8; Heclo 1993). Indeed, instead of looking at the relative weight of ideas, interests, and institutions separately, they will be considered "synthetically and sequentially" (Blyth 2002, 170), as each one of them is constitutive of the others. This chapter claims that these variables help explain what conservative fiscal policies Spain was able to implement.[2]

The chapter proceeds as follows: the first section outlines briefly the economic divergence between both Iberian countries. The second section examines the differences in fiscal performance focusing on three main variables: institutions, ideas, and interests. The last section looks at the balance of payment crisis.

Spain's Fiscal Performance between 2000 and 2007

There is growing consensus that fiscal policies, within the constraints imposed by the SGP, played a central role in Spain's economic performance during the boom years. Since Spain became a founding member of EMU, monetary policy was no longer in the hands of its national governments. It is now widely accepted that increases in government consumption adversely affects long-term growth, and that, while fiscal consolidation may have short-term costs in terms of activity, they can be minimized if consolidation is credible by implementing consistent decisions that deliver solid results.

As we have seen, the Spanish economy experienced a boom in the second half of the 1990s, boosted by the considerable fall in interest rates, when nominal short-term interest rates converged to those set by the ECB. They fell more rapidly than inflation, and the simultaneous processes of financial liberalization and increasing competition contributed to domestic demand increase, in particular housing demand, which boosted the impact further. The economic expansion during these years was largely driven by internal demand. This boom coincided with a period of international expansion. This growth, however, required a concomitant prudent fiscal policy, and Spain was one of the most disciplined countries in Europe, and in the world, and was able to maintain a margin of maneuver that allowed fiscal policy to be used in a countercyclical way (see table 4.1).

Table 4.1 Fiscal Position of Spain before the Crisis (2000–2008)

% of GDP	2000	2001	2002	2003	2004	2005	2006	2007	2008
Structural balance	−1.121	−1.752	−1.118	−0.975	−0.97	−1.599	−1.275	−1.133	−5.034
Net debt	50.265	47.541	44.007	41.319	38.583	34.705	30.53	26.52	30.484

Source: IMF, World Economic Outlook Database, October 2009.

What Explains the Fiscal Performance? Tracing the Role of Institutions, Ideas, and Interests

Spain's experience demonstrates the limits of external pressure and the ability of the acquis communautaire to force change. Institutions, ideas, and interests are crucial in understanding why Spain was able to implement conservative fiscal policies.

Institutions, defined as the set of rules, formal and informal, that actors generally follow, are crucial to understand the behavior of economic actors and policy outcomes. From an institutionalist standpoint, there were a number of factors that helped to account for the limits of convergence.

First, Spain was relatively successful in addressing the problem of temporal inconsistency, which was a key factor for the fiscal performance examined in the previous section. Indeed, in Spain, prior to the crisis, political stability had been the pattern, and the credibility of economic policies (and fiscal policies, in particular) was supported by the relative political stability that prevailed in the country.

Indeed in Spain, as previously discussed in chapter 2, there was remarkable economic policy stability after the crisis of 1992–1993. There were few economic policy shifts throughout the 1990s and the first half of the 2000s, despite changes in government. Between 1993 and 2007, there were only two ministers of finance: Pedro Solbes and Rodrigo Rato;[3] and two PMs.[4] In addition, Pedro Solbes, was minister of finance in the early 1990s and again in 2004. And the power of the minister of finance was reinforced because both of them also served as deputies of the PM.

More importantly, prior to 2011, each of the previous three governments completed its mandate and there were no early elections. This pattern was further reinforced by the ideological cohesiveness of Conservative and Socialists parties and the strong control that party leaders exercised over all members of the cabinet and parliament deputies. In the end, the credibility of economic policies (and fiscal policies, in particular) was supported by the relative political stability that prevailed in Spain during the decades prior to the crisis.

The third factor was the fiscal constitution, which exacerbated the surplus bias. The fiscal constitution includes the institutions enforcing the social contract and incorporates exchange rate regimes, monetary standards, and state revenues. It determines who has the power and under what procedures to legislate on tax issues. In Spain, this process changed with the Aznar administration when they enshrined the principle of budget stability by law. The experience of Spain shows that institutional reforms require active policies by the governments willing to pay the short-term political price for unpopular policies.

The institutional design is of crucial importance to generate incentives to develop and implement optimal policies. The problem of temporal inconsistency in the development and implementation of policies is a problem of institutional design and incentives (Macedo 2003a). Indeed, since Spain joined the EU, the country's institutions have attempted to cope with the new demands from European policies in an increasingly complex context. There have been changes in the forms of governance driven by economic imperatives; socioeconomic modernization; internationalization (e.g., EU networking, liberalization of the economy); lack of convergence; regional decentralization; economic globalization, and Europeanization (e.g., new role for city regions); and new policy changes (e.g., addition of welfare responsibilities and new policy areas, rising demand, and falling political participation), which have led to destatization (e.g., the role of the state as regulator has been rescaling). Yet, while there has been a shift to complex multilevel governance, the pattern has been that of path-dependent institutional evolution, and the state remains the leading actor.

Ideas, defined as "causal beliefs," have been able to counter Spain's long history of "fiscal misbehavior." Ideas define goals and strategies and they shape the understanding of political problems. Indeed, the national discourses that generate and legitimize change in policies remain distinct in Spain and they still matter as primary sources of political behavior. Some of this distinctiveness may be explained by sociological changes. One of the consequences of combined processes of Europeanization and modernization has been what sociologists refer to as the increasing flexible attitudes of Spanish citizens and groups toward norms and social relations as a whole, and the crisis of great ideologies. In the political field, this has been translated into new cleavages, values, and patterns of behavior. In the past, to side with the Left or the Right defined patterns of behavior and affected individuals' ethics, religion, and way of life. Nowadays, there has been an internalization of the value of "tolerance," and options have become more diverse and pragmatic. The result has been the "predominance of the 'made to fit' over the 'made to think,' an affirmation of new craftsmanship of ideas" (Ferreira de Almeida 1998, pp. 161–162). The polarity of social networks and lifestyles that was integral to the ideological divisions of the past has softened, and Portuguese citizens now manage symbols and ideas with much greater "autonomy."

Differences in national discourses extended to the EMU project itself. In Spain there has been for decades strong support for EU and EMU membership. This has facilitated the consensus on the necessary policies to succeed in Europe, and the establishment of sound public policy paradigm, which became dominant and has been supported by the major political parties. In this regard Spain was similar to other countries, like Germany, in which there was growing (and rare) agreement among the Conservative and Socialist parties regarding fiscal consolidation as well as the need to hold firm in the application of restrictive fiscal policies and the achievement of budgetary fiscal surpluses (in Germany a coalition government amended the basic law to include a balance budget objective).

Indeed, in Spain there has been strong consensus about economic policymaking, and the Central Bank has been able to play an important role influencing policy. Since the transition to democracy, domestic elites seized on liberal economic arguments to promote an agenda of institutional reform, influenced largely by domestic politics and interests. Economic reforms served the specific objectives of a small group of reformers within the Central Bank, with long ascendance in Spanish policymaking circles since the last years of the Franco regime. The result was the perpetuation of a pattern of accommodation between state elites and private bankers that had characterized Spanish financial regulation and economic policymaking since the transition to democracy (Pérez 1997).

In addition, in Spain, the policy stability described earlier was reinforced by the shared (and rare) agreement among the Conservatives and Socialists leaders regarding fiscal consolidation (as we have seen the balance budget objective was established by law by the PP), as well as the need to hold firm in the application of conservative fiscal policies and the achievement of budgetary fiscal surpluses. Indeed, this happened to a degree in which Spain became the paradigmatic model of a country applying the budget surplus policy mantra. The Aznar government repeatedly chastised other European governments that were far laxer in their fiscal policies, to a degree to which it created tensions with the richer EU countries, because, although they were in fact running higher deficits, they were net contributors to the EU budget and provided Spain with cohesion and structural funds (i.e., Germany or France). Unsurprisingly, it was hard for them to accept being called irresponsible and to have fingers pointed at them while they were subsidizing Spain through the European solidarity programs.

As discussed in chapter 2, during the height of the crisis, in September 2011, the Socialist and Conservative parties agreed to approve a constitutional amendment, introduced by the Socialist government, limiting the public deficit and pushing for a balanced budget. Its objective was to force public administrations to abide by a maximum deficit.[5]

Also, the role of *interests* is essential to understand the fiscal outcomes described in the previous section. Interest groups attempt to influence policy. Spain is an interesting case to test Gourevitch's (1978) second image reversed and see how international politics affect domestic structures. Rogowski (1990) uses the Stolper-Samuelson theorem to explain domestic cleavages, how the international system affects domestic coalitions, and their struggle for power: trade will help abundant factors and hurt scarce ones. The political implications of this outcome would be that those actors who benefit the most from trade would gain more power.

For Spain a key explanatory factor was the desire by the main political parties and the elites to become a member of the EC/EU, and later a founding member of the EMU in the 1990s. This desire changed the incentives and priorities, and helped to empower the supporters of open trade and sound fiscal policies, such as the Bank of Spain and the Ministry of Finance. At the same time, it eroded the power of entrenched interest groups to exercise effective veto power over any attempt to impose fiscal discipline. The Central Bank played a crucial role in economic policymaking from the outset of democracy (Pérez 1997), and there was a large degree of consensus among the social actors regarding the process of European integration (Royo 2000).

In sum, institutions, ideas, and interests help explain how the opportunity for sustained structural reform was made use of and improvement in fiscal discipline afforded by the euro was largely met, in the case of Spain. Table 4.2 summarizes these findings.

Yet, Fiscal Prudency Was Not Enough

This chapter shows that Spain did not run irresponsible fiscal policies, as Germans and other Europeans critically claimed. In reality, even if Spain had complied with the latest EU fiscal compact approved to prevent future crises (as we have seen, Spain was in fact running structural surpluses before the crisis, just as the compact demands), it would not have saved the country from the current crisis. As claimed throughout the book, Spain had a substantial property boom associated with financial excesses that, fostered by an illusion of prosperity, proved unfounded and unsustainable. It is also important to highlight that the real estate boom was to a large degree financed from abroad, via capital inflows. This contributed to the record current account deficits.

Indeed, the current crisis has exposed the weaknesses in Spain's economy and economic model. Despite the past two decades' significant progress and achievements, the Spanish economy still faces serious competitive and fiscal challenges. Unfortunately, as discussed in chapters 1 and 2, the economic success of the country fostered a sense of complacency, allowing for a delay in the adoption of the necessary structural reforms. Spain still has considerable ground to cover to catch up with the richer EU countries and to improve the competitiveness of its economy. Given the existing income and productivity differentials with the richer EU countries, Spain has to not only continue but also intensify the reform process.

Though Spain entered the crisis in a relatively robust fiscal position, in the end, fiscal prudence, paradoxically, was not enough. When the impact

Table 4.2 A Summary of the Main Findings

Policy domain	Independent variable: EU	Intervening variable 1: Institutions	Intervening variable 2: Interests	Intervening variable 3: Ideas	Dependent variable: Domestic outcome
Fiscal policy	Prior to 1999: TEU, fiscal convergence criteria	Domestic institutional change (1990s onward)	Change in domestic political incentives or external pressure (1990s onward)	Change of fiscal policy paradigm domestically (1990s onward)	Accommodation
	After 1999: SGP	Ministry of Finance strong and stable	No veto power from some groups	Spread of the sound public finance paradigm	Fiscal adjustment in the run up to EMU (1999); conservative fiscal policy afterward until severe fiscal adjustment after 2008
		Fiscal constitution changed	Empowerment of sound fiscal policy supporters (i.e., Bank of Spain and Ministry of Finance)	Economic and political elites had incentives and external pressures to enforce it	Fiscal consolidation and new fiscal constitution
		Addressed the problem of temporary inconsistency and instability		Central Bank and Ministry of Finance have strong influence in sound public policy paradigm	Budget surplus and record low debt
		Failure of semirigid institutional mechanisms like EMS		Paradigm internalized by political elites	
		Strengthening of Central Bank		Consensus among leading parties and unions	
		Decentralization			
		stability and policy continuity			

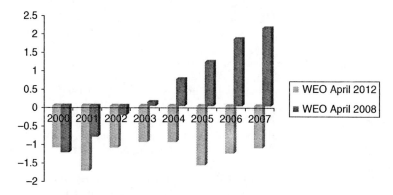

Figure 4.2 Estimates of Spain's Structural Fiscal Balance
Source: IMF, *World Economic Outlook*

of the crisis intensified in 2008, Spain seemed to be in an excellent fiscal position, yet the country's structural or cyclically adjusted deficit turned out to be much higher than its actual deficit (see figure 4.2).[6]

The country's fiscal position worsened sharply as a direct consequence of the global financial crisis and the collapse of the property boom. And Spain's fiscal performance not only deteriorated, as could be expected in the context of such a severe crisis, but it collapsed by more than 13 percent of GDP in just two years. As a result, what had seemed a robust public debt position began to worsen rapidly.

What Should Spain Have Done?

As seen in chapter 1, Spain was one of the European countries that had experienced a huge increase in property prices (the UK and Ireland, being other notable ones) and a boom in property development. That created a big bubble and a very large crash. The big question is what the Spanish government could and should have done about it. One of the main reasons for the boom was the low interest rates following EMU membership. Monetary policy prior to the crisis was far too loose and unsuitable for the Spanish economy. Yet, the government claimed, correctly, that monetary policy was not on its hands, as it was controlled by the ECB. Therefore, the only option they had was to tighten fiscal policy.[7]

Looking at the deficit figures with the insight of time, it could be argued that Spain's structural or cyclically adjusted deficit was much higher than its actual deficit. So the reported excellent figures disguised the truth. The problem is that it is very difficult to know the structural position of a country. Even the IMF, an international prestigious institution that cannot be accused of being controlled by the Spanish government, erred; in 2008, it reported that Spain had run a substantial structural—or cyclically adjusted—fiscal surplus in 2004, 2005, 2006, and 2007. Yet, in 2012 it reviewed the data and reported that it had, in fact, run a substantial structural deficit.

The (incorrectly) reported data drove the government's decisions, and, based on the reported surplus, it was hard to make the case that the country had to run a tighter fiscal policy prior to the crisis. The data and the concomitant policies had the seal of approval from the IMF and European institutions, praising the country for its policies and performance. However, it turned out to be smoke and mirrors because the economic boom led to complacency and a deeply seated misunderstanding regarding the real fiscal situation.

To judge from what happened after the crisis hit the country in 2008, the only way in which Spain could have prevented the deficit disaster that followed would have been to run massive fiscal surpluses of 10 percent or higher during the years prior to the crisis in order to generate a positive net asset position of at least 20 percent of GDP.[8] This, for obvious reasons, would not have been politically feasible. There is no way that the Socialist government, or any government for that matter, could have made the political case for such massive surpluses. Even as it was, there were voices demanding that the government reduce the surplus and invest more.

If a massive fiscal surplus was unrealistic, the only other possible options would have been to increase even more the capital requirements of banks, and/or to establish curbs on bank lending. As will be shown in chapter 6, the Bank of Spain and the Ministry of Finance tried to strengthen the banking regulatory framework and implemented a policy of dynamic provisioning that forced banks to increase their capital provisions. However, yet again as in the case of fiscal policies, the crisis showed that these provisions were clearly insufficient and that banks needed far more capital than available. The second option, curbs on banking lending, would have been politically unacceptable as well, at a time in which the economy was booming and the banks were having record profits. Furthermore, as a member of the Single Market and EMU, and with Spain fully integrated into global capital markets, borrowers would have had access to credit from international lenders as well, and Spanish authorities would not have been able to prevent such inflows under EU rules.

If fiscal profligacy was not the dominant cause for the collapse of the Spanish economy, fiscal discipline cannot be the only cure. In this regard, piling austerity measures, as they are currently doing in Spain (and other countries), on top of one another will not work. The Spanish economy is shrinking at a faster rate than forecasted for reasons outside the country's control; the ratio of Spain debt to its economy was 36 percent when it received the bailout and is expected to reach 84 percent by 2013 (see table 4.3). In this context, further adjustment of the deficit is undesirable and will exacerbate market tensions. Spain needs automatic stabilizers to work this out.

Table 4.3 The Economic Crisis (2008–2013)

Subject Descriptor	Units (%)	2008	2009	2010	2011	2012	2013
GDP, constant prices	Change	0.893	−3.742	−0.322	0.417	−1.538	−1.316
Output gap in percentage of potential GDP	Of potential GDP	2.313	−2.763	−3.389	−3.187	−4.84	−5.145
Total investment	Of GDP	29.114	24.004	22.812	21.541	19.622	18.784
Gross national savings	Of GDP	19.491	19.182	18.29	18.014	17.649	18.636
Inflation, average consumer prices	Change	4.13	−0.238	2.043	3.052	2.44	2.426
Volume of imports of goods and services	Change	7.962	−17.188	9.199	−0.884	−5.697	−2.789
Volume of exports of goods and services	Change	6.721	−10.02	11.258	7.634	2.401	3.536
Unemployment rate	Of total labor force	11.3	18	20.075	21.65	24.9	25.1
General government revenue	Of GDP	37.147	34.863	36.181	35.462	35.711	36.443
General government total expenditure	Of GDP	41.298	46.055	45.546	44.392	42.704	42.116
General government net lending/borrowing	Of GDP	−4.152	−11.193	−9.365	−8.931	−6.993	−5.673
General government structural balance	Of potential GDP	−5.019	−9.021	−7.317	−7.482	−5.389	−3.518
General government primary net lending/borrowing	Of GDP	−3.086	−9.931	−7.945	−7.028	−4.455	−2.21
General government net debt	Of GDP	30.801	42.491	49.805	57.485	78.626	84.43
General government gross debt	Of GDP	40.172	53.917	61.316	69.117	90.693	96.934
Current account balance	Of GDP	−9.623	−4.822	−4.521	−3.526	−1.973	−0.148

*Estimates

Source: IMF, World Economic Outlook Database, October 2012.

Balance of Payment Imbalances and Divergences in Competitiveness

A central argument of this book is that, although the dominant view in Europe is that the crisis in Spain (and the periphery) reflects fiscal indiscipline, the core problem in the case of Spain was excessive lending, divergent competitiveness, and external imbalances. One of the main challenges during the crisis was to agree on the nature and the causes of the illness. It is now widely accepted that the balance of payment is essential to any understanding of the present crisis. Some economists, like Hans-Werner Sinn of CESifo in Munich, have compared it to the crisis of the Bretton Woods System in the years prior to its demise. While the focus during the current euro crisis largely centered on the fiscal challenges, it is essential to note that there is also a crisis of competitiveness.

Many economists agree that the underlying problem in the euro area is the exchange rate system itself, namely, the fact that European countries locked themselves into an initial exchange rate. This decision meant, in fact, that they believed that their economies would converge in productivity (e.g., that the Spaniards would, in effect, become more like the Germans). If convergence was not possible, the alternative would be for people to move to higher productivity countries, thereby increasing their productivity levels by working in factories and offices there. Time has shown that both expectations were unrealistic and, in fact, the opposite happened. The gap between German and Spanish (including other peripheral country) productivity increased, rather than decreasing, over the past decade and, as a result, Germany developed a large surplus on its current account; Spain and the other periphery countries had large current account deficits that were financed by capital inflows. Could Spain become like Germany in its convergence strategies?[9]

As noted before, EMU membership fostered a false sense of security among private investors, which brought massive flows of capital to the periphery. Indeed, membership in EMU led to the convergence of interest rates and the disappearance of risk spreads. At the same time, the birth of the euro took place concurrently with a global credit boom. The consequence of both developments was a surge in cross-border lending to both private and public sectors, which in many countries (such as Portugal or Italy, but not so much Spain) reduced the pressure for fiscal consolidation, and also led to the emergence of balance of payment deficits and divergences in competitiveness.

In this regard, during the years of euphoria following EMU membership, prior to the financial crisis, private capital flowed freely into Spain and, as a result, the country ran current account deficits of close to 10 percent of GDP (see table 4.4). In the case of Spain these deficits helped finance large excesses of spending over income in the private sector (and notably, not so much in the public sector). These capital inflows could have helped

Table 4.4   Trade Balance before the Crisis (2000–2008)

Spain	*2000*	*2001*	*2002*	*2003*	*2004*	*2005*	*2006*	*2007*	*2008*
Current account	−3.959	−3.941	−3.259	−3.509	−5.251	−7.357	−8.972	−9.992	−9.62

Source: IMF, World Economic Outlook Database, September 2011.

Spain (and the other peripheral countries) invest, become more productive, and "catch up" with Germany. Unfortunately, in the case of Spain, they led largely to a massive bubble in the property market, consumption, and unsustainable levels of borrowing. The bursting of that bubble contracted the country's real economy and it brought down the banks that gambled on loans to real estate developers and construction companies. Again, the problem for Spain (and Ireland) was not caused by irresponsible fiscal policy, but instead by irresponsible banking practices leading to the build up of unsustainable liabilities.

At the same time, the economic boom also generated large losses in external competitiveness. As a result, costs and prices increased, which in turn led to a loss of competitiveness and large trade deficits (table 4.4). This unsustainable situation came to the fore when the financial shocks that followed the collapse of Lehman Brothers in the fall of 2007 brought "sudden stops" in lending across the world, leading to a collapse in private borrowing and spending, and a wave of fiscal crisis. The sudden stops (and in some countries, capital flight) in private inflows affected Greece and Ireland first in 2008; then Greece, Ireland, and Portugal in spring 2010; and finally, Italy, Portugal, and Spain in the second half of 2011. These countries were utterly unprepared for the devastating interruption in cross-border finance. In response, the EU chose to impose external adjustment on countries shut out of the markets while financing them through the ECB, which acted as a lender of last resort to banks.

Spain failed to address well-rooted structural problems and the challenge of competitiveness. As shown in chapter 1, while the Spanish economy performed significantly better between 2000 and 2008, this success was a mirage. The collapse of the construction sector that followed the global financial crisis of 2008 had dire consequences because the country had already suffered a sizeable loss of competitiveness. Moreover, the technological capacity of Spain's tradable good industries is weak, and much of Spain's recent investment efforts went into the production of nontradables, particularly buildings. Spain's industries were relatively vulnerable to competition from cheaper wage producers in Central and Eastern Europe, as well as Asia, and productivity growth was low, which will make it harder to restore competitiveness; finally (unlike Portugal), wage bargaining is quite rigid and, above all, unresponsive to conditions in the Eurozone.[10] While unitary labor costs remained fairly stable in Portugal, they increased significantly in Spain, further eroding its competitiveness.

As mentioned in chapter 3 the dogmatism regarding a balanced budget in Spain worked well in the short term and contributed to the credibility of the government policies. The current crisis shows, however, that a more accommodating policy would have been desirable to upgrade the productive base of the country with investments in necessary infrastructure and human capital in order to change the economic model. The maintenance of the balanced deficit paradigm as a goal on its own may have blinded the governments of the benefits of investing in new technology areas in which Spain is still lagging behind. This would have contributed to a faster change in the model of growth and may have reduced the dependency on the construction sector, which is now in the midst of a sharp recession that shows devastating consequences for the Spanish economy.

How can Spain improve its competitiveness? A competitiveness agenda must focus on productivity growth, even more important in Spain than nominal wage growth. To address this shortcoming will demand actions to improve policy across a wide front: higher investment in infrastructure, improvements in land-use planning, efforts to increase the quality of education, rigorous promotion of competition in all areas of the economy, tax simplification, and rationalization of existing regulations.[11] Furthermore, such an agenda will demand a shift from a low-cost, low-skill manufacturing base that relies on technical design and marketing skills from elsewhere, toward a more capital-intensive industry that requires greater skills in the labor force and relies on standard technology; for example, chemicals, vehicles, and steel and metal manufacturers.

In addition, a change in the existing growth model (based on relatively low production costs) in order to build a new framework based on innovation, quality, value-added, and productivity is needed. Small companies must carve out market niches in the global market and develop the technical capacity for short production runs in order to respond to shifting demand. They have to develop their own brands and distribution networks, and create their own customer bases. This will require the development of a technological know-how and marketing techniques. For the Spanish economy, the goal must be to increase productivity by increasing the capital intensity of production.

For Spain, as a member of EMU, its external competitiveness depends on the exchange rate, which is outside its control. Within EMU, it can only seek to improve its competitiveness vis-á-vis its Eurozone partners. That is what Germany did in the 2000s with the Agenda 2010 program and, more importantly, through wage restraint on the part of German labor unions. These reforms remain a challenge for Spain. According to Goldman Sachs ("Achieving fiscal and external balance" March 15 and 22), in order for Spain to achieve a sustainable external position, the country needs a real depreciation of its exchange rate by 20 percent (to place it in perspective: Portugal would need one of 35 percent; Greece one of 30 percent; and Italy one of 10–15 percent; while Ireland was already competitive). Moreover, with average inflation of 2 percent in the Eurozone and, say, zero inflation in currently uncompetitive countries, adjustment would take Spain 10 years (Portugal and Greece 15 years, and Italy 5–10 years). That would also imply 4 percent annual inflation in the rest of the Eurozone. The challenge remains, however, for the core Eurozone countries to accept that competitiveness is necessarily relative, and requires not just structural reforms, fiscal adjustment, and increasing competitiveness and exports from Spain, and other countries in the periphery (e.g., these countries need to become more dynamic, more inventive, and more productive), but also higher demand and inflation from the core countries.[12]

For the crisis to abate, Spain would need to regain its competitiveness and reduce its current account deficit. For this to happen, either the Eurozone runs a bigger surplus with the rest of the world (the question is how) or the Eurozone adjusts via shifts in competitiveness. In other words, the real exchange rates of Spain (and Southern European countries) decline, while those of Northern Europe increase. There are four options: first, aggressive monetary easing, weaker euro, stimulatory policies at the core, and austerity and reform in the periphery to restore growth and competitiveness; second, deflationary adjustment and structural reforms to bring down nominal wages in the periphery; third, financing by the core of an uncompetitive periphery; and, finally, debt restructuring and a partial break-up of the Eurozone. As of summer 2012, there has been a mixture of the second and third options: austerity and financing. Spain could experience an "internal devaluation," in which nominal wages and prices fall, and they become hypercompetitive relative to Germany and other trading partners. Politically, however, this seems unacceptable, hence unlikely. And it seems clear by now that one-sided deflation will fail.

Still, there are important reasons for optimism. Despite the challenging international economic environment, Spanish companies have been quite successful at diversifying their export markets and investments, increasing the technology content of their exports and adding value to their products. Still, to consolidate a new growth pattern based on value-added and productivity, Spain will have to achieve a massive upgrade of its productive base that will allow the country to move up in the value chain. In order to do this, Spain must improve productivity, develop a more flexible economy with a better-educated labor force, achieve higher savings and investment, and develop a more efficient public sector.

Conclusion

This chapter shows that the crisis in Spain was not caused by the profligacy of the public sector. In fact, it was unambiguously generated in the domestic private sector, and fueled by private sector capital inflows. Therefore, the government's options and responsibility to prevent the fiscal crisis were quite limited, as it lacked control of monetary policy and could not limit private sector capital inflows. This challenges the deeply entrenched perception that now dominates European chancelleries and public opinion across Europe. In fact, as noted by Martin Wolf, "if the government could not have prevented the crisis, how can it bear some deep moral fault? Surely, a far more sensible—indeed moral—approach would be to recognize that this is more misfortune than misdeed and offer Spain the help it needs to adjust its economy to the post-crisis reality, without letting it either be pushed into sovereign bankruptcy or humiliated. Yet that is what is now threatened."[13] The primary mistake, according to many observers, may have been the country's decision to join the euro. Had it remained outside, like the United Kingdom, it is likely that even if Spain still suffered a severe recession, its exchange rate and its long-term interest rates would both be far lower as they are in the UK, which has a worse fiscal position than Spain. In any case, it is too late to reconsider that option; the challenge for the country still remains how to survive the crisis within the constraints imposed by membership within a monetary union.

Spain currently faces a situation of lack of credit, fiscal austerity, extreme lack of confidence from the market, and an imploded real state marked. The traditional recipe to deal with such a crisis, a devaluation, is no longer possible: Spain is an EMU member; national and regional austerity are destroying employment; demand stimulus to increase consumption and investment is not possible because fiscal restrictions are a priority and the government lacks the funds and access to cheap credit; increasing debt is not an option in the current context because the markets would not tolerate it and would push yields to unaffordable levels; and monetary policy is in the hands of the ECB. Without credit and demand, there will hardly be a recovery. Hence, the paradox: while austerity will intensify the crisis, expansion is not possible. The Spanish and European governments face the challenge to square this circle.

The experience of the country before the crisis shows that EU and EMU membership have not led to the implementation of the structural reforms necessary to address these challenges. On the contrary, as noted in chapter 2, EMU membership contributed to the economic boom and a real estate bubble (estimated at 30 percent real) fueled by record low interest rates, thus facilitating the postponement of necessary economic reforms. This challenge, however, is not a problem of European institutions, but of national policies. The SGP was unable to address Portugal's fiscal challenges and fiscal prudence and, in the case of Spain, it did not lead to the reforms that should have addressed the country's competitiveness problems (nor did Portugal's "chronic fiscal misbehavior"). Indeed, the process of economic reforms must be a domestic one led by domestic actors willing to carry them out.

As shown, EMU membership brought big early gains to Spain by lowering borrowing costs and removing exchange rate risks. Success, however, led to euphoria and diminished the need for reforms. Governments need to balance prudent policymaking and structural reforms. The most important lesson from Spain is that lower interest rates and the loosening of credit will likely lead to a credit boom, driven by potentially overoptimistic expectations of future permanent income, which, in turn, may increase housing demand and household indebtedness, as well as lead to overestimations of potential output and expansionary fiscal policies. The boom will also lead to higher wage increases, caused by the tightening of the labor market, higher inflation, and losses in external competitiveness, together with a shift from the tradable to the nontradable sector of the economy, which would have a negative impact on productivity.

In order to avoid these risks, a number of measures must be taken: governments should tighten budgetary policies in the case of a boom in demand and/or strong credit expansion. At the same time, they should use fiscal policies in a countercyclical way; budget surpluses should not be driven by higher revenues, as in Spain prior to the crisis; and governments need to address the structural reasons for the deficits and avoid one-off measures that delay reforms. Furthermore, they should guard against potential overestimation of GDP and measure carefully the weight of consumption on GDP, because they may inflate revenues in the short term and create an unrealistic perception of the budgetary accounts. In addition, to avoid unsustainable external imbalances (see table 4.4), countries should also carry out the necessary structural reforms that will increase flexibility and productivity, allowing their productive sectors to respond to the increasing demand and ensuring that their economies can withstand the pressures of membership. They should also set wages based on Eurozone conditions, and not on unrealistic domestic expectations, to ensure wage moderation (Abreu 2006, 5–6). Countries should also take the opportunity presented by the boom to move into higher value-added and faster growth sectors, toward a more outward-oriented production structure. Finally, the current global crisis illustrated the need for tight financial supervision to avoid excessive lending and misallocation of resources.

The Spanish experience shows that EU/EMU membership brings challenges and opportunities. As we have seen, membership by itself did not lead to the implementation of the structural reforms necessary to address fiscal and competitiveness challenges. Success is not automatic and there are no guarantees. Indeed, membership helps those prepared to exploit its benefits. There has to be strong coherence between EU/EMU institutions and domestic policies; hence, governments need to balance prudent policymaking, control labor costs, and implement structural reforms. Fiscal consolidation is not enough.

CHAPTER 5

The Political and Social Concertation Consequences of the Crisis

Introduction

The impact of the global economic crisis has been felt well beyond the economic and financial realms. Spain followed in the path of many other European countries (including Ireland, Portugal, Greece, and France) that saw their governments suffer the wrath of their voters and have been voted out of office (Italy also witnessed the collapse of the Berlusconi administration, which was forced to resign in the face of market pressures and give way to an interim unity government of technical experts led by Mario Monti).

The PSOE was reelected in a general election on March 9, 2008 (see table 5.1). By March 2008, the effects of the crisis were not yet visible, as shown in chapter 2, and the government tried to do everything to minimize it. Since that election, however, economic conditions deteriorated sharply and consequently the government's popularity declined rapidly. Between March 2008 and March 2012, there were a number of electoral contests in Spain at the local, regional, national, and European levels. At the national and European levels the one common pattern was the outcome: the defeat of the Socialist Party and the victory of the PP. And at the regional and local levels the Socialists suffered historical losses, losing control of regional government that they ruled for decades (notably, Castilla-La Mancha and Extremadura), and even losing the election for the first time in one of its historical strongholds, Andalusia (although they were able to reach a coalition with a smaller leftist party to stay in power). This chapter analyzes the outcome of the three most important elections that took place since 2008: the European election of June 2009; the local and regional ones of May 2011; and the national one of November 2011.

At the same time, this chapter examines the impact of the crisis on the social concertation (or social bargaining) process, which emerged in Spain

Table 5.1 General Election Results (2008 and 2011)

Party	Seats 2008	Seats 2011	Votes 2008	Votes 2011	% 2008	% 2011
PSOE	169	110	11,289,335	6,973,880	43.87	28.73
PP	154	186	10,278,010	10,830,693	39.94	44.62
CiU	10	16	779,425	1,014,263	3.03	4.17
PNV	6	5	306,128	323,517	1.19	1.33
ERC	3	3	298,139	256,393	1.16	1.05
IU	2	11	969,946	1,680,810	3.77	6.92
BNG	2	2	212,543	183,279	0.83	0.75
CC-PNC	2	2	174,629	143,550	0.68	0.59
UPyD	1	5	306,079	1,140,242	1.19	4.69
NA-BAI	1		62,398		0.24	
AMAIUR		7		333.628		1.37
COMPROMÍS-Q		1		125,150		0.51
FAC		1		99,173		0.40
GBAI		1		42,411		0.17

Source: The Junta Electoral Central, http://www.juntaelectoralcentral.es/portal/page/portal/JuntaElectoral Central/JuntaElectoralCentral/ResultElect.

during the transition to democracy, and it became a central staple of the policymaking process in the realms of social, economic, and labor policies (see chapter 3). Before the crisis, the process was institutionalized and the social actors (unions, employers' associations, and oftentimes the government) reached dozens of agreements (Royo 2008).

Yet, one of the most devastating consequences of the crisis was the dramatic surge in unemployment, reaching over 24 percent in 2012. Dealing with this record level of unemployment was one of the major goals for both the Socialists and PP administrations, and led to two major labor reforms. Throughout the crisis, the social actors played a central role and were able to reach agreements. However, the crisis also influenced the strategies and negotiating positions of the unions, employers, and governments; in some instances, it also contributed to shift the balance of power among them, thus opening a wider gap among them, which made agreements more difficult (in some instances, impossible). The chapter looks at the evolution of the social concertation process and its outcomes.

The chapter is divided into four main sections. The first examines the electoral impact of the crisis and the outcome of three elections. The second describes briefly the process of social bargaining in Spain, with special emphasis on the year prior to the crisis. The third analyzes the process of social bargaining and its outcomes during the crisis. It closes with an analysis of the motivations of the social actors and the perspectives for the future.

The Electoral Dimension of the Crisis

PSOE came to power in March 2004, thanks in part to the backlash against the PP's support for the war in Iraq, as well as its mishandling of the Madrid train terrorist attacks that took place on the eve of the election. For the following four years, with the economy booming (see chapter 3), it focused largely on social reform, education, constitutional changes in the form of greater devolution, and cultural issues. It proved to be a competent economic manager of the status quo, and the finance minister, Pedro Solbes, was considered a safe pair of hands. Prior to the 2008 election, the government managed to deflect the blame for the economic downturn onto external events: the subprime crisis in the United States, and the subsequent global financial crunch. The opposing PP was unable to articulate a clear and attractive alternative, and in some areas, moved to the Right, thus alienating centrist voters.

Despite the worsening economic environment during the 2008 electoral campaign, both parties competed in showering voters with unprecedented pledges of generous tax cuts; PM Zapatero tried to stimulate the slowing economy and to compensate people for the higher inflation and interest rates by putting more money in their pockets by promising a €400 tax rebate for 13 million wage earners and pensioners, an estimated costs of €5 billion (the equivalent of one-quarter of the government fiscal surplus, or 2 percent of GDP). Opposition parties complained that "it was blatant attempt to buy votes with public monies" or "naked electioneering," and denounced it as "banana republic tactics." And even the leftist union CCOO declared this promise "opportunistic" and dismissed it as a "one-off payment for voting Socialist."

The PP itself had its own controversial plans to cut the tax bill of female workers by €1,000 under the argument that it would encourage them to continue working after they had children by assisting with childcare costs, as well as to raise the tax exemption threshold to €16,000 a year (four out of ten taxpayers would not have to pay taxes). The PP and the PSOE both promised to simplify the tax regime, abolish wealth and inheritance taxes, and reduce the corporate tax rate (at that time, 30 percent) to make Spanish companies more competitive.[1] All these proposals show how unprepared both parties were for what was about to happen to the Spanish economy following the election.

As seen in chapter 1, the economy prospered during the Socialists' first term, but the government was still unloved by the corporate sector, who was anxious at the prospect that Finance Minister Solbes would quit the government after the election, and the government was unable to cash in on the country's economic boom because rapid growth and widespread prosperity had brewed complacency and consumerism, rather than political debate. Furthermore, the slowdown of the economy was already looming, with the construction sector showing definite signs of decelerating.

In the end, the PSOE won the election and increased the number of seats that it already held in Congress (164; the PP had 148), but it did not obtain an absolute majority (it won 169 seats, in the 350 seats' Congress, and the PP, 154) (see table 5.1). This proved to be a significant handicap when economic conditions worsened and the smaller parties were unwilling to support the government's program. This election was a high watermark for the PSOE in the period of analysis; electorally, it would only go down from this peak.

European Elections: June 2009

The electoral erosion of the Socialist government was first manifested in the election for the European parliament on June 7, 2009.[2] There had been six European elections in Spain since the country became a member of the EU. And the June 7 election was the first one since 2000 in which the PP won an election at the national level against the PSOE (prior to this national election, the PP had won a regional election in Galicia, defeating the PSOE-BNG coalition government, and it had made possible a Socialist government in the Basque Country).

Of the 54 seats that Spain holds in the European parliament, the PP gained 23 (in the previous election it had 24); the PSOE 21 (it had 25); Coalición for Europe 2 seats (5.12 percent of the votes); IU 2 seats (3.73 percent); UPyD 1 seat (2.87 percent); and Europa de los Pueblos 1 seat (2.50 percent). The difference between the two main political parties, however, was relatively small: only 3.72 percentage points (42.23 percent for the PP versus 38.51 percent for the PSOE), or 600,000 votes. Yet, the PP's victory was clear: the party received the highest number of votes ever received in this kind of election (previously it had won the European elections three times); while the PSOE lost 5 percentage points compared with the 2004 European parliament elections. Furthermore, the PP won in 11 of the autonomous regions (the PSOE only in 6, and the PNV-CiU won in the Basque Country). It was also a wake-up call for the Socialist government; if the results were extrapolated to the Spanish parliament, the PP would be the leading party with 170 members of parliament, 16 more than the 154 it gained in 2008, and the PSOE would have lost 20 seats (it had 169 originally).[3] The level of abstention, typically higher in these elections, was also significant at 54 percent (it had been 45.14 percent in 2004, and the average in Europe has been 43.39 percent), but it was particularly worrisome in regions like Catalonia where it reached 62.4 percent.

According to exit polls, for the first time the impact of the economic crisis was an important factor in voters' decisions. Despite the fact that the election had a European focus, in reality European issues were absent largely from the electoral campaign, and domestic issues dominated the political agenda. There was also an expectation that the corruption scandals that had been exposed in the months leading to the election (notably the *case* Gürtel, the *suits case* in Valencia, both of which involved the PP; the use of the official plane by PM Zapatero, and other scandals in Andalusia that involved VP Chaves) would have an impact in the election (and the Socialists tried to exploit the scandals extensively throughout the campaign), but it did not happen. In fact, the PP gained more votes in those communities more deeply affected by the corruption scandals (like Valencia or Madrid). If anything, the PSOE's emphasis of these scandals helped to mobilize Conservative voters (and alienated the Socialists ones, who stayed home). In Valencia, for instance, the PP won with 52.3 percent of the votes despite a scandal involving some "gifts" that affected the reputation of the president of the regional government (the difference between the PP and the PSOE in the region widened to 15 percentage points); in Madrid, the difference between both parties was 13 points.[4]

Regional and Local Elections: May 2011

The autonomous and local elections took place on May 22, 2012, and the results were devastating for the PSOE. An unprecedented electoral tsunami of monumental proportions wiped the party away throughout the country; from Barcelona, through Castilla-La Mancha, Extremadura, and Seville, the Socialists lost a slew of regional and local polls en route to the party's worst electoral performance since the democratic transition. It lost 1.7 million votes compared to the 2007 election. The PSOE had earned just 27.8 percent of the vote, trailing the PP by 10 points, which got more than 2 million votes. The PSOE could take only comfort only in the fact that the 37.5 percent share of the vote garnered by the PP would not earn it an absolute majority in Congress (still, in the 1995 local and regional elections won by the PP, which paved the way for its electoral victory in the 1996 general election, it won "only" by 5 percentage points). Yet the Socialists lost historical bastions like Castilla-La Mancha (and eventually Extremadura, where the PP formed a coalition government with the leftist IU), and also lost control over Aragón, Baleares, Asturias (a new election took place in March 2012, in which the PSOE won and formed a collation with a smaller party), and Cantabria. Among the smaller regional parties, a Basque independence party, Bildu, was one of the biggest winners; it gained 1.4 percent of the national vote and secured control of major cities in the Basque Country, including San Sebastian. Finally, despite the apparent public discontent with established parties (articulated by the 15-M movement), the participation rate rose to 66 percent from 63 percent four years earlier.

This was an unprecedented victory for the PP; the party received 400,000 more votes than in 2007 allowing it to accumulate more regional power than ever before. Prior to the election, the PSOE ruled in 9 of the autonomous regions. After the election it would rule only in two: Andalusia (fortunately for the PSOE it held elections in March 2012, and despite the fact that it lost them for the first time ever, it was able to hold to power in coalition with

IU), and the Basque Country (but only temporarily, the October 2012 elections gave the victory to the PNV).[5] The PP would now rule in Cantabria, Castilla-La Mancha, and Baleares, and was able to maintain the substantive majority it already held in La Rioja, Murcia, Madrid, Valencia and Castilla, and León. Two other parties, IU and UPyD, also benefited from the PSOE's collapse and increased their number of representatives in the regional parliaments.

The debacle for the PSOE extended to the concurrent local elections. The PP's victory was also overwhelming in municipalities across the country; the PP ended up with more than 4,500 local city-hall councillors than the PSOE, and its victory extended to traditional Socialists bastions like Seville, A Coruña, and Cordoba, where the PP won with an absolute majority. After the election, the PSOE was able to hold by itself in only four province capitals (prior to the election it ruled in 16 capitals): Toledo, Cuenca, Soria, and Lleida. The PSOE also lost in Barcelona, which it had ruled for the previous 32 years.

The Socialists' attempt during the campaign to focus on local and regional issues to avoid the "punishing vote" that most observers expected failed miserably. Furthermore, PM Zapatero's decision to announce prior to the local and regional elections that he would not run for reelection did not work either. The party's strategy was to use local slogans ("the government of your street") as well as concentrate the communications' strategy and events around their local and regional candidates, while trying to minimize the role of national issues and government leaders. It did not quite work out as expected, because voters were focusing on the economic crisis.

The PP, for its part, eager to remind voters of the perilous economic situation, wanted to brand this election as the first round of the general election, and centered its strategy against PM Zapatero and the government's economic failure. The PSOE was unable to effectively counter those attacks. PM Zapatero and ministers Blanco and Rubalcaba were three of the people more closely associated with the government's response to the crisis and, therefore, the ones more visible in the media throughout the campaign, which played into the PP's strategy. The party also failed to harness the youth discontent that emerged after May 15 (see chapter 2). The PP's message, on the contrary, was simple and direct; it focused on the economic crisis, blamed PM Zapatero for it, and presented the PSOE local and regional leaders as loyal acolytes of PM Zapatero who were similarly responsible for the crisis. There was also interest in knowing the impact, if any, of the 15-M movement, but it was not evident in the results: the participation rate increased by 1 percentage point.[6]

Polls from an exit interview showed that the economic situation had been a determining factor in the electoral outcome. The increasing social and economic effects of the crisis, and in particular the growing number of unemployed (and the fears that unemployment generated), coupled with deep discontent regarding the Socialist's government's handling of the crisis were decisive. In particular, there was profound resentment over the Socialists' change of policies after May 9; when PM Zapatero bended to pressures from the markets, international institutions, and Spain's European partners, and was forced to adopt the most drastic (at the time) budget-cutting measures since the establishment of democracy (see chapter 2). The fact that the government (and PM Zapatero, in particular) was forced to do a complete turnaround as well as implement and publicly defend the opposite of what it had been doing up to that day, was also a major source of discontent and resentment among voters.

The PP quickly claimed that the result of these elections had national implications and, with a general election scheduled within ten months, demanded an early general election. But PM Zapatero refused. The main concern was that the result could add volatility to an already unstable situation, with the government still trying to reassure the markets of its commitment to fiscal austerity. Still, the defeat of the PSOE across the country was expected to make that effort harder. Regional spending was not falling, and the cajas were still deeply intertwined with the regional governments.

General Elections: November 2011

As discussed in chapter 2, PM Zapatero decided later that summer to call for an early election on November 21, 2011, four months in advance. Economic conditions continued deteriorating throughout the country that fall, and the PP used the economic situation as the main argument to attack the Socialists during the electoral campaign. Polls gave the PP an ample victory, but there were doubts as late as mid-November about the magnitude of the victory and whether the PP would obtain an absolute majority.[7] Most polls, however, predicted an overwhelming victory with an absolute majority for the PP.

The PP electoral manifesto was maddeningly vague, beyond generic commitments to austerity (committed to fulfilling the EU deficit target of 4.4 percent in 2012), no tax increases, labor reform, job creation incentives, financial reform to clean up the banks, growth promotion through incentives for small business, and a pledge to be a "competent" and "efficient" government. The party issued a "100-point plan" that included

- Austerity and the elimination of waste to control public spending and stabilize the budget;
- Cleaning up of the balance sheets of the banks to increase liquidity and promote economic recovery;
- Reform of the labor market and collective bargaining;
- Tax breaks for small businesses to promote employment and innovation; and
- Competition in the energy sector to encourage efficiency and protect the environment.

But the details of the substance of these proposals and the implementation plan were omitted. Rajoy himself had been exceedingly cautious during his campaign and avoided firm commitments (except to maintain his "priority": the purchasing capacity of pensions, everything else was up for discussion and could be cut[8]) that would alienate crisis-weary voters and impair his electoral prospects. The PP slogan was "Join the change," but it was not clear what that change entailed (except to oust PM Zapatero). The two leading candidates, Rajoy and Rubalcaba, squared off during a televised debate on November 7, mainly focusing on domestic issues, while largely ignoring the euro sovereign debt crisis looming over Spain. They failed to articulate their plan to square the circle in which Spain found itself: how to combine the austerity demanded by the markets and the EU, with growth (Rajoy's answer was that "it would be difficult," while noting that Spain "never surrenders").[9] He would later realize, when Spain had to request the financial bailout, that surrender was indeed a requirement.

The expectations prior to the election were that the PP would receive a mandate to introduce radical reforms and restore the confidence of the markets after more than three years of crisis. But, as noted in chapter 2, even the prospect of a new Spanish government that would replace the discredited Socialist administration of PM Zapatero could not soothe the markets. Debt costs soared three days ahead of the election: the yield on ten-year bonds reached 6.975, the highest level since 1997, and the premium 499 basis points.[10] Rajoy responded on his last day of campaigning by pleading with financial markets to give his new government enough time in which to turn the Spanish economy around: "I hope this stops, [markets should] realize that there are elections and that the winners must be given a little room for maneuver that should last more than half an hour." He would learn very quickly that markets were not interested in platitudes and would not give his government any time. Even before the election it became clear that ultimately the crisis was not just about Spain (or Italy) but that it was also about Eurozone contagion, which made it very difficult for the Spanish government to turn sentiment around.[11]

The electoral results confirmed the polls' predictions (see table 5.1). The PP decisively defeated the Socialist Party with the best showing since the country's transition to democracy in the 1970s, gaining 10.8 million votes and 186 seats in the 350-seat lower chamber of parliament. The Socialists plummeted to 110 seats from 169. For the Socialists, this was their worst showing since the return to democracy in the 1970s.

Some regional parties were also successful during the election; the Catalan nationalists of CiU gained seats, as did Amaiur, a radical Basque nationalist party, a month after the Basque terrorist group ETA announced that it would stop its campaign of violence.

There were two outcomes that stood out from these results: first, with 44.5 percent of the votes, the PP had 53.1 percent of the seats. Second, it was a more fragmented Congress: the two leading parties, PP and PSOE, now held 84.5 percent of the seats (they held 92 percent prior to the election). This led some to question whether this election would be the beginning of the end of *bipartidism*. It became a legislature dominated by one party, the PP, which does not need to sign agreements with others to pass legislation, but there are also more minority parties in Congress, some more vocal and radical.

Despite the overwhelming victory, there were also risks; the results confirmed the PP victory, but the party had won only less than 600,000 votes (or 5 percent) more than it received in 2008 (when it obtained 154 seats, 32 less than in 2012). These data seem to show that the main reason for the PP's overwhelming victory was the collapse of the PSOE's support: it lost some 4 million votes compared to 2008. Voters were not enthusiastic with the PP, and the results of the election seemed more like an indictment on the PSOE's management of the crisis. Other evidence seems to support that analysis; the degree of loyalty to the PSOE (according to polls it stood at around 40 percent) meant that 60 percent of its voters either abstained or voted for other parties. In previous elections, the majority opted for staying home and not voting. However, in this election, according to the polls, of the 4.8 million votes the PSOE lost, there were 3.9 million who had voted for the PSOE in 2008, who now had decided to vote for other parties, and only 500,000 of them abstained. Of those 3.9 million voters, 700,000 voted for IU, and 800,000 for UPyD. These voters were unhappy with the PSOE, but they were not ready to vote for the PP either. Yet, there were 1.5 million PSOE voters who made the shift to the PP.

Furthermore, a detailed analysis of the data shows that the victory was not as overwhelming as the numbers of seats gained by the PP may make it seem to be. The PP obtained an absolute majority with 459,000 votes less than what the PSOE received in 2008, when it obtained only 169 seats and did not get an absolute majority (which is set at 176 seats). In 2000, the PP obtained a larger percentage of votes (45.24 percent), but obtained fewer seats (183), because the PSOE did not fall by as much as in 2012. In 2012, the PP obtained only 0.7 points more than garnered in 2008. In others words, the PP got an absolute majority largely because of the loss of votes by the PSOE. The PP also benefited from the concentration of its votes, particularly in Andalusia, where it surpassed the PSOE for the first time since the transition; furthermore, Andalusia was the region with the highest number of contested seats.[12]

Indeed, the election does not support the notion that there had been a decisive turn toward the Right that could lead to the establishment of a hegemonic party. The absolute majority gained by the PP was largely configured by an electoral system designed to favor the governability of the country to the party that receives the largest share of votes, which attributed the party 8.5 points more in seats than votes: with 44.6 percent of the votes, the PP obtained 53.1 percent of the seats in Congress. This is the result of the *D'Hont* formula used to assign seats, but also, and more importantly, it is the consequence of the size of the electoral districts in which the general election takes place, based on the provinces. When some electoral districts have only a few seats to distribute, the smaller parties do not get any representatives. Neither the constitution nor the electoral law use population as the key criteria to determine how many seats should be elected on each province. They only establish that each district should have a minimum of two seats (except for Ceuta and Melilla, which have one each), regardless of the population density in that district, setting a floor of 102 seats. Given the 350 seats today, only 248 seats remain for distribution on the basis of population. This exposes the fact that more than half of the districts are small. This favors the party with the largest number of votes, giving the opportunity to add many seats.[13] This is the reason why small- and median-sized parties that run nationally "lose" votes (e.g., they need more votes to gain a seat). The system works to the advantage of small nationalist parties (such as PNV, CiU, and Amaiur in the past election), which typically obtain results very close to the proportionality; they take advantage of the concentration of votes in their provinces and need fewer votes to gain seats. On average, the PP needed 58,230 votes per seat, and the PSOE, 63,399, while UPyD needed 228,048 per seat. The ecologist party Equo did not get anyone elected despite the fact that it received 215,000 votes (it had one person elected in Valencia as part of the coalition Compromís), while other nationalist parties (such as the Galician's BNG, the Canary Islands' CC or Foro Asturias) received fewer votes altogether at the national level, but they were more concentrated within their regions/provinces. This showed that the key to success is a strong base in a well-defined territory, rather than many supporters sparsely distributed across the country.[14]

Finally, although the economic crisis was a crucial factor in deciding the result, the adoption of austerity measures by the regional governments at the autonomous region level did not translate into an erosion of electoral support for those parties/governments. For instance, in Catalonia, which had implemented drastic and painful cuts that had led to significant protests and demonstrations, CiU still gained almost 300,000 votes compared to 2008, and also received increased support at the regional elections. In Castilla-La Mancha, now ruled by the PP, the party received a record 55.85 percent of the votes, despite all the cuts. This seemed to confirm the premise that specific events or decisions are not on their own the driving force in causing the erosion of electoral support, but instead, how those events/decision are managed.[15]

The results of the election showed that Spaniards were eager for change. They endured three years of crisis and expected solutions; thus they decided that the PP and Rajoy would be better than the Socialists at extricating the country from its perilous predicament.[16] Yet, the new government was immediately under pressure from the bond markets to show that it could turn the country's prospects around. The day after, the election yields remained high, with the premium at nearly 470 basis points. Despite its electoral victory, the PP's decision to remain vague on the details of its economic plan may have been a mistake. While it may have worked as a deliberate strategy to boost its electoral prospects, it created uncertainty both within and outside of Spain in an already shaky environment, and generated more resistance and dissatisfaction when the government started to spell out and implement its policies.

The new government faced a situation of lack of credit, fiscal austerity, an imploded real estate market, and extreme lack of confidence from the markets. The traditional recipes would not work: national, local, and regional austerity was destroying employment; demand stimulus to increase consumption and investment was not possible because fiscal restrictions were a priority; increasing debt was not an option; and monetary policy was in the hands of the ECB. Without credit and demand there would be no recovery, and austerity would intensify the crisis. Yet expansion was not possible because there was no money. The new government was forced to confront that impossible challenge, and address what PM Rajoy defined in the closing days of the campaign as "the most difficult economic situation that Spain has faced in the past 30 years."[17] Unfortunately, as described in chapter 2, the results so far (summer 2012) leave much to be desired. And the erosion of the new PP government was almost immediate. By May 2012, 90 percent of citizens expressed their anguish over the crisis, 48 percent censored the government's management of the crisis, and support for the PP decreased by 6 points from the general election (from 46.6 percent to 40.6 percent). With two regional elections scheduled in October 2012, in the Basque Country and Galicia, it remains to be seen whether the PP government is able to stem this haemorrhage (the PP was reelected in Galicia in the October 2012 election, providing a much needed oxygen tank to PM Rajoy).

The next section focuses on another important political process in Spain: social concertation.

Social Concertation in Spain:
A Historically Institutionalized Process

As mentioned briefly in chapter 3, social bargaining became an important component of the economic policymaking process since the democratic transition. It emerged in Spain in the 1970s to address the economic crisis of the second half of that decade. This process was known as "social concertation" (social bargaining) and began with the Pactos de la Moncloa (Moncloa Pacts) of 1977, signed by all major political parties as part of the transition to democracy. From the late 1970s until the mid-1980s, government, unions, and businesses reached five major agreements (Royo 2000, 67–109). Other agreements throughout the 1990s and 2000s followed (Royo 2008).

On balance, the final assessment of these agreements was very positive and set the path for the long-term institutionalization of this process. By fostering consensus and facilitating agreements over the content of the new constitution, the social concertation process provided the foundation on which the transition process was consolidated. In addition, concertation fostered the development of new laws regulating the industrial relations framework, helped mitigate industrial conflict, and contributed greatly to the institutional consolidation of the unions and employers' associations, as well as their recognition as the legal representatives of workers and businesses (Royo 2000, 96–108).

From an economic standpoint, the main contribution of the social bargaining process was that, for the first time, it introduced macroeconomic considerations into collective bargaining. This development made possible the behavior of wages according to inflationary objectives. The combination of social peace, wage moderation, and lower inflation increased the profitability of capital and contributed to higher business profits, which, in turn, fostered confidence, investment, and jobs in the second half of the 1980s (i.e., starting in 1985 investment picked up and increased from 18.9 percent in 1985 to 24.4 percent in 1989, and employment grew an average of 2.9 percent yearly in the second half of the 1980s) (Royo 2000, 96–104).

In spite of its effectiveness, the concertation process broke down after 1986 (Royo 2000, 142–170). It would take almost a decade for social bargaining to resume. The electoral defeat of the Spanish Socialists in the 1996 general election and the victory of the Conservative PP brought about an unanticipated development: the resurgence of national-level bargaining between the government, business, and labor unions on diverse regulatory items are continuing to this day. Indeed, as outlined in table 5.2 although there has not been until recently a return to explicit incomes policy negotiated centrally at the national-level, there was a return to national-level social bargaining in the 1990s and in the first decade of the 2000s under both Conservative and Socialist governments. Between 1994 and 2008, the government, unions, and businesses reached 27 major agreements that covered labor and social reforms, as well as wages since 2002 (Royo 2007, 88–89). Indeed, if one looks at some of the most important social and economic reforms that took place since 1994, the overwhelming majority took place as part of the social bargaining process. Despite occasional breakdowns in this process, the pattern of economic policymaking during the past three decades was largely influenced by this process, helping to account for continuities in economic policymaking (see chapter 3).

Throughout the 1990s and 2000s, social peace and wage moderation fostered by the return of national social bargaining contributed to a new virtuous circle characterized by sustained rapid growth, improving fiscal position, lower unemployment, and higher investment, which, in turn, promoted rapid growth (Royo 2008, 83–100).[18]

Immediately prior to the crisis, the most significant agreement was the 2006 AMCE, signed by the Socialist government and the social actors (CEOE, CEPYME, UGT, and CCOO) (Royo 2007, 90–92). The main objective of this agreement was to address the record levels of temporary contracts. The

Table 5.2 Main Social Pacts, Content, and Leading Signatories (2006–2012)

Agreement	Years	Signatories	Main content
ANC	2006	CEOE, CCOO, UGT	Wage bargaining framework
AMCE	2006	Government, COEO, CEPYME, UGT, CCOO	Reduction of temporary contracts and improvement of the quality of employment
Agreement to Reform the Social Security System	2006	Government, CEOE, CEPYME, CCOO, UGT	Reform of the pension system
ANC 2007	2007	CEOE, CEPYME, CCOO, UGT	Wage bargaining framework
Agreement to Reform the Social Security Reserve Fund. This was the first concerted reform of the SS system since the transition. As a result, the government increased to 15 years (from 12.5) the minimum required to receive a pension.	2007	Government, CEOE, CEPYME, UGT, CCOO	More flexibility to SS reserve fund
Agreement to combat labor accidents	2007	Government, CEOE, CEPYME, UGT, CCOO	Initiatives to reduce the rate of accidents in the workplace
ANC	2008	CEOE, CEPYME, CCOO, UGT	Wage bargaining framework
Commitment to Act to Unblock Pending Collective Bargaining Agreements	2009	CEOE, CEPYME, CCOO, UGT	Finalizing pending collective agreements
AENC	2010, 2011, 2012	CEOE, CEPYME, CCOO, UGT	Wage bargaining framework
Economic and Social Pact against the Crisis	2011	Government, CEOE, CEPYME, CCOO, UGT	Retirement age, collective bargaining system, and active employment policies
Commitment to Act to Unblock Pending Collective Bargaining Agreements	2011	CEOE, CEPYME, CCOO, UGT	Finalizing pending collective agreements
II AENC	2012, 2013, 2014	CEOE, CEPYME, CCOO, UGT	Wage bargaining framework

agreement allowed Spanish firms to convert their temporary workers into permanent ones through a contract of job promotion, with lower dismissal costs. It included initiatives to reduce the temporary rate, such as a period of time (up to December 31, 2007) during which existing temporary contracts could be converted into permanent ones using the so-called contract of promotion of stable employment, with a dismissal cost of 33 days per year of work (as opposed to the regular 45 days per year for regular permanent contracts). After that period, the conversion was extended to regular permanent contracts, giving a powerful incentive to employers to convert their current temporary workers to indefinite ones.

The agreement limited to 30 months the renewal of temporary contracts for one worker. Hence, those workers who served for 30 months in the same position, through two or more temporary contracts, were automatically converted to permanent contracts (with the exception of certain categories of contracts such as training or interim ones). It also established a program of incentives to promote permanent employment, creating subsidies of between €500 and €3,200 per year (depending on the type of contract that is converted into a permanent one) for hiring certain categories of workers. These subsidies were expected to last, on average, four years (as opposed to the previous two years). The accord also included the eventual elimination of subsidies for the conversion of temporary contracts into permanent ones: those contracts signed prior to June 1, 2006, that are transformed into permanent ones had subsidies (€800 for three years) only if they were converted before January 1, 2007.[19]

This landmark pact balanced the demands of employers for lower dismissal costs and Social Security contributions, with those of the unions for increased unemployment benefits and more incentives for permanent jobs. The results of this reform were quite immediate. Yet, the overall impact was limited and the results somewhat disappointing: while the temporary rate decreased to 31.9 percent by November 2007 (a reduction of 2.5 points since the agreement was signed), it was still at the same level as was in 2004.[20] The crisis had a devastating impact over workers on temporary contracts, and both the Socialists and PP governments included provisions in their labor reforms (see below) modifying the limits to the renewal of temporary contracts, thus diluting the potential impact of this agreement.

At the end of 2007, the unions and employers' association signed a new interconfederal ANC to moderate wage growth in 2008. This was the seventh time such an agreement had been signed since the establishment of democracy, thus illustrating the institutionalization of this process,[21] with very positive results; starting in 2002, with the exception of 2006 and 2008, salary increases agreed in collective agreements grew less than inflation (see table 5.3)

For 2008, the social partners agreed to increase salaries 2 percent (the projected inflation), thus rejecting Finance Minister Solbes' demand for increases below inflation. The agreement outlined a set of criteria to regulate

Table 5.3   Results of Eight Years of Interconfederal Collective Agreements

	2002	2003	2004	2005	2006	2007	2008	2009
Inflation (December–December)	4.0	2.6	3.3	3.7	2.7	4.2	1.4	−1.4
Salary increase	3.9	3.7	3.6	4.0	3.6	4.2	3.6	2.67
+/− Number of strikes	690	680	710	669	780	750	810	166
+/− Number of collective agreements signed	5,400	5,500	5,400	5,700	5,800	6016	5304	

Source: Ministry of Labor and Bank of Spain.

the collective bargaining process in 2008 (about 5,000 agreements that include 10 million workers were pending), including a revision clause in case the inflation target was overshot, and allowed for additional increases based on productivity. The agreement also recognized the possibility of contagion from the global financial crisis and alerted about the end of the expansive cycle. It stressed the need to increase productivity.

One of the novelties of the agreement was that, following the approval of the *equality law* the previous March, it requested that collective agreements are adapted to new law (it required that equality plans are negotiated in firms with more than 250 employees) and may include affirmative action initiatives to facilitate women's access to those professions in which they were underrepresented; as well as initiatives to promote a better conciliation between the professional and family life (i.e., regulation of working time, professional classification, promotion, etc.). The agreement also included the commitment to combat labor accidents, previously agreed by the government and the social actors. The social partners also agreed to create a new institution in charge of overseeing safety in small companies (those between 6 and 50 workers), which were not obligated to have enterprise committees. Finally, it included provisions against mobbing and harassment, calling on companies to protect workers and investigate any complaints.[22]

To judge from data published by the National Statistics Institute, labor costs for companies (which include social contributions) increased by 4.2 percent in the third quarter of 2007, compared to the same quarter in 2006, and salary costs increased by 3.8 percent. This was the pattern during the previous years and one of the reasons for the erosion of the country's competitiveness. The impending crisis would showcase this serious shortcoming.

The Impact of the Crisis on Social Concertation

Following his electoral victory in March 2008, Zapatero confirmed his commitment to the social bargaining process. On June 18, 2008, he promised not to apply labor reforms without consensus, and stated his goal to draft a document outlining the issues that would be part of the social bargaining process. The following month he formalized this commitment and announced that he was planning to negotiate all his main policies (not just the social ones, but also the ones on infrastructure, energy, education, health, housing, and public administration) with the social partners.

This commitment was incorporated into the *social dialogue declaration* that was signed by the government, the employers' associations (CEOE and CEPYME), and the main unions (UGT and CCOO) on July 30, 2008. The government stated five main goals for the legislature: the support to companies, the maintenance of social protection, the promotion of women's rights and conciliation, the reform of the Social Security system, and the improvement of the growth potential of the economy.[23] To signal his personal commitment to this process, PM Zapatero decided to be the leading negotiator on the government side (instead of his labor minister, as was traditionally the case). The goal was to start the process the following September.

The crisis, however, would largely influence these plans. The deterioration of economic conditions was already noticeable by that summer, which led to most of the cabinet members' decision to postpone their vacations and to return to Madrid. The government even held a cabinet meeting in mid-August, the first in living memory. Unemployment figures showed that it had grown 24.7 percent the previous year, reaching 2.5 million in August 2008. The social peace, which had been a characteristic of the previous decades, would be severely tested in the months and years ahead.

In November 2008, the first signs of fracture became public; when the leader of the CEOE, Gerardo Díaz Ferrán, called for the lowering of dismissal costs, the unions responded aggressively calling him a "looter." And this was just the beginning of a widening gap. Unions and employers were not able to renegotiate the ANC for 2009. The crisis was already advancing like a hurricane, and the year 2008 ended with a much lower inflation rate (only 1.4 percent, compared to 4.2 percent in 2007). The failure of the negotiation process illustrated the growing gap between employers (who in view of the "exceptional situation" demanded lower wage increases to confront the crisis and thus requested lower wage increases than the inflation forecast: between 0 percent and 2 percent), and the unions (which demanded a 2 percent increase plus productivity, the same criteria used since 2002). Employers also demanded a reduction in Social Security contributions (which the unions adamantly opposed) and dismissal costs, and the elimination of the administrative approval for collective dismissals (the so-called EREs). The negotiations dragged on for much longer than in previous agreements, and in the end they were not able to breach their differences and reach an agreement. For the first time since 2002, there was no agreement.

In light of this new scenario, the Socialist government had to get involved directly to move forward the social concertation process. When Elena Salgado was named finance minister in April, she made it a priority for her to facilitate and lead the social dialogue process; PM Zapatero met with the leaders of the unions and employers' associations to mediate and push for agreements. When the IMF, the BCE, and the Bank of Spain published reports calling for a deep labor reform and the reduction of dismissals costs, PM Zapatero was adamant in publicly resisting those calls, stating that it was not in his government's program "to make dismissals cheaper," and that "it was not the right time for a labor reform."

The bargaining process formally started on May 26, 2009, and within a month there were seven meetings between the unions, the employers, and the government. These negotiations covered four main areas: unemployment protection, social contributions, measures to reactivate the economy, and innovation policies. Other items on the agenda included collective bargaining, professional training, labor mobility, organization of work, work schedules, labor accidents, and public services. In order to facilitate the process, the social actors decided to remove from the bargaining table the most controversial issues: new contract modalities and the reduction of dismissal costs.[24] Negotiations continued throughout the summer, in the midst of growing differences between employers and the unions, which forced the government to play a leading role and to meet separately with the social partners to try to bridge their differences.

The unions established their red lines: the extension of unemployment benefits for a year; the maintenance of Social Security contributions; and the continuing prohibition on temporary work companies to operate in certain sectors. Employers insisted that they wanted a social pact, but not at any price, and stressed the need to reduce Social Security contributions (they demanded a reduction of 5 points, with the government offering half a point, and the unions not accepting any cuts), and decided to include new contract modalities to deal with the crisis into the discussions.

In mid-July, the government announced new concessions to move the process forward: it accepted the unions' demand to extend the unemployment benefits for one year and to pay €420 to those unemployed who no longer received unemployment benefits; and offered employers a reduction of 2 points in their Social Security contributions. At this time, the government decided to take the reins of the negotiations, led by PM Zapatero, and they intensified in the second half of July.

Unfortunately, there was little progress and by the end of the month, PM Zapatero, convinced that the possibility of an agreement was evaporating, declared "war" against the employers' association for their intransigence, and decided to adopt some of the negotiating items unilaterally (like the extension of the unemployment benefits, approved by the government on August 13; or the increase of the lowest pensions and the measures to facility credit to companies). The government blamed the employers' association for the rupture of the negotiations and suspected that the employers had made the decision to wait until economic conditions deteriorated further in the fall to retake the negotiations in a more favorable climate to them.[25] The CEOE responded accusing the government of partiality and of being a "hooligan" of the unions. Afterwards, they invited the unions to new rounds of negotiations in September, with no "red lines." The unions responded negatively, accusing the employers of the third negotiating failure in six months, and asked the government to take unilateral action.

At the regional level, however, things were working better and, in August 2009, the government of Castilla-La Mancha signed an agreement with the unions and employers that included 85 measures and €2 billion to overcome the crisis.

The relationship between the employers' associations and the unions, however, continued deteriorating that fall. The unions resented the blockage in the negotiation of collective agreements at the sectoral and provincial levels (there were 1,500 collective agreements pending), and escalated the verbal confrontation with the employers. The CEOE leaders responded virulently to the government's plans to increase taxes to address the growing deficit, and continued calling for deeper structural reforms. Meanwhile, unions defended the government's management of the crisis, in addition to the tax increases.

At the end of September the leader of CCOO, Ignacio Fernández Toxo, offered employers the possibility of an ambitious wage agreement to address the ongoing crisis that would last for three years, through 2012 (paralleling what they did on the public sector). However, tensions between the government and the employers persisted throughout the fall, with the government calling for a restructuring of the business sector, rather than agreeing on a labor reform, and members of the government (PM Zapatero, ministers Salgado and Corbacho) making very critical comments against the CEOE and its leaders whom they accused on supporting the opposition PP policies. It was definitely not the most constructive environment to reach agreements.

Finally, a breakthrough took place in November when the CEOE accepted the unions' proposal to negotiate a multiannual agreement. On November 18, employers and unions signed an agreement (they called it a *Commitment to Act to Unblock Pending Collective Bargaining Agreements 2009*) to unblock the pending collective agreements, and agreed to negotiate a multiannual agreement before the end of the year. The signed agreement outlined directives to their affiliates to fulfill the salary agreements already signed, which were not being fulfilled (according to the unions there were 135 agreements that affected 1.2 million workers in such a situation). The document also invited the parties to use the mediation organisms for those cases in which the lack of compliance persisted. This was a concession by the employers, who up to that point had pushed for wage increases below 1 percent, while the unions supported increases of between 2 and 3 percent, based on forecasted inflation.[26]

This agreement paved the way for the negotiation of a new agreement on wages and employment. Negotiations among the social actors intensified throughout the end of the year with the government playing an active role by pushing for a new agreement that would include a labor reform. It proposed a new plan to promote youth employment (i.e., with subsidies to hiring) through the possible adoption of the German model, which gave employers the possibility to reduce the number of working hours of their employees with public support to avoid dismissals. Negotiation advanced and both unions and employers agreed on the need for a labor reform.

In December, PM Zapatero, while presenting in Congress the Law of Sustainable Economy (which included a large number of measures to change the productive model), announced a "limited" labor reform that would not reduce dismissals costs, calling on the unions and employers to negotiate it. He outlined the scope: the promotion of the use of part-time work, working hours reduction to promote employment (the German model), and changes to the collective bargaining system. He also made it clear that it would not include a new unitary contract, the reduction of dismissal costs, or the judicial exclusion from labor conflicts.[27] These were all demands from the employers, who still insisted on a labor reform without "red lines." The unions, for their part, organized a demonstration in Madrid on December 12 to pressure employers under the slogan "So they do not take advantage of the crisis" (*Para que no se Aprovechen de la Crisis*). The employers and opposition parties were very vocal against this demonstration for the lack of criticism against the government's policies.

PM Zapatero took advantage of the presentation in January of the annual economic report prepared by the Economic Office of the Government to continue pushing for negotiations. Unions and employers followed through and established a negotiating table to sign a new agreement on collective bargaining, and set the end of the month as the deadline. On a parallel track, they were all trying to negotiate a new labor reform with the aim of concluding it by March. The government planned to announce a labor reform proposal at the end of January, but the unions and employers asked for a delay that would give them time to conclude the collective bargaining agreement. The government agreed to postpone it until February 5, with the hope that the social partners would reach an agreement before the end of April.

During the negotiations, disputes flared regularly, with the employers pushing publicly for lower dismissal costs, and the unions opposing it and rejecting the repeated calls from employers and the Bank of Spain for a reform of the collective bargaining system. Employers viewed the reform as a potential solution to the crisis, and the unions interpreted the crisis as a financial one that made workers suffer. Still, they all publicly called for a rapid agreement.

In February, PM Zapatero gave the social partners a document, approved by the cabinet, outlining the master lines of a proposed labor reform. The main proposals included in the document were the promotion of indefinite contracts by pushing firms to use more often the contract to promote indefinite jobs (which had lower dismissals costs—33 per year worked versus the typical 45 days; but only 17 percent of the contracts used this model); obstacles to the renewal of temporary contracts; more inspections to limit temporary contracts; more young employment through training contracts; more part-time contracts; more flexible working hours in exchange for less dismissals; the revision of subsidies to hiring; and more flexibility within the companies through stronger and more comprehensive collective agreements that would include provisions regarding mobility, productivity, and adaptability.[28] The government also discussed the reform of the pension system. Employers initially expressed their satisfaction with the document, while declaring their displeasure with proposals that, in some cases, did not go far enough. The unions reaffirmed their complete opposition to the proposed changes to the pension system. The government reiterated that "workers would not lose rights," and rejected the option to extend the contract that allowed for dismissals with only 33 days of compensation.

Meanwhile, negotiations to conclude the agreement on collective bargaining and salaries were moving forward, and were concluded on February 8, 2010. The Agreement for Employment and Collective Bargaining (AENC) was signed the day after, and published in the Official Bulleting of State on February 22. The agreement was significant for a number of reasons. First, it would last three years (the previous ones had lasted only one year); second, it established salary increases for each year (up to 1 percent in 2010, between 1 and 2 percent in 2011, and between 1.5 and 2.5 percent in 2012); third, it had a broad and ambitious agenda: to make the economy more dynamic, improve competitiveness and employment, and generate confidence among citizens. Unions accepted wage moderation in exchange for employment. Finally, it set the instruments to achieve these goals: limits to temporal contracts (it opened the possibility to set, as part of a collective agreement, the total volume of temporary contracts allowed); clauses that would allow exceptions to the implementation of the agreement to those companies in serious financial difficulties; and, finally, more negotiations. It included a commitment from the social partners to negotiate a reform of the collective bargaining system within six months; and other issues like flexibility and safety.[29]

The negotiations to reform the labor market continued throughout March, with employers again raising the need to include a new contract with lower dismissal costs, which had already been rejected by the unions and the government. They insisted on their traditional demands to reduce Social Security contributions: to adapt the European directive on services, so that temporary work companies could intermediate in the labor market; and to changes in the collective dismissals process to eliminate the judicial approval. These demands had led to the collapse of the negotiations the previous year. They even proposed a new contract for young workers (up to 30 years old) that would not include any dismissal costs (the reaction to this proposal, labeled a "trash contract," was so negative that they removed it almost immediately). The government responded that they would not negotiate proposals that were not included in the document that they had presented to the social actors; while the unions reacted aggressively against the employer's proposals in addition to the way they made them public. The gap was so large that the government started considering a unilateral labor reform in case the negotiations failed again.

In April, the government introduced a new proposal based on the Austrian model. In Austria, companies established a fund for each worker that would be given to him/her in the case of dismissal, and would complement the state's unemployment benefits. This model promotes labor mobility because the worker takes with him/her the money from the fund that has not been used, accumulated through the workers' professional life. The government continued introducing new drafts, closer to the employer's positions. By mid-April, the unions reached the conclusion that the government was crossing two of their red lines: it sought to extend the contract with 33 days of compensation for dismissals; and it was opening the door to a reduction in the Social Security contributions for companies. They vehemently rejected them. PM Zapatero continued pushing for an agreement and met in person with the leaders of the unions and employers' associations. While all this happened, pressure mounted on Díaz Ferrán to resign due to a growing scandal in the operations of some of his companies. He resisted these calls and pressed on with the negotiations with the unions.

On April 12, the government published a new document to guide the negotiations.[30] It further developed the issues covered in the original document presented in February.[31] The government deadline of April 30 passed by with more meetings but little apparent progress. On the contrary, vitriolic exchanges (and insults) between the unions and employers made the negotiations more difficult. By May, it was becoming more and more evident that an agreement was unlikely and the government, under growing pressure to act from international institutions and the markets, started to prepare its unilateral reform. It announced that it would approve a labor reform on June 16, even if there was no agreement among the social partners. In preparation for such an outcome, the unions started to consider a possible general strike for the same month.

On June 9, after four months of negotiations, the government made a last ditch attempt to reach an agreement and presented a document to the unions and employers with six basis points. In an attempt to satisfy both the unions and employers, the government proposed a new dismissal model that would alleviate the costs for companies without reducing the compensation for the worker: it would resort to the Salary Guarantee Fund to subsidize part of the compensation. In the end, all these efforts were for naught, and the negotiations to reach an agreement failed, largely over significant differences about the causes of dismissals (i.e., when companies could adopt dismissals based on economic conditions with dismissal costs of 20 days per year applicable to all contracts), as well as costs of dismissals (the attempt to move away from the traditional contract based on 45 days of compensation per year worked, and to generalize the one based on 33 days of compensation). The attempt to balance the competing goals to reduce dismissal costs and the temporary rate by extending the contract with a dismissal cost of 33 days, strengthening barriers to temporary contracts, and increasing flexibility within the companies were not enough to satisfy the social partners. That day, after an 11-hours-long meeting, the government concluded that an agreement was not possible, and announced the approval of a new labor reform by decree the following week.

The government, yet again, made the CEOE responsible for the failure of the negotiations. A year earlier, negotiations failed because unions did not accept employers' demands to reduce their Social Security contributions. This time the reasons were more complex: at a time in which there was enormous pressure from within (the Bank of Spain) and outside (the EU, the IMF, the OECD, and the ECB) for a substantive labor reform, employers came to believe that they had a favorable environment to push for a drastic reform and were dissatisfied with the government's moderate proposals. Ultimately, the crisis had contributed to the collapse of the social concertation process. The breaking point was the government's attempt to set more difficulties to hire temporary workers. The unions started to prepare a general strike in response to the government decree.

The government labor reform decree introduced the following changes:

- **Temporary contracts:** the contract for work and service would now have a maximum duration of two years. It could be extended for another 12 months if it was so included in the collective agreement from that sector. The compensation for temporary contracts was increased progressively from 8 to 12 days per year.
- **Objective dismissals causes:** It is now recognized that there may be economic causes to justify dismissals when companies suffer losses. In such a case the compensation would be 20 days per year.
- **Contract to promote indefinite jobs:** It was applied only to workers between 31 and 45 years old, and it was now extended to all workers.
- **Fund to pay compensations:** The government would create a fund that would start in 2012 to subsidize dismissals from contracts to promote indefinite jobs. It would be funded with employers' contributions.
- **Participation of the Salary Guarantee Fund (Fogasa):** During the period before the fund is created, the compensation would be split between the company and the Fogasa.
- **Internal flexibility:** Companies are authorized to change labor conditions (schedules, imposition of different labor turns, or changes in remunerations in accordance with new schedule) during periods of economic difficulties to reduce the level of production and avoid dismissals. If the company and the workers disagreed on these measures, they would have to request a mediator, who would make the final decision.
- **Changes in Subsidies to hiring:** Different subsidies based on the type of contract to promote hiring of certain categories of workers and/or contracts (women, older than 45, indefinite contracts...)

- **Temporary Employment Companies:** the sector is liberalized and these companies can now operate in all sectors to orient, train, and employ workers. These companies would have to guarantee that the workers would have identical conditions in the companies in which they are placed.
- **Absenteeism:** Companies can dismiss workers who miss 20 percent of their working days during two consecutive months, with a dismissal cost of 20 days per year.

The government launched a round of discussions with political parties in parliament to discuss the content of the reform, and only the leftist IU rejected it, thereby taking the unions' side. The government also accepted the PP proposal to have the labor reform processed as a law in Congress. This way the other political parties would have the opportunity to introduce amendments. Still, the government did not receive the support from any other party, and the law was finally approved in September with 168 PSOE votes and 173 abstentions. The decree, however, became effective immediately. In the meantime, PM Zapatero called on the unions to make an effort to understand the context and need for the labor reform, while hoping that the reform would generate a new climate to get out of the recession and create jobs. His calls were not heeded and the unions decided to call a general strike against the labor reform on September 29. After six years of social peace, the unions felt compelled to call the first general strike against Zapatero's government (and the seventh general strike since the democratic transition).[32] In the end, the success of the strike was very uneven with the unions claiming that 10 million workers participated, and the government refusing to enter into a war of numbers and maintaining that in the public sector only 7.52 percent of the workers had participated in the strike.

Following the strike, the government initiated new efforts to reestablish a constructive relationship with the unions (even PM Zapatero was a member of the UGT), and to restart the social concertation process, now focusing on the reforms of the pension and the collective bargaining systems. The government organized a series of meetings throughout the first half of 2010 with the unions and employers. On October 20, there was a cabinet reorganization whereby Valeriano Gómez took over the labor department (see chapter 2). His main goal was to relaunch the social concertation process.

The formal negotiations started on November 12, 2010, when Minister Gómez met with the unions after the general strike. On December 19, the leaders of CCOO and UGT met with PM Zapatero and Minister Gómez, deciding to open a 15-day window to determine whether a pact was possible. The government made the decision to extend the range of issues on the table to try to reach an ambitious agreement that would cover not just the pension reform but also other areas. It was even willing to include other political parties in the agreement, something that had not happened since the Moncloa Pacts in the 1970s. To move the process forward the government also made the decision to involve all of its heavyweights (VP Rubalcaba and ministers Salgado and Gómez) in the process, and they met with the unions on January 8. The social actors were committed to trying to reach an agreement, and initially the goal was to reach an agreement against the crisis quickly. On January 11, CCOO's secretary general, Toxo, launched a proposal to sign an ambitious social pact that would involve the employers as well as the political parties. The agreement would incorporate, in addition to the pension reform, the reform of the collective bargaining system, active labor policies, and aspect of industrial and energy policies. One of the main novelties of this new bargaining round was that the CEOE was now represented by its new president Juan Rosell, who replaced Díaz Ferrán on December 22. His arrival to the CEOE's presidency led to changes in the employers' association approach, which now seemed more open to negotiations and to the possibility to reach an agreement.

Still, the main point of contention was over the proposed delay in the retirement age from 65 to 67 years. The government, lagging well behind in the polls, was under pressure to avoid another failure that could lead to yet another general strike and more social contestation. With the regional and local elections a few months away it became urgent to reach an agreement that could improve its electoral prospects. At the same time, it was under pressure from the markets and international partners to increase the pension age. Therefore, it did not relent on its insistence at the need to increase the retirement age to ensure the sustainability of the system (according to the government's projections, under the current system the balance between expenditures and income could be sustained only through 2023; by 2030, the costs of the pensions benefits would outweigh the contributions). In exchange, it offered the unions some flexibility regarding the transition period.

The negotiations moved forward quickly. Following the approval on January 25 by the Spanish parliament of the new recommendations for the Toledo Pact (which supported the progressive and flexible delay of the retirement age, prioritizing its voluntary character), an agreement on the contentious retirement age was finally reached on January 26 during a meeting with PM Zapatero. According to the agreement, in general, workers would be able to retire at 65 and enjoy the full pension if they had contributed for at least 38 years and 6 months, for the rest of the workers they would have to contribute 37 years to retire at 67 to keep the full pension. It would come into force in 2013, with a transition period that would run through 2027. The agreement also included active employment policies (the government agreed to design a global strategy for workers 55 years old and more, with around €400, which would be administered by the central government)[33] as well as the collective bargaining system (it set the foundations for a reform), which would be articulated and defined later in future negotiations.

The formal agreement was finalized by the social actors on January 31. In addition to the provisions regarding pensions, collective bargaining, and active labor policies, the government included a commitment to recuperate the public function roundtable (an organism to facilitate the dialogue between the government and civil servants), and to further develop the Statute of the Public Function (this was significant because civil servants were already suffering the consequences of the crisis with salary cuts of up to 5 percent). The document also included some statements regarding energy (i.e., the energy mix and the energy sources to be used) and industrial policies. The final decisions on both policy areas would be determined in subsequent negotiations.

The unions were willing to sign in after the government made a number of exceptions to the general rule for women and young people. This was particularly important because young workers typically joined the labor market later (the unemployment rate among young people stood at 52 percent), and typically worked under temporary contracts, which implied that they would have to work more years to meet the minimum requirement to access the full pension. According to the agreement, those who requested leave of absence to take care of their children (the overwhelming majority were women) could add nine months of contributions for each one of them, with a maximum of two years. Internships, for those who have completed their bachelor's degree, would count as part of the contribution period, for up to two years (companies would have to pay for it), and would be applied retroactively for four years. Early retirement at 61 years was strengthened as well; it would be allowed only in cases connected to a "crisis in the company," a concept that still had to be defined. The regular early retirement could still be requested at 63. Partial retirement was also strengthened as well, making it more costly for companies, and thus less attractive. It also included incentives to delay the retirement age. Finally, the agreement also introduced a provision to review these provisions every five years to examine changes in life expectancy, which opened the doors to automatic adjustments to the pension.[34]

This agreement confirmed again the strength of the concertation process, and it was a significant victory for the government, which was able to rebuild its relationship with the unions after the labor reform and the general strike, and was able to present a unified front to Spanish citizens, as well as its European partners and the markets. The government tried to give as much relevance to this agreements as the 1977 Pactos de la Moncloa, which was credited with contributing to the economic recovery of Spain during the transition, thus with the consolidation of the new democratic institutions. PM Zapatero declared that the new pact was "the most important reform since the *Pactos de la Moncloa*," and had it signed in the same room in which those Pactos were signed (the Salón de Tapices of the Presidency). It is worth noting, however, that neither the procedure (in 1977, the political parties were central actors in the negotiations, in addition to the unions and employers) nor the content (the Pactos were not only economic, but also included the reforms of several laws, as well as the approval of syndical and civil rights) nor the context (the Pactos took place during one of the most delicate times of the democratic transition in which much more was at stake: the democratic transition). The economic situation was also different; the key challenge was not so much the unemployment—760,000 unemployed in 1977 versus 4.2 million in 2011—but inflation, which reached 44 percent that year (in 2011 it was 3.5 percent).[35]

This agreement was followed by negotiations to reform the collective bargaining system. The goal was to complete the negotiations by the end of March. The main source of contention was the so-called ultra-activity of the collective agreements (i.e., the indefinite extension when the term of a collective agreement expires and there is not a new agreement to replace it). Other controversial issues included absenteeism (employers wanted to incorporate measures against unjustified absences); internal flexibility (at the time any actions to make adjustments, from furloughs, schedule reductions, salary reductions, or any functional changes within the company, had to be negotiated, with the delay that it implied); blockages in collective agreements; and new modality of contract for young workers. Employers wanted to eliminate that provision, and pushed for the decentralization of collective bargaining, in addition to more internal flexibility. The unions were willing to negotiate in all these areas but disagreed vehemently with the employers on their scope.

Although the goal was to complete the agreement by the end of March, as indicated above, the negotiations stalled and extended throughout May, with PM Zapatero intervening in a few occasions to try to move them forward. The local and regional elections were taking place at that time, and the social actors decided to wait until they were over, with the government setting as a deadline the end of the first week of June. However, significant differences between the unions and employers persisted, with the unions accusing the employers of backtracking from the agreements that they had already reached. The ultra-activity principle and internal flexibility remained as the main contentious issues.

Despite strenuous efforts, including PM Zapatero's participation in meetings, the negotiations failed. Indeed, following four months of negotiation after a last ditch effort to reach an agreement, the social actors announced the breakdown on June 3, 2011. Unions and employers blamed each other for the failure. The unions claimed that the employers kept adding new items to the ones listed in the economic and social pact signed in February to make the agreement impossible; it was a moving target. Employers accused the unions of not being sufficiently ambitious. The government and the unions were convinced that the results of the regional and local elections, which had given an overwhelming majority to the PP, also influenced the OECD's outlook, because employers could now expect that the PP would win the general election scheduled for the following March, and that it would implement a more radical reform.[36]

The failure of the negotiations forced the government to adopt a unilateral reform, approved by the cabinet on June 12, 2011 (see table 5.4). Based on this reform, all collective agreements had to include a mechanism to resolve conflicts. At a minimum, collective agreements must include provisions to name a parity commission of workers and employers that should determine the procedure to effectively resolve the differences that may emerge during negotiations to substantially modify the condition of work and salaries. If that channel failed, the parties could establish procedures, such as mediation or arbitrage for the resolution of collective grievances. Their decision would have legal value and can be appealed only if there are formal issues. The reform also established deadlines for negotiation to prevent blockages; in order to avoid endless negotiations, it set a maximum of 20 months since

Table 5.4 Main Components of the 2011 Collective Bargaining Reform

Area	Description
Unblocking of collective agreements	Neither employers nor unions can block indefinitely the renewal of a collective agreement. They will have 8 months for collective agreements that last 2 years, and 14 months if they last longer. If there is no agreement the parties must resort to arbitrage, whose resolution would be mandatory.
Arbitrator	Arbitrators emerge as a key figure in the reform, both to resolve conflicts in the renewal of collective agreements and conflicts related to internal flexibility.
Internal flexibility	The reform seeks to increase internal flexibility as a way to minimize dismissals. The parties have 15 days to agree in collective substantive changes to working conditions; if they cannot do it, they have to resort to the parity commission and arbitrage. In total they have less than one month to finalize the decision.
Salary adjustments	It is possible for firms to disengage from the salaries set by the sectoral agreement in case of economic difficulties.
Overtime	A percentage of the working day, measured annually, can be distributed throughout the year, based on the needs of the company. The minimum established by the reform is 5%.
Company-level collective agreements	The reform changed the previous framework that privileged provincial collective agreements over company-level ones. Companies that have been using a provincial one (70% of them according to the Labor Ministry), can negotiate a company-level agreement at any time. This would allow companies to adjust more rapidly to shifting market conditions.

Source: *El País*, June 11, 2011.

the communication of the expiration of the collective agreement. Finally, the reform allowed salaries negotiated at the firm level to be lower than those negotiated at a higher level.

Regarding internal flexibility (one of the most contentious issues), the reform established the obligation to include in the collective agreement a maximum and minimum percentage of the working day that is distributed irregularly throughout the year. If nothing is included, that percentage will be 5. If there were differences regarding internal flexibility, the parity commission would decide within seven days. If they did not reach an agreement, the parties could resort to mediation or arbitrage, which became the key instrument of this reform.[37]

Employers and opposition parties (PP and CiU) rejected the reform because they considered it "completely insufficient." The unions, while unhappy with some provisions, were satisfied that some of their key demands, notably the ultra-activity principle, were maintained.

Despite the failure, the social partners continued working together in other areas. The leaders of UGT and CCOO sent a letter to PM Zapatero in August offering the possibility to extend the AENC and to continue moderating wages, in exchange for the unblocking of the collective bargaining process that was preventing the signing of many agreements. At that time, inflation stood at 3 percent and the negotiated increase for new collective agreements was only 1.6 percent.[38] The CEOE, in light of the depth of the crisis, called for the annulment of the salary increases agreed for 2012, which the unions promptly rejected.

These disputes, however, did not prevent parallel discussions to move the agenda forward, and the leaders of the unions and the employers' association met several times throughout the fall to unblock the collective bargaining process. The CEOE prepared a document "Solutions from Employers to Confront the Crisis" that was distributed to the unions and political parties for their review and discussion. It called for the reform of the educational, judicial, and financial systems; opposed tax increases; supported austerity; the simplification of administrative requirements; and insisted on the unity of the market; and encouraged entrepreneurs, among many other things.

These meetings led to a new agreement, similar to the one signed in 2009, to unblock the collective bargaining process. On October 28, 2011, the leaders of the unions and employers' association signed a new agreement titled *Commitment to Act to Unblock Pending Collective Bargaining Agreements 2011*.[39] The main objective of the agreement was, again, to unblock the pending collective bargaining agreements. As in 2009, it outlined directives to their affiliates to fulfill the salary agreements already signed, inviting the parties to use the mediation organisms in those cases in which the lack of compliance persisted. Finally, the agreement called on the signatories to negotiate a multiannual agreement that could renew the AENC signed in 2010.

The Impact of the PP Victory

The end of the November 2011 general election and the PP victory gave a new impetus to the bargaining process. Shortly after the election, PM Rajoy met individually with the leaders of the unions and employers associations and asked them to try to negotiate "urgently" a new labor reform. He gave them until January 6 (they tentatively baptized it the "Epiphany agreement"), and requested that the reform address the following issues: collective bargaining, absenteeism, contracts, and mediation. He also discussed in these meetings pensions and the minimum wage. The government made it clear that it would legislate unilaterally, if the unions and employers failed to reach an agreement.[40]

The pressure of the crisis was such that in a record time the previous labor reform, which had been adopted just a year and a half earlier, had already become obsolete, and the government wanted the social partners to review it and develop a new proposal. PM Rajoy used, as an argument to push for an agreement, a letter that had been sent from the BCE to Spain requesting a competitive devaluation of salaries to regain competitiveness. Unions and employers met throughout the end of 2011 and beginning of 2012 with the government pressuring them with the threat of a unilateral reform.

The effects of the 2010 reform were still not visible. It sought to address the following problems: first, the duality of the labor market. However, the percentage of temporary contracts was still increasing despite the 2010 reform; 95 out of 100 contracts were temporary, and between 2010 and 2011, there were 14 new million contracts with only 1 million of them indefinite.[41] Second, the reduction of dismissals costs generalizing the 20 days per year compensation and the number of workers who used the so-called express dismissal (with 33 days, instead of the 45) dropped by more than 60,000 between January 2010 and November 2011. Third, with the creation of the capitalization funds, it wanted to give workers funds that would travel with them throughout their professional careers (this one was one of the highlights of the previous reform), but it could not be implemented for lack of funds. Fourth, increase internal flexibility: the new reform sought to facilitate collective mobility, the substantive modification of working conditions (changes in functions, schedule, position, etc.); and the adoption of clauses to unhook from higher level collective agreements. But it was too early to know the substantive effect (the new collective agreement in the chemical sector seemed to indicate that the reform allowed for more internal flexibility). Fifth, by strengthening the temporal collective dismissals ERE process; expedients to temporarily regularize employment (suspending or reducing the working day) became one of the best instruments to avoid dismissals, through internal flexibility. However, in 2009, they affected 485,000 workers and in 2011, 196,000 (the expedient to regulate employment-ERE extinction expedients affected only 63,000 in 2010 and 50,000 in 2011). Sixth, promotion of young employment with subsidies (the previous reform had been able to create only 8,000 new training contracts).[42] Given these paltry results, the new reform sought to move forward in all those areas, in a rapidly deteriorating labor market context.

On January 25, the unions and the employers' association signed the second AENC for three years: 2012, 2013, and 2014.[43] The negotiation had started the previous summer, but the electoral campaign made progress very difficult. The agreement established a maximum salary increase of 0.5 percent for 2012, and of 0.6 percent for 2013. In 2014, salaries would increase 0.6 percent if the economy grows less than 1 percent; and 1 percent if it grows between 1 percent and 2 percent. If it grows faster than 2 percent, the increase would be 1.5 percent. These increases were subject also to the evolution of inflation, and with safeguards clauses it would exceed 2 percent (but the rate of inflation used would be the Eurozone one, if the Spanish one exceed the Eurozone one). The agreement also included provisions regarding the structure of collective bargaining and the internal flexibility of companies in cases of economic crisis to try to avoid dismissals. It also called for the contention of top managers' salaries, as well as basic product prices.

Regarding internal flexibility, the new agreement called on the parties to increase the 5 percent minimum of time allowed to enterprises to reallocate the working hours (it was established during the previous labor reform in the Worker's Statute), to 10 percent. It also introduced more flexibility regarding overtime, allowing the collective agreements to include objective criteria that would allow companies to request overtime under urgent circumstances. Finally, the agreement included provisions regarding the structure of collective bargaining: both parties agreed to promote firm-level collective bargains, while maintaining provincial level agreements. The agreement did not include the thorniest issue: the cost of dismissals.[44]

Despite progress in all these areas, the government still felt that a deeper reform was needed and continued working toward that goal. PM Rajoy was heard at an EU summit stating that his labor reform would cost him "a general strike," and finance minister, Guindos, was on record stating that the reform would be "extremely aggressive."[45] The government still insisted, however, that there would not be a single contract because it was not unconstitutional (despite contradictory messages, including an article from Minister Guindos in the *Wall Street Journal* defending such a model). This was opposed both by the unions and employers. It also denied that it intended to reduce unemployment benefits.[46]

The new labor reform was announced on February 10. According to the government, its main goals were to reduce the duality in the Spanish labor market between temporary and indefinite contracts, as well as increase the internal flexibility for the companies. It generalized to 33 days of compensation for dismissals with a maximum of 24 months. It also added flexibility to the criteria under which employers could use the model of dismissals with a cause (the so-called *despido procedente*), which was subject to a lower compensation of 20 days per year worked and a maximum of 12 months; it allowed companies to pay 20 days when the company had "actual or forecasted losses," or a "diminution of sales during three consecutive quarters." By defining more clearly other objective causes for dismissals, the goal was to reduce the judicial flexibility that existed up to that point, in which labor courts made the determination (typically in favor of the worker). The result was when firms admitted that a dismissal was not justified they typically adopted the so-called express dismissal process that forced them to pay a higher compensation to the dismissed workers (in 2011 60 percent of the dismissals adopted this model) (see table 5.5). The reform eliminated that option.[47]

The reform also eliminated the administrative approvals for expedients of employment regulation or EREs, which applied to collective dismissals. Before the reform, firms that wanted to adopt an ERE had to request approval from the Ministry of Labor; and it was essential that there was agreement between the unions and the employers. Since it was very difficult to reach an agreement, companies tended to increase the amount of compensation and pay more than the 20 days and 12 months established by the law. The reduction in compensation for dismissals would also affect existing ordinary contracts (protected by 45 days prior to this reform). After the reform two scales would be applied: if a worker is dismissed he/she would get compensated for 45 days per year that she/he worked at the company for the period prior to the reform; and for 33 days for the period after the reform has been approved and published (February 11, 2012). The reform also eliminated the so-called *salarios de tramitación* (transition salaries) that workers received while they were appealing a dismissal until a judge made a final decision. Now they would receive them only if the company loses the case and readmits the worker.

In order to address youth unemployment, the government created a new indefinite contract for SMEs that combines unemployment benefits with a salary, and it reinstated the prohibition suspended by the Socialist government to renew temporary contracts for more than 24 months starting on December 31. The new contract for entrepreneurs establishes a reduction in labor costs SMEs of less than 50 workers who hire an unemployed worker aged 30 years old or younger. These workers will continue receiving 25 percent of the unemployment benefits, and the employer will not

Table 5.5 Evolution of Dismissals by Type (2009–2011)

Year	Labor court	Express dismissal	Objective cause	Conciliation	ERE	Other
2009	1.84	70.09	14.97	3.74	7.83	1.52
2010	2.45	65.53	17.97	3.23	9.09	1.93
2011	1.86	57.94	24.73	2.68	10.33	2.47

Source: Ministry of Employment.

have to pay 50 percent of the benefit accrued to the employee for up to a year, even if this period coincides with the trial period established in the new contract. In addition to this contract, the government modified the bonuses to the Social Security quotas: companies can save up to €3,600 when they hire with indefinite contracts young workers of between 16 and 30 years of age. The bonus increases along with the tenure of the worker in the company.

One of the most surprising components of the reform was the provision allowing employers to reduce workers' salaries without the need of an agreement, based simply on reasons of competitiveness or productivity. The decree that published the reform included "salary quantity" as one of the work conditions that the company can modify based on "technical, organizational, or production reasons," defining these reasons as "those that are related with competitiveness, productivity, or the technical organization of work of the company." It would affect workers with salaries above the minimum ones set in their collective agreement. Whenever they do, this new provision opened the door to salary reductions at the discretion of the company, which could now reduce salaries to lower costs, and/or to punish workers who are not performing adequately (e.g., it would be relatively easy to allege competitive reasons to reduce salaries).[48]

This was a crucial provision that responded to domestic and external demands for an "internal devaluation," now that a traditional devaluation was no longer an option because the country was a member of the EMU. According to many observers economic conditions would not improve in Spain until nominal wages fell (in Ireland they had already fallen by 25 percent, and this factor was credited with the faster recovery of the Irish economy). Unions and employers agreed to salary increases of only 0.5 percent in 2012 and 2013, in exchange for a generic commitment to maintain employment. This decision was based on what happened in 2009 when the economy and unemployment sank while salaries increased. The agreement tried to address that. But many observers insisted that it was insufficient and argued that salaries would have to decrease by between 5 percent and 15 percent. This would contribute to increase the competitiveness of Spanish firms and help increase exports, which would be critical in a context of depressed internal demand. Unions, however, resisted it and pointed it to the fact that in 2012, for the first time, companies' income (46.2 percent) was higher than workers' (46 percent).[49]

In the area of training, the labor reform undertook a substantive reform of the professional training system, and established that workers have the right to 20 hours of training paid by their companies. Furthermore, the maximum age to qualify for a training contract increased to 30 years until the unemployment rate decreases to 15 percent, which is not limited to only one sector. In addition, the reform allows temporary work companies to operate as employment agencies. For groups that have been particularly hit by unemployment, like women, the reform established aid of up to €4,500 for companies who employ unemployed women older than 45 years of age for the first three years of the contract depending on the sector (€1,500 per year). This assistance was reduced to €4,200 in the case of men. In the case of temporary suspension of work for a deterioration of activity, the reform introduced a 50 percent bonus in the companies' Social Security contributions for those workers affected by the reduction in their working hours, with a maximum duration of 240 days, and conditioned to the maintenance of employment for at least one year. If the companies eventually eliminated the position, the unemployment benefits for the employee would not be affected. The reform, surprisingly, did not simplify the existing wide range of temporary contracts.

The reform also dealt with collective bargaining; it limited to two years the extension of collective agreements expired, thus eliminating the so-called principle of "ultra-activity" that allowed for indefinite extension of collective agreement after they expired. If the social partners do not reach an agreement to renew it within those two years, the workers will be covered by the one adopted at the higher level (from the company to the provincial, autonomous region, and sectoral), and if they do not exist, by the Workers Statute. It also included provisions that outlined the causes to declare a collective agreement inactive; it incorporated part of the recently signed AENC 2012, 2013, 2014, which established the prevalence of company-level contracts over the sectorial ones. The reform also further developed the agreement between the social partners, establishing that in those cases of conflict in which there was no solution and the arbiter could not come to a resolution, they would be decided by the National Commission of Collective Agreements (the Comisión Nacional de Convenios), in order to ensure there would be a final decision.[50] These provisions sought to add incentives to force the social partners to reach agreements.

This was an ambitious reform that was expected to set a new period (a "before and after") in the labor relations arena. It responded to longstanding demands from the CEOE to reduce dismissal costs and the intervention of the administration, to increase the internal flexibility of companies, to eliminate the principle of ultra-activity, and to give priority of company-level collective agreements. They declared the reform as "deep," "substantive," and "helpful to create jobs." Even the German chancellor, Angela Merkel, supported the reform and applauded the government's determination to address the country's economic problems.[51] It aligned dismissal costs in Spain with those of its European partners; no other country compensated dismissed workers with as many as 45 days per year worked with a maximum of 42 months (in Germany, it is 18 months).[52]

Unsurprisingly, the unions reacted negatively, immediately announcing a plan of incremental mobilizations that would start on February 19 against the reform. They accused the government of lowering dismissals costs (something that, as we saw in chapter 2, they had promised not to do), reducing the administrative and judicial oversight of dismissals, and to opening the door to reduce salaries. According the union leaders the reform would "accelerate the destruction of employment with the reduction of dismissal costs, the easy criteria established to justify losses, and the lowering of criteria that determines the objective causes for dismissals," declaring the reform "radical," "useless," "unbalanced," and "tremendously damaging to workers' rights."[53] The decision to postpone a possible general strike was based on political calculations (there were regional elections scheduled in March in Andalusia and Asturias); economic (the government still needed to approve the budget for 2012); and strategic (the very dire situation of the Spanish economy, and the high unemployment level, which typically contribute to demobilizing workers).[54]

The PSOE declared its resounding opposition to the reform, classifying it as a *decretazo* (a massive decree) that would serve only to incentive dismissals, and would not create employment. It decided to challenge its constitutionality because it violated articles 24 (effective judicial protection) and 37 (collective bargaining).[55] The Spanish citizens' reaction was more nuanced. In a poll published before the final text of the reform was published, most of the respondents (66 percent, including 56 percent of the PSOE voters) felt that a reform was necessary (both the unions and the Socialists declared that it was not); 73 percent supported the possibility to allow workers to reach agreements with employers outside of the collective agreements' framework, and 42 percent felt that the unions were largely concerned with those who already have jobs (the "insiders) and were hindering reforms (46 percent would support a general strike, and 50 percent reject it). Yet, 70 percent opposed salary reductions. The concern about the economy was translated to an erosion of support for the EMU: 27 percent supported a return to the *peseta* (67 percent supported the euro).[56]

The demonstrations called by the unions on February 19 under the slogan "*Not to a labor reform unfair to workers, inefficient for the economy, and useless for employment,*" were relatively successful: the unions declared that more than half a million people participated in the demonstration in Madrid; 400,000 in Barcelona, 150,000 in Valencia. But the government challenged those figures. Following that success, the unions moved forward with their mobilizations' agenda, and called for new demonstrations on March 11 (widely criticized because of the coincidence with the anniversary of the terrorist attack in Atocha), and for a general strike on March 29. The general strike of March 29 culminated with massive demonstrations in cities across the country, with strong participation in Madrid (about 170,000 people) and Barcelona (275,000).

The processing of the reform through Congress, to be approved by law, led to further changes that deepened some of its provisions (bringing them even closer to the CEOE's preferences). The limit to the indefinite extension of collective agreements that had not been renewed was reduced from two years to one; in addition, it gave even more power to the employers to change unilaterally working conditions, by allowing them to control up to 10 percent (1,750 hours) of the annual working time (as opposed to the existing 5 percent), and the worker only needs to be informed 5 days ahead. In a signal to the unions, the PP negotiated with CiU and amendment to increase the supervision by the administration in cases of collective dismissals (in which they can advise and mediate; and the Labor Inspection service has to elaborate a report about collective dismissals to make sure that companies fulfill the legal obligations of information and negotiation). And, the contract created to allow companies with less than 50 workers to hire workers with a trial period that could last up to one year, in which they can be dismissed without any compensation, would be legal *only as long as* the unemployment rate stays above 15 percent, under the argument that it is a "crisis contract" (unemployment stood at 24 percent at the time, and it was not expected to get under 20 percent until 2017 at the earliest). Other changes included a new definition of the objective cause based on the annual reduction of production: a persistent fall of income as a base of objective dismissal with 20 days of compensation would be accepted when ordinary income falls during three consecutive quarters relative to the same period the year before. The same rule applies, but based on only two quarters, to cases in which the employer is trying to change substantive labor conditions (salary, schedule, transfers, etc.). It also included more bonuses for autonomous workers who hire relatives (50 percent of the Social Security contribution for 18 months). And finally, it allowed companies with profits and with more than 100 workers who dismiss workers 50 years old or older (preretirement) to pay the unemployment cost (before it applied to companies with more than 550 workers).[57]

Just a few months after the adoption of the reform, its pernicious impact was already noticeable (although it is difficult to isolate the impact of the reform from the impact of the crisis). By March 2012, the number of objective dismissals (with lower compensation) had already surpassed the number of nonproceeding ones, 35,480 versus 32,590; and the number of collective dismissals, which no longer required administrative approval, had doubled from 6,500 to 11,064 compared with the previous year (although the crisis had also intensified). Objective and disciplinary dismissals increased between 20 and 30 percent, according to some sources. Prior to the reform, there had also been an increase in the judicialization of cases, which increased by 50 percent between 2009 and 2012, with the expectation that they would increase even more after the reform.[58] Finally, the negotiation of collective agreements fell down to record lows after the reform; between January and August, only 1,113 agreements were signed, the lowest number in record since 1981. The number of workers covered in collective agreements also fell to 2.9 million, the lowest since 1994.[59]

Conclusion

The crisis had an impact both electorally and in the process of social concertation. Electorally, Spain has followed the path of many of its neighboring countries. Following the Socialist reelection in March of 2008, when the impact of the crisis on the Spanish economy was not yet visible, the incumbent government has suffered the ire of Spanish voters and has lost every single major election that has taken place since the effects of the crisis intensified throughout the second half of 2008. This erosion of electoral support culminated in November 2012 when the Socialist Party suffered the worst electoral results since the establishment of democracy, and the PP won with an absolute majority.

While the PP's popular support has suffered dramatically in only a few months in power (see chapter 2), this decline has not been accompanied by better prospects for the Socialists, who are still blamed for the initial denial and lack of action to address the crisis, as well as for the consequences of the crisis, and the government's programmatic shift to deal with it. It seems they have a long way to go to regain the voters' confidence.

From a social concertation perspective, the record is more nuanced. While there have been two unilateral labor reforms and two general strikes in 2012 against the government's policies (the last one took place on November 14), there have also been significant instances of cooperation and agreement among the social partners. The economic crisis has clearly impacted the approach and the leverage that unions and employers brought to the bargaining table. The devastating effect of the crisis and the dramatic increase in unemployment, in particular, severely weakened the unions and strengthened the hand of employers throughout the crisis. This chapter has shown how employers changed tactics and hardened their position, the weaker the unions and the Socialist government positions became (i.e., after the local and regional elections when they were negotiating the reform of the collective bargaining system). In many cases, the political agenda and calendar (i.e., the prospect of a PP victory in 2011) were instrumental in setting the negotiating agenda, and contributed to the breakdown of negotiations.

Notwithstanding these differences, the crisis has also showed the resilience of a bargaining process that has already been institutionalized for decades. Even when the social partners' negotiations ended in rupture, their initial approach was to negotiate and to try to find a negotiated solution.

Why Are the Social Actors Still Interested in Social Concertation?

As I have discussed elsewhere (Royo 2008), the interest of social partners pushes them toward negotiations. Successful coordination depends not only on the organization of the social actors but also on their interests and strategies. Social bargaining is a political process; therefore, it is necessary to examine the political settlements that motivate the social actors. Spanish firms decided that while competitiveness was contingent on the increasing flexibility of labor and firms, it also depended on the ability of the national system in which they operate to provide collective goods—namely, education, training, wage coordination, and labor cooperation. Hence, they acknowledged that the crucial problem for their firms was the need to institutionalize further the production of collective goods. Consequently, firms gave priority to continuing social concertation and supported cooperative strategies as instruments to further competitiveness. They understand that the most effective way to achieve wage moderation, increase competitiveness, and liberalize the labor market is through the acquiescence of unions. Confrontation led to higher wages and the partial paralysis of the reform and liberalization processes in the second half of the 1980s and first half of the 1990s because unions mobilized in opposition to these reforms and were able to exercise a de facto veto power. Concertation, on the other hand, has resulted in wage moderation and offered a gradual and stable path toward reform and liberalization of the labor market (Royo 2008, 227–228). The state has played a crucial role in these processes facilitating (and participating in) the bargaining process, providing incentives to the actors and enacting legislation to implement the agreed reforms.

For the unions, tripartite bargaining was as a defensive strategy to retake the initiative and influence policy outcomes (Royo 2008, 242–243). In addition, the resurgence of social bargaining was fostered by a process of institutional learning, which led union leaders to conclude that previous confrontational strategies were detrimental to the interest of their constituencies, and threatened their own survival. Indeed, with their support for these agreements, unions sought to mitigate the decline in their bargaining power at the workplace level. With these pacts they have also tried to counteract the reduction in their capacity for collective action, which has been a consequence of being sidelined by employers and governments, as well as the erosion of their influence in the policymaking process.

Furthermore, a process of institutional learning fostered the resilience of social bargaining, despite the crisis, learning, and increasing autonomy by unions from political parties (Royo 2008, 278). This development also reflects an attempt by the social actors to reconcile the need to control costs through more flexibility in hiring practices and the need for cooperative relations at the firm level in order to remain competitive. In other words, these agreements have constituted an institutional mechanism to support business competitiveness through consultative practices.

What Can We Expect of the 2012 PP Labor Reform?

It is important to note that Spain has a long history of unilateral reforms imposed by the governments that have not produced the desired results.[60] Indeed, since the Workers Statute was adopted in 1980, it has been revised almost 50 times, almost one change every half a year, to try to address the main weaknesses of the Spanish labor market since the democratic transition: the duality of the labor market (with over 30 percent, the highest rate of temporary work among the developed countries); and the high level of unemployment (as we have seen, Spain was among the fastest job creators in the EU during the boom year, mostly through temporary contracts, yet it has also been the fastest destroyer of jobs since the crisis started and has, by far, the highest rate of unemployment in the EU). To address these problems that has been multiple reforms (notably in 1992, 1994, 1997, 2002, 2010, and 2012). Nothing, so far has really worked.

Some analysts (and most employers) have claimed that the problem has been that the reforms have never gone far enough, that they have not been able to transform a labor market structure and regulatory framework that was largely inherited from an authoritarian regime. According to this view, the labor market has been a drag on the modernization of the country's economic structure. Unions (and other analysts) claim that the problem is not the regulation of the labor market, but instead the economic activity, the flow of credit (or lack thereof), and the productive model, which so far was largely able to create temporary jobs. This debate has not been merely political or academic, but it has also been contested in the streets through multiple general strikes: so far in 1978, 1985, 1988, 1992, 1994, 2002, 2010, and twice in 2012.

Most observers agree that the 1984 labor reform may have been possibly the most transformational one because it was the one that introduced the use of temporary contracts (lowering dismissal costs was politically unfeasible at the time, and this provided a backdoor flexibility mechanism to address unemployment). Successive reforms have tried to address the problems created with that decision (e.g., the dualization of the labor markets between *insiders* with indefinite contracts and more protection; and *outsiders* with temporary ones and less protection, or unemployed), but they have done so largely on the margins and have tried to limit the temporary rate.

The 1994 reform eliminated the temporary contract without cause, allowed individual dismissals for objective cause, as well as reformed the content of collective bargaining. However, the unions resisted it (it led to another general strike) and paralyzed it in collective bargaining. It took almost three years (after PM González lost the election) to observe substantive changes in the content of collective bargaining. This was yet another instance in which the lack of consensus led to the inadequate and insufficient implementation of a labor reform, which ended failing to address its intended goals.

Aznar introduced in his first reform the contract to promote permanent employment with a lower dismissal cost of 33 days (a principle generalized by the PSOE reform of 2010), but failed to really dent the temporary rate (which remained over 30 percent); in 2001, the PP imposed an eight-day compensation per year worked to temporary contracts, with a similar result, and the PSOE tried again in 2006 with bonuses for hiring permanent workers, with very limited improvements. Only the current crisis worked (the temporary rate has been reduced to 25 percent), but at the expense of employment (the unemployment rate exceeded 24 percent in the summer of 2012).

The lack of consensus to reform substantially the structure of collective bargaining has been yet another important factor to account for the insufficient internal flexibility for companies, and for the stickiness of salaries, which tend to be unresponsive to economic conditions, and which, in turn, has often led to more dismissals during periods of crises. And here the responsibility is shared. Contrary to many misconceptions, employers have not been traditionally supportive of giving primacy to company-based collective agreements. On the contrary, as proved by their last agreement with the unions in 2012 in which they agreed to maintain provincial level collective agreements, they supported an articulated structure that would suit their organizational strengths.

All these examples show the limited efficacy of unilateral reforms and the benefits of social concertation. It remains to be seen what the impact of the PP February 2012 reform will be. It has been in many ways a much more radical reform than the previous ones, yet if history is of any value, we should temper our expectations.

CHAPTER 6

The Crisis and the Spanish Financial System

Introduction

This chapter aims to examine changes in Spain's national financial system and the extent to which Spain has been affected by the international financial crisis (see Royo 2013a and 2013c).[1] It seeks to address two complementary questions: how has the Spanish financial system been affected by the global financial crisis and why? and how did it respond to it and why? As we have seen throughout the book, by the summer of 2008, the effects of the global crisis were evident in Spain, and since then the country has suffered one of the worst recessions in history. In the summer of 2012, Spanish financial institutions seemed to be in the brink of collapse and the crisis of the sector had forced the EU in June (2012) to devise an emergency €100 billion rescue plan for the sector. However, during the first stage of the crisis (2008–2010) its impact on the financial sector was limited, and particularly the large banks performed relatively well compared with their counterparts in other countries.

Indeed, between 2008 and 2010 the Spanish financial system, despite all its problems, was still one of the least affected by the crisis in Europe. During that period, of the 40 financial institutions that received direct assistance from Brussels, none was from Spain (as of June 2010, a dozen were from Germany, five from the UK, six from the Benelux, and four from Ireland). Furthermore, the public amounts that were committed to support those institutions were astronomical: 3,300 billion or 28 percent of the EU's GDP, in capital injections (315 billion), the purchase of damages assets (103 billion) and guarantees (2900 billion). In contrast, the support provided to Spanish institutions (loans at 7.7 percent interest rate) only reached 30 billion (just 1 percent of the total).[2] In December 2010 Moody's ranked the Spanish banking system as the third strongest of the Eurozone, only behind

Finland and France, above the Netherlands and Germany, and well ahead of Portugal, Ireland, and Greece. Finally, Santander and BBVA had shown new strength with profits of €4.4 billion and €2.8 billion, respectively, during the first half of 2010. How do we explain this (short-lived) performance? This paradox needs to be explained.

This chapter shows that Spanish regulators had put in place regulatory and supervisory frameworks, which initially shielded the Spanish financial system from the direct effects of the global financial crisis. Indeed, the Bank of Spain had imposed a regulatory framework that required higher provisioning, which provided cushions to Spanish banks to initially absorb the losses caused by the onset of the global financial crisis.

Nevertheless, this success proved short lived. When the crisis intensified, the financial system was not able to escape its dramatic effects. Indeed, the collapse of the real estate market eventually led to a traditional banking crisis fueled by turbo-charged lending by market-based banking on the liability side of the Spanish banks' balance sheets. In order to explain this outcome the chapter focuses on the following variables: first, the regulatory framework; second, the institutional features of the banking system, including the role of the Bank of Spain; and, third, the impact of macroeconomic developments, such as the collapse of the real estate sector and the economic crisis, on banks' accounts.

Finally, Spain is rather unique that the largest banks have not faced massive problems so far. Indeed, as late as August 2012, analysts and markets are still drawing a distinction between strong and weak banks and trying to recognize the management and lending standards of the so-called Big Three—Banco Santander, BBVA, and La Caixa—as opposed to those of many cajas, which were often run by politicians with little (if any) financial and banking experience. While the cajas were struggling under the weight of bad mortgages and loans to construction companies, the Big Three's exposure to toxic assets associated with the Spanish real estate sector has been a relatively small problem for them; BBVA and Santander have diversified internationally giving them access to greater resources, funding, and capital, which has allowed them to liquidate the toxic property assets at a lower price than their rivals, and with limited damage to their earnings. Net profits for the first quarter of 2012 at Santander (€1.6 billion and 1 billion respectively) were more than ten times greater than their nearest rival, La Caixa, which lacks the international diversification of the other two and depends largely on a powerful branch network that is located in a market mired in recession.[3] The real problems in Spain have been largely at the next level down, with the cajas. In this regard Spain is different from Germany, where both the large private banks and the Landesbanks were badly impacted by the global financial crisis.

The chapter proceeds as follows. Section one outlines some of the main features of the Spanish financial system. Section two analyzes the initial impact of the crisis on the Spanish financial system during the 2008–2010 period, and the initial responses of the government and the Bank of Spain to the crisis. Section three looks at the reasons that explain how and why the Spanish financial system responded to the crisis the way it did. Section four examines the deteriorating performance of Spanish institutions in the latest stages of the global financial crisis and explains this reversal, which led to the EU financial rescue of June 2012. It looks in particular at the collapse of Bankia, as it symbolizes the main problems that plagued most of the cajas. The chapter concludes recounting some brief lessons from the Spanish experience.

The Structure of the Spanish Financial System

Since Spain joined the EU on January 1, 1986, the Spanish financial system has been adapting to the European context. The regulatory organs of the Spanish financial system are all the institutions with competences to dictate legal norms (i.e., the government, Congress, and the Ministry of Economy); while the supervisory organs are the Bank of Spain and the CNMV. The Bank of Spain is the central supervisory institution. Regulated by the 13/1994 Law of Autonomy of the Bank of Spain (which has been subsequently partially modified), the Bank is in charge of the supervision of all credit institutions. It shares some competences with the Autonomous Communities, which also have supervisory power over the savings banks (Cajas de Ahorros) and credit cooperatives. Finally, The CNMV, created by the 24/1988 Law, is the institution in charge of supervision and inspection of stock markets and the activities of legal and physical people involved in these markets.

Most of the cajas were established in the nineteenth century as pawnshops with the support of the Catholic Church and/or local municipalities with the aim of redistributing their profits through social work (they dedicated a significant portion of their provisions, typically over 20 percent to social causes). Over time, most of them came under the control of the regional and local governments that often used them to advance their political agendas. They were regulated by both the national government (in charge of the basic norms), and by the autonomous communities governments (in charge of the application and development of the rules established by the central government). Political institutions (parties and unions) participated in the governing bodies of the cajas.

The distinctive regulatory framework that separates cajas from commercial banks is a crucial factor in explaining the differences in performance between the cajas and commercial during the crisis. Indeed, in the past decades cajas made a push to increase their market share, and they expanded aggressively beyond their traditional markets, competing with traditional commercial banks to offer real estate loans. When the real estate bubble collapsed after 2007, many of them accumulated billions of euros of loans at risk of default, and were forced to require state support.

Prior to the liberalization of the late 1980s and 1990s, the Spanish financial systems (like those of Greece and Italy) was a typical credit-based Mediterranean system, characterized by extensive interventionism, state control over the banking system, and underdeveloped capital markets (Pérez and Westrup 2010). The role of financial institutions was to provide funding toward the process of economic development and industrialization (Pérez 1997; Lukauskas 1997), and bank deposits were turned into low-interest credit for industrial enterprises and the government (Deeg and Pérez 2000). The oligopolistic nature of the sector generated significant costs for Spanish firms outside the finance sector (Pérez 1997).

The liberalization of the sector started in the second half of the 1980s, driven by the country's integration in the European Community and the subsequent European single market program. In Spain's case the process of financial liberalization was also part of the Bank of Spain's effort to achieve effective disinflation (Pérez and Westrup 2010). The European integration process, and particularly the creation of the Single Market and the EMU, has been a driving factor in subsequent developments. While financial regulations are still the responsibility of the national governments, in reality over the past two decades there has been a harmonization process throughout all the member states. This process led to the liberalization, modernization, consolidation, and opening up of the system.

Yet, the degree of financialization[4] of the sector was relatively low prior to the crisis and the majority of banks assets were loans to customers, and a significant part of bank assets involved Spanish government securities, which were considered among the safest possible asset investments. This relatively low degree of financialization of Spanish banks (like Italian and Greek ones) can be explained by the slow evolution of the national financial system and Spanish banks' reluctance to change a business model that has been consistently successful for decades. Credit institutions concentrate approximately 94 percent of the credit process, which illustrates the high relative weight of financial intermediation in the Spanish economy. Indeed the Spanish financial system is considered as highly banckarized (*bancarizado*) given the strong direct or indirect weight of credit institutions, particularly banks and cajas.

According to the Bank of Spain data on the liabilities side, Spanish banks have traditionally been very active in capital markets (though not relative to other countries), relaying particularly on the interbank markets for their funding (on an average about 20 percent of the total), while cajas and credit cooperatives, which have been more successful capturing resources from their customers, have not been so dependent on those markets (only around 7 percent). Spanish banks lend more than what they get in deposits, which forces them to rely on wholesale markets to fill the gap. This has forced them to rely heavily on the ECB during the crisis, as we discuss below.

Furthermore, the ECB data shows that customer loans as a percentage of assets were 67.31 percent at the end of 2007, a much higher percentage compared to other countries, such as the UK, Germany, or France. This would place Spain very low on a "market-based banking graph."

However, securitization provided collateral for about 16.9 percent of bank lending in Spain, suggesting that much of this bank lending was financed from the market. This is actually moderately high in comparative terms (for instance, in France it is only 2.9 percent). Thus, a lot of the Spanish credit boom was fed by the securitization of liabilities, which allowed Spanish banks to lend more. This was not off–balance sheet, but the result (increased lending) was similar to what we have seen in other countries like the UK (although about 50 percent less in GDP terms). Thus market-based banking is still pretty important to Spain. According to the IMF, at the end of 2007, cross-border liabilities as a percentage of GDP represented only 60.6 percent, a much lower figure than that of countries such as France (157.6 percent) or Germany (143.3 percent). International liabilities as a percentage of total liabilities represented 24.1 percent (versus 66.1 percent in the UK or 77.7 percent in Ireland). This seems to suggest low market-based funding.

How Was the Spanish Financial System Affected by the Global Financial Crisis between 2008 and 2010?

Spanish banks and cajas have been unable to escape the crisis. The weak underbelly has been principally the cajas, unlisted and regionally based and often politicized savings banks, which account for half of the financial sector's assets. During the boom years they successfully captured market share from the banks, investing heavily in the real estate (lending to consumers, developers, and constructions companies). They are now facing the consequences of the collapse of that sector.[5]

And the crisis has extended to commercial banks as well. Banif suffered the collapse of Lehman Brothers because it had invested more the €500 million from its investors in Lehman's bonds. Under threats of litigation from its customers, Banif decided to compensate them partially, with the overall result that they lost 40 million past year. Bankinter, BBVA, Bancaja, Altae (Caja Madrid) and Banco Sabadell also sold these products to their investors and lost money as well. In addition, Banco Santander and BBVA have also been immersed in the Madoff fraud case: customers of Optimal, Banco Santander's Swiss-based hedge funds management, may have lost up to €2.3 billion through investments with Madoff; and BBVA has announced that it may have lost up to €300 million. Santander has already announced that it will compensate its clients.

The crisis is also affecting the banks' profitability, particularly in the Spanish market where their benefits have been decreasing since 2008 (for instance, they declined 10 percent in 2009). Spain's largest banks have been helped by their geographical diversification as they were very active with foreign acquisitions during the past two decades in the United States, Mexico, Brazil, and the UK, among other countries. This has limited their exposure to the weak economy of the home country and helped them when the crisis struck: for instance, about a fifth of Santander's profits come from Brazil and another fifth from the UK. This is in contrast with France and other Central European banks that have not benefited so much from their international expansion, and in the case of Austrian banks, have been severely impacted by the crisis in Eastern Europe.

The biggest threat for Spanish banks in the medium term has been their heavy exposure to the Spanish property crash, and their dependence on international wholesale financing (40 percent of their balance depends on funding from international markets). The delinquent rate increased to 5 percent in 2009 and it reached 7 percent in 2010, and over 8 percent in 2012. During the crisis the exchange of debt for unpaid real estate assets at fictitious prices became a somewhat typical instrument to hide their real delinquent rates for many institutions. According to some estimates, commercial banks have exchanged debt for real estate assets valued at €10,000 million; and according to UBS, if Cajas de Ahorros (saving banks) had done the same, their delinquent rate would have been 5.6 percent, and not the stated 4.6 percent. Initially cajas tried to preserve the accounting value of these assets through operations like *Aliancia*, a society established by eight saving banks to manage €200 million in real estate assets, with the acknowledged objective to take these assets out of their balance accounts and "not to lose money." Given this degree of "manipulation" it is not surprising that many analysts estimated that the delinquent rate was only half of what it should have been if their accounts had been more transparent.[6]

At the same time, the fast-growing unemployment (it reached 20 percent by 2010) and the collapse of the real estate market, which constituted 60 percent of the banking loans (i.e., loans to families, to enterprises in the real state sector, or direct real estate assets), have contributed to increase the loan delinquent rate. In Spain there is a crucial link between unemployment and the health of the banking sector. The degree of bankarization of the Spanish economy (i.e., the proportion of active and passive financial assets from all economic actors with banking intermediaries) is one of the highest of the OECD; and the source of business funding outside of the three main financial institutions (banks, cajas, and credit cooperatives) is the lowest in the OECD. Therefore, not surprisingly, the dramatic surge in unemployment has caused significant damage to financial institutions because it has led to further deterioration in the quality of their assets and their capacity to absorb additional risks (more than half of the aggregated assets of the Spanish banking system are linked directly or indirectly to real estate assets). This dire situation was expected to be compounded by the decrease in revenues caused by the collapse of interest rates and the lower volume of business.

In June 2009 the Spanish government created the FROB, to pave the way and help fund the restructuring of the Spanish financial sector: its €9 billion could be leveraged up to 99 billion. The ultimate goal was to force a series of merges of cajas. Initially this consolidation process met with significant political resistance as well as concerns about the EU's role (the former competency commissioner, Neelie Kroes, demanded in November 2009 that the Spanish government should define clearly the role and functioning of the FROB, and, therefore, there were questions on whether each merger would have to be approved by the EU to make sure that it would not violate European laws[7]), and it moved very slowly. The first phase of consolidation included partnerships among the following institutions: Caja Duero with Caja España and Caja de Burgos in Castile-León; Caixa Catalunya with Manresa and Tarragona; and Tarrasa, Sabadell, Girona, and Manlleu in Catalonia; Unicaja initiated the process to absorb Cajasur and Caja Jaén in Andalusia; and Caja Navarra and CajaCanarias, from Navarra and the Canaries, planned a holding to share business and their risk and capital policies.

The situation continued deteriorating throughout 2009–2010 (there were ten cajas with delinquent coverage lower than 40 percent, which represented 29 percent of the sector's assets) and the Bank of Spain was forced to use the requirement for higher provisions to push for the consolidation. Pressures for consolidation were also driven by the conviction that the cajas were overstaffed: banks have almost the same market share but use 20,000 employees and 9,000 branches less.

The Bank of Spain continued exercising pressure on the cajas to restructure the sector, and they started to respond to these pressures. By the beginning of that year, 27 cajas (of the original 45) were involved in merge processes. Many cajas also started to downsize their staff and reduce costs (for instance, Caixa Girona announced on March 31, 2010, that it would reduce its staff by 5 percent and would close 15 nonprofitable branches). And, according to Rodrigo Rato (president of Caja Madrid), by the end of the crisis, only 20 cajas would exist in the country.[8] In Galicia the regional government announced at the end of March the predisposition to merge Caixanova and Caixa Galicia; and Caja de Extremadura initiated a merge process toward a so-called virtual merge (*fusión virtual o fusion fria*) using the SIP, which did not force the merged institutions to eliminate their administrative boards or the branch network, but required them to merge their risk models, computer systems, capital, and at least 40 percent of the benefits. It also forced them to sign a mutual solvency commitment, and to be part of the merged institution for a minimum of ten years; as well as to combine some activities and functions like the politics to manage risks. In Catalonia the boards of the cajas Catalunya, Tarragona, and Manresa approved their merge in May 17, 2010, and they received the approval to merge from Brussels. BBK started working to create a SIP with CAM to establish the third largest caja in Spain, which failed; and later Cajasur, CAM, Caja de Extremadura, and Caja Cantabria announced a SIP merge. Caja Navarra, CajaCanarias and Caja Burgos created Banca Cívica; and CajaSol and Caja Guadalajara also started negotiating a SIP. In December 2010, Unicaja (which had already absorbed Caja Jaén) and Ibercaja announced negotiations to merge, and La Caixa announced its intention to explore the possibility to become a bank. Even the labor unions supported the restructuring of the sector: CCOO announced publicly on April 3, 2010, that it would support the entrance of private capital in the cajas.

Yet, the delinquent rate continue increasing, reaching 5.38 percent by February 2010 (1.17 point higher than in 2009), while financial institutions experienced increasing difficulties raising funds in international markets, forcing the ECB to play a crucial role providing liquidity: the debt of Spanish financial institutions with the ECB reached €81.88 billion in March 2010, representing 15 percent of the total debt of the Eurozone with the ECB.

Meanwhile, the consolidation process continued with the Bank of Spain playing a leading role, while still finding significant resistance: for instance, on May 22, 2010, the Bank of Spain was forced to seize Cajasur, a small caja based in Cordoba, Southern Spain (it accounted for 0.6 percent of Spain's banking assets), a peculiar institution controlled by the Catholic Church and chaired by a priest. By end of 2009 Cajasur's bad loan ratio reached 10.2 percent of its assets, double the Spanish average and its tier one capital ratio was just 1.94 percent below the legal minimum requirement and it faced a capital shortfall of €523 million. The board of Cajasur rejected in May 2010 the merge with Unicaja, a decision that led the Bank of Spain to intervene to sell it to the highest bidder after recapitalizing it with the €523 million. With this decision the central bank was trying to send a clear message that it would not tolerate further delays restructuring processes among the unlisted cajas past the established deadline of June 30, 2010.

Nonetheless the implications of this intervention were severe: bank stocks were marked down globally and the euro was also pushed down. This crisis illustrated the global implications of a local crisis and highlighted how slow Spanish (and European authorities) had been in cleaning up the banking sector. The failure of Cajasur also showcased the dire state of Spain's property market, to which the saving banks were severely exposed, as we have seen. In addition, it illustrated not merely the financial institutions' exposure to individual countries, but also the interlinked nature of their exposure, because many of these bad loans were packaged as covered bonds or mortgage-backed securities and sold them to German, French, and other investors.[9] This seizure rushed other cajas, who were eager to unveil coordination agreements in an attempt, to stave off a similar fate.

Within days of the Cajasur seizure decision, four cajas (Caja Mediterráneo, Cajasur, Caja Extremadura, and Caja Cantabria) announced plans to pool their operations in a joint holding group, and Caixa Girona started negotiating with La Caixa. By May 2010, 34 of the 45 cajas were involved in merging and restructuring discussions, and it was expected that that would lead to the creation of 11 new cajas. In June Caja Madrid and Bancaja announced their merge through the creation of a SIP, BFA, which led to development of the largest Spanish financial institution based on the volume of assets. They were joined by five smaller cajas (Caja Insular de Canarias, Caja Avila,

Caixa Laietana, Caja Segovia, and Caja Rioja). BFA became the major share-holder of Bankia (48 percent of its capital, as described below, was placed in the stock market in July 2011 though a public offering). The operation was promoted by the Bank of Spain, supported by the Zapatero's Socialist government, authorized by the PP regional governments of Valencia and Madrid, and blessed by the boards from all the participating cajas.[10] This merge would prove disastrous, as we will see later. Meanwhile, the financial performance of the cajas continued deteriorating during the first quarter of 2010: Caja Madrid announced a fall of almost 80 percent in revenues, and La Caixa 11.4 percent.

All this merging activity notwithstanding, deteriorating economic con-ditions led to downgrades of the country's debt. In April 2010 Standard & Poor downgraded Spanish sovereign debt following the country's sluggish outlook for economic growth, a decision that was followed by Fitch in May, which forced the government to approve a €15 billion package in spending cuts (see chapter 2). The government also enacted reforms aimed at bolster-ing the cajas and designed to dilute the influence of local governments in these institutions. On July 9, 2010, the government approved a royal decree of the LORCA, which represented the most sweeping reform of the sector in 170 years (it was approved by the Spanish Congress on July 20).[11] As a result of this reform, elected and government officials were banned from sitting in the boards of these cajas. Furthermore, if the cajas wanted to stay in banking they need to demutualize and establish shareholders structures in which the largest stakes would be capped at 40 percent. Cajas would also be able to sell up to 50 percent of their equity to private investors.[12]

This reform established four possible models for the cajas: maintain their condition of caja, with the new quota regime, adapting their statutes to the corporate governance regulations; become part of the SIP, popularly known, as we have seen above, as a "cold merge": through which a caja could main-tain its status as caja but transferring all its banking businesses to a bank, while maintaining 50 percent of the subsidiary's stock and keeping the social work and the industrial portfolio within the caja; or they could become a foundation transferring all its business to a bank in which the caja holds a participation of less than 50 percent.[13] The new law also affected Spanish banks: it gave powers to the Bank of Spain and the Ministry of Finance to impose "the obligation to have available a minimum amount of liquid assets that would make it feasible to confront potential fund exits derived from commitments and liabilities, including in the case of stress, and to maintain an adequate structure of financial sources and maturities." The aim of this reform was to avoid a repetition of the current situation in which banks were facing liquidity tensions due to the closure of international financial mar-kets. This measure was considered an advance of the Basil III regulations, approved later that summer.[14]

In June the Spanish government admitted that the country's banks were on the brink of a funding crisis because they were struggling to gain funding from the international capital markets. Again, there were particular concerns surrounding the cajas, still exposed to the ailing property sector. A financial crisis was becoming a sovereign crisis. These concerns were illustrated by the rising cost to borrow for Spain in the debt markets, and the rise in the costs for the country and the banks to insure their bonds against default. In June 2010 it cost Spain twice as much to borrow from capital markets over two years as it did in the middle of April. The increase in costs fueled concerns that the country would be forced to use emergency funds from the recently created EU €440 billion from EFSF. However, any move by the country to tap the fund would further undermine the confidence of investors in the market, which led Spanish and European leaders to stress, yet again, that "financial markets shouldn't make the mistake of establishing and equivalence between Greece and Spain."[15] Fortunately, markets settled down and Spanish bond yields remained relatively stable in June: the benchmark ten-year bond yields rose 6 basis points to 4.73 percent. This respite would not last long.

In July the Bank of Spain made public the results of the "stress tests" that the main European financial institutions had undergone in 2010: only 5 of the 17 cajas had failed them: Banca Cívica, Banca Espiga, Caja Catalunya's group, Unnim, and Cajasur. Spain had subjected 95 percent of its banking system to these stress tests (the average in the EU was 50 percent). The overall good result of the Spanish financial system seemed to confirm the benefits of the countercyclical capital regime (see below). The response of the markets to these results was very positive and helped to push down the country's risk premium. Unfortunately, this optimism proved unjustified and short lived.[16] The crisis continued affecting the bottom line of the financial institutions: Spanish cajas earned 26 percent less in the first six months of 2010 than in the first semester of 2009.

The consolidation process of the cajas intensified throughout the summer. In July CAM announced its intention to move forward with the merge with Cajasur despite the opposition of the labor unions. In Catalonia, Caixa Catalunya, Tarragona, and Manresa created Catalunya Caixa; and in September the assemblies of seven cajas (Caja Madrid, Bancaja, Caja Insular de Canarias, Caja Segovia, Caixa Laietana, Caja de Ávila, and Caja Rioja) approved their integration and the creation of a bank that would start operations in 2011. As of December 2010, there were 16 cajas left versus the 45 that existed just 6 months before when the merging process started.

Overall, and contrary to their counterparts all over the world, during the first stage (2008–2010) of the global financial crisis, most Spanish banks appeared to have escaped the worst direct effects of the global financial crisis. Furthermore, as late as mid-2012, Spain still has two of the most credit-worthy banks in the world, Banco Santander and BBVA, and the crisis has not affected their solid foundations. On the contrary, they have continued generating profits. Moreover, while their main competitors in other countries have been severely affected, and in many cases had to be rescued by their governments, in Spain Santander and BBVA have not needed state assistance nor liquidity injections. In contrast, Spanish banks have emerged as rescuers in foreign markets; Santander has invested in the United States, UK, and Germany, and BBVA and Banco Sabadell in the United States. By November 2009 only one financial institution had collapsed due to liquidity problems after overextending itself in loans to local projects and had to be taken over by the Bank of Spain, Caja Castilla-La Mancha. But it only represented 1 percent of total assets. *How do we account for this initial performance?*

Why Did Spanish Banks Perform Better during the First Stage of the Global Financial Crisis?[17]

First, *the institutional setting*: As we have seen, Spain has a well-coordinated regulatory framework, in which the Bank of Spain plays a crucial role as a supervisory body, but works closely with the consumer protection agency and the finance ministry.[18] The Bank of Spain discouraged lenders from adopting risky "off–balance sheet" accounting methods and from acquiring toxic assets. At the same time, the Bank's onsite supervisors, who are posted in the head offices of commercial banks and cajas, were overseeing risk decisions. Also, the Bank of Spain was instrumental in forcing financial institutions to focus on quality of capital, limiting their leverage and the debt to equity ratio.

Second, *the regulatory framework* was also crucial: prior to the crisis, the Bank of Spain implemented a "dynamic provisioning system," which established a countercyclical capital regime for banks. On the basis of this regime, starting in 2000, banks had to make provisions for latent portfolio losses, which allowed for the creation of a buffer in the form of a reserve deducted from capital in good times and released in times of downturn. At the same time, the Central Bank also prevented the provision of dividend increases at times of growth that might undermine banks' solvency in the long term. Finally, the Central Bank prevented off–balance sheet activities. This framework provided Spanish banks with a countercyclical mechanism that has been essential to overcome the first stage of the current crisis.

An additional factor to explain the performance of the Spanish banks was *the historical learning process* that took place in the decades prior to the crisis. Spanish central bankers learned from the crisis of the 1970s, 1980s, and early 1990s and they adopted measures to prevent the repetition of these crises. The idea of an anticyclical fund was an old one and had been a source of constant confrontations with the banks. The economic crisis of the early 1990s and the collapse of Banesto in 1993, which the Bank of Spain was almost powerless to prevent, illustrated the need to deepen the preventive measures. This crisis led Luis Angel Rojo, governor of the bank at that time, to establish such provisions in an internal document (a "circular"); his successor, Jaime Caruana (2000–2006), started to implement them in 2000.

Strategic decisions were also important. Spanish banks have focused largely on retail and commercial banking, and they ignored the risky attractions of opaque investment banking operations that became so widespread in other countries. The strategic decision to diversify internationally, primarily in Latin America, was also crucial for the larger bans because it has allowed them to compensate for the poor performance in the Spanish market. For instance, in 2011, Santander received nearly 70 percent of its profits from economies that do not use the euro currency.

Finally, some Spanish bankers attribute the behavior of the country's financial institutions to *cultural factors*. While the evidentiary basis for this claim has been challenged, it still seems plausible. Indeed, Spanish bankers are usually considered boring and conservative bankers who focus on their responsibility to customers, employees, and shareholders, not just on quarterly financial reports. Spanish banks, like Santander, kept their risk management separate from business areas and with independent reporting lines; had risk policies decided at board level; and their risk management was focused on knowing the customer. In addition, Banco Santander board's risk committee meets for half a day twice a week, and the board's ten-person executive committee meets every Monday for at least four hours, devoting a significant proportion of that time to assessing risk and approving transactions.[19]

The Canary in the Coal Mine: How More "Traditional" Problems Led to a Greater Banking Crisis

As we have seen in the previous sections, in the run up to the crisis, the Bank of Spain and the regulators earned themselves a fine reputation. MAFO stated in October 2008, after the collapse of the banking system in many other countries, that "the sector is in a strong starting position, and the Bank of Spain has the capacity and the tradition to know how to resolve the most complex situations without trauma for the depositors, or the overall economy." He added: "I am convinced that our entities, which knew how to manage the expansive cycle, will also know how to adopt the management decisions and implement the adequate strategies that will allow them to confront the difficulties with success."[20] They did not and neither did the Bank of Spain and the Socialist governments. They would come to regret such complacency.

Indeed, the relative success in dealing with the crisis proved short lived. When the economic crisis deepened, it led to a traditional banking crisis caused by the collapse of the real estate market, unemployment records, increasing government debt, and difficulties accessing credit in wholesale markets. The real estate boom-bust cycle, which materialized in particular in the cajas sector, exposed weaknesses in the policy and regulatory frameworks, as well as the sector's overreliance on wholesale funding. In the end the financial system could not decouple from the economic cycle and the huge macroeconomic crisis that has besieged the country. This section seeks to account for this reversal.

The deteriorating situation is illustrated by the interest margin of the Spanish banking system—the difference between what they earn on loans and the cost of funding—which fell about 20 percent since July 2007 to 0.86 percentage points at the end of 2011, the lowest since at least 1970 when the Bank of Spain started to compile the data. For the first time since 1985, return on equity was negative at the end of 2011, as a result of the economic crisis and increasing provisions against losses on real estate debt.

It is undeniable that there has been significant progress in trying to address the consequences of the crisis. By the summer of 2012, banks have accumulated €112 billion in extra provisions for bad property loans since 2007, which are expected to increase to €147 billion by the end of 2012, or the equivalent of 14 percent of GDP; they have higher capital ratios; 5,700 branches have been eliminated, a 12 percent cut (as a result, 2,656 little towns have lost their branches and 4.8 million citizens will not have branches in their municipalities), and a 10 percent cut in staff (30,172 jobs have been lost between 2008 and 2012 in the financial sector; and the consolidation efforts described above have resulted in the absorption through mergers of 30 weaker institutions, all but two of them cajas: as of September 2012 there were only 9 cajas left, as a result of this consolidation process (from the original 45), and all of the them but 2 small ones (cajas de Ontinyent [Valencia] and Pollença [Mallorca]), had transferred to banks their financial businesses.[21]

Yet, by September 2012, the problem with real estate toxic assets had resulted in the intervention and nationalization of eight financial institutions. Between 2009 and 2010 two cajas were intervened (Caja Castilla-La Mancha and Cajasur), in 2011 four more were nationalized (CAM, Unnim, Catalunya Caixa, and Novagalicia Banco). Banco de Valencia (controlled by Bancaja) was intervened in 2011 and nationalized in 2012. Finally, Bankia was nationalized in 2012. Altogether, by May 9, 2012, the reorganization of the sector had involved €115 billion from the Spanish government. Of this, half are guarantees, 19.3 billion were used to buy assets, 14.346 have been direct assistance from the FROB, and 400 million are the losses from Cajasur, which were absorbed. Finally, the financial institutions themselves used €119 billion of their own capital to clean up their accounts and comply with new provision requirements.[22] As we have seen, the main problem has been with the cajas (see table 6.1).

The most important intervention was the partial nationalization of BFA, the Bankia matrix: On Wednesday May 9, 2012, the government was forced to nationalize Bankia, the country's largest real estate lender, which again validated the concerns about insufficient regulatory oversight, and the perception that banks and the Bank of Spain had played down the risk posed by real estate loans. This was the largest bank nationalization in the country's history. Its nonperforming loan rates were running at 8 percent at the time

Table 6.1 A Chronology of Crony Capitalism among *Cajas*

Caja	*Collapse*	*Features*	*Problems*	*Controversies*	*Outcome*
Caja Castilla-La Mancha	–March 29, 2009. –It had 26.38% of defaulted loans; deposits down by 12.51%, 1.68 billion in land holdings. –Costs of collapse: 2.475 billion in loan guarantees and 1.3 billion in capital –Lost 75% of the assets accumulated for decades –It has broken the legal requirements regarding risk	Group of 5 cajas. Ranked twelfth in the sector, and with €19 billion in assets	Inefficient and outdated risk assessment systems, excessive investment in the real estate sector; rapid expansion outside of its region, particularly in Levante; very dependent on wholesale funding.	–Rumors about its collapse led to deposit withdrawals in Yébenes. –Campaigns attributed to the PP against the solvency of the caja, and to promote deposit withdrawals. –Merging attempts with Ibercaja and Unicaja failed –PwC report found a whole 3 billion in the accounts. –Bank of Spain refused to lend it 2 billion to merge with Unicaja. –Confrontation between Bank of Spain and the Junta de Andalucía over the merge with Unicaja –FGD paid for the losses (FROB did not yet exist). –The risks were known but the supervisors did little to address them.	Nationalized and later absorbed by Cajasur –FGD paid 4.125 billion, and later when it was absorbed by Cajasur (which is now part of the Liberbank group), it received 1.493 billion from the FROB.
Cajasur	–May 21, 2010 –596 million in losses in 2009, and 1.1 billion in losses in 2010	Controlled by the Catholic Church: It had six priests on the board, and it was presided	–Excessive investment in real estate. –As early as 2004 the default rate was 3.5% (the average in the sector was 0.6%).	–Massive deposit withdrawals –The board refused to heed the Bank of Spain request to merge with Unicaja –Its president requested the Bank of Spain intervention, in effect killing the caja, instead of approving the merge with Unicaja (he had	–Sold to the Basque BBK –752 employees dismissed –It received 800 million in loans from the FROB that it has to repay.

	–In 2009 1.7 billion in the real estate sector (4,000 houses and 2 million square meters in land holdings).	over by a priest for 30 years (Miguel Castillejo, who was replaced in 2005 for another one, Santiago Gómez Sierra).	–In 2010 it reached 10.4%, doubling the average. –Excessive concentration of credit in questionable individuals (Rafael Gómez: 400 million in 2004), and construction companies (Prasa: 209 million, and Sánchez Ramade: 143 million), exceeding the legal concentration of risk (25%)	a difficult relationship with Braulio Medel, president of Unicaja) –Worked with promoters, like Rafael Gómez, who were later indicted for their involvement in real estate scandals –Bank of Spain opened expedients against 38 former board members. –Four CEOs between 2007 and 2009. –Bank of Spain inspections (four between 2005 and 2008) not enough to force changes.	–BBK requested 392 million from the FROB to confront the losses from bad loans.
CAM	–July 22, 2011 –From 244 million in benefits in 2009 to 2.713 billion in losses in 2010	Ranked fourth in the sector. 137 years old and the result of 20 mergers	Excessive investment in real estate sector (doubled it between 2003 and 2005, participating in 66 societies and 104 projects in that sector); lack of professionalism in top leadership; insufficient internal controls; political instrumentalization. Only caja that issues cuotas participativas	–Former managers indicted –Questionable investment in amusement park (the ruinous Tierra Mítica), and the Ciudad de la Luz –Soft loans to board members (161 million between 2004 and 2010 at a 0% interest rate). –Failed merger attempt in 2010 with Cajasur, Caja Cantabria, and Caja Extremadura. –Multimillion salaries and payoffs to managers: the former CEO Carlos López Abad and another five top managers retired with 15.5 million in pensions. His successor, Maria Dolores Amorós, had a €600,000 salary and a lifelong pension of €369,497 without the approval of the	–Intervened and Nationalized –It received 2.3 billion in capital from the FROB (it acquired 80% of the institution, and then 100%), and 3 billion in liquidity. –Banco Sabadell absorbed it in December 2011 with an initial aid package of 5,24 billion from the FGD.

continued

Table 6.1 Continued

Caja	Collapse	Features	Problems	Controversies	Outcome
			(participative quotas, or tittles similar to stock but without political rights).	appropriate supervisory boards. –Amorós was fired on September 2011, for among other reasons, falsifying financial accounts. –The last president, Modesto Crespo, did not receive an official salary, but he had arranged to receive an annual retribution of €300,000 through a CAM affiliate, TI Participaciones. –75,000 people affected by the problems with preferential stock and subordinated debt.	
NCG	–In 2011, 169 million in losses –It needed a 1.162 billion loan from the FROB for the merger; and later on another one for 2,465 billion to meet the recapitalization requirements imposed by the Zapatero administration.	–Result of the merge between Caixa Galicia and Caixanova. –Ranked fifth in the sector. –70 billion in assets –They held 40% of the market in Galicia	Excessive investment in the real estate sector; rapid expansion outside of Galicia; risky investment in the Mediterranean coast; associated with controversial constructors like El Pocero; politicized boards; insufficient controls; dependence on wholesale markets for funding	–After the merge, it announced a gross benefit of 2.67 billion between 2010 and 2015 –Purchase of the Sálvora Island. –Compensation and rewards scandals for their top managers: José Luis Méndez (sailboats and a 16.5 million pension package) –Julio Fernández Gayoso, leader of Caixanova, was able to manipulate the rules with the support of the Galician government to stay in the job past the legal age (he was 81). –The merged institution was valued at €1.714 billion. After accounting adjustment, this was revised to 181 million.	–Nationalized. FROB owns 93% of the capital (the rest was left to the caja to fund the foundation activities). Novacaixagalicia Banco –1,200 people preretired and 300 branches had to be closed –Still needs €4.5 billion –Transferred €5 billion to the bad bank. –On December 2012, the lender had a negative economic value of €3 billion. –Social capital will convert into equity and the state will become the owner of 100 percent of its stock.

				–FROB expected to inject €5,425 billion from the MEDE funds.
Catalunya Caixa	Second caja in Catalonia. It resulted from the merge in 2010 of Caixa Catalunya, Manresa and Tarragona.	Excessive exposure to the real estate sector; dependence on wholesale markets for funding; very lax risk control systems (sometimes the collateral was simply the expected reevaluation of the real state asset, and 32% of the mortgages were granted for an amount that was more than 80% of the value of the real estate asset); expansion outside of their territory; corporate board played very limited role in decisions	–CC planned to promote more than 4 million square meters in the Mediterranean arch and Madrid working with local companies, in which it participated with 50% of the investment (Prasa, Armilar, and Jale). It also expanded to Portugal. These alliances imploded when the real estate market collapsed and the caja assumed 100% of the investment. –CC opened 300 new branches between 2003 and 2007 in other regions (Madrid, Andalucia, Valencia, and Murcia). –Bank of Spain has postponed its sale until they know for certain the capital needs of the institution (estimated to be at least 5 billion). –The former president of CC, Narcís Serra, has stated that when he took over the position in 2005 he had to impart one-hour classes to the members of the board because "they did not have the basic skills to understand the caja's accounts." –Compensations: former president left CC with a 10-million package and his successor, Todó, negotiated a "postoccupation package" of 3.55 million.	Nationalized FROB owns 89.9% (injected 1.7 billion to increase the group's capital). –The Catalonian government is interested in having Banco Sabadell buy it. –Transferred €6.7 billion to the bad bank. –On December 2012, the lender had a negative economic value of €6,674 billion. –FROB expected to inject €9,084 million from the MEDE funds.
	–September 30, 2011 –CC had 1.33 million in losses in 2011 –Toxic assets estimated at 12 billion –CC closed 2008 with the highest loan default rate in the system growing from 1% to 5.28% in one year			
Unnim	Resulted from the merge in 2009 of the	Expansion outside of their territory; excessive investment in	–In 2004 Sabadell and Terrasa decided to invest on each other's territory (breaking an informal understanding that had lasted over a century).	Nationalized (FROB controlled 100%), and later acquired in March 2012
	–It received 380 million loan from the FORB to merge,			

continued

Table 6.1 Continued

Caja	Collapse	Features	Problems	Controversies	Outcome
	and 568 after nationalization. −1.75 billion in real estate assets; and 3.598 billion in loans to developers. −55 real estate societies. −469 million in losses in 2011.	Sabadell, Terrassa, and Malleu cajas	the real estate market; excessive opening of branches; left aside their industrial participations; political meddling; lack of financial skills among top managers (many came from cultural entities and the municipalities)	−In 2004 Caja Sabadell with 12.4 billion assets had 284 branches all over Catalonia; four years later it had opened 95 more, 16 of which were in Madrid, 9 in the Valencia region, and 1 in Andalusia; Caja Terrasa with 11.7 billion in assets grew from 232 branches in Catalonia to 268 with 11 in Madrid and 2 in Aragón; and Caja Malleu grew from 92 in Catalonia and 1 in Madrid, to 101 in Catalonia and 3 in Madrid. −Caixa Girona was going to be part of the merged institution but the local leaders of two nationalist parties rejected the merger because it would dilute their share (despite the fact that it would be 23% with only 7.8 billion in assets). Shortly after it was absorbed by La Caixa. −As the crisis intensified and its capital needs increased, Unnim negotiated possible mergers with Banca Cívica, Ibercaja, and the Basque cajas, but they all failed. −After it was nationalized, it still rewarded its loyal customers in 2011 with trips to Turkey in high-standing hotels	for 1 euro by the BBVA (and 953 million in aid from the FROB). 530 employees have been dismissed. BBVA has proposed an additional reduction of 1,265 employees (it had 3,076 in summer of 2012), and the closing of 314 branches.
Banco de Valencia	Nationalized in 2011 after identifying a 548 million whole in its books. Valued at 1,09 billion.	−Founded in 1900. It funded industrial, electrical, railway, and urban projects.	Politicized leadership; excessive concentration of risk in the real estate sector: it reached 65.8% (the average in	Loan default rate of 16.4%, double the average in the sector, solvency ratio of 1.7% (well below the legal limit of 8%). −Ongoing criminal accusations for illicit enrichment against the former CEO, Domingo Parra.	Nationalized. FROB injected 1 billion in 2012 to acquire 91% of the capital. −Acquired by Caixabank. −Transferred €1.92

Bought by the Caja de Valencia (later Bancaja) in 1994.
-It was part of the Bankia group when Bancaja merged with Caja Madrid.

the sector was 59%); political intervention from the regional government that replaced technical criteria for political one; close links with real estate developers; expansion of the branch network

-Branch network increased 82% between 2000 and 2008, well above the sector.
-Partnership with dubious characters like Eugenio Callabuig (it bought its company Costa Bellver for 107 million, when it had assets only of 10 million).
-It gave loans to Jaume Matas, former president of the Balearic government, who was later sentenced for corruption.
-Dispute with Rodrigo Rato, president of Bankia, when he requested an audit in February 2012 after the merge between Caja Madrid and Bancaja.
-Compensation scandal: Aurelio Izquierdo, former president of Banco de Valencia, had negotiated a compensation package of 14 million (later he declined part of it and received "only" 7.6 million).

billion to the bad bank.
-On December 2012, the lender had a negative economic value of €6.3 billion.
-FROB expected to inject €4.5 billion from the MEDE funds.

Sources: Developed based on information from "Agujeros negros' del sistema financiero 1–7," *El País*, June 24–29, 2012; "Parte de guerra: Ocho entidades intervenidas o nacionalizadas en España," *El País*, May 9, 2012; and "La banca nacionalizada, recapitalizada y liberada de 'activos tóxicos,'" *El País*, December 27, 2012.

of the nationalization. The cost of the nationalization is expected to reach between €7 and 10 billion. This nationalization shows that some of the caja mergers that the Bank of Spain and the previous government pushed for were dysfunctional. Billed as the "leader of the new banks" and as evidence of the success of the Socialist government's crusading banking reforms, Bankia has proved to be a monumental fiasco, and it showed the refusal to acknowledge the true extent of the country's real estate problem. In many ways Bankia symbolizes the problems with the cajas and also with the government's response to the crisis. *What led to its collapse?*

The Bankia Nationalization: Chronicle of a Collapse Foretold[23]

The nationalization of Bankia in the spring of 2012 represents most of what had been wrong with the financial system and Spanish cajas. As we have seen, Bankia was the result of the merge between Caja Madrid, Bancaja and five smaller cajas. Its problems, however, started well before the creation of the new institution.

By 2009 Caja Madrid was already in financial difficulties and the institution was in the midst of a political fight that symbolizes the political interferences that were so characteristic at the cajas. The president of the Madrid regional government, Esperanza Aguirre, was trying to oust Caja Madrid's president Miguel Blesa who had been in that position for 13 years, and wanted to have him replaced by her own VP of the Madrid regional government, Ignacio González. Blesa had gotten the job because of his personal friendship with PM Aznar (they went to school together), and he had engineered the ousting of his predecessor, Jaime Terceiro, who had been named president of the Caja in 1988 by the Socialists. But Blesa had no previous experience in the financial sector. The major of Madrid, Alberto Ruiz Gallardon, opposed Aguirre's decision and tried to block it (both the regional government and the city had representatives in Caja Madrid's board), while supporting Rodrigo Rato's candidacy (who had been a VP and minister of finance in the Aznar's government, and a former manager director at the IMF).[24]

In the end Rato won the battle and was appointed as president of Caja Madrid. This was presented as a nonpolitical decision, notwithstanding the fact that he had been one of the leaders of the PP for years, and the fact that the PP controlled both the Madrid regional government and the city hall). Rato continued the pattern initiated by Blesa to increase his salary when he was appointed president (he made €1 million more than Blesa, and Blesa had multiplied his salary by 18 compared with his predecessor, Jaime Terceiro), as well as the salaries of his top executives, while doubling the per diem of the members of the board. This was just another example of the kind of abuses that became so pervasive among the cajas.

At that time, Caja Madrid was already experiencing severe difficulties marked by a significant decline of the institution's financial margins, its enormous indebtedness with international lenders, as well as its dependence on the constructions sector and real estate mortgages, because it has given huge loans to construction and promotion companies. By 2009 its operating profits had fallen by 68 percent, and the caja was obligated by the Bank of Spain to increase provisions by €500 million. It was only the caja's investments in Telefónica, the selling of its stock in Endesa, financial and treasury operations (which were even more profitable than its retail network), and its profitable investments in industrial companies and Mapfre, that gave the institution some breathing room. The rating agencies were already alarmed by the situation, and Moody's classified its bond emission as B2 (junk) out of concerns about the ability of the institution to pay the interests on its debt.

Rato inherited this problematic situation. His first priority was to recapitalize the institution, which was floundering under the weight of insufficient capital. His tenure was marred by this problem, which in the end led to the nationalization of Bankia. During his first year he charged €4 billion against capital to avoid losses, with the approval from the Bank of Spain. At the same time, given that he was not a finance expert, it was expected that he would name one as his CEO. However, it took him a year and a half to do so. And when he named Fernando Verdú from Banca March, it happened just a month before Bankia's public offering in the stock market. Rato's lack of experience was compounded by the facts that he surrounded himself with a group of people at the top, none of which came from within the institution or were financial experts, and that he largely ignored the board. These decisions proved to be a significant handicap as the crisis intensified.

Six months after Rato became president of Caja Madrid, he announced the merge with Bancaja, another large caja based in the Valencia region, and five smaller cajas. Through this merge they created Bankia, the third largest financial group in Spain behind Santander, and BBVA. However, the financial situation of Bancaja was even worse than that of Caja Madrid, as it was highly leveraged with construction loans, and was also short in provisions and liquidity (the Valencia region has been suffering one of the worst crises in the country driven by the collapse of its construction and real estate sectors). The reasons for the merge remain to be explained. Many in the PP government now blame the Bank of Spain for forcing it in order to shrink the number of cajas and build larger institutions that would be able to withstand the crisis better. At the same time, the Bank of Spain is also accused of not knowing the real magnitude of Bancaja's problems. In addition, the company responsible for auditing both cajas' accounts, Deloitte, was also in charge of estimating the value for the merger, and this may have been a problem as well, as some claim it may have had vested interests in the decision. The reality was that two cajas with significant problems merged, and one of the lessons, nowadays finally widely accepted, is that you do not create a solid bank by merging two bad ones. At the time of the merge, however, there was little opposition. The blame game intensified after the nationalization of Bankia and Aguirre has gone as far as to claim that the merge took place "under a barrel of a gun."[25]

The merge decision also shows the high degree of political interference in the cajas' decisions, one of the main reasons for their problems. Both regional governments, Madrid and Valencia, were controlled by the PP and the party leaders wanted to create a large national bank. At that time the regional governments were power centers of their own, and there was little question of their actions and decisions (the Valencia government was immersed in a series of corruption scandals that also involved the president of the Generalitat and the regional PP-Francisco Camps). In that context, some of the cajas had become, essentially, political instruments to achieve political goals. Only the crisis brought these issues to the fore.

In this regard, it is worth highlighting that Rato had been a candidate to replace PM Aznar when he decided to step down and not run for a third mandate in 2004. The internal contest within the PP pitted him against Mariano Rajoy, and Aznar eventually handpicked Rajoy as his successor. Rato was the loser but according to many people he never quite accepted the outcome. Henceforth Rato never stopped his political activities during his tenure in Caja Madrid/Bankia and he continued participating in some of the party's public events. Many observers have interpreted his actions as dominated by political considerations, and as part of a political strategy to emerge as a potential alternative to PM Rajoy. According to this perspective the merger would give him the platform to do so.

However, the merger did not address the subjacent problems, the banks' exposure to toxic real estate assets, which continued growing as the crisis intensified, and the construction and real estate sectors continued deteriorating. In March 2011, Bankia requested €4,465 billion from the FROB, and intensified the process of slashing costs by reducing branches and staff, which reduced costs by €550 million and was considered a significant achievement. However, it proved to be insufficient to make up for the bank's huge problems.

At the same time, Rato pushed for the decision to move ahead with a public stock offering, which took place in the midst of the economic crisis and was also controversial. Bankia announced it to potential investors with the advertising slogan "our future together," a message that just a year later proved prescient when the bank was rescued. This decision proved to be ruinous for the institution and its investors.

Again, the rationale for this decision is mired in controversy. Some claim that it was required in order to fulfill the conditions of the financial reform approved by the Socialist government, which requested less capital from entities listed in the stock market. However, others interpreted the decision in political terms, yet again: Rato was convinced that PM Zapatero wanted to hurt him because he was from the PP. Hence he announced to the board that he would not wait for the government demands and that he had decided to become independent, not relying on government's funds, by issuing public stock. This decision took place while the merging process was still ongoing and it was perceived as a huge gamble, as there were serious concerns that the public offering could be a failure. To avoid that, the government went as far as to pressure institutional investors to buy stock from the new institution that would prevent a public relations fiasco for Spain.

Immediately following the public offering Bankia had to confront the collapse of Banco de Valencia, a subsidiary (see table 6.1). The problems of this entity had not been recognized until a few weeks before its collapse. In an unprecedented decision, the Bank of Spain decided to allow the collapse of a subsidiary: Bankia, the matrix company would not rescue it, and it would be absorbed by the FROB. This fiasco led to the final confrontation between Rato and the president of Bancaja, José Luis Olivas, who was forced to resign.

The PP victory and the beginning of 2012 did not bring positive news for the institution. Rato tried to negotiate a possible merger between Caja Madrid and its main historical competitor, the Catalonian La Caixa, which had the support from the Rajoy government. News of the possible merger were filtered to the press, and it was perceived as a positive solution given the healthier status of La Caixa, which would have made it easier for the new institution to absorb the losses from the construction sector and would have alleviated Bankia's shortage of capital. Yet, in the end, Rato decided not to move forward out of concerns for his own role in the new institution (La Caixa was a larger institution and a stronger caja) and over the control of the new entity. Nevertheless, Rato still looked for other alternatives and pushed for new mergers. He proposed one with the Asturias' Liberbank and later another one with the Andalusian Unicaja. Both were rejected by the Bank of Spain.

On May 11, 2012, Finance Minister Luis de Guindos ordered banks to set aside provisions equivalent to 45 percent on the nation's €307 billion ($387 billion) book of loans linked to real estate developers. This new additional demand proved to be devastating for Bankia, as it did not have the capital to meet it. On May 18, 2012, it requested government assistance, and the Spanish government was forced to nationalize it in an effort to restore investors' confidence in the Spanish banking sector. Even though the government had made a sweeping declaration that no more public money would be put into Spain's banks as late as February 2012, it changed tack in light of Bankia's problems, and recognized that it would have collapsed had it not been rescued. The government approved an injection of €23.5 billion of state aid in exchange for a 90 percent control of Bankia, what has become Spain's biggest bank nationalization. The bulk of the money would be used to boost provisions against real estate losses to get a coverage ratio of nearly 49 percent, in line with other Spanish banks. Following the nationalization, Bankia's parent group BFA restated its 2011 results to reflect an astonishing €3.3 billion loss, rather than the reported 300 million profit. Rato's successor, José Ignacio Gorigolzarri, uncovered a whole of €23 billion in Bankia's accounts that would need to be covered with public funds.

Initially the government announced that it would inject its own government debt into Bankia, issuing government guaranteed debt in return for equity, thus allowing Bankia to deposit those bonds with the ECB for cash. However, the ECB rejected this plan because it would potentially breach the EU ban on "monetary financing," or central bank funding of governments, and informed the Spanish government that it would have to proceed with a proper capital injection for Bankia. This was yet another public relations disaster for the Spanish government, and it reinforced the pattern of improvisation and contradictions that had characterized its decisions from the beginning of its tenure in December 2011. In the end, Bankia's nationalization was the tipping point that led to an EU bailout package to rescue the ailing Spanish banking system (see below).

When Rato forced Olivas out, he stated that "all the financial leaders that have taken the cajas to their current predicament should assume their responsibilities." This sentence proved prescient in the end, as it was applied to him. It would serve as his own epitaph. The magnitude of the disaster is still difficult to grasp: BFA and Bankia had 11.5 million clients, 4,000 branches spread all over the country, and a 10 percent market share; and initially Bankia's stock was valued at €3.75 per share. In 2007 Caja Madrid had €2.86 billion in profits and Bancaja 491 million. In 2011 BFA lost €3.318 billion, and by the end of 2012 its stock was less than €1 (€0.55 in December, down more than 80 percent from the flotation price), and it continued falling. The FROB announced on December 17, 2012, that Bankia had a negative economic value of €4.15 billion. As a result, the FROB announced that it planned to increase BFA's capital by €13.46 billion before the end of 2012, in addition to the €4.5 billion that it received the previous September. As a result, Bankia's 350,000 retail shareholders were expected to lose practically all their investments because their share of equity would be practically wiped out.[26]

The combination of the devastating effects of the crisis on the cajas, with the dramatic impact that it had on loan defaults, particularly on those (like Caja Madrid and Bancaja) that had relied heavily in mortgages; their reckless investment decisions in the real estate sector and developers; the decision to merge cajas with similar problems; and the inadequate profile of the managerial teams that lacked the necessary experience to make the right decisions when the crisis exposed their underbellies, all led to the worst disaster of Spain's financial history.[27] The whole fiasco has led to lawsuits from investors and is being investigated by the courts. When the investigating court questioned Rato in December of 2012, he declared that he would not have taken the decision to move forward with Bankia's public offering, had he not been forced to do it; and he blamed the Zapatero and Rajoy governments for all the problems that led to the nationalization of Bankia.[28] It seemed, once again, as noted in the Introduction, that no one was responsible for anything.

In the end, concerns about Spanish banks' undercapitalization led to the announcement of an EU banking bailout for Spain in June 2012.

The Banking Bailout

Bankia's rescue highlighted concerns that the level of provisions that Spanish banks had taken against distressed property portfolios were too low. At the same time, apprehensions about the fiscal situation of the country (public debt had doubled since the crisis started from 35.5 percent of GDP at the end of the first quarter of 2008 to 72.1 percent at the end of the first quarter of 2012), and the interconnectedness between sovereign issuer and banks pushed Spanish yield up and intensified concerns about the need for a bailout. The intensification of the financial crisis was leading to a deepening sovereign crises. Spain's banking system was perceived as systemically important for the Eurozone because the country had about €450 billion of deposits from foreign companies and individuals.

Investors perceived those concerns and they were punishing Spanish banks and Spain's sovereign. The performance of Spanish banks' stock reflected those worries as well: between mid-March and the end of June of 2012 Santander and BBVA's stock declined about 30 percent. At the same time, Spain's cost of borrowing kept increasing and the spread on Spanish ten-year bonds over German Bunds hit new European highs in late May 2012, climbing to 511 points; while yields of ten-year bonds moved above 6.5 percent (reaching 6.9 percent on June 14), and moving closer to the 7 percent level that was widely considered unsustainable, and which led to bailouts for Greece, Portugal, and Ireland.

Yet, despite these alarming signs, as late as May 28, the Spanish government and PM Rajoy insisted that the country would not need international bailout for its banks. On April 12, Mr. Rajoy stated that "talking about a rescue makes no sense...Spain is not being rescued; Spain can't be rescued. There is no intention and no need and so Spain will not be rescued." Rajoy was also on record stating that "we are not going to let any regional government fall, or any bank fall, because they can't...if that happens the country will fall." This followed the repeated statements of the members of the government that Spain would not take any form of international rescue.

By early June 2012, however, it was becoming clear that despite all the denials, a recue was inevitable and that Spain would in fact need a bailout. The government's attempts to force the BCE's hand (the budget minister, Cristobal Montoro, responded to a question about whether Spain needed a bailout with a veiled threat: "those with the most interest in whether Spain does all right are the holders of debt, who have to be repaid in full and have that right," and Minister Guindos was on the record stating that the battle for the euro was going to be waged in Spain), and its insistent demand for help from its European partners only exasperated them, and intensified concerns in European capitals that it was only considerations over the political stigma associated with a bailout, rather than the policy constraints that Brussels would include on it, that was keeping the Spanish government from accepting aid that was on the table.

Spain's risk premium—the difference between its bond yields and those of Germany—continued soaring after the Bankia nationalization, adding pressure to the government, and Bankia's shares plunged. By June 5, the severity of the situation was finally creeping in and the government was already admitting (in the words of Mr. Montoro) that given the high perceived risk of its sovereign debt Spain did "not have the doors of the markets open," and this despite the fact that it was planning to auction up €2 billion of bonds that same week. Mr. Rajoy, for his part, continued insisting on the need for a banking union and Eurobonds, stating during a senate session that Europe "needs to support those that are in difficulty . . . The most important thing is we have a problem of financing, of liquidity and debt sustainability." Germany still refused to provide aid unless there was a formal request from the Spanish government.

Finally, on June 8, VP Soraya Sáez de Santamaría, in response to a question about a possible request for a bailout, answered: "there are some things that cannot always be answered as if they were test questions." A day after, on Saturday June 9, following a few days of fierce official negations, the government finally asked the EU for funds to recapitalize its struggling banking sector at a conference call between the Eurozone's 17 finance ministers. It agreed to accept a bailout of up to $125 billion, nearly three times the $46 billion in extra capital that the IMF said it was the minimum the banking sector needed to guard against the deepening of the country's economic crisis. The decision also aimed at quelling rising financial turmoil ahead of the Greek parliamentary election schedule for June 17. This decision made Spain the fourth and largest European country to agree to accept emergency assistance (albeit in this case for the country's financial sector).

The European statement on the aid gave few details, which initially allowed the government to claim that it was not a "rescue" package, and that it was not subject to the conditionality and supervision by the troika (EU, IMF, and ECB) that characterized the other three rescue packages of Greece, Ireland, and Portugal. In Spain the announcement was made by Minister Guindos, which caused a political storm and forced PM Rajoy to give an impromptu press conference the day after, on Sunday, June 10, before he departed to watch the Spanish football national team play a Eurocup game in Poland. Guindos announced that "what we are asking is financial support, and this has absolutely nothing to do with a full bailout," and added that the terms of the emergency loan would be "very favorable," and that "the problem that we face affects about 30 percent of the Spanish banking system." The amount of the financing was expected to be completed after the two consulting firms had been hired to look at the bank accounts published their audit report on June 21. The funds would be channelled through the Spanish bank bailout fund, the FROB, and the Spanish government would ultimately be responsible and had to sign the memorandum of understanding and the conditions that came with it.

The market's response to the bailout package was initially sanguine. While observers praised the decisive preemptive action of European leaders (something relatively unusual during the crisis), and the fact that the aid was directed to the banks and that the amount was much larger than estimated to give some margin in the case of further need, there was disappointment regarding the failure to inject the money directly into the banks as equity.[29] The model proposed for the aid failed to recognize the crucial link between sovereign debt and the banks. Spanish banks accounted for a third of Spanish sovereign bonds, nearly double the tally before the crisis started (they had purchased €83 billion between December 2011 and June 2012). As in Greece where the sovereign debt dragged down the banks, this made them very vulnerable to a potential sovereign debt crisis, which was becoming increasingly more likely in Spain, thus intensifying the "doom loop." Consequently, after an initial market rally, the Spanish bond continued jumping higher and reached a new record, very close to 7 percent, just four days after the announcement of the bailout, demonstrating that investors were growing increasingly anxious about Spain's ability to pay back its debts.

Still, even with the bailout, much remains to be done in the Spanish financial sector. According to the rating agencies, Spanish banks' problems include adverse operating conditions due to the economic crisis; the reduced creditworthiness of the Spanish sovereign, which impacts banks' stand-alone profiles and affects the capacity of the government to support banks; rapid asset-quality deterioration because nonperforming loans to real estate companies are increasing rapidly and mortgages continue deteriorating; and restricted market funding access in wholesale markets; and, finally, growing investor concerns about Spanish banks and the sovereign.

How Do We Account for the Deteriorating Performance of Spanish Banks, Which Led to the Financial Bailout?

There are a number of factors that help account for the deteriorating performance of the Spanish banks after 2009 (see Royo 2013c). The first is *the effects of the devastating economic crisis* on Spanish banks. As we have seen, since 2008 the country has suffered one of the worst recessions in history: in 2010, Spain's GDP fell by 3.6 percent, the worst performance since data has been compiled; the public deficit reached over 11 percent; public debt increased from 36 percent to 50 percent; and housing construction fell by 20 percent. In 2012, the deficit is expected to reach 5.3 percent; unemployment stands at over 24 percent with more than 5.6 million people unemployed; and the debt is expected to reach 79 percent of GDP. These deteriorating economic conditions have a severe impact on the banks' balance sheets. Indeed, the second recession in three years and the record-high unemployment, close to

25 percent in mid-2012 (and 50 percent for those 25 years old and younger), is triggering new loan losses in the Spanish mortgage market and increasing the percentage of nonperformance loans (see below).

Second, banks are also being severely affected by *concerns over the country's sovereign debt*. As we have seen throughout the book the crisis in Spain did not originate with wildly mismanaged public finances. On the contrary, Spain had a budget surplus between 2005 and 2007, and public debt stood at 36 percent of GDP before the crisis. The crisis has largely been a problem of ever-growing private sector debt, compounded by reckless bank investments and loans, particularly from the cajas (to developers and construction companies rather than to home buyers), as well as aggravated by competitiveness and current account imbalances. Spain still has a relatively low ratio of public debt (70 percent in 2011, compared with 165 percent for Greece or 120 percent for Italy), but the nonfinancial private sector debt is 134 percent of GDP, higher than any major economy in the world with the exception of Ireland (and in the case of Ireland, figures are skewed because of the outsized presence of foreign multinationals). Many corporations took advantage of the record low-interest rates that followed Spain's accession to the EMU and gorged on cheap debt to expand domestically and internationally. To place the problem in perspective, the gross debt of household increased dramatically in the decade prior to the crisis, and by 2009 it was 20 percentage points higher than the Eurozone average (86 percent of GDP versus 66 percent). In the previous two years, it has fallen by 5 percentage points but it is till now (May 2012) a little less than 16 percentage points higher than the Eurozone average (about 81 percent). In addition, the gross debt of Spanish companies is 29 percentage points higher than the Eurozone's (134 percent of GDP versus 105 percent). Yet, it is worth emphasizing that the debt of financial institutions is lower than the Eurozone average (102 percent versus 128 percent). Their main problem is not the level of debt, but where it is invested: in real estate assets.

The austerity policies implemented since May 2010 are aggravating the fiscal position of the country. The ratio of Spain's debt to its economy was 36 percent before the crisis and is expected to reach 79 percent in 2012, and 84 percent by 2013 (and this is even based on optimistic growth assumptions). The shrinking economy will continue raising the debt, as well. The European Commission announced in May 2012 that Spain is likely to miss its deficit reducing targets for 2012 and 2013 by wide margins: it is now projected at 6.4 percent of GDP for 2012 (the original government projection was 5.3 percent) and 6.3 percent for 2013 (it was 3 percent). The premium Spain pays to borrow over Germany reached an euro-era record of over 600 basis points in the summer of 2012 and yields on government bonds have increased to over 7 percent. There are also concerns about the fiscal situation of the autonomous regions: four of them (the equivalent of 35 percent of GDP) have a public debt classified by the rating agencies as junk bond (Castilla-La Mancha, Valencia, Murcia, and Catalonia). The government announced that the 2011 deficit from Madrid (1.3 percent of GDP, which is now 2.2 percent), Valencia, and Castile-León was higher than expected, which had pushed the country's deficit up to 8.9 percent (it had been originally estimated at 6 percent and then the new government increased it to 8.5 percent), further eroding the credibility of the country's finances. Finally, Catalonia and Valencia had to request a bailout from the central government at the end of the summer (2012).

In sum, Spain seems to have fallen into the "doom loop" that has already afflicted Greece or Portugal and led to their bailout. The sustainability of the Spanish government debt is affecting Spanish banks (including BBVA and Santander) because they have been some of the biggest buyers of government debt in the wake of the ECB long-term refinancing operation liquidity infusions (the percentage of government bond owned by domestic banks reached 30 percent in mid-2012).

An additional crucial factor that helps explain the current financial crisis has been *the collapse of the real estate sector*. Spain, similar to other countries such as the United States, stands out in 2012 in having a huge property burst, a significant fiscal deficit, and a current account deficit. Indeed, the country is facing a very traditional banking crisis largely driven by bad property lending (in some cases caused by political cronyism). Land prices increased 500 percent in Spain between 1997 and 2007, the largest increase among the OECD countries. The country's credit boom peaked in 2008 when the supply of cheap, and largely external, finance began to dry up. The real estate sector fit like a glove in a financial sector that was seeking rapid growth at all costs. At the end of 2010, the IMF reported that Spain had the largest real estate bubble in the developed world.

But the global financial crisis burst it. Indeed, by the end of 2011, land prices, adjusted for inflation, had fallen about 30 percent from the 2007 peak, and home prices were off about 22 percent. Housing prices fell by 11.2 percent in 2011. Only in Madrid, prices were down by 29.5 percent. And many analysts estimate that house price adjustment is still less than halfway complete, and expect that real estate prices will fall to mid-1990s levels. The implosion of the real estate market is exposing the vulnerability of the banking sector to that market, which constituted 60 percent of the banking loans. Consequently, Spain has been suffering a property-linked banking crisis exacerbated by financing obstacles from the international crisis.

Four years after the crisis started, the quality of Spanish banks' assets continues to plummet. The estimated losses for banks are in and the Spanish banks still hold €308 billion in total real estate assets. The Bank of Spain classified €180 billion as troubled assets at the end of 2011, and banks are sitting on 656 billion of mortgages and 2.8 percent are classified as nonperforming. Credit to the real estate sector is still (in the summer 2012) the Achilles heel of the Spanish banking system. The toxic assets associated with the construction sector continue growing and there are more and more of them in the banks' balance sheets. Of the 180 billion declared problematic by the Bank of Spain, more than 100 billion are risky loans and around 80 billion are properties and assets collected by banks on defaults. Banco Santander has already absorbed €75 million in new bad loan provisions, half of what it expected to need for 2012; and Banesto's profits fell 88 percent in the first quarter of 2012 compared to the previous year. Bad loans, reached almost 8 percent in 2012, the highest level in 18 years as percentage of total lending.

Spanish banks are also suffering the consequences of their dependence on *wholesale funding* for liquidity since the crisis started, and, in particular, their dependence on international wholesale financing, as 40 percent of their balance depends on funding from international markets, particularly from the ECB. The debt with ECB reached €81.88 billion in 2012, and Spanish banks have increased their ECB borrowings by more than six times since June 2011, to the highest level in absolute terms among euro area banking systems as of April 2012.

The crisis has also exposed *weaknesses in the policy and regulatory framework*. The most evident sign of failure has been the fact that the country has already adopted five financial reforms in three years, and it has implemented three rounds of bank mergers:[30]

1. *June 2009*: The government approved the FROB and the first round of "cold" mergers. The FROB was funded with €9 billion to clean up the balance accounts of the entities most affected by the real estate crisis, in exchange for preferential stock that could be returned in five years. As a result of this process, there were seven groups of newly merged cajas that asked for support; more than 30 cajas were involved in merging discussions that led to the reduction in the number of cajas from 45 to 22.
2. *February 2011*: In anticipation of the requirements that would be established by Basil III, the government approved a decree that increases to 10 percent the capital provisions for all entities that fund more than 20 percent of their needs in the markets (for the others the minimum is established at 8 percent). If they did not meet the new requirements, they had two weeks to present a capitalization plan to the Bank of Spain. They either found new partners or they had to issue stock. In addition, there was another round of mergers, and the number of cajas was reduced to nine.
3. *February 2012*: The new Conservative government increased the capital provisions to €50 billion to clean up the real estate assets. This amount was the result of increasing to 80 percent the percentage of land covered against a possible nonpayment (and to 65 percent for unfinished houses, and 35 percent for finished ones). The banks had until the end of 2012 to comply. The government also increased the FROB funding to €15 billion and capped the salaries of executives from institutions that had received public aid.

4. *May 2012*: In response to the intensifying crisis and pressures from the IMF, ECB, Brussels, and the markets, the government approved a new reform, the fourth since the crisis started. As part of this reform, the government has ordered banks to set aside an additional €30 billion in provisions against bad loans to ensure that banks had provisions of 52 percent of the value of loans made for land purchases. Those banks unable to meet the new provisioning rules would be able to borrow the additional money in the form of state-backed convertible bonds carrying a 10 percent interest rate. Furthermore, banks could transfer their riskiest assets to state-guaranteed asset management companies to help speed the sale of real estate assets the bank holds. Each bank would be forced to create a bad bank into which it will put physical property assets at marked down valuations, in preparation for potential sales to outside investors. Finally, the government agreed to ask two independent firms—Roland Berger y Oliver Wyman—to audit the banks' real estate portfolios. Following this reform, four Spanish banks (Banco Mare Nostrum, Liberbank, Unicaja, and Ibercaja) announced that they were working on a merger to create the country's fifth largest lender, with assets of €270 billion.[31]

5. *August 2012:* A new financial reform was approved in response to the EU financial rescue package. It created a *bad bank* that could absorb the toxic assets from the real estate sector, and had the authority to buy and sell all kind of assets and to issue bonds. The reform reinforced the role of the Bank of Spain in the creation of the bad bank. The Bank of Spain was also assigned a central role in the decisions regarding the assets that would be transferred from each individual financial institution to the bad bank, and more importantly, in the pricing of these assets before their transfer. It also established a new process to restructure and liquidate financial institutions and it gave a central role in that process to the FROB and the Bank of Spain. Finally, the reform reduced the role of the regional governments in the restructuring and liquidation of cajas and saving cooperatives

Prior to the last reform (it is still too early to assess it), the results of these reforms have been questionable at best. The fact that Spain has had five reforms in less than three years, instead of one that really fixed the problem, says it all. They have been largely perceived as "too little and too late," and they failed to sway investors' confidence in the Spanish financial sector. The approved "low-cost" reforms have not solved the problems. Both the Socialists and Conservative governments have been reluctant to admit the depth of the liquidity and solvency problems of many institutions (particularly the cajas, where politics has continued to play a role throughout the crisis) and the reforms have been insufficient to address them. At the same time, the attempt to force restructuring through mergers has also backfired, as proved by the Bankia fiasco. The governments have also failed to recognize that merging weak banks do not create a strong one. The €100 billion assigned to deal with the crisis seemed woefully insufficient and investors seem to be waiting for additional funding (and reforms) once the external auditors complete their work. The IMF also recently announced the regulatory weaknesses that need to be addressed (IMF 2012a): the banking and securities regulators' independence needs to be strengthened; the insurance and securities regulators need to gain financial and budgetary independence; the bank of Spain needs further authority to address preemptively the build-up of risk in the system; and the sanctioning regime in banking and securities supervision needs to be strengthened.

The current crisis can also be blamed on the *actions (and inactions) of the Bank of Spain*.[32] As we have seen above, at the beginning of the crisis, the Bank of Spain's policies were all praised and were taken as model by other countries. Time, however, has tempered that praise and the Bank of Spain is now criticized for its actions and decisions (or lack thereof) during the crisis.

The Bank of Spain anticipated the potential pitfall from the real estate bubble as early as 2003, when it alerted in one of its Economic Bulletins that the magnitude of the bubble could be "as high as 20 percent." This caused a conflict with the Conservative government, and Rodrigo Rato, the minister of finance at the time, questioned the report. This was the first instance of a battle that marked the course of action in subsequent years and this, despite the Autonomy Law, which protected the Bank of Spain against political interference. Indeed, the conflicts between the government and the Bank of Spain, between the political and the financial powers, are crucial to understanding what has happened as well as why the Bank of Spain failed to act to burst the real estate bubble, and to address the recapitalization of the cajas until it was too late. Naturally, any action to bust the bubble was opposed by the governments (both the PP and PSOE ones) because of the negative impact it would have had on economic growth.

Despite the Bank of Spain warnings, mortgages continued growing at a fast pace: a 20 percent annual rate. Yet, banks and cajas continued to ignore its recommendations. Pushed by intensifying competition for growth and market share BBVA increased its mortgages by 17 percent; La Caixa by 23.4 percent; Caja Madrid by 24.9 percent; and Banco Santander by 14.9 percent. The herd logic, once again, triumphed.

Governor MAFO has also been severely criticized. A Socialist Party militant who had served in government in different capacities since the 1980s, he had scant financial experience when he became governor of the Bank of Spain (this shortcoming has been used by many observers to explain the deficiencies in the design and implementation of the financial reforms). Prior to assuming the governor's position, Governor Ordoñez had played a very prominent and public role in Spanish media criticizing the country's growth model and its dependence in the construction sector. However, he failed to heed his own advice when he became governor. Facing strong opposition from the politicians and regional governments that controlled the cajas and were very reluctant to relinquish their power, he was not able (or did not dare) to confront them. This was a key factor in explaining the delays in the Bank of Spain's intervention, which often waited too long and/or acted when it was too late, resulting in the problems getting out of hand (as it happened with the cajas from the Valencia region, the Galician ones, or even with Caja Madrid).

The arguments often mentioned by the Bank of Spain—that it lacked control of monetary policy (which was in the hands of the ECB), that it would have been counterproductive to burst the bubble because it was already declining, and that it did not have the tools to burst the bubble—seem disingenuous at best.[33] It is true that the establishment of the countercyclical regime was costly for the Bank of Spain and led to significant confrontations with the banks that complained bitterly that it placed them at a disadvantage with their international competitors because it reduced their profit margins. There was also a sense of complacency that the regime would provide a sufficient cushion if the real estate sector fell down. Yet, it was the Bank of Spain itself that approved the high concentration of risk in the real estate sector. Moreover, there were other actions that the Bank of Spain could take, and should have taken, to reduce the risk and dependence from the construction sector, such as increasing the required provisions together with the ECB, or strengthening the regulatory framework. Political considerations (both governors, Caruana and MAFO, wanted to avoid a confrontation with the PP and the PSOE) and concerns over potential litigation drove the agenda and precluded more decisive action to address the problem.

Even the new governor of the Bank of Spain, Luís María Linde, admitted in congress (in the summer of 2012) that the Bank of Spain had acted "insufficiently or inadequately" to the crisis, and recognized that it "was not successful in what we call *macro-prudential* supervision." He added: "we did not made the decisions that now we finally realize would have been necessary to address the large increases in indebtedness, and later on, we failed to contain and correct the strong deterioration of the banks accounts, which followed the collapse of the real estate bubble," while recognizing the fact that the Bank of Spain was "not the only European supervisory entity that made these mistakes, that was not of much consolation." Under questioning from MPs he acknowledged that "it would be absurd not to recognize mistakes in the oversight of banks," and that the euphoria associated with the economic boom made it more difficult to "see the risks that we were accumulating. It was as if no one wanted to foresee the possibility of a recession, of interest rates increases, or the collapse of funding." He still gave credit to his predecessors for introducing the anticyclical provision system in which the Bank of Spain "was a pioneer," but recognized that the main flaw of that system was "its timidity and its insufficiency in containing the excessive growth of credit," and admitted that the Bank of Spain had not gone far enough and had to "curtail its aspirations."

He was also very critical of the Sistemas Institucionales de Protección (the so-called cold mergers) introduced by his predecessor, because they were not "the solution" and did not produce the "desired results"; "they tried to overcome the political difficulties that emerged from the regional governments, as well as other difficulties raised by the cajas themselves to the mergers and integration" of these institutions. Yet, the resulting mergers were not very positive and contributed, contrary to the original goal, "to delay decisions and adjustments." Finally, he admitted that the banking stress tests were not sufficiently strong either, but argued that "almost no one was able to anticipate the depth of the crisis, something that affected the quality of the stress tests." He even admitted the possibility (which had already been mentioned by Joaquín Almunia, the EU Commissioner, and rejected by the PP government) to proceed with an "orderly resolution" of institutions that do not have a "strong pulse." But he was immediately corrected by the minister of finance, Luís de Guindos, who reaffirmed the government's position against the "liquidation of any Spanish financial institution."[34]

In the end, the Bank of Spain chose the path of least resistance: alerting about the risks but failing to act decisively, despite the fact that there were people within the bank who had been very critical of such inaction and lack of leadership. The Inspectors Association of the Bank of Spain published in May 2006 a letter to the minister of finance, Pedro Solbes, criticizing Governor Caruana's passivity in the face of the accumulated and growing risk associated with the real state sector. They attributed the extraordinary growth of the real estate prices to the "excessive growth of bank lending," and accused the governor of "lack of determination" in demanding "rigor" from financial institutions "when assuming risks."[35] This experience shows that in the absence of appropriate leadership supported with the necessary regulatory and financial controls, the actions of the Bank of Spain were influenced by political considerations, which ended up undermining its role. If anything, it shows the increasing concentration of power away from the Bank of Spain, in the hands of the government, and the banks.

The consequences (by the end of 2012) were nothing short of calamitous. On November 25, 2012, Minister Guindos requested €37 billion for the nationalized cajas (Bankia-almost 18 billion, Novagalicia, Catalunya Caixa and Banco de Valencia), and it was expected that four additional institutions (Ceiss, BMN, Caja3 and Liberbank) would request an additional €5 billion in support, which would increase the total bailout amount to around €45 billion. In exchange for this financial support the European Commission requested draconian measures: a 60 percent cut in the assets from nationalized cajas, a very painful restructuring plans that would include thousands of dismissals, the selling off of affiliates and their participation in industrial companies, the prohibition of loans to construction developers, and a request to retreat to their original region of operations. By the end of 2012 the nationalized cajas had already transferred €36 billion of their toxic assets to the newly created "bad bank" (called Sociedad de Gestión de Activos

Procedentes de la Restructuración Bancaria-Sareb), and it was estimated that they would have to sell the adjudicated assets for an average discount of 63 percent of their gross book value.[36]

Conclusion

There is consensus that the stern regulations of the Bank of Spain played a key role in the initial positive performance of Spanish banks. It made it so expensive for financial institutions to establish the off–balance sheet vehicles that had sunk banks elsewhere that Spanish banks stayed away from such toxic assets, and it also forced banks to set aside during the good years "generic" bank provisions, in addition to the general provisions for specific risks. Still these measures proved insufficient. As the crisis intensified and the real estate market worsened, the banking sector could not escape its dramatic effects. Deteriorating economic conditions, the implosion of the real estate market, the dependence on wholesale funding, weaknesses in the regulatory framework, and the role of the Bank of Spain all help explain this reversal.

As noted throughout the book, from the beginning of the crisis, Spanish governments have underestimated the country's property crash, the increasing unemployment rate, the rising debt-to-GDP ratio, and the impact that these factors would have on the banking sector. Furthermore, since the crisis intensified, Spain's policymakers and regulators have been indecisive. There was still a feeling in the country that the country and the banks are being unfairly picked by the markets and the EU.

The experience of the Spanish financial sector shows that it is impossible for banks not to be affected from a collapsing bubble in real estate. Spain had very high levels of securitized lending (i.e., banks transforming mortgages into ABS) that contributed to the property market bubble. In the end, the Spanish government (and the Bank of Spain and the ECB) failed to cope with the asset bubble and its imbalances. Hence, the Spanish experience shows that financial stability cannot be divorced from economic policy: while regulation matters, macroeconomic factors too do. The banks are still dealing with their toxic assets and need to learn from the lessons of other countries: their toxic assets need to be cleaned up, not just merged into a bigger problem. Bankia is a perfect example of that failure. In the end, Spain did not heed the lessons from previous crisis: do not lend excessively to property developers; burst the bubble before it is too late; recognize that retail banking is not a low-risk activity; avoid overconcentration in property loans; and remember what happened in earlier instances.[37]

Conclusion:
Lessons from Spain

To be ignorant of evils to come, and forgetfull of evil past, is a merciful provision in nature, whereby we digest the mixture of our few and evil dayes, and our delivered senses not relapsing into cutting remembrances, our sorrows are not kept raw by the edge of repetitions.

—Sir Thomas Browne

Introduction

This chapter outlines some of the main lessons that can be learned from Spanish experience before and during the crisis. As shown throughout the book, the crisis has so far devastated the Spanish economy, and there is consensus that the situation will only get worse before it gets any better. It is expected that by the end of 2013 the economy will start to grow again helped by the decline in unitary labor costs and inflation, which will allow Spanish products to gain competitiveness, and by the fall in the *Euríbor* interest rates, which will alleviate the financing of the debt for individuals and companies. By the end of 2012 some data was still discouraging: unemployment kept rising throughout the year, reaching new highs (the crisis destroyed 2,000 employments per day throughout 2012), and is expected to increase to 28 percent in 2013 (to an astonishing 6 million people); poverty and inequality indicators continued deteriorating; social conflict intensified; inflation reached 2.9 percent at the end of the year driven by the tax increases; real estate prices continued declining driven by the record unemployment, lower purchasing capacity, excess stock, and higher taxes and financial costs (average housing prices fell 7 percent in 2012, with an accumulated decline since the crisis started of 33 percent) with the deleterious effect that this has on banks' loans; and the economy was still expected to contract between 1.3 and 1.5 percent in 2013.[1] Still, there were also some positive indicators, as well: the sovereign bond yields stabilized at the end of the year (after reaching a record 7.5 percent in the summer), thus allowing the government to postpone the decision regarding a possible EU sovereign bailout; investment was flowing back into the country and capital flight was stemmed; the adjustment of the country's external debt continued improving (it went down from a record 170 percent of GDP in 2010, to 165.7 percent in September 2012); unemployment went down by 59,094 people in December 2012 after four consecutive months of increases; and the reduction in unitary labor costs and improving productivity were contributing to an "internal devaluation" that was allowing Spain to regain its competitiveness and increase its exports.

This book underscores that the economic crisis in Spain has not been solely caused by the global financial crisis. Indeed, Spain has been facing a severe economic and social crisis, which coincided in time with the global (and Eurozone) financial crisis. The latter one has been deepening and intensifying the severity of the domestic crisis, but the global and Eurozone crises cannot serve as an excuse to minimize the domestic components of the Spanish one. On the contrary, Spain faces a crisis caused largely by two simultaneous disequilibria: the unsustainable growth of the real estate/construction sector and excess consumption, both driven by very low interest rates, which took the trade deficit to an unprecedented 11 percent of GDP just before the crisis, the highest of the OECD countries. And it would be disingenuous to claim that the crisis was a surprise, because international and domestic observers and institutions were alerting all that it would not come for a few years. It is essential to accept these premises to diagnose and address the crisis adequately.

The Socialist and Conservative governments have implemented several rounds of structural reforms and budget cuts to address the crisis. These measures attempted to respond to some of the fundamental imbalances in the Spanish economy that precipitated the crisis in the first place. Unfortunately, these reforms are hindered by budgetary constraints, which have (and will continue to) hampered the government's efforts to address historical shortcomings that are at the root of the crisis of the Spanish economy and its lack of competitiveness (e.g., low productivity and insufficient innovation). In addition, rounds of austerity are making it impossible for the government to gain much popular support to implement the ambitious regulatory and institutional reforms that should be introduced. On the contrary, the growing scarcity of resources results in greater conflict among interest groups scrambling to receive a larger portion of a shrinking pie. Conflict also intensifies with the regional governments in charge of implementing social and education policies, yet lack the financial resources to do so.

Spain still faces a situation of lack of credit, fiscal austerity, extreme lack of confidence from the markets, and an imploded real estate market. The traditional recipes are not working: national and regional austerity are destroying employment, demand stimulus to increase consumption, and investment is not possible because fiscal restrictions are a priority while increasing debt is not an option in the current context, and monetary policy is in the hands of the ECB. Without credit and demand, there will be hardly a recovery. While austerity will intensify the crisis, expansion is not possible due to misguided EU and market pressures. The Conservative government still faces the challenge of how to square this circle. In its first six months, the PP government negotiated with Germany and the EU liquidity in exchange for austerity and reform, and tried to develop and implement a credible program in order to regain the confidence of external and domestic investors, including the cleaning up of the financial institutions, fulfilling the fiscal consolidation program, and deepening reforms. So far (as of the end of 2012), the positive outcomes have not materialized.

At the European and global levels a main structural problem still persists, which needs to be addressed: the mismatch between global economics and local politics. Global capitalism and the power of mobile capital have outstripped the capacity of national governments to manage it. As a result of the crisis in Europe (and elsewhere), inequalities and structural unemployment have been increasing within and across countries. Yet, governments have failed to protect citizens against these insecurities because they do not have the money and/or the tools. The subsequent discontent has been fueling the rise of rightwing populism, the anticapitalism on the left, and the politics of identity. In response, most governments increasingly have been looking inward focusing on their narrow national interests.

However, despite the crisis, laissez-faire capitalism has not been discredited. Indeed, expectations that the role of governments would be rehabilitated as key actors in economic management have not materialized. On the contrary, fury against the bankers has not been translated into renewed faith in the state; and throughout Europe (and in Spain) the center-right swept elections (with France being one of the few exceptions). The excesses of markets have not translated into public confidence in the state, and there is still not much consensus on its role, efficiency, or size. Voters seem to blame both bankers' greed as well as public borrowing. In this regard, the occupy movement that emerged in most countries during the crisis has many threads—anticapitalism and antiglobalization—but it has lacked cohesion, and has been unable to articulate clear alternatives. Finally, countries have been lacking decisive leadership and a "grand plan" to move forward.

In order to address the global financial crisis, European governments need to focus on the following: achieving macroeconomic stability; fixing their financial systems with better regulation and management, avoiding the buildup of leverage, developing better shock absorbers, and protecting their citizens from predatory practices; addressing unemployment and inequality through fiscal redistribution, access education, job subsidies, and by focusing on growth; reforming corporate governance so companies focus on stakeholders rather than shareholders, and providing better incentive systems that focus on the long term; reforming tax systems to generate the resources to provide public goods and improving corporate taxation, making taxes more progressive and shifting from incomes to consumption and wealth; and last but not least, preserving democratic politics so citizens still feel like they have a voice and appropriate channels to articulate their demands and grievances.

Indeed, well-calibrated government activism is needed to provide the collective goods, such as training and infrastructure that countries (and companies) require to succeed in a global economy. It is also important to emphasize that although we can blame global finance and worldwide corporations for the crisis, we should also save some blame for the "insatiable consumers and investors that inhabit in almost every one of us."[2] Indeed, throughout the crisis (in Spain and elsewhere) there has been a widespread tendency to point fingers in all directions, but not quite enough soul searching to reflect in how our own individual behavior contributed to the excesses that led to the crisis in the first place (or how we failed to hold accountable those responsible for it). Who forced people to buy houses and get mortgages that they could barely afford?; to consume beyond their means?; or to spend, rather than save or invest? The crisis has exposed that many Spanish people (if not the country itself) were living beyond their means, and the necessary ongoing corrections are being brutal, with many innocents suffering the consequences of the crisis and its devastating social outcomes.

But governments must be patient. History shows that the aftershocks of these crises are long and painful (Reinhart and Rogoff 2009). Finally, as important as it is to deleverage, more than just austerity and fiscal discipline is needed. Austerity on its own will not address the lack of competitiveness and the deficits in the current accounts. Indeed, how can economies rebound if the private and public sectors deleverage at the same time? In Spain, banks are writing down billions of euros in their portfolio investment. In the public sector, initially the deficit was projected to be 8.5 percent in 2011, with unrealistic goals to reduce it to 5.3 percent in 2012 and 3 percent in 2013. In effect, this meant an incredible 5.5 percent adjustment over two years, and in the middle of a recession. This pattern (repeated all over Europe over and over again throughout the crisis) to seek credibility with incredible and unrealistic goals and projections, has only undermined trust and credibility. In their desperation to placate the insatiable markets, they have sacrificed the little credibility that Spanish governments had left.

Can the Spanish economy grow before the end of the decade? Will reforms increase confidence and produce growth? Ultimately governments will need to determine how to balance austerity and growth. Spain needs a program forcing the private sector to deleverage over the next 3–5 years, while maintaining robust public sector deficits and implementing structural reforms. The focus must be shifted to the public sector deficit only after the private deleveraging is complete. This would accelerate the adjustment. Presently, Spain is stuck in a debt trap and may end up where Portugal is now: under a rescue umbrella.

Unfortunately for Europe, the euro crisis has been a return to zero-sum politics. If anything, collective interest and cooperation at the domestic and European level have been battered. The crisis has led to a new age of nationalism and to the erosion of solidarity, one of the founding principles of the process of European integration. So far during the crisis, agreements among countries at the EU level have been largely transactional ("I give you some-thing in return for something"), rather than the "enlightened self-interest" that primed European actions in previous decades ("I am helping another country because that helps me and my own citizens"). This has led to a grow-ing (and very risky) North-South wedge within the EU, a pervasive sense of political powerlessness for governments and citizens alike, and, overall, to a crisis of EU governability. Yet, often during the crisis governments seemed to forget their citizens, obviating that the crisis was largely not their fault. In many countries, including Spain, this has led to growing social fracture and unrest.

Many European governments, not just Spain, are trapped in a sovereign debt trap; for their governments, the challenge is how to confront an age of austerity. And this in a context during which Europe faces significant chal-lenges: not just the current crisis, but also the lack of trust in the EU; the ineffectiveness of EU institutions; the demographic crunch; immigration; feeble growth; the sustainability of the welfare state; and the lack of strong leadership at the EU level.

The book has stressed that the crisis in Spain, while conditioned and deeply affected by the global and Eurozone economic crises, is substantially a "homegrown" crisis that was the consequence of a series of domestic struc-tural problems, which were not properly addressed, as well as policy errors from successive governments, many predating the global financial crisis. *What can we learn from the Spanish experience?*

Lessons from Spain's Experience

Nominal Convergence Takes Place Faster than Real Convergence

Spain's economic record for the past two decades shows that nominal con-vergence is faster, but that real economic convergence is a slow process.[3] As shown in chapter 1, the process of financial liberalization, economic reforms, and the significant decline in real interest rates permitted Spain to meet the Maastricht convergence criteria. Hence, on January 1, 1999, the coun-try became a founding member of the EMU, despite the fact that as late as 1997 it was considered an outside candidate for joining the Eurozone. Yet, it fulfilled the inflation, interest rates, debt, exchange rate, and public deficit requirements established by the Maastricht Treaty. This development confirmed the nominal convergence of the country with the rest of the EU. However, while nominal convergence has largely taken place, the income levels of Spain increased at a much slower rate and they remain behind the EU27 average (see table C.1).

More importantly, Spain still lags behind many of the EU's richest coun-tries in terms of their GDP per capita (as of 2011): Germany (120 percent); the Netherlands (131 percent); Austria (129 percent); Sweden (126 percent); France (107 percent); and even Ireland (127 percent) are still well ahead of

Table C.1 Divergence of GDP Per Capita (1980–2011)

	1980	1985	1990	2000	2007	2011
EU totals (%)	100.0	100.0	100.0	100.0	100.0	100.0
Spain	74.2	72.5	77.8	81.0	98.0	99.0

Source: EU.

Spain. The analysis of the nominal convergence data since Spain joined the EU shows that it has advanced at a faster pace than real convergence, and that it has experienced a cyclical evolution in Spain with significant increases during periods of economic expansion and sharp decreases during economic recessions. Furthermore, Spain's relative performance has been comparatively worse than that of other new member states. For instance, in the first 15 years since the adhesion of Spain to the EU in 1986, per capita income increased "only" 11.5 percent, and in Portugal's to 14.2 percent. Ireland's, in contrast, increased 38 percent. Only Greece with an increase of 6.8 percent had a lower real convergence than Spain in that period.

Indeed, 26 years of membership (as of 2012) have not been enough to catch up with the richest EU countries, and Spain's European integration revealed both convergence and divergence, nominal and real. Possible explanations for this development include: inflation differentials (i.e., since 1997, inflation in Spain exceeded the EU average every year); differentials in economic growth; higher levels of unemployment in Spain (it has always been among the highest in the EU, even during the boom years); comparatively lower rates of labor participation (i.e., active population over total population, which stood at 50 percent in Spain); inadequate education of the labor force (i.e., only 28 percent of the Spanish potential labor force has at least a high school diploma, in contrast with the EU average of 56 percent); low investment in R&D and information technology (among the lowest in the EU); and inadequate infrastructure (i.e., road mile per 1000 inhabitants in Spain is 47 percent of the EU average, and railroads is 73 percent). Finally, prior to the crisis, the inadequate structure of the labor market with high dismissal costs, a relatively centralized collective bargaining system, and a system of unemployment benefits guaranteeing income instead of fostering job search may have also hindered, in the eyes of many observers, the convergence process.[4]

It Is Essential to Prepare for EMU

Spain's EU and EMU membership was considered a success during the boom years. As we discussed in chapter 1, EU integration was the catalyst for the final conversion of the Spanish economy into a modern Western-type economy. The idea of Europe became a driving force that moved reforms forward was a fundamental factor for bringing together political stabilization and economic recovery. It also facilitated the modernization the country's economy, as well as the implementation of the microeconomic and macroeconomic reforms that successive Spanish governments undertook throughout the 1980s and 1990s (Tovias 2002).

In a context of strong support among Spanish citizens for integration, membership became a facilitating mechanism that allowed successive governments to prioritize economic modernization and pursue difficult economic and social policies (i.e., to reform its labor and financial markets), with short-term painful effects. Moreover, as a result of enlargement, Spanish producers gained access to European and world markets, providing additional incentives for investment and allowing for the development of economies of scale. This resulted in increasing competitiveness (albeit with the problems outlined in chapters 1 and 5), which contributed to attract investment and helped to build new industries. Not surprisingly polls demonstrated that Spaniards were among the staunchest supporters of the process of European integration.

However, as positive as this process has been, the crisis has also shown that countries need to undertake the necessary structural reforms to fully adapt to the demands of a single market and a monetary union. In this regard, the crisis fully exposed the vulnerabilities of the country's institutional and economic model, as outlined throughout the book. Somehow there was an expectation that membership on its own would force structural reforms, and this (naturally) did not happen. On the contrary, the crisis has shown the limits of EU/EMU membership in imposing institutional reforms in other areas (e.g., the labor market, the financial sector, or competition policy) and to balance domestic and external economic objectives. It took a crisis of historical proportion for the country to finally undertake some the structural reforms that were needed to operate in a monetary union. Institutional reforms require active policies by the governments that are willing to pay the short-term political price for unpopular policies.

EMU Membership Carries Risks

The Spanish experience also provides an interesting insight into the pitfalls of integration into a monetary union. As noted by Vítor Constancio, the ECB VP (and former governor of the Bank of Portugal), one of the main lessons from Portugal's experience (which also applies to Spain) is that "countries used to high inflation and high interest rates are likely to experience an explosion in consumer spending and borrowing" upon joining a monetary union.[5] This spurt will make the downturn inevitable, particularly in countries such as Spain that are vulnerable to higher oil prices and increasing competition from developing countries such as India and China. In Spain, the strong domestic demand stemmed from the sharp fall in interest rates. Demand, however, was not followed by a parallel increase in supply, as it was hindered by low productivity growth, leading to a significant increase in imports, as well as high external deficits and debts. External indebtedness, in turn, has led to lower domestically available income.

In this regard, a very important lesson is that lower interest rates and the loosening of credit will likely lead to a credit boom, driven by potentially overoptimistic expectations of future permanent income, which in turn may increase housing demand and household indebtedness, as well as lead to over-estimations of potential output and expansionary fiscal policies. The boom will also lead to higher wage increases, caused by the tightening of the labor market, higher inflation, and losses in external competitiveness, together with a shift from the tradable to the nontradable sector of the economy, which would have a negative impact on productivity (Abreu 2006, 5).

In order to avoid these risks, countries should develop stringent budgetary policies in the case of a boom in demand and/or strong credit expansion. At the same time, they should guard against potential overestimation of GDP, and measure carefully the weight of consumption on GDP, because they may inflate revenues in the short term and create an unrealistic perception of the budgetary accounts, as in the case of Spain. Furthermore, to avoid unsustainable external imbalances, countries should also carry out the nec-essary structural reforms to increase flexibility and productivity, as well as improve innovation in order to allow their productive sectors to respond to the increasing demand and to ensure that their economies can withstand the pressures of increasing competition. They should also set wages based on Eurozone conditions to ensure wage moderation, instead of on unreal-istic domestic expectations and/or domestic inflation (Abreu 2006, 5–6). Countries should also take the opportunity presented by the boom to move into higher value-added and faster growth sectors toward a more outward-oriented production structure. Finally, the current global crisis illustrated the need for strict financial supervision to avoid excessive lending and misal-location of resources.

Indeed, EMU membership is not a panacea. On the contrary, Sweden, which is not an EMU member, has been one of the most successful European economies during the past decade. Much of the credit is based on the struc-tural reforms and spending cuts that reduced a 12 percent of GDP deficit into a balanced budget. The single most important reason for Sweden's success, however, may have been the country's decision to abandon the European fixed currency exchange rate regime and switch to a floating exchange rate, and give independence to its National Bank. This decision allowed for the decline of the currency value, which helped to restore competitiveness and decreased the budgetary cost of unemployment. At the same time, it allowed the National Bank to focus its monetary policy on a 2 percent inflation target, instead of just trying to use monetary policy to maintain a fixed exchange rate. The subsequent economic growth allowed the government to use fiscal policy as a tool of economic reform and income distribution. The current global financial crisis exposed the weaknesses of the EMU. Sweden is a sobering example of the benefits of a floating exchange rate and strict inflation targeting, options that are not available to Eurozone countries.[6]

Not All Problems Were Fiscal Problems

This book analyzes the debt crisis in Spain and shows that it was not caused by the profligacy of the public sector, but rather, as shown in chapter 4, by the fact that in Spain the crisis did not originate with wildly mismanaged finances. Indeed, the crisis in Spain has largely been a problem of ever-growing private sector debt, compounded by banks' reckless investments and loans (particularly to developers and construction companies, not so much to home buyers), and aggravated by competitiveness and current account imbalances. Therefore, the options that the government had to prevent the fiscal crisis were limited, as it lacked control of monetary policy and could not limit private sector capital inflows.

Fiscal Discipline Matters, but It Is Not Enough

It is now widely accepted that increases in government consumption adversely affect long-term growth; also that while fiscal consolidation may have short-term costs in terms of activity, they can minimized if consolidation is credible by implementing consistent decisions that deliver solid results. In this regard, differences in fiscal policies, within the constraints imposed by the SGP, played a central role in countries' performance prior to the crisis (Royo 2012). Unsurprisingly, of the cohesion countries, the ones that performed better in the decade and a half prior to the crisis were those who maintained fiscal discipline: Ireland and Spain. Both countries either maintained a budget surplus or reduced their budget deficits to comply with the SGP, while reducing their total expenditures vis-à-vis GDP. Prior to the crisis, Spain was perceived as one of the most fiscally disciplined countries in Europe. Initially, fiscal surpluses allowed the country to use fiscal policy to be used in a countercyclical way to address the global financial crisis.[7]

As noted above, when nominal short-term interest rates converged to those set by the ECB the Spanish economy experienced a boom during the second half of the 1990s boosted by the considerable fall in interest rates, which fell more rapidly than inflation. The impact of this development was further boosted by the simultaneous processes of financial liberalization, which contributed to increased domestic demand, and, in particular, housing demand. The expansion of the Spanish economy during these years was largely driven by internal demand, and this boom coincided with a period of international expansion. This expansion would have required a concomitantly prudent fiscal policy.

However, as shown in chapter 4, although Spain entered the crisis in 2008 in an apparent excellent fiscal position, the country's structurally or cyclically adjusted deficit turned out to be much higher than its actual deficit. As a result of the crisis, the country's fiscal performance collapsed by more than 13 percent of GDP in just two years. This shows that Spain's structurally or cyclically adjusted deficit was much higher than its actual deficit, and illustrates how difficult it is to know the structural position of a country.

In order to avoid such a situation, as noted in chapter 4, countries should further tighten budgetary policies in the case of a boom in demand and/or strong credit expansion. It is also important that they use fiscal policies in a countercyclical way to be prepared for recessions; finally, higher revenues, as in Spain prior to the crisis, should not drive budget surpluses. On the contrary, governments need to address the structural reasons for the deficits and avoid one-off measures that simply delay reforms but do not address the long-term budgetary implications. In addition, in order to avoid what happened in Spain (revenues were inflated in the short term as a result of the bubble, which created an unrealistic perception of the budgetary situation of the country), governments should also guard against potential overestimation of GDP and measure carefully the weight of consumption on GDP. Finally, the current global crisis also illustrates the need for tight financial supervision to avoid excessive spending and misallocation of resources.

But we need to challenge the orthodox view that has taken root in Europe based on the unlimited positives of austerity. On the contrary, by now it should be clear that harsh austerity measures during a recession tend to deepen the downturn. Even the IMF has recognized as much. Looking at the experiences of advanced economies that have faced public debt burdens as high, or higher, than those prevailing today, and the way that they responded to those crisis, the IMF has drawn the following lessons (IMF October 2012c):

1. Successful debt reduction requires fiscal consolidation *and a policy mix that supports growth.* Key elements of this policy mix are measures that address structural weaknesses in the economy and supportive monetary policy.
2. Fiscal consolidation must emphasize persistent, structural reforms to public finances over temporary or short-lived fiscal measures. In this respect, fiscal institutions can help lock in any gains.
3. Reducing public debt takes time, especially in the context of a weak external environment. (My italics)

The EU still needs to take note of these conclusions. If anything, the crisis has shown that fiscal policy should not be treated as an accounting exercise. Indeed, higher tax rates in the context of a shrinking economy do not necessarily increase tax revenues; in addition, spending cuts do not necessarily result in lower expenses because they may cause additional outlays on unemployment benefits and other social programs. In the case of Spain, the problem has been aggravated because the crisis unveiled an unexpected degree of fiscal laxity and financial mismanagement by most of the 17 regional autonomous governments in addition to hundreds of the municipalities.[8]

However, as noted before, credibility still seems to trump any other goal; when countries miss their deficit targets, the expectation is that they must overcompensate the next time around and make additional cuts to meet the goals. Nevertheless, the evidence so far is that this approach is not working: in Spain, the EU target included a 3.2 percent of GDP deficit correction for 2012. For 2012 and 2013, the targeted fiscal adjustment is 5.5 percent of GDP, one of the biggest fiscal adjustments ever attempted by any industrialized country; put in perspective, a reduction of the deficit from 8.5 percent to 5.3 percent represents between €53 and 64 billion, which seems simply impossible. Yet, any announcement that the country may miss the deficit targets garnered a response by the Rajoy government (and previously the Zapatero one) of renewed commitment to meet the stated goals, and/or a new pledge to take any additional steps to make further cuts. However, new announcements of cuts often provoke the opposite response from the markets and investors, and instead cause panic, and push bond yields further up because of concerns over the impact that additional cuts may have on the country's (lack of) growth prospects, which in turn would make the deficit goals even more unrealistic. Finally, the notion that structural reforms can help in this context is also questionable, because they take time to implement and come to fruit. So far (as of the end of 2012), austerity and reforms are not having the effects predicated throughout the crisis.[9] We still need a growth strategy and a New Deal at the European level.

Address Deficiencies in the Policymaking Process and Challenge the Dominant Paradigm

Prior to and during the crisis, there was strong consensus in Spain among economic elites, as well as among Conservatives and Socialists leaders, regarding fiscal consolidation and the balance budget objective. Indeed, prior to the crisis (as we have seen in chapter 4), Spain presented itself as the model of a country applying the budget surplus policy mantra. This consensus may have worked well in the short term, because it contributed to the credibility of the government policies, and allowed the country to become a founding member of EMU, but a more accommodating policy would have positively contributed to upgrading the productive base of the country with investments in necessary infrastructure and human capital that may have contributed to a faster change in the model of economic growth, as well as reduced dependency on the construction sector.

As a matter of fact, the real state bubble during the decade prior to 2007 helped minimize and mask the structural problems of the Spanish economy (see chapter 1). This development was a result of the consensus among Spanish political and economic elites regarding the neoliberal market-oriented policy paradigm, according to which the liberalization and deregulation that followed the process of European integration were highly advantageous for the country and resulted in a positive economic performance. Consequently, as examined in chapter 3, both parties in government, the PSOE and the PP, applied policies that were largely consistent with this paradigm, which was never fully challenged, despite indications that there were reasons for skepticism. Robert Fishman (2012) eloquently discusses the mediocre performance of the Spanish economy between 1974 and 1999, highlighting the structural inability of the Spanish economy to address the unemployment problem, which remained persistently high even during the boom years (the lowest point was reached in May 2007, still 7.7 percent, comparatively high).

It was this inability to create enough jobs, despite the consensus over the apparent reasons for the persistent unemployment (which largely focused on the rigidities in the labor market, labor costs, and the role of trade unions), as well as the repeated failure of successive neoliberal labor reforms to address it (see chapter 5) that should have led to a more critical review of the dominant policy paradigm. Yet, this did not happen for the reasons examined in chapter 3.

On the contrary, the fixation with the neoliberal paradigm blinded the country's leaders from the need to address other structural problems that hindered job creation and productivity growth, such as the insufficient access to capital for entrepreneurs as well as for SMEs, rooted on the oligopolistic nature of the financial sector (Pérez 1997), which hindered their ability to innovate or to create new companies and new jobs (Fishman 2010, 293–299). The country's competitiveness and productivity have also been hampered by insufficient (and/or inadequate) reforms in other areas such as education, vocational training, R-D-i, the incorporation of women into the labor force, and the work-life balance.

In the end, it was the endemic inability of the Spanish political system to generate alternative policy responses to address economic challenges, and develop and implement the necessary structural reform to tackle them that has led the country to its current predicament. Policy stability and consensus over a flawed policy paradigm, which focused largely on the liberalization of the labor market as the solution to all the country's problems, did not deliver the necessary reforms that the country needed, and this failure has intensified the current crisis. Unfortunately, the ongoing fixation with austerity (imposed by the EU but also fervently supported by the Rajoy government, and previously by the Zapatero one) is threatening to worsen Spain's structural problems because it impedes investment in areas such as R-D-I, education, vocational training, and social services that are crucial to provide short-term stimulus and long-term competitiveness.

Learn from Traditional Financial Crises

The financial crisis in Spain did not involve subprime mortgages, collateralized debt obligations, SIVs, or even investment banks. In many ways, the financial crisis in Spain has strong similarities with traditional banking crisis. For instance, there are some strong parallels with the United States' savings and loans crisis over two decades ago, which ended up costing $100 billion; or the recent Irish one. In Spain, as in the United States and Ireland, real estate lending became during the boom years the new fashion of the times for banks and cajas. Excess lending, as well as insufficient regulation and supervision, led to overleverage and a real estate bubble. In the end, this property bubble aggravated by excessive concentration of risk in one sector of the economy (the construction sector) led to hubris (Royo 2013a).

In this regard, the similarities with Ireland are striking: both countries experienced an enormous property price bubble before the 2008 global financial crisis. But the Irish financial system imploded earlier than the Spanish one and hence there is already a longer record of dealing with it. The three lessons one can draw from Ireland's experience in dealing with the current crisis are as follows: "present an accurate estimate of the bad loans (and bring in outside independent consultants with credibility); force banks to face up to losses, possibly through the creation of a so-called 'bad bank;' and finally, share as much of the losses as possible with bank bondholders."[10]

Fortunately for Spain, as noted in chapter 6, the bubble was smaller than in Ireland; property prices rose in Spain about three times between the mid-1990s and the 2007 peak, compared with 4.5 times in Ireland, and real estate loans peaked at 77 percent of the Irish economy, compared with 29 percent in Spain. Moreover, the crisis so far (as of December 2012) has largely affected the second tier of Spanish banks. Santander and BBVA diversified far more and hence major international operations were substantively less affected. At the same time, Spain, unlike Ireland, established a recapitalization instrument and process based on the FROB. The problem, of course, is that it lacked enough funds, leading to the EU financial bailout. However, this bailout has represented "only" 9 percent of the Spanish economy, compared with 43 percent for the Irish one (or €63 billion).

In the end, as noted in chapter 6, Spain did not learn from its previous crisis: banks should not lend excessively to property developers; governments and central bankers should be proactive in bursting the bubbles before it is too late; bankers should recognize that retail banking is not a low-risk activity, and should avoid overconcentration in property loans; and finally, governments and central bankers should avoid any complacency (as it happened in Spain), and instead need to be vigilant and proactive to avoid the mistakes of the past and to anticipate all possible scenarios, including the most negative ones.

In Spain, the misplaced and excessive confidence on the strength of the financial sector, and the almost unquestioned belief in the regulatory and oversight prowess of the BoS, led to hubris. Indeed, as noted in chapter 6, the financial sector regulatory framework and the BoS had been widely praised at the outset of the crisis for their heavy handed approach. However, there were serious deficiencies that came to the surface later, the most important of which was the inadequate regulatory framework that ruled the cajas. Cajas were mutually owned banks supervised under a mixture of national and regional charters that allowed them to grow rapidly into commercial property in search of market share and higher profits. This regulatory framework allowed for undue political interference (often compounded by the lack of experience and in many cases ineptitude of the politically appointed managers), and the cajas were often pushed by local and regional governments to make loans. These loans were not off–balance sheets, they were very much on display, yet the cajas' managers and the regulators largely ignored their risks (including the IMF, which was on record praising the strengths of the Spanish banking sector and the ability of Spanish banks to absorb losses from adverse shocks without systemic distress).

The BoS and the government also failed to burst the real estate bubble, or to limit deposit-funded lending institutions.[11] The notion that banks (even "conservative" Spanish ones who claimed for years that they had mastered risk management) can best judge on their own how much to expose themselves to property has proven to be a fallacy. The Spanish experience shows that, in a context of growing real estate prices, banks are not capable of restraining themselves. They need even more oversight and regulation.

Financial Regulation Matters

Regarding the experience of the Spanish financial sector during the crisis, there are also several lessons (see chapter 6) (Royo 2013a). First, there is consensus that the stern regulations of the Bank of Spain played a key role in the initial positive performance of Spanish banks, because it forced banks to set aside during the good years "generic" bank provisions in addition to the general provisions for specific risks. In addition, it made it so expensive for them to establish off–balance sheet vehicles that Spanish banks stayed away from such toxic assets. The 'Spanish Method' is now being generalized all over the world. There has been also growing consensus that banks were under-capitalized in the run up to the crisis and hence most counties are now subjecting their banks to higher capital requirements. At the same time, they are also making regulatory rules less procyclical, tightening liquidity requirements, trying to ensure that governments and regulators pay closer attention to the buildup of risk across the financial system as a whole, finally preventing off–balance sheet activities.

Second, no model is perfect. Indeed, the experience of the Spanish financial sector shows that it is impossible for banks not to be affected from a collapsing bubble in real estate. The collapse of wholesale funding for Spanish banks eventually had a knock-on effect on Spanish bank lending, thus leading to the bursting of the asset price bubble (by the end of 2011 land prices, adjusted for inflation, fell about 30 percent from the 2007 peak; and home prices are off about 22 percent) and a seemingly more "traditional" banking crisis. As a result, Spain is still suffering a property-linked banking crisis exacerbated by financing obstacles from the international crisis. The Bank of Spain announced in 2012 that bad loans on the books of the nations' commercial banks, mostly in the real estate sector, reached 7.4 percent of total lending.

Third, the Spanish government (and the ECB) failed to cope with the asset bubble and its imbalances. Hence, the Spanish experience shows that financial stability cannot be divorced from economic policy; while regulation matters, macroeconomic factors do too. And they had options: the government should have eliminated housing tax breaks and/or establish higher stamp duty on property sales, or higher capital gains tax on second properties.

Fourth, the performance of Spanish banks shows the need for conservative risk management. Bankers should stress the need to be obsessive about credit quality, avoid noncore activities such as proprietary trading, learn from past experiences, learn that geographical diversification may help to limit the banks' exposure to the weak economic performance of a particular market, all the while realizing that the nature of the diversification is important as proved by the performance of other European banks who diversified and experienced problems (i.e., French banks diversified by investing into Greece and also in dodgy securities funded by wholesale borrowing with negative results).

Fifth, the structure of mortgages can make a major difference in how a collapse of the real estate sector plays out. In Spain, refinancing is very unusual because mortgage loans are typically made at variable rates and there is no need to refinance if rates decline. In addition, mortgage loans are not bundled into securities to be sold to foolish investors and there were no "originate-to-distribute-strategies." On the contrary, banks expected to profit from these loans and gave few mortgages to investors looking to rent or flip homes. Moreover, typically there are no home equity lines of credit and borrowers cannot take out cash to spend on other things. Consequently, even if prices decrease, homeowners still have equity in their homes. Finally, mortgages are recourse and buyers cannot walk away if they have other assets[12] (Norris 2011). All these factors help explain why, despite the collapse of the real estate market, a relatively low percentage of loans appear to be in trouble (according to the Bank of Spain in September 2011, it was only half a point less than in mid-2009).

The experience of Japan in the 1990s also shows that zombie banks keep lending to troubled borrowers to avoid recognizing losses from bad loans, and that they do not extend credit to borrowers that need it to support the economy. The challenge is how to recognize a "dead bank walking." EMU banks are using ECB loans to buy government bonds, helping countries service their debt and making a profit. The risk, however, is that this strategy makes them even more exposed to governments bonds. Ultimately, the onus will be on the governments; if they regain the trust of investors, it will automatically improve the health of banks by increasing the value of their holdings of sovereign bonds.

Finally, the crisis has also illustrated how critical the flow of credit is for the functioning of economies. There has been widespread (and justified) resentment in Spain (and elsewhere) about the rescue of financial institutions. The reality is that if you want to help small and medium-sized companies it is essential to recapitalize banks. That is the only way to restart credit. The ECB funding efforts in this regard, have been instrumental, but unfortunately they have not been sufficient to increase credit to consumers and SMEs.

It Is the Politics, Stupid

Throughout the crisis the focus has been largely on the economic dimension of the crisis, as well as on its economic causes and consequences. It would be a mistake, however, to underplay the political dimensions of the crisis, and not just at the Spanish national level, but also at the European and global ones. This has been as much a political crisis as an economic one, and as much a failure of the markets, as a failure of politics. Political decisions have marked the course of the crisis.

At the domestic level, as discussed in chapter 2, the responses to the crisis from both the Socialist and Conservative governments have left much to be desired. So far (December 2012), transparency, decisiveness, and cooperation between the major parties have been sorely lacking. The Introduction chapter discussed the growing gulf between politicians and society and the responsibility of the elites (both political and economic) in the current predicament the country finds itself in. As of December 2012, more than 300 politicians had been charged in corruption scandals.[13] Recent polls confirm this estrangement: in December 2012 to the question "do you approve or disapprove in the way that institutions and social groups carry on their functions?" only 9 percent approved the way politicians carry on their functions (88 percent disapproved); 10 percent approved the way political parties carry on their functions (89 percent disapproved); 16 percent approved the way Parliament carries on its functions (81 disapproved); 20 percent approved the way the government carries on its functions (74 disapproved); and 29 percent approved the way trade unions carry on their functions (69 percent disapproved).[14] Therefore, the political dimension of the crisis cannot be minimized. It demands the overhaul of the structures established during the democratic transition in the late 1970s.

The handling of the Bankia crisis and the subsequent bailout were symbols of this political crisis. The government's reputation took a big hit: sweeping declarations (i.e., "no more public money to banks," "no bailout") were followed by 180-degree turnarounds; published figures had to be corrected (i.e., the size of Spain's budget deficit was revised upwards twice in the first six months of the government's tenure); and decisions were not appropriately vetted and run by European authorities before they were made public (i.e., the announcement that the projected deficit for 2012 would be 5.9 percent had to be lowered to 5.3 percent when the European authorities approved it; or the decision to inject government bonds into Bankia to pay for the rescue, which the ECB rejected). This all seemed to reinforce a pattern of incompetence and improvisation already established by the previous Socialist administration, damaging for the country throughout the crisis. The PP government, however, insisted in highlighting its reformist credentials (demonstrated by the overhaul of the labor market, the financial sector reform, its effort to impose austerity and reduce expenditures, and the first full-scale attempt to control spending by Spain's regional governments) insisting somehow that there was a method to the madness, while complaining that Spain was not being rewarded for "doing its homework." It still needs to learn that sweeping declarations are not enough.

Need to Address Current Account Deficits and Competitiveness

While the focus during the Eurozone crisis largely centered on the fiscal challenges, it is essential to note that we are also are dealing with a crisis of competitiveness (see chapter 4). As we have seen, EMU membership fostered a false sense of security among private investors, which brought massive flows of capital to the periphery. As a result, costs and prices rose, which in turn led to a loss of competitiveness and large trade deficits. Indeed, below the public debt and financial crisis there was a balance of payment crisis caused by the misalignment of internal real exchange rates. The crisis will largely be over when Spain regains its competitiveness.

Between 2000 and 2010 the loss of competitiveness vis-à-vis the Eurozone deteriorated: 4.3 percent if we take into account export prices and 12.4 percent if we take into account unitary labor costs in the manufacturing sector. Even though salaries in Spain were among the lowest in the Eurozone, Spain had a problem of "high relative labor costs." And compared to the OECD countries (the 30 more developed economies); the loss of competitiveness was even larger: 7.5 percent in export prices and 28 percent in unitary labor costs in the manufacturing sector. Although Spain was considered a "virtuous" country prior to the crisis for its fiscal policies, it had serious competitiveness problems that originated in the credit boom, and its consequences in the price-salaries relationship. In this regard, the solution will not be just to reduce salaries, but to guarantee that salary increases are connected with productivity. The collective bargaining structure did not sufficiently address that link because salaries were largely determined at the sectoral or provincial levels and applied to all companies within that sector/province, regardless of productivity, hence generating inflationary pressures and damaging competitiveness.[15]

However, it is important to emphasize that it would be simplistic to claim that the large trade deficit in Spain was caused exclusively by high relative salaries and low competitiveness. Other countries, such as the United States, also experienced very large trade deficits prior to the crisis as well, and it cannot be argued that the United States is not a very competitive country (the

Global Competitiveness Report ranks it five in the world). Indeed, trade deficits cannot be explained without reference to the policies of export-led countries in Asia (particularly China), and Europe (Germany). The aggressive export policies of these countries that pushed down domestic consumption intervened to keep exchange rates down and accumulate foreign reserves, generated huge current account surpluses, and then recycled them into capital outflows (in Asia, currency reserves in these countries rose by $5,300 billion in July 2008) led to intense disequilibria in the global economy, as well as global economic imbalances between savings and investment. The "global savings glut" in emerging economies pushed down rates on government bonds and led investors to search for higher yields, which resulted in a reduction of risk premiums and lower market discipline. In Southern Europe (and Spain) this massive flow of capital was a crucial factor to understanding the real state bubble

In this regard, it is essential to remember the role of payment imbalances: dependence of output in one country on demand in others. If Spain is to become more competitive, Germany must become less so. In effect, this means that southern European nations need to reduce their current account deficits, while northern European nations reduce their surpluses. Either the Eurozone runs a bigger surplus with the rest of the world (but it is not clear how this may happen), or the adjustment in the Eurozone takes place via shifts in competitiveness: the real exchange rates of Southern Europe decline, while those of Northern Europe increase. This would require countries with surpluses, such as Germany, boost their domestic demand, which would demand that countries address the intra-EU imbalance: Germany should adjust its export-led model. This is particularly important in the absence of additional cohesion funds.

Eurozone countries have four options:

1. Aggressive monetary easing, weakening euro, stimulatory policies in the core, and austerity and reform in the periphery to restore growth and competitiveness;
2. Deflationary adjustment and structural reforms to bring down nominal wages in the periphery;
3. Financing by the core of an uncompetitive periphery; and
4. Debt restructuring and partial breakup of the Eurozone.

So far (December 2012), there is a mixture of the second and third options: austerity and financing. But, as noted throughout the book, there is growing consensus that one-sided deflation will fail. In the absence of devaluations, countries need structural reforms and growth. An "internal devaluation" through a decrease in prices and salaries is socially and politically very difficult. Governments can opt to reduce their Social Security contributions and increase their VAT; reduce other nonsalary costs such as the energy and infrastructure ones; or increase productivity and labor quality. The challenge with these latter options, however, is that they will further reduce consumption thereby making matters worse, at least in the short term. They also require time—something that countries such as Spain lack. Finally, again, a growth strategy is still missing.

Need to Control Labor Costs to Remain Competitive

The experience of Spain within EMU also shows that there have been lasting performance differences across countries prior to the crisis. These differences can be explained at least in part by a lack of responsiveness of prices and wages, which have not adjusted smoothly across sectors, and which, in the case of Spain, have led to accumulated competitiveness losses and large external imbalances. While Germany (and other EMU countries) implemented supply-side reforms to bring labor costs down, through wage restraint, payroll tax cuts, and productivity increases, making it the most competitive economy with labor costs 13 percent below the Eurozone average, Spain continued with the tradition of indexing wage increases to domestic inflation rather than the ECB target, and it became one of the most expensive ones with labor costs going up to 16 percent above average (Portugal leads with 23.5 percent, Greece with 14 percent, and Italy with 5 percent).[16] A lesson for EMU members has been that it is critical to set wages based on Eurozone conditions, and not on unrealistic domestic expectations, to ensure wage moderation (Abreu 2006, 5–6).

Not surprisingly the countries that have controlled unitary labor costs during the crisis are doing better. Poland, for instance, is the EU's fastest growing economy: the country recorded a 15.8 percent cumulative expansion from 2008 to 2011 (during this period the EU's GDP shrank by 0.5 percent), and is expected to grow by 2.7 percent in 2012. One of the reasons is Poland works longer hours than its European neighbors: Polish work an average of 1,975 hours a year, more even than the French (1,670 hours) and the Germans. And while German workers are still twice as productive as Poles, Polish salaries are a fifth of German pay.[17]

In the absence of the possibility to devalue as a way to reduce the price of its exports and regain competitiveness, the only option for Spain (and the other EMU members in crisis), has been through an "internal devaluation" (i.e., by lowering labor costs). While the country is barely surviving the pain of adjustment, there are already positive signs on that front. According to government's figures its trade deficit has been shrinking, and it was down 28 percent for the first ten months of 2012, to €28 billion, compared to the same period a year earlier; the lowest level since 1972. Moreover, according to Eurostat, by December 2012, over all, Spain's unit labor costs were down 4 percent since 2008; and average hourly labor costs stood at €20.60, which was well below Germany's €30.10 and France's €34.20. One of the consequences of this positive development has been the increase in industrial competitiveness: for instance, in 2012 the Spanish labor market was 40 percent cheaper than those of Europe's largest car-making countries, Germany and France. As a result carmakers committed in 2012 to new plants or expansion in the country, totalling as much as €2 billion (and exports represent 90 percent of Spain's car production).[18]

Be Aware of New Players in World Trade and the Erosion of Comparative Advantage

As examined in chapters 1 and 4, a crucial problem for Spain has been the dramatic erosion of its comparative advantage. The emergence of major new players in world trade, like India and China, as well as the eastern enlargements of the EU have been particularly damaging to the Spanish economy because those countries have lower labor costs and compete with Spain traditional exports (as exporters of relatively unsophisticated labor-intensive products), leading to losses in export market shares (aggravated by the appreciation of the euro and the increase of unit labor costs relative to those in its trading competitors). At the same time, Spain's attempt to specialize in medium- and higher-technology products was also hindered by the accession of the Eastern European countries into the EU, which were already moving into those sectors specializing in these products.

In the end, Spain's ability to keep the lid on unitary labor costs prior to the crisis was insufficient to generate enough growth in exports to compensate for increasing domestic demand. While easy access to cheap credit had boosted domestic demand for households, it has also caused a shift of resources from tradables to nontradables services. This shift was further hastened by high wage increases, also in the public sector, caused by a tighter labor market in the second half of the 1990s, which further hampered external competitiveness and productivity. The result was an imbalanced economy sustained by strong domestic demand that translated into higher imports and external deficit.

Furthermore, some Spanish sectors of the economy did not prepare well for the WTO liberalization of sectors with major economic impact in the country, particularly footwear and textiles. The situation was compounded by the Asian crisis of the late 1990s, which led to the devaluation of these currencies, further eroding the competitiveness of Spanish exports. As a result, Spanish exports of footwear and textiles fell with the concurrent wave of dismissals and closures, which further dampened expectations and caused social problems.[19]

Finally, in order to avoid unsustainable external imbalances (see chapter 4), countries should also carry out the necessary structural reforms to increase flexibility (particularly internal flexibility that may be even more important for companies to allow them to deeply effect their human capital, than the external one, despite the traditional fixation on dismissal costs) and improve productivity. This would be the most effective way to allow their productive sectors to respond to the increasing demand and to ensure that their economies can withstand the pressures of membership to a single market. Finally, countries should also take the opportunity presented by the boom to move into higher value-added and faster growth sectors, toward a more outward-oriented production structure.

Learn from Previous Crises

As we have seen throughout the book, when the crisis first hit Spain at the end of 2007, most Spanish politicians and economist claimed, yet again, that "this time was different," and that the impact of the global financial crisis would be limited. They argued that the old rules no longer applied and that the new situation bears little similarity to past crises. In their seminal book, Reinhart and Rogoff (2009) examine eight centuries of government debt defaults (fittingly going back to the Spanish empire) from around the world, and conclude that claims that this time is different are invariably proven wrong. They show that while financial crises come in different ways, they are not mysteriously born of unexpected events. On the contrary, they are the result of frequently occurring events that can be identified and even managed if regulators and governments are sufficiently alert and know what to look for.

In the case of this global financial crisis we ignored, again, precrisis patterns that have recurred with eerie consistency in previous crises, and we failed to heed the lessons of history. Human nature and human mistakes were again at the heart of the disaster. If anything, the crisis has shown the critical need to relearn the forgotten lessons of the past.

For instance, the similarities between the current crisis in Europe and the Latin American sovereign debt crisis of the 1980s are striking.[20] Both in Europe and in Latin America, debts were issued in a currency over which the borrowing countries had no control: in the case of the large European countries, the euro, and in the case of Latin America, the US dollar. Furthermore, in both cases the crisis followed a period of easy credit. Spain (Ireland, Greece, and Portugal) experienced a boom of capital inflow and lending following accession to the Eurozone when interest rates reached record low levels. Similarly, Latin American countries were inundated with petro dollars in the 1970s, which were recycled into cheap loans to Latin American countries with little few conditions and or assessment of credit worthiness. In the 1970s, loan syndication was supposed to reduce risk; in the 2000s, securitization was also designed to reduce risk. In both cases, they did not. Finally, both crises took place concurrently with a global recession. In 1981, it was driven by the US Federal Reserve's decision to increase interest rates to 20 percent to control inflation. A year later, Mexico defaulted when it could no longer serve its $80 billion foreign debt. In 2009, the global crisis was precipitated by the collapse of Lehman Brothers. Two years later, both Greece and Ireland were compelled to ask for bailouts.

The similarities also extend to the responses to the crisis. In 1982, the initial solution centered on the goal to restore economic growth, because it was thought that growth would allow countries to restore their fiscal balance and pay back their debts. For that reason, the initial bailouts to Latin American countries were designed to buy time, so they could grow again. However a combination of deflating wages and shrinking economies ended up hurting growth. The crisis was misdiagnosed as a liquidity problem, when in reality it was a solvency one. It was only when Latin American countries accepted that premise, after Brazil stopped paying interest on its debt, that the solution to the crisis focused on debt forgiveness, as articulated by the 1989 Brady Plan: in return for debt relief, bank debt was turned into so-called *Brady bonds* backed by US Treasuries as collateral that reassured investors. In exchange, Latin American countries agreed to implement a series of economic reforms articulated around the Washington consensus. If the Latin American experience is a blueprint we can expect haircuts and collateral sweeteners (instead of US Treasuries, new Eurobonds?) in Europe.

One of the lessons from this comparison is that it takes time to get the right diagnosis and come up with the appropriate responses. Then, as now, policymakers muddled through and tried different options. When they failed, they tried new policies until finally the found the right ones. Time is essential because it provides the room to identify the roots of problems, allowing policymakers to come together, overcome resistances, and finally reach a measure of consensus to implement the right policies. Finally, time is also instrumental because it gives lenders the capacity to rebuild their capital to absorb further losses (they need to build up their capital buffers). For instance, according to the IMF, in the case of Latin America, in 1982, loans accounted for more than twice the capital base of US banks. Early debt write-off would have been impossible, as they would have devastated the US banking system. Similarly, according to the Bank for International Settlements, the accumulated debt claimed of foreign European banks in 2010 on Greek, Irish, Portuguese, Spanish, and Italian debt was almost €1,800 billion (twice as much as the US banks' exposure during the Latin American crisis).

Some of the important lessons from the current crisis are that countries should not liberalize their financial sector too fast; they should moderate borrowing, increase savings, focus on the real economy, invest in education and productivity, and remember that not all innovation (particularly in the financial sector) is useful.

We Need a Balanced EU Response

The solution to the crisis in Spain cannot come only from within Spain. The country is still in deep trouble despite all the reforms and budget cuts. The solution must also come from Europe. So far (December 2012) the EU response to the crisis has focused largely on buying time, and it has centered around five pillars:

1. Setting up large pools of money to provide emergency loans;
2. A move toward a closer fiscal union that would allow for the eventual creation of Eurobonds;
3. The development of a limited unified system for overseeing European banks;
4. ECB purchasing of sovereign debt in secondary markets; and
5. ECB lending to the Eurozone's banks as a lifeline to prevent a bank run and to allow them to continue to finance purchases of sovereign bonds.

Up to summer 2012, the EU strategy was to provide controlled financial support to debtor countries hoping to buy time to implement structural reforms that allow them to grow and reduce their deficits. Yet, while firewalls provide time, they do not solve problems. In addition, the short-term problem was that structural reforms deepen recessions. How long will structural reforms take to filter through to the real economy? So far, as seen in the case of Spain, austerity policies contributed to a sharp contraction of the debtor countries' economies; this has led to a "rolling crisis" as the EU keeps giving aid to countries that do not meet goals, such as Greece.

Furthermore, the crisis shows that the time horizon of rescue programs may be too short. Countries need time to implement a sustainable adjustment program, especially EMU members without the recourse to devaluations and with large accumulated external deficits. In this regard, taking countries away from the markets for a few years may not be optimal. It may help with short-term liquidity challenges, but it raises doubts about their ability to stand on their own, thus discouraging private investors. It is also important that adjustment programs include details of the specific structural policies necessary to sustain the macroeconomic adjustment and they specify the reforms needed, which should be frontloaded and subject to monitoring. Finally governments should remember that debt restructuring can be very damaging for other countries because there is the risk that investors will dump European governments bonds, which would intensify the crisis. The Greek problems showed that it should an option of last resort and, if possible, it should be avoided through privatizations.

Finally, prior to summer 2012, the ECB response may have been insufficient as well. So far, the role of the ECB was not as stimulating as that of the FRB) in the United States. Indeed the FRB spent hundreds of billions of dollars buying bonds, and amassed more than $1.6 trillion of federal debt to supply banks with massive amounts of cash they could use to lend to borrowers. The ECB was lending to banks, but they had to post collateral against the funds borrowed; hence the effect was less significant, and its sovereign bond-purchasing program was limited.

The ECB's decision, announced on September 6, 2012, to purchase Eurozone countries' short-term bonds in the secondary markets as part of the new program dubbed OMT may be a step in the right direction. It may lay the groundwork for a more coherent and sustainable solution that the previous ECB's program of limited bond buying. However, for this plan to be implemented governments must apply for aid from the Eurozone rescue funds with compliance of the conditions in exchange for support. In December 2012, Spain was still considering whether or not to apply for this aid.

Address EMU Institutional Constraints

The crisis has shown that the EMU is a flawed construction. Mario Draghi, president of the ECB acknowledged as much when he noted that it was like a "bumblebee" and declared "it was mystery of nature because it shouldn't fly but instead it does. So the euro was a bumblebee that flew well for several years." Lately it has not been flying well, and according to him, the solution should be "to graduate to a real bee."[21]

The crisis in Spain has illustrated the EMU's institutional shortcomings: Spain had a huge bubble that crashed with the crisis. The "bumblebee" flew for a while and convinced investors that they could invest (and lend) massively within the country, thus money poured into Spain. However, when the crisis hit, the country could not count on the EU to guarantee the solvency of its banks, or to provide automatic emergency support. And when unemployment soared and revenues plunged, the deficits ballooned. As a result, investors' flight followed and drove up borrowing costs. The government's austerity measures and structural reforms so far only contributed to deepen the country's slump. The country needs relief with its borrowing costs and hopes that the ECB plan will help (but resists the conditionality attached to it). It also needs support with its exports. Europe has so far largely come short on both accounts.

Outside of the Eurozone, high-income countries can support their economies because they have a central bank in charge of monetary policies and an adjustable exchange rate, allowing them the ability to run large fiscal deficits to compensate for the private sector deleveraging. However, the Eurozone lacks these mechanisms; when private external funding dried up, it left countries in the periphery with funding needs and a mechanism for adjusting their external accounts. This is a fundamental institutional flaw to deal with a global crisis.

Indeed, Greece has been the "canary in the coalmine." How can such a small country, representing only 2 percent of the Eurozone's GDP, threaten the whole EMU? This demonstrates the fragility of an institutional framework that tried to balance fiscal sovereignty with a monetary union. This model failed to combine flexibility, discipline, and solidarity. Fear is what is keeping it all together. But is fear enough to hold it together? If anything, the crisis exposed the shortcoming of EMU institutions. This is replication of the mistakes of the gold standard (Ahamed 2009).

At the financial level, the crisis also showed that there are countries like Spain (and Ireland) that are ill-equipped to regulate their banks effectively and lacked the adequate funding for the bailouts needed to guarantee deposits or prevent bank runs. In this regard, the Commission recently presented a plan that would have the ECB supervise banks across the Eurozone. However this plan has been met with stiff opposition, particularly from Germany that was concerned about the impact on its regional banks and about overstretching the ECB.

The crisis has also exposed the gap between the political power of national governments and EU institutions, on the one hand, and markets on the other. It has shown the different speeds at which they operate. National and European level political institutions have had a hard time reconciling the rapidly shifting expectations of financial markets with their own power limitations to act. The ECB and European institutions have shown that they need time to make decisions, resolve lingering differences, and deliver solutions to address the crisis. More often than not, the perception has been that they were doing too little too late. Moving forward, this deficiency needs to be addressed and decision-making mechanisms should be improved.

Discipline and Austerity Are Not Enough

Can an expansionary fiscal contraction work? The problem for Spain is the feeble outlook for growth: the Spanish economy is expected to contract by 1.7 percent in 2012 (and between 1.5 and 1.7 percent in 2013); the country has high external indebtedness; and it has a tremendous private sector debt. As a result, Spain's sovereign debt was repeatedly downgraded throughout the crisis. Unemployment also reached record levels at over 24 percent (and the unemployment problem is particularly acute among young people at over 50 percent). Furthermore, deep-seated structural weaknesses are still holding back growth and weighting on market assessment: overregulated product and labor markets, poor productivity, and low education achievement in international tests. There is also a funding gap; Spain faces billions of euro debt repayment in 2013. As a result of all this, many investors lost confidence in Spain's ability to return to sustainable growth under its currents constraints.

And the effects of austerity are affecting not only Spain: by the end of the 2012 summer the Eurozone was no longer stagnating, but contracting; GDP fell from April through June 2012 by 0.2 percent from the previous quarter of the 17 Eurozone member countries, and in Spain it shrank. 4 percent. So much for the notion that austerity could get these countries out of the recession! On the contrary, governments' budget cuts were one of the main reasons for this contraction, which was expected to become a full-fledged recession by the end of 2012. In other words, Europe is paying the consequences of an erroneous strategy based on budget restrictions across the Eurozone and inflexible controls over budget deficits, with very little to compensate and stimulate growth.

Can a government committed to reform turn around investor sentiment? The crisis has been a rollercoaster. There were times in which it seemed Spain could avoid the risk of contagion from the other countries already bailed out, but so far discipline has not been enough to decouple Spain from them in the eyes of investors. Even so, Spain still was (in the summer of 2012) in a considerably better fiscal position than Greece (e.g., the deficit target for 2012 was 5.3 percent in Spain, while for Greece, it was 6.8 percent; and the debt was expected to reach 70 percent in Spain and 190 percent of GDP in Greece). Yet, the yield on Spanish bonds reached 7.5 percent in July of 2012, a record since the country joined the Eurozone.

In this regard, if there was ever an assumption that financial markets act rationally, it has been shattered by this crisis. Any perception that markets are rational players imposing budget discipline in politicians must be placed into question in light of recent events. If anything, the crisis showed that nothing is measurable; in addition, investors' decisions are as much driven by fear as they are by rational considerations. Otherwise it is hard to explain why bond yields have behaved so erratically, or why rates periodically surged for troubled countries such as Spain, while they have hovered near negative levels for other such as the United States (with a larger deficit and debt than Spain) or Germany. Risk attracted profits and markets' concerns are becoming self-fulfilling; for instance, concerns over Spain's possible default have been driving up yields, yet by increasing the country's borrowing costs, markets make it more likely that the country will default. As a consequence, no matter what the government does (and most acknowledge that it has done a lot both in cutting costs and with structural reforms) it has not had as much impact because the market seems pretty much convinced that Spain needs a full-fledged financial bailout from the EU.[22]

It is also important to emphasize, as analyzed in chapter 4, that sloppy lending and irresponsible private borrowing were crucial factors leading to the crisis, not fiscal irresponsibility. If fiscal profligacy was not the dominant cause for the collapse of both economies, fiscal discipline cannot be the cure. In this regard, piling austerity measures on top of one another will not work. The Spanish economy is shrinking at a faster rate than forecasted for reasons outside the country's control; the ratio of Spain debt to its economy was 36 percent when it received the bailout and it is expected to reach 84 percent by 2013. In this context, further adjustment of the deficit is undesirable and will exacerbate market tensions. Spain needs automatic stabilizers to work. The challenge remains how to balance austerity and growth.

In this regard, the contrast with the United States is striking. Since 2007, the US Congress passed the equivalent of three stimulus bills:

a. A bipartisan $158 billion package of tax cuts signed by President George W. Bush in early 2008
b. A $787 billion bill pushed by President Obama as he took office in 2009 in the wake of the financial system's collapse

c. A tax cut and unemployment fund extension agreement reached by President Obama and Congressional Republicans in December 2010.

Many studies show that these measures are a key reason why the unemployment rate is not in double digits now in the United States.

Is Leaving the Eurozone an Option?

Since Spain is part of EMU, devaluations are no longer an option. The pain from the crisis has led some people to contemplate the possible benefits of abandoning EMU. This option, however, overlooks the benefits of EMU membership. Indeed EMU membership has been sheltering Spain from some of the worst effects of the global financial crisis. It helped prevent further capital flight (which took place in the past when investors tried to find refuge in countries with stronger currencies) and avoid a repetition of the attacks on the *peseta* that led to the devaluations of 1992 and 1993. Indeed, there is no doubt that without the euro the crisis would have already led to massive capital flight, a devaluation of the *peseta*, an inflationary spiral, in addition to the implementation of more restrictive monetary and fiscal policies. Hence, it is not surprising that, so far (December 2012), there is widespread support for EMU membership in the country. Therefore, the question should not be whether to leave the Eurozone, but instead how to use this crisis as an opportunity to move away from the preceding unsustainable growth model.

The siren calls for abandoning the euro should not be heeded. The effects of this decision would be potentially disastrous, and not just for Spain. The breakdown of the Eurozone would result in a depreciation of the original currency, the *peseta*, vis-à-vis the dollar and the euro (according to some estimates by as much as 30 percent). Since a significant proportion of Spain's debt is denominated in euros and dollars, this would force the country to default, which would close the country's access to international markets for years to come (as happened to Argentina after 2001). Furthermore, since Spain imports 77 percent of its energy, this devaluation would provoke a sharp increase in inflation, with the subsequent impoverishment and loss of purchasing capacity of the country's citizens, who would in turn demand higher wage increases, further eroding the competitiveness of Spanish firms and eliminate most of the advantage that may have been obtained from the devaluation. In addition, leaving the euro is likely to create a substantial banking crisis as depositors race to move their savings elsewhere. Finally, the most important objection, this decision would not resolve the country's economic problems, its external indebtedness, nor its lack of competitiveness, and would destroy the (already diminished) country's credibility.[23]

What Does All This Tell Us about VoC in Spain?

The focus of the VoC literature is on how national institutional differences condition economic performance, public policy, and social well-being; and whether national institutions will survive the pressures for convergence generated by the crisis. This book contributes to this literature by highlighting the synergy between the different components (labor and product markets, fiscal and financial institutions) on the development of the crisis (i.e., how national institutional differences condition economic performance); but it is too early to answer the second part (i.e., whether Spain are moving toward a LME model).

As outlined in the Introduction, according to the VoC literature, Spain is characterized by strong strategic coordination in financial markets, but not so in the field of labor relations. In countries such as these, there have been historically high levels of state intervention, and the coordination of labor relations was led by the state (i.e., the minimum wage or the ability to translate a wage increase in a firm to the entire sector). Hence, some VoC scholars argue that as states become more reluctant to coordinate labor relations in these countries, they will become less coordinated.

The crisis shows that LMEs and CMEs are surviving the crisis and that differences between both models are not being erased. Initially there was more active government intervention in most countries to mitigate the impact of the crisis, yet it proved short-lived (particularly in the LMEs). In this sense, the VoC literature is moving away from distinctions based on the level of state intervention. In the case of LMEs (like the United States), the relative increase in government activism (for instance, during the first two years of the Obama administration) does not diminish the fact that they are still LMEs. The responses of these countries to the crisis parallel differences between CMEs and LMEs because reforms are tailored to particular political economies; in the United States and the United Kingdom, the focus has been on stimulating consumption and rely more on tax cuts rather than spending increases (the ratio is 4 to 1, whereas in CME it is 1 to 2). On the contrary, in Germany the focus has been on subsidies for part-time work to avoid unemployment (a key for firms to retain high skilled labor). In Spain, originally the government focused on investment in infrastructure and short-term hiring, which reinforced the Spanish model. In the financial sector, the government and the Bank of Spain's initial decisions strengthened the existing model and further consolidated the strategic coordination in the country's financial markets.

Furthermore, the VoC literature stresses that institutional arrangements come in packages that cannot be easily unbound; as such, arrangements in one domain are dependent on arrangements in another. It does not specify which institutional arrangements can shift independently of others. Reforms in one area would demand reforms in other areas. Hence, institutional change is problematic and for countries that do not have coordinated institutional arrangements it is very difficult to develop them. Therefore, the most likely route for economic success for such countries would be to move to the LME model. Contrary to this prediction, prior to the crisis, the Spanish institutional model had not been converging toward an Anglo-American model (Royo 2008). It is true, however, that the more recent reforms seem to be pushing the country in a more LME direction. Spain was already characterized by weak strategic coordination in the field of labor relations, and the last two labor reforms will, if anything, accelerate the erosion of coordination. Yet, as analyzed in chapter 5, the social bargaining process is institutionalized and it will be interesting to observe how it adapts to the latest labor reform.

Furthermore, in the financial sector the initial response to the global financial crisis showed that cross-national differences persisted. While financial capitalist states converged as a result of the combined processes of globalization and European integration rendered the "Mediterranean" financial model far less distinct from other models than before, in the case of Spain as we examined in chapter 6, the crisis initially led to extensive regulatory intervention that served to reinforce the preexisting model, and changes in the years immediately preceding the financial crisis were not reversed. However, it is likely that the radical restructuring of the Spanish Financial System in the last year will accelerate its convergence toward a less bankarized model, more based on the markets.[24]

Yet, it is important to stress that the process of institutional change is not linear and that there is also strong path dependency; therefore, it is still too premature to confirm any definitive outcomes. In addition, the analysis of the Spanish experience with the crisis confirms the thesis that coordination is a political process and that strategic actors with their own interests design institutions (Thelen 2004). Institutional change is a political matter because institutions are generated by conflict, they are the result of politics of distribution, and, hence, they are politically and ideologically construed and depend on power relations (Becker 2006, 9). Institutions are important for firms because they influence interests and impact coalitions, and in a context of structural changes we have to examine the political settlements that motivate the social actors. In other words, institutional change is driven by politics. I agree with Thelen (2004, 73) that the focus on the "political dynamics" helps to underline that coordination is not just a "thing that some countries have and others lack." Indeed, the Spanish experience prior to the crisis showed that coordination is possible in countries that "lack" the appropriate institutional setting, and it can be sustained over a period of time (Royo 2008). The crisis has a profound effect on power relations and the interests of actors. The (yet undetermined) outcome(s) of these changes will, in turn, influence the process of institutional change. But it is still too premature to make definite conclusions.

Conclusion: Unfinished Economic Business

The book's Introduction discussed the political and institutional dimensions of the crisis. From an economic standpoint, the current crisis is the result of a combination of disequilibria led by private (not public) indebtedness, the real estate bubble, and inflation. These factors were compounded by the global financial crisis, and the adoption of policies that sharply increased the deficit led to a dramatic deterioration of the fiscal position of Spain, which in turn led to the loss of confidence from investors and higher borrowing costs.

There are many reasons for the current crisis in Spain: from policy mistakes, to the subprime crisis in the United States that led to a global financial crisis, to collective irresponsibility, to corruption, to institutional rigidities, to the flawed EMU design that lacked a fiscal union, among others. But the book stresses that the crisis in Spain is not one of fiscal irresponsibility and of profligate spending, as many have portrayed. The reality as seen throughout the book is far more complex than that. Moreover, the crisis in Spain is not just a Spanish economic crisis but also a European one. The EU was a political project that emerged in a particular context with a set of defined goals. Over time, as it has grown larger, those goals became increasingly diffused; one of the consequences is a further erosion of the identity of this project. Intensifying resentment, parochialism, and social conflict across the Union is only exacerbating the tensions. Europeans need a frank discussion about what it means to be European and where the EU is headed.

In Spain, this crisis may still present an opportunity to move away from the preceding unsustainable growth model. A competitive devaluation is no longer an option, while a new competitiveness agenda will have to focus on productivity growth, which is even more important in Spain than nominal wage growth. To address this challenge will demand actions to improve policy across a wide front: higher investment in infrastructure, improvements in land-use planning, efforts to increase the quality of education, rigorous promotion of competition in all areas of the economy, tax simplification, and rationalization of existing regulations. Furthermore, such an agenda will demand a shift from a low-cost, low-skill manufacturing-base that relies on technical design and marketing skills from elsewhere toward more capital-intensive industries requiring greater skills in the labor force and relying on standard technology (e.g., chemicals, vehicles, steel and metal manufacturers), as well as a change in the existing growth model (based on relatively low production costs) in order to build a new framework based on innovation, quality, value-added, and productivity.

The goal must be to increase productivity by increasing the capital intensity of production. Innovation and higher productivity will require the following four main conditions: first, investment in capital technology (i.e., information systems and telecommunications); second, a new culture of entrepreneurship, innovation, and risk; third, human capital with strong skills and the flexibility to adapt to new technologies and processes, based on a model of continuous training; and lastly, a flexible and adaptable industrial relations framework. The support for innovation and entrepreneurship has to be firm and unequivocal. Spain must close the gap with its competitors; venture capital represents a sad $4.6 per inhabitant (versus $70 in the United States or $140 in Israel).[25]

Spain needs now to reinvent itself. But there is much to build upon and the country has already proved that it can do it by extricating itself from equally grave crisis. Indeed, the history of the country since the transition to the country in the 1970s is a history of success without parallel in virtually any other country (with the only possible exception of South Korea). According to the OECD, when Spain joined the organization in 1962, per capita income was the lowest of the member states at $3,800. By 1986, when it joined the EU, it almost tripled it to $10,000 and by 2012, despite the crisis, reached $27,000. The GDP gap with Germany also closed in 30 years from 2.5 points to 1.06 in 2012. Spaniards need to abandon their fears of the future, embrace change, and convince themselves to invest in new technologies and education to reinvent the country and build a new future based on innovation and entrepreneurship. This will require collective an individual efforts, in conjunction with private and public cooperation.

There are reasons for optimism: since 2002, the country's exports have increased by 70 percent (up 26 percent from their 2009 levels and still exceed by 7 percent the precrisis heights achieved in 2008); and unitary labor costs have been reduced as noted before, helping improve competitiveness (it is expected that business will regain in two years the competitiveness lost between 1998 and 2008). At the same time, the corporate base of the country remains strong and an analysis of the sales, research, internationalization, and financial strength of most of the companies listed in the Ibex 35 Madrid stock shows comparative success. Firms like Inditex emerged as one of the world's fashion industry leaders and is the only European firm entered the Fortune 500 list since 1975. Finally, some of the recent reforms, like the pensions one, will help the country's fiscal position and make it more sustainable. The last financial reform, the most ambitious so far, is also expected to finally clean up the sector and help rebuild the confidence of investors.

Still, much remains to be done in other areas, including: the reform of the energy sector; the elimination of barriers to the single market; the strengthening of the role of supervisory and regulatory institutions; the reform of the educational system to improve educational outcomes; the liberalization of the professional associations; the development of new funding instruments for SMEs; and the support the autonomous regions with their liquidity problems. Much is at stake; the course of these reforms will largely determine the future prospects of the country. Restoring confidence (and liquidity) will be key.

The country's challenges are not only financial and economic, but also political and institutional. Spain needs to modernize a structure of government that was designed for a different era in which the country was emerging from decades of dictatorship. It needs new institutions that will respond to the demands of its increasingly diverse and vibrant society. Spaniards have been protected economically for centuries by the army, the state, and the Catholic Church. Who will protect them now? They must ask themselves whether they want to shape their own future or have others shape it for them. As painful as the crisis has been (and will continue to be), it would be far worse in the long term if the country does not use it as an opportunity to build a sustainable future.

So far the crisis has led to a severe loss of hope and self-esteem throughout the country.[26] Moreover, the misdiagnosis of its causes and the tendency to blaming Spanish society for all the problems has intensified that pattern. In addition, they have facilitated the justification (and implementation) of failed austerity policies that not only are generating social conflict and despair, but also eroding hope in the future because the cuts in education, training, R-D-I, and social policies are undermining the pillars that should constitute the basis of a sustainable recovery. It is time for the Spanish government (and the EU) to recognize that austerity and reforms need to be complemented with a new growth plan that addresses the competitive and social challenges that the country faces.

As this book goes to press, at the end of 2012, the debate is still about how long it will take the Spanish (and European) economy to recover and what must change to avoid further crises. After the announcement in September of the ECB plan to buy bounds, Spanish bond yields have stabilized and have not yet succumbed to contagion from Greece, retreating from the summer 2012 levels that threatened the country with bankruptcy. However, while the crisis seems to have calmed down somewhat, its underlying causes have not been eliminated. This period of relative calm is giving European leaders (who finally accepted that the crisis was not just about Greece, or Spain, but about fundamental design flaws that needed to be addressed) the time to continue developing the institutional structure needed to make the euro credible and sustainable. The question remains, however, whether this period of calm will hold long enough for European leaders to complete the institutional reforms (and the European and national levels), for economic growth to resume, for structural reforms to come to fruit, and for banks to clean up their balance sheets and resume lending.[27]

In the coming months Europe (and the rest of the world) will be watching closely to see if Spain formally asks for support from the European rescue fund (MEDE) in order to qualify for support from the ECB, which would buy Spanish bonds to help lower the country's borrowing costs. Much will hinge on this decision. However, regardless of this decision, Spain will have to adjust its standards of living and productivity. Otherwise the country risks a lost decade, or longer. It will not be easy, but while the picture is rather grim, there are strong reasons for optimism. In the end, the success of the Spanish economy will hinge on its ability to balance the positive legacies of the past with the reforms needed to meet the challenges of the future.

Notes

Introduction: Spain at a Crossroads

1. Paul Krugman, "Europe's Austerity Madness," *New York Times*, September 28, 2012.
2. "Spanish Leader Unveils Fresh Overhauls," *Wall Street Journal*, September 26, 2012.
3. "Dancing towards a Spanish Rescue," *Financial Times*, September 24, 2012.
4. John Plender, "Spain's Debt Crisis Has Exposed the Limits of ECB Help," *Financial Times*, April 11, 2012.
5. "Lagarde Endorses Spain's Economic Reforms," *Financial Times*, August 2, 2012 and "Christine Lagarde cree que las medidas del Gobierno son 'muy, muy valientes,'" *El País*, October 3, 2012.
6. "Spain's Finances Prompt Fear of Resurging Debt Crisis," *New York Times*, April 11, 2012.
7. Pedro Solbes, "How Spain Will Return to Strong Growth," *Financial Times*, September 9, 2008.
8. José Ignacio Torreblanca, "Rajoy tiene un plan: hacer un 'hail Mary,'" *El País*, November 11, 2011 and Victor Mallet, "Rajoy Poised for 'Hail Mary Manoeuvre,'" *Financial Times*, November 18, 2011.
9. "El FMI prevé que España prolongue la recesión a 2013 con una caída del 0.6%," *El País*, July 16, 2012.
10. "Las ayudas a la banca disparan el déficit y la deuda del estado," *El País*, September 29, 2012.
11. "La patronal pronostica una caída en 2013 que triplica la prevista por el gobierno," *El País*, September 19, 2012.
12. "A Complacent Europe Must Realize That Spain Will Be Next," *Financial Times*, April 11, 2011.
13. "Property Market in Spain and Italy Close to Collapse," *Financial Times*, August 12, 2012.
14. "UGT acusa a la reforma laboral de haber empeorado las condiciones de trabajo," *El País*, September 17, 2012.
15. "The Spanish Patient," *Economist*, July 29, 2012.
16. From Andrés Ortega, "La desmoralización de España," *El País*, September 11, 2012.
17. "Ricos más ricos, pobres más pobres," *El País*, November 12, 2011.
18. "La crisis retrasa ocho años la convergencia con Europa en riqueza por habitante," *El País*, December 14, 2012.

19. "Spain's Crisis Reignites An Old Social Conflict," *New York Times*, August 24, 2012.
20. "Spain Recoils as Its Hungry Forage Trash Binds for a Next Meal," *New York Times*, September 25, 2012.
21. "Fears Rising, Spaniards Pull Out Their Cash and Get Out of Spain," *New York Times*, September 4, 2012.
22. "El Banco de España cifra la caída real de los depósitos en 55,000 millones," *El País*, September 19, 2012.
23. "La banca sufre perdidas record de 10,535 millones hasta junio por las provisiones," *El País*, August 17, 2012.
24. "La mayor caída del crédito en 50 años," *El País*, September 18, 2012.
25. "La morosidad en la banca marca un nuevo máximo y roza el 10% en julio," *El País*, September 18, 2012.
26. "La prima de riesgo asfixia la financiación de las pymes españolas," *El País*, September 10, 2012.
27. "Spanish Bank Test Confirm Need for 60bn in New Capital," *Financial Times*, September 29–30, 2012.
28. "La banca española necesita 53,745 millones de capital para sanearse," *El País*, September 29, 2012.
29. The Nobel Prize winner Paul Krugman compares the Spanish case with that of UK when that country returned to the gold standard. UK returned with a currency overvalued by around 20 percent and with a large debt from World War I. Similar to Spain, it proceeded to pursue a policy of harsh fiscal austerity, reaching primary surpluses around 7 percent of GDP, and internal devaluation through deflation. As a consequence, it suffered prolonged stagnation and failed to reduce its debt. If this comparison holds, it bodes poorly for the Spanish economy. See http://krugman.blogs.nytimes.com/2012/10/03/the-economic-consequences-of-mr-rajoy/?smid=tw-NytimesKrugman&seid=auto.
30. Angel Laborda, "La mejora de la productividad requiere reformas," *El País*, June 22, 2008.
31. See http://reports.weforum.org/global-competitiveness-report-2012–2013/. See also "Competition Gap Grows in Europe, Study Says," *New York Times*, September 6, 2012.
32. William Chislett, "Expect the Pain in Spain to Continue," *Financial Times*, April 12, 2011.
33. Data from the OECD. See "Estado de la educacion 2012," *El País*, September 14, 2012.
34. "Cataluña se destaca como la comunidad mas endeudada de España," *El País*, September 14, 2012.
35. "Lagarde endorses Spain's economic reforms," *Financial Times*, August 2, 2012.
36. "Shut Out of the Dent Markets, Catalonia Asks Madrid for Emergency Aid," *New York Times*, August 29, 2012.
37. "Catalonian Independence Would Not Be Plain Sailing," *Financial Times*, September 27, 2012.
38. David Gardner, "Financial Crisis Stokes Fires of Spanish Identity," *Financial Times*, September 27, 2012 and "Spain's Leader Fails to Reach Deal with Catalonia," *New York Times*, September 21, 2012.
39. "Catalan Teachers Add Voice to Anti-Austerity Noise," *Financial Times*, September 28, 2012; David Gardner, "The Catalan Champion with Spain's Future in His

Hands," *Financial Times*, September 29–30, 2012; and David Gardner, "Separatism Is a Genuine Threat to the Future of Spain," *Financial Times*, September 7, 2012.

40. See "In Euro Crisis, Fingers Point in All Directions," *New York Times*, August 25, 2012.
41. Interview with Soraya Rodríguez, "Quien da motivos para que salgamos a la calle es el PP," *El País*, March 1, 2012.
42. From Cesar Molinas, "Theory of Spain's Political Class," *El País*, September 12, 2012.
43. Joaquín Estefanía, "¿Como hemos llegado hasta aquí?," *El País*, June 9, 2012.
44. "Alarm Sounds Over Spain's Rising Public Debt," *Financial Times*, March 9, 2012.
45. From Cesar Molinas, "Theory of Spain's Political Class," *El País*, September 12, 2012.
46. "La reforma sin forma," *El País*, September 23, 2012.
47. "In Spain, a Symbol of Ruin at An Airport to Nowhere," *New York Times*, July 19, 2012. A giant statue along the entrance road to the airport has an aluminium model airplane on top, the closest an airplane has come to the airport. The statue, 79 feet tall, costing $375,000, was designed to honor the instigator of the airport initiative, Carlos Fabra, longstanding head of Castellón's provincial government, who is under judicial investigation in connection with several cases of corruption and tax evasion.
48. "First a Building Spree, Now the Axe Is Falling," *New York Times*, July 9, 2012.
49. "Luxury Hotels Built in Name of Progress Declared Illegal," *Financial Times*, July 6, 2010.
50. See "a Culture Clash Overturns a Spanish Savings Bank and Its Captain," *New York Times*, August 21, 2012.
51. See Cesar Molinas, "Theory of Spain's Political Class," *El País*, September 12, 2012
52. "La banca española sufre en julio una fuga record de depósitos," *El País*, August 28, 2012 and "El Banco de España cifra la caída real de los depósitos en 55.000 millones," *El País*, September 19, 2012.
53. See Fernando Vallespin, "¿Súbditos o ciudadanos?," *El País*, September 14, 2012.
54. "La evolución de la percepción económica y los principales problemas," *El País*, September 11, 2011.
55. From Andrés Ortega, "La desmoralización de Espanha," *El País*, September 11, 2012.
56. "El 72% da por seguro que las decisiones económicas se tomarán desde Bruselas," *El País*, September 9, 2012
57. Ignacio Torreblanca, "Fracasos colectivos," *El País*, July 13, 2012.
58. See David Gardner, "The Silent Rajoy Is Deaf to the Spanish Emergency," *Financial Times*, August 6, 2012 and "Merkel Says Europe Is 'in a Race with the Markets,'" *Financial Times*, June 15, 2012.
59. "Politics Is Adding to Spanish Woes," *Financial Times*, July 25, 2012.
60. From Andrés Ortega, "La desmoralización de España," *El País*, September 11, 2012.
61. See Joaquín Estefanía, "La democracia aletargada," *El País* September 13, 2012.
62. "La banca española sufre en julio una fuga record de depósitos," *El País*, August 28, 2012.

63. "Spain Post-Franco Institutions Battered by Contact with Politics," in *Financial Times*, July 23, 2012.
64. "Todos quieren calendar el otoño," *El País*, September 22, 2012.
65. Ignacio Torreblanca states it very succinctly: "All sides prefer to live with mal-functioning institutions rather than one that may work against them," in "Spain Post-Franco Institutions Battered by Contact with Politics," *Financial Times*, July 23, 2012.
66. David Gardner, "The Silent Rajoy Is Deaf to the Spanish Emergency," *Financial Times*, August 6, 2012
67. From "Parapetados tras las vallas," *El País*, September 15, 2012.
68. "Madrid Attacked Over Meddling at Broadcaster," *Financial Times*, August 9, 2012.
69. "Spain Post-Franco Institutions Battered by Contact with Politics," *Financial Times*, July 23, 2012.
70. From Stefanie Claudia Müller and Roberto Centeno, "Alemania debe de condicionar la ayuda económica a España," *El Confidencial*, September 6, 2012. See http://www.cotizalia.com/opinion/disparate-economico/2012/09/06/alemania-debe-condicionar-la-ayuda-europea-a-espana-7390/.
71. From Miguel Jiménez, "Herencias y falacias," *El País*, July 11, 2012
72. Bankia announced losses of €4.4 billion in the first half of 2012, which forced the government to inject cash. "Ousted Bankia Chief Blames Central Bank and Politicians," *Financial Times*, July 27, 2012 and "Spanish Bank's Ex-Leader Defends Record There," *New York Times*, July 27, 2012. The case has been brought to court by a small political party, UPD, and a judge has ordered Mr. Rato and three dozen former Bankia directors to respond to criminal fraud and accusations regarding their management of the institution. Other cajas are also immersed in judicial proceedings: in Barcelona, judges are investigating the compensation packages of former executives of CatalunyaCaixa; the FROB has also initiated legal action against former directors of Banco de Valencia over possible management irregularities; and antifraud investigators have filed a lawsuit against five directors of NovacaixaGalicia over the terms of their retirement benefits. See "In Spain, a Banking Crisis Goes to Court," *New York Times*, July 15, 2012.
73. "Caja Madrid concedía prestamos a clientes sin capacidad de pago," *El País*, September 23, 2012.
74. Andrés Ortega, "La desmoralización de España," *El País*, September 11, 2012.
75. Andrés Ortega, "La desmoralización de España," in *El País*, September 11, 2012.
76. "Chastened King Seeks Redemption, for Spain and His Monarchy," *New York Times*, September 29, 2012.
77. From "Spain's Jobless Rely on Family, a Frail Crutch," *New York Times*, July 29, 2012.
78. This helps to account for one of the country's biggest paradox record unemployment levels with relatively low civil unrest. The open secret is that unemployment figures are not real. Hundreds of people claim unemployment benefits while they work in the underground economy. Evidence of this is that when unemployment fell down to 8.5 percent during the boom years, employers could not find workers. Successive governments have launched campaigns against the black economy with little success. The number of jobs in the underground economy has increased from about 1.5 million in the early 1980s to 4 million in the three years to 2008. Some of the reasons to explain include high rate of

taxation and the regulatory burden, weak rule of law, low confidence in the state, and low social capital. See Victor Mallet and Guy Dinmore, "Negative Effects," *Financial Times*, June 9, 2011. The PP government's latest antifraud plan has found 57,457 illegal employments in the first six months of 2012, an increase of 11.86 percent compared with the same period in 2011. In addition, inspectors reported 30 percent more infractions from employers than in 2011 and identified 6,943 workers who were receiving their unemployment benefits but did not meet the criteria, a 50 percent increase. See, "El plan antifraude permite aflorar 57,457 empleos sumergidos hasta septiembre," *El País*, October 3, 2012.

79. For instance, the Corporacion Catalana de Medios Audiovisuales has 2,800 employees, 6 TV channels, and several radio ones. See "El fiasco de las teles autonómicas," *El País*, September 15, 2012.

80. From Stefanie Claudia Müller and Roberto Centeno, "Alemania debe de condicionar la ayuda económica a España," *El Confidencial*, September 6, 2012, http://www.cotizalia.com/opinion/disparate-economico/2012/09/06/alemania-debe-condicionar-la-ayuda-europea-a-espana-7390/.

81. Tony Barber, "Unfinished Business," *Financial Times*, September 21, 2012.

82. See Paul Krugman, "Europe's Austerity Madness," *New York Times*, September 28, 2012.

83. "Ireland Leads Way on Labour Costs," *Financial Times*, July 21, 2012.

84. "The Many Crises Confronting Spain," *Financial Times*, September 28, 2012.

85. James Mckintosh, "Lessons for Rajoy from My Spanish Phrase Book," *Financial Times*, September 20–30, 2012.

86. "Political Hurdles Clog Spain's Path Out of Debt," *New York Times*, September 11, 2012.

87. "Waiting for Rajoy," *Economist*, September 15, 2012.

88. "Spain Eyes 40bn Euros of Cuts in Fresh Reforms," *Financial Times*, September 28, 2012.

89. "Despite Public Protests, Spain 2013 Budget Plan Includes More Austerity," *New York Times*, September 28, 2013.

90. See Wolgang Munchau, "Welcome Back-Again-to the Eurozone Crisis," *Financial Times*, October 1, 2012.

91. "La recapitalización de la banca española puede ser insuficiente, según Moody's," *El País*, October 1, 2012.

92. "La prima de riesgo reflejara si las pruebas son creíbles," *El País*, September 29, 2012.

93. Ignacio Torreblanca, "Fracasos colectivos," *El País*, July 13, 2012.

94. See Joaquín Estefanía, "El lado oscuro del ajuste," *El País*, September 17, 2012.

95. See "Spain Post-Franco Institutions Battered by Contact with Politics," *Financial Times*, July 23, 2012.

96. It borrows from the framework and analysis developed for the special volume "Europeanisation in the 'Southern Periphery' Tracing the EU's Impact on Domestic Political Economies." See Royo 2013b.

1   From Boom to Bust: A Miraculous Decade (1997–2007)?

1. "Zapatero Accentuates Positives in Economy, But Spain Has Other Problems," *Financial Times*, April 16, 2007, 4 and "Spanish Economy at Its Best for 29 Years, Says Zapatero," *Financial Times*, April 18, 2007, 3.

2. "El paro se sitúa en el 7.95% y alcanza su nivel más bajo desde 1978," *El País*, July 27, 2007.

3. "La economía española se hace fuerte," *El País*, March 25, 2007 and "La economía repuntó al 3.9% en 2006 tras el mayor avance de la productividad en nueve años," *El País*, February 22, 2007.

4. Guillermo de la Dehesa, "La Próxima Recesión," *El País*, January 21, 2007.

5. "Spain's Bold Investors to Offset 'Gentle Slowdown,'" *Financial Times*, February 22, 2007.

6. From "Modernised Nation Faces Uncharted Territory," special report, *Financial Times*, June 21, 2007, 1.

7. Emilio Ontiveros, "Redimensionamiento Transfronterizo," *El País*, July 15, 2007.

8. "Siesta's Over for Spain's Economy," *Los Angeles Times*, April 7, 2007.

9. Deloitte's business poll, "Barometro de Empresas," from "Un año de grandes resultados," *El País*, January 14, 2006.

10. "Spanish Bulls," *Financial Times*, February 20, 2007.

11. According to the *Financial Times*, 17 percent of those polled selected Spain as the country where they would prefer to work ahead of the United Kingdom (15 percent) and France (11 percent). See "España vuelve a ser diferente," *El País*, February 19, 2007 and *Financial Times*, February 19, 2007.

12. Calavita provides a detailed analysis of the immigration experience in Spain and exposes the tensions associated with this development. She also highlights the shortcomings of governments' actions with regard to integration and the impact of lack of integration on exclusion, criminalization, and radicalization.

13. "Tolerant Spain Is Booming as It Absorbs Flood of Foreign Workers," *Financial Times*, February 20, 2007, 3.

14. "Spanish Bulls," *Financial Times*, February 20, 2007. Still, 59 percent thought that there were "too many foreigners" in the country.

15. "Immigrants Boost British and Spanish Economies," *Financial Times*, February 20, 2007, 3.

16. "El paro baja hasta el 8.3% en 2006, la mejor tasa desde 1979," *El País*, January 26, 2007.

17. Guillermo de la Dehesa, "La Próxima Recesión," *El País*, January 21, 2007.

18. "La Economía española creció en la última década gracias a la aportación de los inmigrantes," *El País*, August 28, 2006.

19. See Martin Wolf, "Pain Will Follow Years of Economic Gain," *Financial Times*, March 29, 2007.

20. José A. Herce, "La Política de Cohesión," *El País* November 15, 2006, 4–Negocios.

21. Nevertheless, while acknowledging the critical role played by EU funds in the success of Spain, it is also important to stress that successful integration is not only a budgetary issue. On the contrary, the Spanish experience demonstrates that the main benefits of integration derive from the opportunities it generates in terms of trade and FDI. Indeed, receiving EU funds is by no means a guarantee of success, and Greece is just one example of this.

22. According to the latest data (2007) from the *World Bank Governance Indicators* (http://info.worldbank.org/governance/wgi/sc_chart.asp), Spain is ranked in the 75–100th country's percentile ranks in control of corruption, government effectiveness, regulatory quality, rule of law, and voice and accountability.

23. According to Martinez-Mongay and Maza Lasierra, "The outstanding economic performance of Spain in EMU would be the result of a series of lucky shocks, including a large and persistent credit impulse and strong immigration, underpinned by some right policy choices. In the absence of new positive shocks, the resilience of the Spanish economy to the financial crisis might be weaker than that exhibited in the early 2000s. The credit impulse has ended, fiscal consolidation has stopped, and the competitiveness gains of the nineties have gone long ago."

24. "Fears of Recession as Spain Basks in Economic Bonanza," *Financial Times,* June 8, 2006.

25. Angel Laborda, "El comercio en 2006," *El País,* March 11, 2007, 20.

26. Wolfgang Munchau, "Spain, Ireland and Threats to the Property Boom," *Financial Times,* March 19, 2007 and "Spain Shudders as Ill Winds Batter US Mortgages," *Financial Times,* March 21, 2007.

27. "Spanish Muscle Abroad Contrast with Weakling Status among Investors," *Financial Times,* December 11, 2006.

28. "La Comisión Europea advierte a España de los riesgos de su baja competitividad," *El País,* February 4, 2007.

29. See "The EU 'Is Losing Battle on Competitiveness,'" *Financial Times,* January 13, 2003, 3. Spain has lost 3 positions (and is listed at number 20) in the last Globalization Index published by *Foreign Policy* (January–February), no. 134 (2003): 60. In addition, the World Economic Forum has placed Spain among the least competitive countries in the EU (with only Greece behind) in its "Report on Global Competitiveness." This report examines economic conditions in 80 countries focusing on two main indexes: MICI, which measures the quality of business development, and the GCI, which examines growth prospects in five to eight years based on macroeconomic stability. Spain is listed twenty-ninth in the latest Globalization Index, which measures economic integration, personal contact, technological connectivity, and political commitment, published by *Foreign Policy* (November–December 2007).

30. Daniel Gros, "Will EMU Survive 2010?" *Centre for European Policy Studies,* January 2005, www.ceps.be.

31. Oficina Económica del Presidente, *Convergencia y Empleo: Programa Nacional de Reformas de España,* Madrid: OEP, October 2005, 27–28.

32. "Almunia Says Inflation Dampens Spain's Potential Growth Level," *El País,* English Edition with *International Herald Tribune,* February 18, 2006 and "Angel Laborda, 'La inflación se nos va,'" *El País,* November 18, 2007.

33. The surge of immigration, which resulted in a sharp increase in the participation rate, has led to a decrease in average remuneration per worker (about 3.7 percent between 2002 and 2004).

34. "Los expertos piden cambios en la política de I+D," *El País,* December 18, 2006.

35. "Diez años con el mismo sueldo," *El País,* November 27, 2007.

36. See Jesús Benegas Nuñez, "Innovación, Productividad y Empleo," *El País,* July 10, 2005.

37. IESE, *Euroíndice Laboral* (Adecco), December 12, 2006. From "Bruselas considera insostenible la deuda exterior de España," *El País,* December 19, 2006.

38. "Garbage Jobs Stifle Spanish Innovation," *Financial Times,* October 21, 2005, 3.

39. "La OCDE señala el alto número de repetidores como 'punto débil' de la educación en España," *El País,* September 12, 2006.

40. Philippe Aghion, Mathias Dewatripont, Caroline Hoxby, Andreu Mas-Colell, and André Sapir, "Why Reform Europe's Universities?" *Bruegelpolicybrief*, www.bruegel.org.
41. "Zapatero Accentuates Positives in Economy, But Spain Has Other Problems," *Financial Times*, April 16, 2007, 4.

2 Responding to the Crisis: A Chronicle of a Foretold Failure

1. "Spain Looks to Rebuild after Property Crash," *Financial Times*, April 9, 2008.
2. See J. Wart, "A ver si nos enteramos," *El País*, October 12, 2008, p. N31.
3. See "La crisis corre más que su medicina," *El País*, November 9, 2008, p. 26
4. Yet, as shown in chapter 6, Spanish banks and cajas were unable to escape the crisis. Their biggest weakness was their heavy exposure to the Spanish property crash and dependence on international wholesale financing. *Banco Santander* and BBVA have also been immersed in the *Madoff* fraud case: customers of Optimal, *Banco Santander's* Swiss-based hedge funds management, may have lost up to €2.3 billion through investments with Madoff, and BBVA announced that it may have lost up to €300 million. *Santander* has already announced that it would compensate its clients.
5. "Zapatero Backs Fresh Round of Public Spending," *Financial Times*, March 27, 2009.
6. "Spain's Finance Minister Sees No Room for Fiscal Stimulus," *Financial Times*, March 28–29, 2009
7. Victor Mallet, "Spain Needs to Find Permanent Solution to Its Temp Problem," *Financial Times*, April 30, 2009.
8. "Spanish Realism Takes Over from 'Green Shots,'" *Financial Times*, June 16, 2009.
9. "Spain Eyes Tax Rise to Plug Deficit," *Financial Times*, September 1, 2009.
10. "Spain Raises Taxes to Tackle Deficit," *Financial Times*, September 28, 2009.
11. "S&p Negative on Spanish Deficit," *Financial Times*, December 10, 2009.
12. "Spain Promises Austerity and Return to Growth," *Financial Times*, December 10, 2012.
13. "Spain Seeks Credit with Harsh Budget," *Financial Times*, January 30–31, 2010.
14. Victor Mallet, "Spain Risks Joining Greece at Bottom of Deficit Class," *Financial Times*, February 2, 2012.
15. "Spain and Portugal Under Strain," *Financial Times*, February 6–7, 2012.
16. "Spain: A Legacy in Limbo," *Financial Times*, April 11, 2010.
17. "Zapatero Denies Talk of imf Rescue," *Financial Times*, May 5, 2010
18. "Spain Seen as Moving Too Slowly on Crucial Reforms," *New York Times*, May 4, 2010.
19. "El gobierno baja el sueldo de los funcionarios, congela las pensiones y elimina el 'cheque bebe,'" *El País*, May 12, 2010.
20. "Dos minutos que cambiaron España," *El País*, May 16, 2010.
21. "Spain's Reforms Given Urgency by Debt Crisis," *Financial Times*, June 16, 2010.
22. "Endure Cuts for the Sake of Spain, Zapatero Urges," *Financial Times*, July 15, 2012.

23. "Tax Rise on Rich in Spain's 'Austere' 2011 Budget," *Financial Times*, September 25–26, 2010.
24. "Spain's Socialists and Unions, Battered by Economic Crisis, Struggle to Adapt," *The New York Times*, October 10, 2010.
25. "Embattled Zapatero Resorts to Cabinet Reshuffle," *Financial Times*, October 21, 2010.
26. "Spain Defiant Amid Bank Turmoil," *Financial Times*, November 27–28, 2010.
27. "Portugal and Spain Talk Down Fiscal Problems," *Financial Times*, November 19, 2010.
28. "Zapatero Joined by Business Elites in Promise of Reform," *Financial Times*, November 29, 2010.
29. "Spaniards Tighten Belts for Another Bleak Christmas," *Financial Times*, December 21, 2010.
30. "Catalonia's Credit Crunch Undermines Spain," *Financial Times*, February 1, 2011.
31. "Zapatero Warns on Regional Spending," *Financial Times*, January 17, 2010.
32. This was not an easy process: in early April an important merger of four cajas fell apart.
33. "Reluctant Retrencher," *Financial Times*, January 17, 2010.
34. "Spain Reduces Motorway Speed Limit to Save Fuel," *Financial Times*, February 26–27, 2011.
35. "Spanish Downgrade Revives Fears Over Weaker Eurozone Economies," *Financial Times*, March 11, 2011.
36. "Spain's Zapatero to Stand Down at Election," *Financial Times*, April 4, 2011 and "Spanish Premier Says He Won't Seek New Term," *New York Times*, April 4, 2011.
37. "Spain Walks Debt Tightrope after Portugal Seeks Aid," *Financial Times*, April 12, 2011.
38. "IMF 'Decouples' Spain from Periphery," *Financial Times*, April 14, 2011.
39. "Madrid Backtracks on Claims of 9bn Euros Chinese Injection into Cajas," *Financial Times*, April 15, 2011.
40. "Migrant Surge Adds to Spain's Resentment of German Strength," *Financial Times*, April 13, 2011.
41. "Pain in Spain Drives Young People's Protest," *Financial Times*, May 20, 2011 and "Despite Ban, Protests Continue before Spanish Vote," *The New York Times*, May 22, 2011.
42. This movement led to the emergence of similar mobilizations across the world, such as the anti–Wall Street demonstrations, the Occupy movement, and the "We are the 99" in the United States.
43. Victor Mallet, "Spanish Blame Game Over Deficit Targets Hides Dual Culpability," *Financial Times*, June 10, 2011
44. For instance, the Spanish Associations of Pharmaceutical Companies and Medical Equipment suppliers claimed that they were owed €5.2 billion and €4.3 billion respectively by the health system, now in the hands of the regional governments. See Victor Mallet, "Spanish Blame Game Over Deficit Targets Hides Dual Culpability," *Financial Times*, June 10, 2011.
45. "Madrid's Finances Under Fire," *Financial Times*, June 8, 2011.
46. "Spain Approves More Cuts to Public Spending in 2012," *Financial Times*, June 26–27, 2012.

47. IMF, "Spain—Staff Report for the 2011 Article IV Consultation; Public Information Notice; Statement by the Staff Representative; and Statement by the Executive Director for Spain," July 2011. IMF Country Report No. 11/215.

48. "IMF Warns Spain of Setbacks," *Financial Times*, June 22, 2011.

49. "Spanish Protesters Turn Their Vitriol against Brussels," *Financial Times*, June 20, 2011.

50. "Zapatero Declares 'Tranquillity' Over Finances," *Financial Times*, July 13, 2011.

51. "Spain in 5bn Euros Budget Pledge," *Financial Times*, August 9, 2011.

52. Victor Mallet "Early Spanish Polls Unlikely to Soothe Fears of Investors," *Financial Times*, August 1, 2011.

53. See "Rajoy Unveil Programme of Austerity and Rapid Reform," *Financial Times*, December 20, 2011.

54. See "Spain Warns of Deficit Overshot," *Financial Times*, December 31/January 1, 2012.

55. "Doubts Emerge on Spain's Prospects from Brisk Growth," *New York Times*, March 24, 2012.

56. "Spain Plans to Breach EU Goals," *Financial Times*, March 3/March 4, 2012.

57. Mortgage holders had to meet the following criteria: all members of the household have to be unemployed (at that time there were 1.5 million households in that situation); the mortgage payment should exceed 60 percent of the family income; and they should own only one house. There was also a price range based on the size of the city where the house was located. The "delayed" interest rates charged could not be more than 2.5 percent higher over the rate applied to the mortgage. See "El gobierno establece reglas para los desalojos que incluyen la dación en pago," *El País*, March 9, 2012.

58. See "Foreclosure Protesters in Spain's Cities Now Go Door to Door," *New York Times*, July 16, 2011.

59. "Madrid Vows to Pursue Reforms Despite Strike," *Financial Times*, March 30, 2012.

60. According to the government's plan, "black money" can be returned from tax havens or elsewhere with no questions asked, in exchange for a fee of 8–10 percent of the money "regularized."

61. "Spain Unveils Toughest Budget Since 1970s," *Financial Times*, March 31/April 1, 2012.

62. "Spanish Banks Need No Bailout, EU Insists," *Financial Times*, March 29, 2012.

63. "Spain and EU Reject Talk of Bailout," *Financial Times*, April 11, 2012.

64. "Stop Blaming Spain, Rajoy Tells Eurozone Leaders," *Financial Times*, April 12, 2012.

65. "Spain's Finances Prompt Fear of Resurging Debt Crisis," *New York Times*, April 11, 2012.

66. Spain has four levels of government: central, regional, provincial, and municipal. The *Circulo de Empresarios*, a business lobby group, published a report on devolution in 2011 in which it showed that the number of public employees in Spain had risen from 2.2 million to nearly 3.2 million since 1996, far more than necessary based on the population size. See "Madrid Vows to Curb Regional Excess," *Financial Times*, April 13, 2012.

67. "Spain Weak Spot," *New York Times*, April 25, 2012.

68. "Spain Falls into Recession Again," *Financial Times*, April 24, 2012.

69. From "Additional Fiscal Measure Undertaken by the Spanish Government on July 13, 2013." Ministry of Economy and Competitiveness, http://www.thespanisheconomy.com/en-GB/Paginas/home.aspx

70. "Spanish Borrowing Costs Drop as Economy Minister Warns on Debt," *New York Times*, July 17, 2012.

71. "Montoro: 'Si no sube la recaudación esta en riesgo el pago de las nóminas'," *El País*, July 8, 2012.

72. The FLA was a liquidity instrument created by the central government (through the Royal Decree 21/2012) to assist the regions with problems in paying their debts, modelled on the European stability fund. 6 billion would come from the public entity that runs the national lottery system.

73. The Catalans, which contributed more to the central government than they received, were pushing for a model similar to the Basque one in which they would collect their own taxes. See "Madrid in Duel with Regions for Aid," *Financial Times*, July 24, 2012.

74. "Deteriorating Outlook Drives Spain's Borrowing Costs Near Euro-Era Highs," *Financial Times*, July 21–22, 2012.

75. "Berlin Hosts Talks on Spanish Crisis," *Financial Times*, July 25, 2012 and "Policy Makers Patient Despite Spanish Pain," *Financial Times*, July 25, 2012.

76. "ECB Resists Madrid's Plea for Help," *Financial Times*, July 25, 2012.

77. "Draghi Triggers Rally with Binds Talk," *Financial Times*, July 27, 2012 and "Stocks Soar after Pledge to Support Euro Zone," *New York Times*, July 27, 2012.

78. "Schäuble and Geithner Urge Reforms," *Financial Times*, July 30, 2012.

79. "El Código Penal incluirá cárcel para quienes falseen cuentas públicas," *El País*, July 28, 2012.

80. "El PP se desploma en un mes," *El País*, July 28, 2008.

81. "El PP pierde cuanto puntos de estimación de voto desde abril," *El País*, August 6, 2012.

82. "After Unity Rally in Europe, Reality Check from Spain," *New York Times*, July 28, 2012.

83. IMF, "IMF Executive Board Concludes 2012 Article IV Consultation with Spain." Public Information Notice No. 12/87, July 27, 2012, http://www.imf.org/external/np/sec/pn/2012/pn1287.htm.

84. "A Legacy in Limbo," *Financial Times,* April 12, 2010.

3 The Challenges of Economic Reforms: Zapatero and Continuities in Economic Policymaking

1. See Walter Münchau, "Spain, Ireland and Threats to the Property Boom," *Financial Times*, March 19, 2007.

2. The Spanish economy also benefited from a favorable conversion rate of the peseta vis-à-vis the euro. When the national currency was fixed to the euro at the end of 1998, the Spanish peseta was converted at a rate of 166 pesetas to one euro.

3. Elena Salgado held the post until the PP came to power following the party's victory in the November 2011 elections. She was replaced in December of 2011 by Luis de Guindos, who, for the first time in decades, did not hold the VP position

4. There is also consensus on the important role that technocrats (the "economic technopols" and "trinitarios") from the Ministry of Commerce, the Bank of Spain, or the Ministry of Foreign Relations (or the Ministry of Relations with Europe) have played on economic policy stability since the transition (De la Dehesa 1994, 139–140).

5. The decision to support the Budget Stability Act was a surprise and a sign of Solbes's clout in the new government. The Socialist Party had objected strenuously to this law while it was in opposition and had gone as far as to challenge its constitutionality in court supporting the challenge presented by regional governments in which the party was in power. Solbes, a fervent supporter of balanced budgets and zero deficits during the cycle, refused to follow the party line. It was only the agreement with ERC, in June of 2004 that led the government to make changes to the law in 2006. In exchange for Esquerra's support for the budget, the government agreed to avoid a budget surplus in 2006 and 2007.

6. For instance, Joan Guitart (2008) points out that "the share of wages in national income reached in 2006 a historic level of 46.4 per cent of GDP, or a fall of 3.2 points in ten years; the operating surplus increased by 0.2 per cent to 45.1 per cent and net taxes on production and imports, essentially borne by the workers increased by 2.9 per cent to 11.5 per cent. On the other hand taxation represented in 2007 41 per cent of GDP, or four points below the European average.... The 35 biggest Spanish companies registered profits of 24,508 million Euros in the first quarter of 2007."

4   The Limits of Fiscal Convergence

1. See Martin Wolf's blog: "What Was Spain Supposed to Have Done?," June 25, 2012, http://blogs.ft.com/martin-wolf-exchange/2012/06/25/what-was-spain-supposed-to-have-done. Accessed June 25, 2012.

2. This chapter borrows from the framework and analysis developed for the special volume "Europeanisation in the 'Southern Periphery' Tracing the EU's Impact on Domestic Political Economies." See Royo 2013b.

3. Prior to them Carlos Solchaga had been in the position between 1995 and 2003.

4. Prior to them Felipe González was PM for almost 14 years, between 1982 and 1996.

5. The PSOE, however, did not support the "budgetary stability law" obliging Spain to cut its annual budget deficit to zero by 2020, approved by the PP in April of 2012 to implement this constitutional amendment. It claimed it went beyond the approved constitutional amendment.

6. See Martin Wolf's blog: "What Was Spain Supposed to Have Done?," June 25, 2012.

7. From Martin Wolf's blog: "What Was Spain Supposed to Have Done?," June 25, 2012.

8. From Martin Wolf's blog: "What Was Spain Supposed to Have Done?," June 25, 2012.

9. Simon Johnson's blog: "The End of the Euro: What's Austerity Got to Do With It?" June 21, 2012.

10. Martin Wolf, "Struggling to Tackle Bad Fiscal Behaviour," *Financial Times*, April 8, 2008, 1–2 (special section on "Investing in Portugal").

11. See Martin Wolf, "Britain Must Get to Grips with Lackluster Productivity Growth," *Financial Times*, November 8, 2005.
12. See Martin Wolf, "Why the Bundesbank is Wrong," *Financial Times*, April 10, 2012.
13. Martin Wolf's blog: "What Was Spain Supposed to Have Done?," June 25, 2012

5 The Political and Social Concertation Consequences of the Crisis

1. "Rivals Shower Tax Pledges on Spain's Voters," *Financial Times*, January 30, 2008.
2. At the European level, Conservative and Eurosceptic parties won the election.
3. "Los resultados darían un vuelco total a la composición del Congreso," *El País*, June 8, 2009.
4. "La crisis impulsa al PP a un triunfo claro," *El País*, June 8, 2009.
5. The PSOE was also able to rule in Asturias after a snap election in March 2012.
6. "El tsunami del 22-M ahoga al PSOE," *El País*, May 23, 2012 and "El castigo," *El País*, May 23, 2012.
7. The socialists claimed on November 13 that the distance was being reduced and some polls seemed to show that possibility. See "¿Se mueve algo en las encuestas?," *El País*, November 14, 2011.
8. Interview with Rajoy: "Mi prioridad son las pensiones. A partir de ahí habra que recortar en todo," *El País*, November 16, 2011
9. Victor Mallet, "Spain's Party Leaders Indulge in Navel-Gazing as Crisis Rages," *Financial Times*, November 9, 2011.
10. "Spanish Debt Costs Soar Ahead of Election," *Financial Times*, November 18, 2011.
11. "Rajoy Begs Markets for More Time," *Financial Times*, November 19–20, 2011 and "Rajoy on Verge of Sweeping Poll Victory in Spain," *Financial Times*, November 21, 2011.
12. From "El PP debe la mayoria absoluta más al colapso del PSOE que a su resultado," *El País*, November 21, 2011.
13. For instance, in Andalusia the PP did not receive 50 percent of the votes but gained more than half of the seats; in Valencia it obtained 61 percent of the seats with 50 percent of the votes and in Castilla León, 65 percent with 55 percent of the votes.
14. From "El bipartidismo entra en crisis," *El País*, November 28, 2011.
15. For instance, the defeat of the PP in 2004 following the terrorist attack of March 14 was caused not by the attack itself but by how the Aznar government administered it. See, "El PP debe la mayoria absoluta más al colapso del PSOE que a su resultado," *El País*, November 21, 2011.
16. Despite its enormous struggles with the economy, PM Zapatero's government was credited for the social change that it had brought to Spain: for promoting women's rights, for pushing changes to the abortion laws, for legalizing same-sex marriage, and for brining in the end of ETA's terrorists campaign. See "Spain Voters Deal a Blow to Socialists Over the Economy," *The New York Times*, November 21, 2011.

17. "El PP baja a 11 puntos la ventaja sobre el PSOE y el 48% censura su gestión," *El País*, May 9, 2012.
18. See M. Wolf, "The Gain in Spain," *Financial Times*, July 7, 1999, 10. See also IMF, *Public Information Notice* 99/65, June, 1999.
19. See "Gobierno y agentes sociales cierran la reforma laboral tras más de un año de negociaciones," *El País*, May 4, 2006.
20. See "La conversión de contratos temporales a fijos se triplica," *El País*, September 1, 2006 and "Diez años con el mismo sueldo," *El País*, November 27, 2007
21. http://www.empleo.gob.es/es/sec_trabajo/ccncc/D_AspectosNormativos/AcuerdosInterconfederales/index.htm.
22. "Patronal y sindicatos alertan de que la crisis puede contagiar a España," *El País*, December 14, 2012.
23. "Zapatero destaca el crecimiento, el empleo y la protección social como ejes del dialogo," *El País*, July 29, 2008.
24. "Contactos en serie para el dialogo social," *El País*, June 28, 2009
25. "Zapatero declara la Guerra a la CEOE," *El País*, July 26, 2009.
26. "CEOE y sindicatos abren la puerta a tratar una reforma laboral en 2010," *Cinco Días*, November 12, 2009.
27. "Zapatero anuncia una reforma laboral limitada sin abaratar el coste del despido," *El País*, December 3, 2009.
28. See the document "Líneas de actuación en el mercado de trabajo para sus discusión con los interlocutores sociales en el marco del dialogo social," published by the government on February 5, 2010. http://www.lamoncloa.gob.es/actualidadhome/2009-2/050210enlacedocumento. See also "El Gobierno centra la reforma en los jóvenes y la contratación indefinida," *El País*, February 6, 2010.
29. "Patronal y sindicatos pactan un alza salarial máxima del 1% para 2010," *El País*, February 9, 2010 and "Tres años para mejorar la calidad del empleo," *El País*, February 10, 2010.
30. "Dialogo social: Sobre actuaciones en el mercado de trabajo," published by the government on April 12, 2010. http://www.empleo.gob.es.
31. A group of 100 Spanish economists published a manifesto demanding substantive reform that would include a single contract with a dismissal compensation that would grow based on the years of work.
32. The other general strikes took place on April 5, 1978 (a European-level strike called against the unemployment caused by the oil crisis); June 20, 1985 (against the PSOE government pension reform); December 8, 1988 (against the PSOE youth employment plan); May 28, 1992 (against the reduction on unemployment benefits and a proposed law to regulate strikes); January 27, 1994 (against the PSOE labor reform); and June 20, 2002 (against the PP labor reform).
33. The government also negotiated a "full force" plan to facilitate the hiring of young workers and long-term unemployed. The objective was to subsidize part-time contracts (which were rarely used in Spain) so that companies would have incentives to hire young workers that way. The plan would last one year and was expected to benefit 100,000 workers. During that time companies would be exempted from paying 100 percent of the Social Security contributions (75 percent if the company has more than 250 workers) in exchange for hiring a worker for a minimum of six months and for a schedule that would be equivalent to at least half of the regular schedule. There were no salary directives, and each

company would apply the salaries included in the collective agreement. An additional measure was the decision to replace the €420 (which was given to unemployed at that time) with a new subsidy of around €400, to unemployed who, in addition to participating in a training program, have family responsibilities. See "Varias facilidades de contratación beneficiarán a 100,000 jóvenes," *El País*, January 31, 2011.

34. "El acuerdo de pensiones da paso a un gran pacto social," *El País*, January 29, 2011.

35. See "Del gran pacto de la democracia al de la crisis," *El País*, February 3, 2011.

36. "Gómez ve 'una influencia clara' de las elecciones en la ruptura de la reforma de convenios," *El País*, June 6, 2011.

37. "Los convenios incluirán por ley un mecanismo de desbloqueo," *El País*, June 8, 2011.

38. "Toxo y Méndez ofrecen más años de moderación salarial," *El País*, August 19, 20011.

39. http://www.empleo.gob.es/es/sec_trabajo/ccncc/D_AspectosNormativos/Normativa/contenidos/Compromiso2011.htm.

40. "Rajoy pide un acuerdo sobre la nueva reforma laboral para Reyes," El País, November 30, 2012.

41. Because of the crisis, the Socialist government had been forced to suspend the limits to the sequencing of temporary contracts.

42. "Primera reforma con 'contrarreforma,'" *El País*, January 22, 2012.

43. http://www.empleo.gob.es/es/sec_trabajo/ccncc/D_AspectosNormativos/Normativa/contenidos/Acuerdo2012.htm.

44. "Empresarios y sindicatos revisarán los sueldos si la inflación supera en 2%," *El País*, January 24, 2012.

45. "Guindos: 'La reforma laboral será extremadamente agresiva,'" *El País*, February 9, 2012

46. "Báñez: 'No va a haber contrato único en este país porque es inconstitucional,'" *El País*, February 7, 2012.

47. "Despidos baratos con la venia del juez," *El País*, February 22, 2012. Prior to the reform, since going to court was typically risky because they tended to side with the workers, within 48h after the dismissal, companies could recognize that it was not justified (*la improcedencia*) and deposit the compensation in the labor court, which paralyzed the *salarios de tramitación*. The reform seeks to address this abused process and clarify the objective reasons for dismissals, so they are based on real and certain causes.

48. In those cases in which the reduction of salaries or the modification of substantive working conditions affected a large number of employees (more than 30 in number or more than 10 percent of staff), companies would have to open a round of consultation, after which the company would be allowed to modify the working conditions that are not explicitly covered in the collective agreement. If they are covered, they would need to open a process that could end up being decided by a mediator or by the National Consultive Commission of Collective Agreements. "La reforma laboral abre paso a una rebaja general de los sueldos," *El País*, February 11, 2012.

49. "A falta de devaluación, bajada de salarios," *El País*, February 17, 2012.

50. From "El Gobierno facilita que las empresas se acojan al despido más barato de 20 días." "El Gobierno generaliza el contrato de 33 días y permite cobrar el paro

y un sueldo." "La reforma facilita y abarata el despido," *El País*, February 10, 2012.

51. "Merkel alaba la reforma laboral española," *El País*, February 13, 2012.

52. "España se acerca al coste de despido en Europa, pero las trabas aún son menores," *El País*, February 13, 2012. According to the 2012 *Doing Business* report from the World Bank, Spanish companies give an average compensation of 15 weeks of salary (Germany gives 12 weeks). But the prenotification requirement of 2 weeks is among the lowest.

53. "Los sindicatos convocan marchas contra la reforma el 19 de febrero," *El País*, February, 11, 2012.

54. "Los sindicatos aplazan la huelga general," *El País*, February, 12, 2012.

55. "Caldera califica la reforma aprobada por el Gobierno como un decretazo," *El País*, February, 10, 2012. A labor court in Madrid also started the proceeding to elevate the labor reform to the Constitutional Court—questioning the formula adopted by the government to approve the decree (a royal decree, which would be later ratified by Congress—it was being processed as a law project and formally approved that summer), dismissals' regulations, the authority of companies over the *salarios de tramitación*. As well as, for the discrimination that may be caused between workers with the right to unemployment benefits and those who do not have them, see "Un juzgado de Madrid duda de la constitucionalidad de la reforma laboral," *El País*, March 15, 2012.

56. "La mayoria ve necesaria una reforma laboral pero no una bajada de sueldos," *El País*, February, 11, 2012.

57. The law still had to be ratified by the Senate at the time of finishing this manuscript. "El PP endurece la reforma laboral al acortar la prórroga de los convenios," *El País*, May 2, 2012.

58. "Reforma laboral: Primera fase," *El País*, May 20, 2012.

59. "La negociación de convenios cae al mínimo tras la reforma laboral," *El País*, August 5, 2012.

60. This section borrows from "Un fracaso detrás del otro," *El País*, June 6, 2010.

6   The Crisis and the Spanish Financial System

1. This chapter borrows from Sebastián Royo, "How Did the Spanish Financial System Survive the First Stage of the Global Crisis?" *Governance* (forthcoming 2013a); and Sebastián Royo, "A 'Ship in Trouble' The Spanish Banking System in the Midst of the Global Financial System Crisis: The Limits of Regulation," in Iain Hardie and David Howarth, eds. *Market-Based Banking, Varieties of Financial Capitalism and the Financial Crisis*, New York: OUP, (forthcoming 2013c).

2. "¿Por qué Berlín ataca a España?," *El País*, June 20, 1010.

3. "Two Tiers, One Crisis for Spanish Banks," *Financial Times,* May 18, 2012.

4. Financialization is defined as the trading of risk, and it is operationalized by looking at Spanish banks' assets (i.e., the size of the trading book and the presence of toxic assets) and liabilities (i.e., the funding base of banks—their reliance on wholesale market rather than retail deposits for funding, the securitization of lending, and the use of SIVs).

5. A recent study from Vicente Cunat and Luis Garicano shows that the main difference between banks and cajas is not so much the latter's political nature but

the lower level of professionalization of their managers: only 31 percent of their presidents have postgraduate degrees—half of them have banking experience and half of them have occupied political positions before becoming presidents. According to them this development means that cajas could have saved €12,000 million have they had better prepared and qualified managers without a political past. Cajas with a political president have on an average 0.93 points more of delinquent loans than those that do not, 0.98 points more if the president does not have postgraduate degrees, 0.93 points more when there is no financial experience, and 2.84 points more if there are those who meet all the three conditions. See "La Politizacion eleva la morosidad de las cajas en 12.000 millones," El País, October 31, 2010.

6. Vicente Cuñat and Luís Garicano, "¿Para cuando la restructuración del sistema financiero español?" El País, September 13, 2009.

7. Iñigo de Barrón, "El supervisor mete presión a las cajas," El País, October 18, 2009.

8. "Rato vaticina que al final de la crisis sólo quedaran 20 cajas," El País, April 14, 2010.

9. "Leaning Lenders," Financial Times, June 4, 2010, 9.

10. "Balance de un fracaso," El País, June 8, 2012.

11. As in Germany, the autonomous governments' willingness to support the cajas (the Landers and the LBs in the case of Germany) frustrated the central government's attempts to restructure the sector.

12. "Spain to Let Cajas Sell 50% of Equity," Financial Times, July 9, 2010,17.

13. "El Gobierno abre la puerta a la privatización total de las cajas," El País, July 10, 2010.

14. "El Banco de España exigirá a la banca un nuevo coeficiente de liquidez," El País, July 14, 2010.

15. Jean-Claude Juncker, chairman of the Eurozone finance ministers group, in "Turmoil in Spain sparks fear of crisis spreading," Financial Times, June 16, 2010, 15.

16. "Todos los bancos españoles aprueban los exámenes de resistencia en Europa," El País, July 23, 2010; "Los bancos y cajas disponen aún de un 'colchón" extra de 20,000 millones," El País, July 26, 2010, 15; and "Premio a la transparencia española," El País, July 27, 2010, 18.

17. From Royo, "How Did the Spanish Financial System Survive the First Stage of the Global Crisis?".

18. Emilio Botín, "Why Banks Must Adopt a 'Back-to-Basics Approach," Financial Times: Future of Finance, October 19, 2009.

19. See Emilio Botín. "Sage Advice." Financial Times, October 16, 2009; Emilio Botín, "Why Banks Must Adopt a 'Back-to-Basics Approach.'" Financial Times: Future of Finance, October 19, 2009; and "Retrato del Poder," El País, October 20, 2010.

20. He also warned of the need to cleanup the bad loans in "Tres años, cuatro reformas y varios cadáveres por el camino," El País, May 11, 2012.

21. "Spain Bank Chief Faces Reform Battle," Financial Times, April 16, 2012 and "El cierre de cajas dejará sin oficina a casi cinco millones de españoles," El País, July 16, 2012.

22. "Parte de guerra: Ocho entidades intervenidas o nacionalizadas en España," El País, May 9, 2012.

23. This section borrows heavily from "Así fue la caída del coloso," El País, May 13, 2012. Also "Balance de un fracaso," El País, June 8, 2012.

24. The battle was so nasty that at some point Aguirre was inadvertently recorded saying that "we have given another seat [in the board] to *Izquierda Unida* [United Left, the political party], and we have taken it away from the son of a bitch [referring to Gallardon]."

25. From "Así fue la caída del coloso," *El País*, May 13, 2012.

26. "Bankia valuation deals blow to retail investors," *Financial Times*, December 12, 2012.

27. "Balance de un fracaso," *El País*, June 8, 2012.

28. "Rodrigo Rato culpa a Zapatero y a Rajoy del deterioro económico de Bankia," *El País*, December 20, 2012.

29. See Patrick Jenkins, "'Doom Loop' Takes the Fizz Out of Madrid's Brief Euphoria," *Financial Times*, June 12, 2012, 2 and Andrew Ross Sorkin, "Why the Bailout in Spain Won't Work,' *New York Times*, June 12, 2012, B1.

30. "Tres años, cuatro reformas y varios cadáveres por el camino," *El País*, May 11, 2012.

31. The reaction from the markets to this reform has been quite mixed. While there is a sense of relief that Spain is finally coming to grips with its banking difficulties, there is the sentiment that it failed to sway investors: banks' shares fell sharply and borrowing costs rose again over levels seen before as unsustainable (6.3 percent for 10-year bonds). Investors seem to think that this reform is not the definite cleanup that that the market expected. Standard & Poor downgraded 11 of the country's largest banks on April 30, 2012, and Moody's downgraded 16 of the banks on May 18, 2012.

32. This section borrows from "El día que el Banco de España se doblegó," *El País*, March 13, 2011; and "Un gobernador entre dos fuegos," *El País*, May 13, 2012.

33. The Bank of Spain defended itself with seven arguments: that it lacked the appropriate instruments to address the crisis until 2009; that the economic deterioration was far longer and intense than anticipated; that the government had decided to reject the creation of a "bad bank"; that international banks were unable and unwilling to participate in the merge and acquisition process that was taking place in Spain because of the crisis; that they could not use the traditional tool to liquidate banks, namely forcing bondholders to take loses because of the potential contagion effect to other banks and cajas; that the corporate governance system of *cajas* was very deficient and politicized; and that the autonomous governments refused to approve the merges during the restructuring process. See "El Banco de España se defiende de su lentitud con siete argumentos," *El País*, June 11, 2012.

34. "El Nuevo gobernador critica la gestión de sus predecesores en el Banco de España," *El País*, July 17, 2012.

35. "Los inspectores del Banco de España culparon a Caruana de los problemas de la banca con el 'ladrillo'," *El País*, February 21, 2011.

36. "La banca nacionalizada traspasa al banco malo activos por valor de 37.110 millones," *El País* December 26, 2012.

37. John Gapper, "Bankia Fiasco Carries the Same Old Lessons," in *Financial Times*, May 30, 2012.

Conclusion: Lessons from Spain

1. "Un año más en recesión," *El País*, December 30, 212.

2. Robert Reich, "The Biggest Risk to the Economy in 2012, and What's the Economy for Anyway?," http://robertreich.org/post/16773820312.

3. While there is significant controversy over the definition of real convergence, most scholars agree that per capita GDP is a valid reference to measure the living standards of a country.
4. From "La Convergencia Real a Paso Lento," *El País*, February 14, 2000.
5. Interview with Vítor Constancio in *Financial Times*, May 16, 2008, 2.
6. Lars Wohlin, "Swedish Lessons Cannot Be Applied to Euro Zone," *Financial Times*, June 15, 2010.
7. Interview with Vítor Constancio, governor of the Bank of Portugal, "Concerns about Divergence 'Overlook Ability to Change,'" *Financial Times*, May 16, 2008: 2.
8. "A Gathering Gloom," *Financial Times*, March 23, 2012.
9. Wolfgang Munchau, "Spain Has Chosen to Accept Mission Impossible," *Financial Times*, April 16, 2012.
10. "Irish tell Spain to Imagine the Worst in Banking Bailout," in *Bloomberg*, June 14, 2012.
11. In Hong Kong for instance, the HK Monetary Authority adjusts the loan-to-value ratios under which local banks can make mortgage loans to mitigate property bubbles. See John Gapper, "With Bankia We Must Dust Off Old Lessons on Bad Loans," *Financial Times*, May 31, 2012, 9.
12. Floyd Norris. "Spain's Banking Mess," *New York Times*, September 23, 2011, B1.
13. "Más de 300 políticos españoles están imputados en casos de corrupción," *El País*, January 2, 2012.
14. See Barómetro de Metroscopia, *El País*, December 29, 2012.
15. "España pierde competitividad por los precios y los salarios," *El País*, April 4, 2010.
16. Stefan Collignon, "Germany Keeps Dancing as the iceberg looms," *Financial Times*, January 20, 2009, 13.
17. "Poland's Growth Defies Eurozone Crisis as Hard Work Pays Off," *Financial Times*, July 2, 2012.
18. This is also a result of the flexibility and consensus that characterize employer-union relations in the sector, which employs 280,000 people in Spain (85 percent of them on long-term contracts), and accounts for a tenth of the country's output. See "In Cars Spain Sees Potential for Growth," *New York Times*, December 28, 2012.
19. It was similar for Portugal; see Abreu 2006, 3–4.
20. From "Eurozone Can Learn Grim Latin Lessons," *Financial Times*, December 22, 2010.
21. Paul Krugman, "Crash of the Bumblebee," *New York Times*, July 30, 2012.
22. "Bond Traders in Europe Deal in High Expectations, and Fear," The *New York Times*, August 4, 2002.
23. See Guillermo de la Dehesa, "No habrá una ruptura del euro," *El País*, August 17, 2012 and Carmen Alcalde "Los daños de salir de la moneda única," *El País*, August 17, 2012.
24. Emilio Ontiveros, "La más intensa transformación," *El País*, December 30, 2012.
25. From Javier Santiso "España 3.0," *El País*, August 17, 2012. The crisis has led to the emergence of new venture capital initiatives and new start-ups, and the crisis is leading to the emergence of new entrepreneurs with a different profile: not only young people but also professionals who have been working for decades in their sectors are leaving their companies to create new start-ups. Of the dozen

start-ups with revenues of over €100 million in Europe, two of them are from Spain: Privalia (which focuses on online sales) and Odigeo (online travel).

26. See "A lo único que debemos temer es al miedo," *El País*, December 30, 2012.
27. "In Europe, focus begins to shift to the speed of a nascent recovery," *New York Times*, December 31, 2012.

Bibliography

Abreu, Orlando. "Portugal's Boom and Bust: Lessons for Euro Newcomers." *ECOFIN Country Focus* 3, no. 16 (2006): 1–6.

Acemoglu, Daron, and James Robinson. *Why Nations Fail: The Origins of Power, Prosperity and Poverty*. New York: Random House, 2012.

Ahamed, Liaquat. *The Lords of Finance*. New York: Penguin Books, 2009.

Albert, Michael. *Capitalism against Capitalism*. London: Whurr, 1992.

Alesina, Alberto, and Francesco Giavazzi. *The Future of Europe: Reform or Decline*. Cambridge, MA and London: MIT Press, 2006.

Almarcha Barbado, A., ed. *Spain and EC Membership Evaluated*. New York: St. Martin's Press, 1993.

Alston, Lee J., Thrain Eggertsson, and Douglass C. North. *Empirical Studies in Institutional Change*. New York: Cambridge University Press, 1996.

Alvarez-Miranda, Berta. *El Sur de Europa y la Adhesion a la Comunidad: Los Debates Politicos*. Madrid: CIS, 1996.

Amable, Bruno. *The Diversity of Modern Capitalism*. Oxford: Oxford University Press, 2003.

Analistas Financieros Internacionales. *Guia del sistema financiero español*. [Guide to the Spanish financial system]. Madrid: AFI, 2005.

Aoki, M. Toward a Comparative Institutional Analysis. Cambridge: MIT Press, 2001.

Asensio Menchero, Maria. *El Proceso de la Reforma del Sector Publico en el Sur de Europa: Estudio Comparativo de España y Portugal*. Madrid: Instituto Juan March, 2001.

Barrón, Iñigo. "Lehman no ha hecho daño hasta ahora…" [Lehman did not hurt up to now…]. *El País*, September 13, 2009.

Barry, Frank. "Economic Integration and Convergence Process in the EU Cohesion Countries." *Journal of Common Market Studies* 41, no. 5 (2003): 1–25.

Bentolila, Samuel, and Juan J. Dolado. "Labour Flexibility and Wages: Lessons from Spain." *Economic Policy* 9, no. 18 (1994): 55–99.

Bentolila, Samuel, J. Segura, and L. Toharia. "La Contratación Temporal en España." *Moneda y Crédito* 193 (1991): 225–265.

Bermeo, Nancy. *Unemployment in the New Europe*. New York: Cambridge University Press, 2002.

Blanchard, Olivier J., J. Andrés, C. Bean, E. Malinvaud, A. Revenga, D. Snower, G. Saint-Paul, R. Solow, D.Taguas, and L.Toharia. *Spanish Unemployment: Is There a Solution?* Madrid and London: Consejo Superior de Cámaras de Comercio, Industria, y Navegación/Center for Economic Policy Research, 1995.

Blanchard, Olivier J., and Juan Jimeno. "Structural Unemployment: Spain versus Portugal," *American Economic Review* 85, no. 2 (1995): 212–218.

Blanco, Roberto. "The Securization Market in Spain: Past, Present and Future." In M. Chavoix-Mannato "Working Party on Financial Statistics: Proceedings of the Workshop on Securitisation." OECD Statistics Working Papers (2011/03), OECD Publishing, 2011.

Blyth, M. "An Approach to Comparative Analysis or a Sub-discipline within a Sub-field? Political Economy." In *Comparative Politics. Rationality, Culture and Structure*, 2nd ed., edited by M. I. Lichbach and A. S. Zuckerman, 193–219. Cambridge: Cambridge University Press, 2002.

Boix, Carles. *Political Parties, Growth and Equality. Conservative and Social Democratic Strategies in the World Economy.* New York: Cambridge University Press, 1998.

Botella, Joan, Richard Gunther, and Josè Ramón Montero. *Democracy in Modern Spain.* Yale University Press: New Haven and London, 2004.

Bover, Olympia, Pilar Garcia-Perea, and Pedro Portugal. "Labour Market Outliers: Lessons from Portugal and Spain." *Economic Policy* 31 (2000): 381–428.

Calavita, Kitty. Immigrants at the Margins: Law, Race, and Exclusion in Southern Europe. Cambridge: Cambridge University Press, 2005.

Cameron, David. "Unemployment, Job Creation, and Economic and Monetary Union." In *Unemployment in the New Europe*, edited by Nancy Bermeo, 7–51. Cambridge: Cambridge University Press, 2001.

Carballo Cruz, Francisco. "Causes and Consequences of the Spanish Economic Crisis: Why the Recovery Is Taken so Long?" *Panoeconomicus* 3 (2011): 309–328.

Carreras, A., and X. Tafulell. *Historia Económica de la España Contemporánea (1789–2009).* Barcelona: Crítica, 2004.

Closa, C., and P. Heywood. *Spain and the European Union.* New York: Palgrave, 2004.

Crouch, Colin. *Capitalist Diversity and Change.* New York: Oxford University Press, 2005.

De la Dehesa, G. "Spain." In *The Political Economy of Policy Reform*, edited by J. Williamson, 123–140. Washington DC: Institute for International Economics, 1994.

———. *La Primera Gran Crisis del Siglo XXI.* Madrid: Alianza Editorial, 2009a.

———. "Momento para dos reformas necesarias." *El País*, September 29, 2009b.

De la Fuente, A., and R. Demenech. "Ageing and Real Convergence: Challenges and Proposals." In *Spain and the Euro: The First Ten Years*, edited by J. F. Jimeno, 191–273. Madrid: Banco de España, 2010.

Duran Munoz, Rafael. *Contencion y Transgresion: Las Movilizaciones Sociales y el Estado en las Transiciones Espanola y Portuguesa.* Madrid: Centro de Estudios Politicos y Constitucionales, 2000.

Dut, A. K., and J. Ross. "Aggregate Demand Shocks and Economic Growth." *Structural Change and Economic Dynamics* 18, no. 1 (2007): 75–99.

The Economist. "The Party's Over." November 8 (a special report), 2008.

Editorial Board. "The Economic Policies of the Zapatero Government." *Revista de Fomento Social* 247, 2007.

Eichengreen, Barry. *The European Economy since 1945.* New Jersey: Princeton University Press, 2007.

Esping-Andersen, Gosta. *Social Foundations of Postindustrial Economies.* Oxford: Oxford University Press, 1999.

———. "Who Is Harmed by Labor Market Regulations?" In *Why Deregulate Labor Markets?*, edited by G. Esping-Andersen and M. Regini, 66–98. Oxford: Oxford University Press, 2000.

Esping-Andersen, Gosta, and Marino Regini, eds. *Why Deregulate Labor Markets?* Oxford: Oxford University Press, 2000.

Estefanía, Joaquín. *La Larga Marcha: Medio Siglo De Política (Económica) Entre La Historia Y La Memoria.* Barcelona: Ediciones Península, 2007.

Estrada, A., J. F. Jimeno, and J. L. Malo de Molina. "The Performance of the Spanish Economy in EMU: The First Ten Years." In *Spain and the Euro: The First Ten Years,* edited by J. F. Jimeno, 83–138. Madrid: Banco de España, 2010.

Etchemendy, Sebastián. "Revamping the Weak, Protecting the Strong, and Managing Privatization: Governing Globalization in the Spanish Takeoff." *Comparative Political Studies* 37, no. 6 (August 2004): 623–651.

——. *Models of Economic Liberalization: Business, Workers, and Compensation in Latin America, Spain, and Portugal.* New York: Cambridge University Press, 2012.

Fernández Méndez De Andes, Fernando, ed. *La Internacionalización de la Empresa Española: Aprendizaje y Experiencia.* Madrid: Universidad Nebrija, 2006.

Fernández Ordóñez, Miguel. "The Challenges to the Spanish Banking System in the Face of the Global Crisis." Lecture on the occasion of the 50th anniversary of ESADE. Barcelona, October 30, 2008.

Field, Bonnie. *Spain's 'Second Transition'?: The Socialist Government of Jose Luis Rodriguez Zapatero.* New York: Routledge, 2011.

Fishman, Robert M. "Rethinking State and Regime: Southern Europe's Transition to Democracy." *World Politics* 42 (1990a): 422–440.

——. *Working Class Organization and the Return of Democracy in Spain.* London: Cornell University Press, 1990b.

——. *Democracy's Voices.* Ithaca: Cornell University Press, 2004.

——. "Rethinking the Iberian Transformations: How Democratization Scenarios Shaped Labor Market Outcomes." *Studies in Comparative International Development* 45, no. 3 (2010): 281–310.

——. "Democratic Practice after the Revolution: The Case of Portugal and beyond." *Politics & Society* 39, no. 2 (2011): 233–267.

——. "Anomalies of Spain's Economy and Economic Policy Making." *Contributions to Political Economy,* April 2012.

Fishman, Robert M., and Anthony Messina, eds. *The Year of the Euro.* Indiana: University of Notre Dame Press, 2006.

Fondo de Restructuración Ordenada Bancaria (FROB): http://www.frob.es/index_en.html.

Frieden, Jeffry, and Ronald Rogowski. "The Impact of the International Economy on National Policies: An Analytical Overview." In *Internationalization and Domestic Politics,* edited by Robert O. Keohane and Helen V. Milner, 108–136. New York: Cambridge University Press, 1996.

Führer, Ilse Marie. *Los Sindicatos en España.* Madrid: CES, 1996.

Galí, J. Comments on "The Performance of the Spanish Economy in EMU: The First Ten Years." In *Spain and the Euro: The First Ten Years,* edited by J. F. Jimeno, 139–146. Madrid: Banco de España, 2010.

García Mora, Alfonso. "El gran ausente" [The big absence]. *El País,* November 22, 2009.

Garrett, Geoffrey. *Partisan Politics in the Global Economy.* New York: Cambridge University Press, 1998.

Goldthorpe, John A., ed. *Order and Conflict in Contemporary Capitalism.* New York: Oxford University Press, 1984.

González, A., and E. Gutiérrez. "Spain: Collective Bargaining and Wage Determination." In *Wage Policy in the Eurozone,* edited by P. Pochet, 217–238. Brussels: Peter Lang, 2002.

Guillén, Mauro. *The Rise of Spanish Multinationals*. Cambridge: Cambridge University Press, 2005.

Guitart, Joan. "Zapatero: Left in Form, Right in Essence." *IV Online Magazine*, IV402, July, 2008.

Gunther, Richard, Jose Ramon Montero, and Joan Botella. *Democracy in Modern Spain*. New Haven: Yale University Press, 2004.

Gunther, Richard, Giacamo Sani, and Goldie Shabad . *Spain after Franco: The Making of a Competitive Party System*. Berkeley: University of California Press, 1986.

Haggard, Stephan, and Robert R. Kaufman, eds. *The Politics of Economic Adjustment*. Princeton: Princeton University Press, 1992.

———. *The Political Economy of Democratic Transitions*. Princeton: Princeton University Press, 1995.

Hall, P. A. "The Eurocrisis and Beyond: The Challenges for Germany and Europe." Presented at the Annual Conference of the International Association for the Study of German Politics. London, May 16, 2011.

Hall, Peter, and Danbiel Gingerich. "Varieties of Capitalism and Institutional Complementarities in the Macroeconomy: An Empirical Analysis." MPIfG Discussion Paper 04/5. Cologne: Max Plank Institute for the Study of Societies, September 2004.

Hall, Peter, and David Soskice. *Varieties of Capitalism*. New York: Oxford University Press, 2001.

Halleberg, M., R. Strauch, and J. von Hagen. "The Design of Fiscal Rules and Forms of Governance in European Union Countries." ECB Working Paper No. 419, December 2004.

Hamann, K. *The Politics of Industrial Relations: Labor Unions in Spain*. New York: Routledge, 2012.

Hancké, B. "The Political Economy of Wage-Setting in the Eurozone." In *Wage Policy in the Eurozone*, edited by P. Pochet, 131–148. Brussels: Peter Lang, 2002.

Hancké, B., M. Rhodes, and M. Thatcher, eds. *Beyond Varieties of Capitalism: Contradictions, Complementarities, and Change*. Oxford: Oxford University Press, 2007.

Hardie, Iain, and DavidHowart. "Market-Based Banking and the Financial Crisis." Mimeo: Paper presented at the University of Victoria, 2011.

———, eds. *Market-Based Banking, Varieties of Financial Capitalism and the Financial Crisis*. New York: Oxford University Press (forthcoming 2013).

Harrison, J., and D. Corkill. *Spain: A Modern European Economy*. Burlington: Ashgate, 2004.

Hassel, A., and B. Ebbinghaus. "From Means to Ends: Linking Wage Moderation and Social Policy Reform." In *Social Pacts in Europe—New Dynamics*, edited by G. Fajertag and P. Pochet, 61–84. Brussels: European Trade Union Institute, 2000.

Heclo, H. "Ideas, Interests and Institutions." In *The Dynamics of American Politics: Approaches and Interpretations*, edited by L. C. Dodd and C. Jillson, 366–392. Boulder, CO: Westview, 1993.

Huber, Evelyne, and John D. Stephens. *Development and Crisis of the Welfare States: Parties and Politics in Global Markets*. Chicago: University of Chicago Press, 2001.

———. *Democracy and the Left*. Chicago: University of Chicago Press, 2012.

IMF (International Monetary Fund). *World Economic Outlook*. Washington, DC: IMF, Various Years.

———. IMF Spain—Staff Report for the 2011 Article IV Consultation. Country Report No. 11/215 (July 2011).

————. *Spain: The Reform of Spanish Savings Banks Technical Notes*. IMF Country Report No. 12/141, 2012a.

————. *The Good, the Bad and the Ugly: 100 Yeas of Dealing with Public Debt Overhangs*. Washington: IMF, October 2012b.

Iversen, Torben. *Capitalism, Democracy and Welfare*. New York: Cambridge University Press, 2005.

Jenson, J. "Ideas and Policy: The European Union Considers Social Policy Futures." American Consortium on European Union Studies, ECAS Cases, No: 2010/2, 2010. Available at transatlantic.sais-jhu.edu/bin/y/d/2010.2_ACES_Cases_Jenson.pdf.

Jenson, J., and F. Mérand. "Sociology, Institutionalism and the European Union." *Comparative European Politics* 8, no. 1 (2010): 74–92.

Jordana, J. "Reconsidering Union Membership in Spain, 1977–1994: Halting Decline in a Context of Democratic Consolidation." *Industrial Relations* 27 (1996): 211–224.

Katzenstein, Peter. *Small States in World Markets*. Ithaca: Cornell University Press, 1985.

Kesselman, Mark. *The Politics of Globalization*. Boston: Houghton Mifflin, 2011

Locke, Richard M. *Remaking the Italian Economy*. Ithaca: Cornell University Press, 1995.

López, Julia. *Un Lado Oculto de la Flexibilidad Salarial: El Incremento de la Judicializacion*. Albacete: Bomarzo, 2008.

Lukauskas, Arvid. *Regulating Finance*. Ann Arbor: Michigan University Press, 1997.

Macedo, Jorge Braga de. "Portugal's European Integration: The Limits of External Pressure." In *Portugal: Strategic Options in a European Context*, edited by J. A. Tavares, F. Monteiro, M. Glatzer, and A. Cardoso, 61–97. Lanham, MD: Lexington Books, 2003a.

————. "Portugal's European Integration: The Good Student with a Bad Fiscal Institution." In *Spain and Portugal in the European Union*, edited by Royo Sebastián and Paul Manuel. 169–194. Portland: Frank Cass, 2003b.

————. "A Mudança do Regime Cambial Português: Um Balanço 15 anos Depois de Maastricht." UNL WP 502, 2007.

Mallet, Victor. "Prudence Pays Off for Big Banks." In "Investing in Spain," special report, *Financial Times*, October 2, 2009, 3.

Maravall, Jose Maria. "Politics and Policy: Economic Reforms in Southern Europe." In *Economic Reforms in New Democracies: A Social-Democratic Approach*, edited by Luiz Carlos Bresser Pereira, Jose Maria Maravall, and Adam Przeworski, 77–131. Cambridge: Cambridge University Press, 1993.

————. *Regimes, Politics and Markets*. New York: Oxford University Press, 1997.

Marks, M. *The Formation of European Policy in Post-Franco Spain*. Avebury: Brookfield, 1997.

Martin, Cathy, and D. Swank. *The Political Construction of Business Interests: Coordination, Growth, and Equality*, New York: Cambridge University Press, 2012.

Martinez-Mongay, Carlos, and Luís Angel Maza Lasierra. "Competitiveness and Growth in EMU: The Role of the External Sector in the Adjustment of the Spanish Economy." *Economic Papers*, no. 355 (October 2009).

Matín Aceña, Pablo. *Universia Business Review-Actualidad Económica: 150 Aniversario Banco de Santander*, November 5, 2007.

Mauro, Filippo, and Katrin Forster. "Globalisation and the Competitiveness of the Euro Area." Occasional Paper Series, No. 97, European Central Bank, 2008.

McDonough, Peter, Samuel Barnes, and Antonio López Pina. *The Cultural Dynamics of Democratization in Spain*. Cambridge: Harvard University Press, 1998.

McGuire, Patrick, and Goetz von Peter. "The US Dollar Shortage in Global Banking." *BIS Quarterly Review,* March, 2009.

Menz, Georg. *Varieties of Capitalism and Europeanization: National Response Strategies to the Single European Market.* New York: Oxford University Press, 2005.

Molina, O., and M. Rhodes. "Conflict, Complementarities and Institutional Change in Mixed Market Economies." In *Beyond Varieties of Capitalism,* edited by B. Hancké, M. Rhodes, and M. Thatcher, 223–253. Oxford: Oxford University Press, 2007.

Morlino, Leonardo. "The Europeanisation of Southern Europe." In *Southern Europe and the Making of the European Union,* edited by António Costa Pinto and Nuno Severiano Teixeira, 237–260. New York: Columbia University Press, 2002.

Morlino, Leonardo, and José Ramón Montero. "Legitimacy and Democracy in Southern Europe." In *The Politics of Democratic Consolidation,* edited by Richard Gunther, P. Nikiforos Diamandouros, and Hans-Jürgen Puhle, 231–260. Baltimore: Johns Hopkins University Press, 1995.

OECD. *Economic Surveys: Spain.* Paris: OECD, 2010.

Olson, Mancur. *The Logic of Collective Action Public Goods and the Theory of Groups.* Cambridge, MA: Harvard University Press, 1965.

———. *The Rise and Decline of Nations.* New Haven: Yale University Press, 1982.

Pérez, Sofía A. *Banking on Privilege.* New York: Cornell University Press, 1997.

Pérez, Sofía A., and Philippe Pochet. "Monetary Union and Collective Bargaining in Spain." In *Monetary Policy and Collective Bargaining in the New Europe,* edited by Philippe Pochet. Brussels: Peter Lang, 1999.

Pérez, Sofía A., and Jonathan Westrup. "Finance and the Macroeconomy: The Politics of Regulatory Reform in Europe." *Journal of European Public Policy* 17, no. 8 (2010): 1171–1192.

Pérez Díaz, Victor. *The Return of Civil Society.* Cambridge: Harvard University Press, 1993.

Plender, J. "Respinning the Web." *Financial Times,* June 22, 2009, 5.

Pontusson, Jonas. *Inequality and Prosperity.* Ithaca: Cornell University Press, 2005.

Porter, Michael. *The Competitive Advantage of Nations.* New York: Free Press, 1990.

Pridham, Geoffrey. "European Integration and Democratic Consolidation in Southern Europe." In *Southern Europe and the Making of the European Union,* edited by António Costa Pinto and Nuno Severiano Teixeira, 183–207. New York: Columbia University Press, 2002.

Regini, Marino. "Still Engaging in Corporatism? Recent Italian Experience in Comparative Perspective." *European Journal of Industrial Relations* 3, no. 3 (1997): 259–278.

Rhodes, M. "Globalization, Labour Markets and Welfare States. a Future of Competitive Corporatism?" In *The Future of European Welfare,* edited by M. Rhodes and Y. Meny, 178–203. New York: St. Martin's Press, 1998.

Reinhart, Carmen M., and Kenneth Rogoff. *This Time Is Different: Eight Centuries of Financial Folly.* New York: Princeton University Press, 2009.

Rogowski, Ronald. *Commerce and Coalitions: How Trade Affects Domestic Political Alignments.* Princeton, NJ: Princeton University Press, 1990.

Rojo, L. A. "Spain's Membership of EMU: Lessons for 2009." In *Spain and the Euro: The First Ten Years,* edited by J. F. Jimeno, 27–30. Madrid: Banco de España, 2010.

Rothstein, Bo. *Social Traps and the Problem of Trust.* Cambridge: Cambridge University Press, 2005.

Royo, Sebastián. *From Social Democracy to Neoliberalism.* New York: St. Martin's Press, 2000.

————. *A New Century of Corporatism?* Westport: Praeger, 2002.

————. "The 2004 Enlargement: Iberian Lessons for Post-Communist Europe." In *Spain and Portugal in the European Union: The First 15 Years*, edited by Sebastián Royo and Paul Manuel, 287–313. Portland, OR: Frank Cass, 2003.

————. *Varieties of Capitalism in Spain*. New York: Palgrave, 2008.

————. "After the Fiesta: The Spanish Economy Meets the Global Financial Crisis." In "Southern Europe and the Financial Earthquake: Coping with the First Phase of the International Crisis," South European Atlas special issue, *South European Society & Politics* 14, no. 1 (March 2009a): 19–34.

————. "Reforms Betrayed? Zapatero and Continuities in Economic Policies." In "Spain's 'Second Transition'? The Socialist Government of Jose Luis Rodriguez Zapatero," Special Issue, *South European Society & Politics* 14, no. 4 (December 2009b).

————. "Portugal and Spain in the EU: Paths of Economic Divergence (2000–2007)." *Análise Social* 45, no. 195 (2010): 209–254.

————. "Lessons from Portugal and Spain in the EU after 25 Years: The Challenges of Economic Reforms." In *Spain and the European Union: The First Twenty-Five Years (1986–2011)*, edited by Joaquín Roy and María Lorca-Susino, 155–292. Miami: Jean Monnet EU Chair, University of Miami, 2011.

————. "How Did the Spanish Financial System Survive the First Stage of the Global Crisis?" *Governance* (forthcoming 2013a). [Article first published online: November 6, 2012. DOI: 10.1111/gove.12000].

————. "Portugal in the European Union: The Limits of Convergence." *South European Society & Politics* (forthcoming 2013b).

————. "A 'Ship in Trouble' The Spanish Banking System in the Midst of The Global Financial System Crisis: The Limits of Regulation." In *Market-Based Banking, Varieties of Financial Capitalism and the Financial Crisis*, edited by Iain Hardie and David Howarth. New York: Oxford University Press (forthcoming 2013c).

Royo, Sebastián, and P. Manuel, eds. *Spain and Portugal in the European Union*. Portland: Frank Cass, 2005.

Scharpf, Fritz, and Vivien Schmidt. *Welfare and Work in the Open Economy: From Vulnerability to Competitiveness*. Oxford: Oxford University Press. 2000.

Schmidt, Vivien. *The Futures of European Capitalism*. New York: Oxford University Press, 2002.

Schneider, Ben Ross. *Business Politics and the State in Twentieth-Century Latin America*. New York: Cambridge University Press, 2004.

Sebastián, Miguel. "Spain in the eu: Fifteen Years May Not Be Enough." Paper presented at the conference "From Isolation to Europe: 15 Years of Spanish and Portuguese Membership in the European Union," Minda de Gunzburg Center for European Studies, Harvard University, November 2–3, 2001.

Serra Ramoneda, A. *Los Errores de las Cajas: Adiós al Modelo de las Cajas de Ahorro*. Barcelona: Ediciones Invisibles, 2011.

Steinmo, Sven, Kathleen Thelen, and Frank Longstreth, eds. *Structuring Politics. Historical Institutionalism in Comparative Analysis*. New York: Cambridge University Press, 1992.

Streeck, Wolfgang, and Kathleen Thelen, eds. *Beyond Continuity: Institutional Change in Advanced Political Economies*. New York: Oxford University Press, 2005.

Swank, Duane. *Global Capital, Political Institutions, and Policy Change in Developed Welfare States*. New York: Cambridge University Press, 2002.

Thelen, Kathleen. *How Institutions Evolve: The Political Economy Skills in Germany, Britain, the United States and Japan*. New York: Cambridge University Press. 2004.

Tilford, Simon, and Philip Whyte. *The Lisbon Scorecard X. The Road to* 2020. Brussels: Centre for European Reform, 2010.

Toral, Pablo. *The Reconquest of the New World: Multinational Enterprises and Spain's Direct Investment in Latin America.* Great Britain: Ashgate, 2001.

Torcal, Mariano. "Political Dissatisfaction in New Democracies: Spain in Comparative Perspective." PhD Dissertation, Ohio State University. 1999.

Torres, Francisco. "A Convergência para a União Económica e Monetária." In *Em Nome da Europa. Portugal em Mudança, 1986–2006,* edited by Marina Costa Lobo and Pedro Lains, 97–120. Cascais: Principia (ICS), 2007.

Tovias, Alfred. "The Southern European Economies and European Integration." In *Southern Europe and the Making of the European Union,* edited by António Costa Pinto and Nuno Severiano Teixeira, 159–81. New York: Columbia University Press, 2002.

Traxler, F. "The Logic of Social Pacts." In *Social Pacts in Europe,* edited by G. Fajertag and P. Pochet, 27–36. Brussels: European Trade Union Institute, 1997.

Williamson, J., ed. *The Political Economy of Policy Reform.* Washington, DC: Institute for International Economics, 1994.

Wolf, Martin. *Why Globalization Works.* New Haven: Yale University Press, 2004.

Zysman, John. *Governments, Markets, and Growth: Financial Systems and the Politics of Industrial Change.* Ithaca, NY: Cornell University Press, 1983.

Index